WHAT WE HOLD IN COMMON

An Introduction to Working-Class Studies

EDITED BY JANET ZANDY

THE FEMINIST PRESS AT THE CITY UNIVERSITY OF NEW YORK
NEW YORK

Published by The Feminist Press at The City University of New York
The Graduate Center, 365 Fifth Avenue, Suite 5406, New York, NY 10016
feministpress.org

First edition, 2001
09 08 07 06 05 04 03 02 01   5 4 3 2 1

Portions of this book originally appeared in *Women's Studies Quarterly* 23 (spring/summer 1995) and
26 (spring/summer 1998).

Library of Congress Cataloging-in-Publication Data
What we hold in common : an introduction to working-class studies / edited by Janet Zandy.
        p. cm.
    Includes bibliographical references.
    ISBN 1-55861-258-0 (cloth: alk. paper)—ISBN 1 55861-259-9 (paper: alk. paper)
        1. Working class—United States—History. 2. Working class women—United States—History.
3. Working class writings, American—History and criticism. 4. Working class—Study and teaching—United States. 5. Working class—Research—United States. I. Zandy, Janet, 1945-

    HD8066 . W48 2001
    305.5'62'0973—dc21
                                                                              2001023591

The Feminist Press is grateful to Mariam K. Chamberlain, Florence Howe, Joanne Markell, and
Genevieve Vaughan for their generosity in supporting this publication.

Text design by Dayna Navaro
Composition by Stratford Publishing Services
Printed in the United States of America on acid-free paper by McNaughton & Gunn

For Florence Howe, builder and sustainer of The Feminist Press
For Sara Cahill, a writer's editor
In memory of Constance Coiner (1948–1996), pragmatic visionary

And for Tillie Olsen

Solidarity is not a matter of sentiment, but of fact, cold and impassive
as the granite foundation of a skyscraper.

—Eugene V. Debs

Rochester regional transit workers, Amalgamated Transit Union Local 282, Regional Transit System, 1990. By Marilyn Anderson.

Contents

New Initiatives, Syllabi, and Resources

Acknowledgments

Solidarity, as Eugene V. Debs clearly understood, is not a given in a society that prizes competition and individual gain. Debs scoffed at showy, empty displays of sentiment, and struggled for what he called the basic elements of solidarity: "identity of interest, clarity of vision, honesty of intent, and oneness of purpose."[1] It is customary to think of solidarity in terms of labor struggles, but less so in terms of cultural expression. Even less likely is the recognition of the continuous solidarity it takes to sustain a small press, especially one with such an audacious name, The Feminist Press. In its thirty years, The Feminist Press has been in the vanguard of every critical intersection of progressive social movements and cultural expression. In particular, under the leadership of Florence Howe, The Feminist Press has had an intuitive recognition of the power and importance of working-class culture. This new edition of the first edited working-class studies collection would not exist without the class-conscious foundations of The Feminist Press. I want to acknowledge all the writers, editors, designers, marketing specialists, assistants, and cultural workers, past and present, who believe in the importance of sustaining the shared vision of The Feminist Press, and particularly, Florence Howe, Jean Casella, and Sara Cahill.

NOTE

1."A Plea for Solidarity." *Eugene V. Debs Speaks*, ed. Jean Y. Tussey (New York: Pathfinder Press, 1970), 206.

Preface to the New Edition

In 1983 I began teaching a course called Working-Class Literature to evening students at a community college in Rochester, New York. I returned home after each session exhilarated. We read books by Agnes Smedley, Studs Terkel, Tillie Olsen, Harriette Arnow, and Maxine Hong Kingston. Students wrote work narratives, conducted oral histories, and viewed labor films such as *Salt of the Earth*. Even after an eight-hour workday, students arrived early, stayed late, and were energized by the confluence of reading, experience, and powerful memories the course evoked. When I encounter former students from that class, they still reminisce about it, and it remains the best teaching experience I've ever had. Why? I think what made the class so memorable was the emergence of uncontrived community created through the readings and conversations and through the process of affirming and reclaiming our denied and erased labor legacies, as well as a realization that our collective studies and readings, so unrecognized by the academic or business institutions in which we worked, were really important. What we began to build then is now an established field, "Working-Class Studies."

In 1995, I spoke about "traveling working class," at the Working-Class Lives/Working-Class Studies Conference in Youngstown, Ohio.[1] A memorable, rare, and, for me, jubilant occasion where personal ideas met a receptive, public audience, this conference attested to the possibilities of working-class cultural and intellectual presence within the academy. We recognized a new trajectory for ourselves and our students—an alternative to the forget-who-you-are-if-you-want-to-succeed message covertly and overtly delivered to working-class students for generations. We validated the importance of carrying the best of working-class values, ethos, and knowledge into the academy and of using that rich, complex, even discordant heritage to expand what constitutes knowledge. And we realized that we were no longer working in isolation. We had allies, builders from inside and outside working-class lived experience.

It was at this Youngstown conference that the 1995 issue of *Women's Studies Quarterly*, straightforwardly called "Working-Class Studies," first appeared. This issue, assigned as a class text and sold steadily at conferences over the years, is now out of print. Editors at the Feminist Press, especially publisher emerita Florence Howe, have long recognized the power and importance of working-class studies and encouraged this reprinted and expanded issue of the *Quarterly* into a complete book, *What We Hold in Common*, which includes all the original works and more than fifty pages of new resource material.

In the meantime, in the real world, as students like to say, the landscape of work shifted, and, for some, was destroyed. Instead of polluting steel mills employing thousands, we have wasted hulks, shadowed by new prisons. A handful of skilled and industrial workers have now become tour guides in reconstructed mills and mines. According to a *New York Times* 1996 labor analysis, "more than 43 million jobs have been *erased* [emphasis added] in the United States since 1979.[2] *Erased* is an important linguistic distinction; these jobs were not lost or misplaced; they were cut and workers were eliminated. And as

William J. Wilson argues in *When Work Disappears*, inner-city neighbors have been disproportionately affected by joblessness.[3] In the city of Rochester, a culturally and historically rich corporate city, 89.2 percent of all school children qualify for free lunches. That number was 22 percent in 1980.[4] Despite the low unemployment figures (numbers which beg for deconstruction), and the new service and technological industries, there is little doubt that we are witnessing a shifting of work and wealth of historic proportions. The rich are enormously richer, the working class—the majority class[5]—must continue to struggle to make it from paycheck to paycheck, and the poor endure societal invisibility, increasing criminalization, a threadbare safety net, and real hunger. It is not an exaggeration to describe the United States as a landscape of economic apartheid. As a new political regime takes power, we face the bitter fruit of undemocratic capitalism. Not everyone has struck gold on the dot-com frontier.

Recalling those hard-working students in my 1983 Working-Class Literature course, I wonder how they have traversed the changes in the worlds of work, whether they survived the latest round of deindustrialization and downsizing, found a place in the new technical or service economy, or were lucky and retired early. In a dusty file, I find this commentary: "Working-Class Literature seems to be concerned with basic issues and needs. The simple questions of survival are important, not philosophical arguments. . . . W.C.L. can be described as an art form which enlightens people by revealing an aspect of the working class: their strivings, defeats, gains, attitudes, desires, needs, offerings, concerns, and convictions." In a note, the writer defines the working class as "those who have little control over the things they do at work or the results of their work" and adds in bold letters "GOOD LUCK IN FILLING THE CLASS NEXT YEAR."

From isolated courses to an established field, working-class studies—as a democratic force as well as a curricular and cultural movement—is driven by a joint consciousness: an awareness of the materiality of lived class experience and a belief in the power of education and culture to effect change. We are cautious about our claims. Pushing against the insularity of academic circles, we know that the *language* of transformation, transgression, and theory cannot suffice. The struggle is larger than texts. Working-class studies resists compartmentalization and seeks to sustain the dual meanings of *juncture*—as critical point in time and as joining seam. We are using our spaces and opportunities to build linkages between democratic ideals and curricular and cultural practices. An antidote to cynicism, working-class studies is an "expanded relational vision"[6] that draws energy from its reclamation of the past as it fully participates in the building of the future.

All the contributors to *What We Hold in Common* offer the reader multiple tools, interventions, and models for connecting the visionary with the possible in different locations and circumstances. Through scholarship, creative writing, educational initiatives, syllabi and bibliographies, the contributors bring a wide variety of perspectives to working-class studies. While retaining all the original material from the 1995 issue of *Women's Studies Quarterly*, I have expanded the "voice" section to include the first national publication of "El olor de cansansio"

("The Smell of Fatigue") by Melida Rodas, the elegiac poem "For Giacomo" by Edvige Giunta, and a brilliant essay on class difference by Carolyn Chute. The syllabi in the new resource section offer a range of possible ways of practicing working-class studies in different institutional locations. Laura Hapke draws on mining as metaphor and pedagogical entry port, and Todd Vogel offers a creative historical weaving of texts on slavery, consumption, and labor. Julia Stein suggests how a unit on working-class literature can be compressed into a day, and Will Watson reshapes a graduate course on proletarian literature from a working-class studies perspective. A course on women's history has distinct class accents as taught by Peter Rachleff, and Chuck Barone underscores the reality of class oppression in his courses on the poor and capitalism. Edvidge Giunta reflects on the power of memoir writing for urban, working-class students, and Larry Smith explores the possibilities of combining working-class literature and film and provides selected student narratives about their own working lives and families.

No collection on working-class studies would be complete without Sherry Linkon and John Russo's account of the building and sustaining of the first Center for Working-Class Studies at Youngstown State University. Doug Noble describes another approach to working-class studies in linking teachers, professors, and union workers in developing a work-based curriculum project for middle and high school students in Rochester, New York. The resource sections conclude with Tom Zaniello's astute filmography of labor documentaries and Nicholas Coles's carefully edited selected bibliography of American working-class literature.

I include the original introduction to the 1995 issue of *Women's Studies Quarterly* because it introduces the selections and describes a vision of a curriculum—an epistemology—grounded in the knowledge and experiences of working people. That 1995 issue was recognized as runner-up for best special issue by the Council of Editors of Learned Journals. It is my fervent hope that this expanded edition will be a useful tool to a new generation of teachers and scholars of working-class culture. To be sure, this is not a mere trend. Working-class studies is an answer to the controlling elite, a means of resistance to injustice, and a respectful honoring of the invisible many who sustain us all.

Janet Zandy
Rochester, New York
January 2001

NOTES

1. "Traveling Working Class" was first published in the 1998 issue of *Women's Studies Quarterly*, "Working-Class Lives and Cultures" edited by Renny Christopher, Lisa Orr, and Linda Strom, vol. 26 (spring/summer 1998): 228–42.

2. *The Downsizing of America* (New York: Times Books, 1996), 4.

3. See William J. Wilson, *When Work Disappears: The World of the Urban Poor* (New York: Vintage, 1997).

4. John Klofas, Department of Criminal Justice, College of Liberal Arts, Rochester Institute of Technology, "Metropolitan Forum," http:/www.rit.edu/www.~jmk.gcj and http://www.rit.edu/la/cj/facstaff.

5. See Michael Zweig, *The Working Class Majority* (Ithaca, N.Y.: ILR Press, 2000).

6. For a more detailed description of working-class studies see my "Toward Working-Class Studies" in *The Heartlands Today/The Urban Midwest*, vol. 7, ed. Larry Smith (Huron, Ohio: Firelands Writing Center, 1997), 158–62.

Introduction

Let us imagine what it would be like if the history and culture of working-class people were at the center of educational practices. What would students learn? What would they carry with them from elementary school to high school and college, and then into their jobs and community organizations? Surely they would know the long history of class warfare in the United States, what some historians call "the other Civil War." They would see the stubborn power of capital in relationship to labor from the beginnings of the Industrial Revolution to the growth of transnational corporations. They would have a sense of workers' culture—oral traditions, songs, literary expression, murals, sculpture, and photography. They would understand that culture is created by individuals within social contexts and that they themselves could produce it as well as consume it. They would be engaged in their communities, collecting oral history, participating in study groups.

Confronted by the complexity of working-class experience, students would develop an intellectual elasticity and a tolerance for difference. Conscious of the many intersections of class and ethnicity and gender and race, working-class studies would cultivate a capacity for reciprocal vision. Isolated issues would be seen in relational terms. Instead of being pitted against each other in competition for scarce jobs, students would be insisting on a workers' democracy. If capitalism still existed, they would be politically engaged in demands for full employment, a shorter workday (four hours seems about right), more vacation time (the United States currently has the least amount of vacation time for its industrial workers of any developed country). They would learn early in their lives that the "pursuit of happiness" should take precedence over the "protection of property." They would be subjects, not objects or things. They would insist that technology should be in service to humanity, not the other way around.

I write this brief utopia on the first day of 1995. It's a small indulgence to celebrate the end of 1994, a particularly mean-spirited year. I write from Rochester, New York, where on a daily basis the newspaper reports last night's shooting, this month's corporate downsizing, and the latest statistics on class polarities. According to today's newspaper, for example, one-third of all children in Rochester now live below the poverty line.

I view this collection as emerging out of the reality of this present to prepare the ground for the important work of building and sustaining working-class studies. I include *sustaining* because even though we are at the beginning of creating officially sanctioned programs of study, working-class studies rests on old cultural practices of self-education and group study, union organizing, summer schools for workers, and cultural expression. What is new is the emergence of this field in an academic context, in solidarity with women's, African American, ethnic, and labor studies. Our understanding of class identity is incomplete without the interplay of these other identities, but these other subjectivities cannot be properly studied without a class dimension.

The contributors span three generations. They are from different geographic and cultural places. Whether they speak with an intimate personal voice or a more distanced, often academic voice, they are all engaged in the process of witnessing. Each writer demonstrates a sense of connection to others across time, and a desire—even a responsibility—to use this occasion to provide a space where the silenced many may be heard and seen. In other words, whether the form is a poem, a syllabus, an oral history, or a theoretical essay, the connecting tissue is a collective class consciousness and a solidarity with working people.

We begin with personal voices. Rooted in the writing voice of Wilma Elizabeth McDaniel are the internal migrations of American workers looking for work, and the desire for culture and beauty, bread and roses. Lisa Orr and Kristin Kovacic speak of the labor of their parents, of factory closings, of corporate and university downsizing, of betrayed expectations and promises. Barbara Horn and Joann Quiñones pay homage to the work of mothers and grandmothers, to production and reproduction. In her feisty lyrics and music, Pat Wynne sings for the invisible many—those who work their way through school or have to pawn their possessions for food.

What distinguishes working-class cultural studies from canonical histories and literatures is the emphasis on a collective sensibility. Often this involves the interplay of three narrative voices: the personal *I*, the referential *they*, and the collective *we*. One of the interesting paradoxes of working-class writing (especially women's writing) is that although it relies heavily on autobiography as a genre, its subject is rarely isolated or romanticized individualism. Rather, its raison d'être is to recall the fragile filaments and necessary bonds of human relationships, as well as to critique those economic and societal forces that blunt or block human development. This is evident in Maida Springer-Kemp's oral history, in Jo Sinclair's *The Seasons*, and in the stories of women workers at the Bryn Mawr Summer School. Even when the narrative is located in the recesses of the individual psyche and the writer (Jo Sinclair or Cy-Thea Sand) is fighting depression and despair, the emerging narrative—and the confidence to write it—comes out of, as Florence Howe shows, *working* class consciousness into the text.

Another important dimension of studying working-class culture is examining the double, even multiple, work of cultural production. It is important to recognize how working-class stories and subjectivities enter bourgeois institutions and become part of a larger intellectual conversation. Often this falls on the will and more privileged circumstances of the next generation—those from working-class families who acquired an education—to see that the experiences of the majority of the people are not forgotten. This is evident not only in the work of oral historians and publishers, but also in the careful scholarship of bibliographers like Cheryl Cline and in the labor of creating space for working-class texts and history in the classroom, which we see reflected in the work of Linda Strom and Laura Hapke.

What is crucial to retrieving and producing working-class culture is the reciprocal and dialogic dimension of the process. We are generationally interdependent: the past is given voice in our work, but our work would not exist without this class history. It is a conversation of multiple voices across time. Working-class histories, stories, and images are not *taken* to be sold in the marketplace of ideas but rather *claimed* as a valuable inheritance. The poets who write about the Triangle fire of March 25, 1911, have poetic voice because of the power of the tragic story. We have the stunning photographs of working people in this volume because of Marilyn Anderson's sense of kinship with her subjects; these are pictures given, not stolen.

Finally, the suspicion with which many practitioners of working-class studies regard theory is justified if theory is no more than an abstract, albeit playfully linguistic, reduction of reality. Purposeful theory and criticism are not divorced from the physicality of working-class lived experience. Working-class cultural theorists recognize the protean nature of working-class texts and how they cannot and should not be dominated, corralled, or mastered by the bullying voice of theory. We now have a developing theoretical practice addressing the body of working-class literature and history in print. Carole Anne Taylor's study of *The Maimie Papers* asks, appropriately, "how the world of writing relates to lived experience and why it matters." The "habitat" of working-class writing is further explored in Roxanne Rimstead's pioneering work on "anti-Theory" and the subjectivities of marginal women. Lisa Orr offers a moving and insightful reading of the cultural inheritance of Tillie Olsen's *Yonnondio*, and Julie Stein provides an important overview of working-class poetry and a necessary intervention into the gendered world of "industrial music." Constance Coiner's concluding essay offers a pragmatic model for reading working-class texts. Her essay is a map of the U.S. working-class literary landscape, essential cartography for any future study of working-class literary expression.

I have always felt that if working-class culture became merely an object of study, and not a means of struggle, then it would lose purpose. Let us hope that, in a small way, this collection will advance our resolve to continue the struggle of earlier generations for economic justice for us all.

Janet Zandy
Rochester, New York
January 1995

Working-Class Voices

School Clothes

Wilma Elizabeth McDaniel

Summer was Oklahoma hot and humid. Maybe it was a little worse than average.

People working in the fields had to carry extra jugs of water and knock off work at the height of midday heat. One fellow had to be carried out of the field.

Red-faced, with galled armpits, all agreed, "This here has been a scorcher."

Chickens responded miserably to the heat. They drooped around in yards and pens searching for a spot of shade, sometimes gasping with open mouths.

Mrs. McCarver was careful to keep fresh water in the pen for her chickens. It got almost scalding hot during the day.

She said, "That is the least that I can do. It is no wonder the poor things are not laying eggs."

She met her crippled neighbor, Orveta Walker, at the mailbox on the road the next day.

She mentioned the chickens' poor laying record during the heat and added, "I don't try to save enough eggs to fry. I keep all of them for baking. With my big family, I bake cookies or cake or some kind of dessert every day."

Orveta was painfully thin and pale and wore a sack dress of a print whose pattern was almost faded to extinction.

She said, in a voice that matched her appearance, "I don't bake nothing except one-egg cakes. I'm saving them to buy school clothes for Anice. I have managed to save four eggs each day."

She added, with quiet determination, "I aim to start my girl off to school decent. None of them old faded hand-me-down dresses. They are always too long or too short. Some of the buttons are off, and you never can match 'em. The braid is all frayed out. No, indeed—I aim to start her in a spanking-new dress."

She worked toward her goal faithfully all summer. Each Saturday she caught a ride to town with the mailman and sold her week's collection of eggs.

She limped home, always saying happily, "I am proud to have a one-way ride. It sure beats walking both ways."

Two weeks before school began Mrs. McCarver invited Orveta to go with her to town. Everyone crowded into the McCarver's Model T sedan. Orveta had to hold Anice on her lap to make room, and seven-year-old Wanda McCarver scrunched down on the floorboard at her mother's feet.

They jolted excitedly over the rough roads to the small town of Depew, turned right at the railroad and up the slight hill to the one main street.

Mr. McCarver turned the group loose in front of Harrington-Pettigrew's Mercantile and said good-humoredly, "We leave for home at 1:30 in this car, unless someone wants to walk."

Mrs. McCarver and Orveta hurried inside the Mercantile with Wanda and

Anice at their heels. The women parted, and Mrs. McCarver went back into the hardware department.

Orveta went straight to the dry goods department and stopped at the big barrel that held countless remnants. Wanda had followed her with great interest and stood beside the barrel, but Anice went exploring the aisles and recesses of the store on her own.

Orveta began methodically to lift out the many odds and ends of cloth. She examined each piece carefully and laid it on a counter, so that she would not lose time handling the same piece twice. Once she straightened up and sighed deeply, then bent over the barrel and began to dig out the remnants again.

Wanda was sorting through the remnants on the counter and thinking that there were only drab pieces of brown and navy blue and calico prints of black and white. Nothing there for girls her age.

The stack on the counter grew high with the depressing remnants. Finally, Orveta brought up a sausagelike roll of purple-and-white striped gingham. It had a piece of paper pinned to it.

Orveta stood holding the roll in her hand, staring at it in unbelief. She said, "Wanda, I cain't believe it. There is one yard and a half in this remnant, and it is marked 'Ten Cents' in big letters. Plenty to make Anice a dress and bloomers."

She looked around and asked, "Where did Anice go? Probably a-gabbing with someone in the store."

Wanda said, "There she is over in the shoe department, sitting in a chair like she was a customer." Orveta said, "What did I tell you? That child don't meet no strangers. It worries me sometimes." She took her precious find to a clerk and paid for it with two nickels tied up in a knotted handkerchief.

Wanda stood beside her, savoring the magic smell of bolts of cloth on the shelves. Orveta said, "This will work up fast. I have got a pattern that the preacher's wife give to me. When I get home I'll clear the table and get started on this before night."

She added, "Lord have mercy! Look over there at Anice. She is having that clerk try shoes on her just like she was gonna buy some. Well, she is gonna be disappointed there, if she thinks I can buy her new shoes. But she will have a nice dress and bloomers."

Mr. McCarver was a man of his word. At 1:30 sharp he started the Model T, and everyone scrambled to crowd in again.

The women's purchases filled the nostrils of the occupants with some of the magic aromas from back at the Mercantile.

As the car jolted over the worst of the road, Mrs. McCarver opened a sack and gave each child a stick of striped candy, saying, "I don't think this will spoil your supper." Wanda looked closely at her stick of candy. It was white with delicate purple stripes. From her floorboard seat she said, "Mama, this candy is exactly like Anice's new dress is going to be."

Anice spoke up from her mother's lap. "My candy is yellow striped." Little Hal, the McCarver's youngest, said "I think I got me a black stripe. I don't like it."

"Boy, you don't know what is good!" Mr. McCarver said heartily. "That is a licorice stripe. You pass that up here to me and ask your mother to give you another color." Little Hal reached his candy over to his older brother Kosh, sitting in front. "Here, you give this to Papa."

Wanda plagued her mother with her perennial question. "Mama, may I stop at Anice's house and play awhile? Please."

Mrs. McCarver said somewhat sternly. "You had better ask Orveta first. I don't want you to wear your welcome out."

Pleadingly, Wanda asked Orveta, "Do you mind if I stop and play with Anice awhile?" Orveta laughed heartily. It sounded almost robust, coming from her thin throat. She said, "No, I don't care one bit. Anice needs company to help her learn the ways of the world."

"Alright, Wanda," said Mrs. McCarver. "You start down the road by five o'clock."

Mr. McCarver pulled up the hill and stopped in front of Orveta's shotgun house. She got out slowly with her precious purchase. Anice and Wanda stumbled out after her. Orveta stood beside the car and spoke slowly. "I am sure obliged to you folks for taking us into town with you, like we was kinfolks. You know I don't have nobody of my own in this place except Anice."

The McCarvers said, almost simultaneously, "It is our pleasure to help a neighbor." The Model T gave a lurch and drove on down the Shamrock Road toward the McCarver's sharecroppers' house.

Anice and Wanda immediately decided to go seining for minnows at the rock-bottom sink below the barn. The water would be high from the last rain. They grabbed an old colander and some fruit jars and rushed off through the grove of blackjacks that ended sharply in a clearing around the sink.

Orveta swung into action immediately. She cleared the table of the spoon holder and sugar bowl and peppersauce bottle and laid out the candy-striped cloth. Pinning the pattern to the cloth, she cut out the dress, quickly, expertly, losing no time. Within a few minutes she was sitting at the treadle sewing machine, whizzing the garments together.

When Anice and Wanda returned, sunburned and tired, they found Orveta already smocking the dress with purple embroidery thread. The girls sat and cooled off with the doors open, drinking cold buttermilk.

Wanda, in particular, watched Orveta's nimble fingers adorning the dress with the embroidery so popular just now. She finished the dress and hung it on a line above her ironing board, where it fluttered ever so slightly in a breeze wafting in through the front door.

Wanda said, "Look Anice! Your dress is just like that purple striped candy. It looks so good you want to eat some of it."

Anice barely looked up. Gulping down the remainder of her buttermilk, she said, "Boy, howdy, we caught us a tub of minnows." Orveta stood and looked at the dress. She picked up the small matching bloomers from the ironing board. "I will give these a good pressing, along with the dress, when I heat up the sadirons. It is time to start a fire and fix supper, anyway."

Wanda knew that Orveta did not have a clock and was too poor to buy one.

"Don't you think it is about time for me to start home? Are the shadows about right?"

Orveta answered, "Yes, it is just about five o'clock, the time your mother told you to start home." Adding, aloud to herself, it appeared to Wanda, "There. Nobody can say that I didn't make an effort to start my girl off to school decent. People will know that I care about her schooling and the way I raise her up."

Abruptly, she changed the subject. "I have let myself run out of water. I'll have to go to the well before I cook supper."

As Wanda left the yard, she saw Orveta limping toward the well, which seemed an unreasonable distance from the house. She carried a large bucket. Wanda felt sorry for Orveta. That bucket was really too heavy for a crippled woman. Orveta had a hard row to hoe. She had heard her parents say so, many times. But she had really worked and managed to buy cloth and make Anice a beautiful dress.

Wanda thought about that dress as she walked slowly home down the dusty road. It seemed to her that Anice had a very special dress, different from any she had ever had herself, or ever would have.

She reasoned that her parents were sharecrop poor, but she had a *father*. He had not died when she was a baby, as Anice's father had.

A father could get credit all year until the crops were harvested; buy groceries, liniment, lanterns, tools.

His wife could go into Harrington-Pettigrew's Mercantile and buy a whole bolt of gingham and muslin to make clothes for her family.

Yes, the purple striped–candy dress was one to be remembered always.

The picture of it was implanted in her mind for all time as she opened the gate and entered her own safe yard.

Go See Jack London

Wilma Elizabeth McDaniel

This incident was so critical to me, I found myself writing about it fifty years later. Nothing has changed except a bit of poetic license with Rosa's name. It was actually plain Rose.

My childhood friend and schoolmate Windy Tolliuer shared all of my interests except one. She did not care for literature and never read anything for pleasure except the Sunday funny papers when they were circulated in the neighborhood. She was crazy about "Little Orphan Annie" and the "Toonerville Trolley" section. That represented *all* her literary choices.

This difference in our tastes didn't seem too vital until the summer of 1927. That was the year that our hound-dog, hardscrabble community had a writer move in among us—Rosa Paolita. Actually, she was an artist also, painted in oils and watercolor. Someone reported to my family, "That woman is a female Zane Grey. She writes like a man, and they say she has a copy of every book Jack London ever wrote."

The words caused a cold prickling sensation up and down my spine. I had to see that woman! It might not be easy. Her tar-papered shack sat well off the road. I recalled from a previous tenant that the clothesline was in back of the house, and even a rough plank table for summer eating.

I couldn't saunter along the road and pretend to be studying ants or picking daisies and watch her eating or hanging up her wash. I began to have dreams of flying about her house invisibly and seeing her working at an easel under the host oak trees.

I attempted to convey some of my feelings to Windy on her way to the minnow pool. I said, "Windy, I am going to see a writer and artist who has all Jack London's books."

Before I could ask her to go with me, she slapped a mosquito on her leg, and answered acidly, "Go see Jack London, I don't care," and marched out of the yard toward the minnow pool where we usually fished together. I didn't attempt to follow her.

Anyway, Mama called me to wash the fruit jars for canning little yellow tomato preserves. It was a bumper crop for them. I don't think there has been or ever will be such a crop again, and Mama tried not to lose a single tomato. I ardently wished the vines would dry up before I had to wash another tub of fruit jars.

It was after lunch before Mama finished screwing the lids on the last hot sticky jar. She was carefully wiping each with a wet dishcloth, when Mr. Barkus knocked at the door.

He said, "No Ma'am, I can't come in. My wife and I took our new writer neighbor Mrs. Paolita to the doctor yesterday. She fell across an old cultivator and broke her left arm. I thought you neighbor women ought to know about it. You will probably want to cook something and take it to her."

Mama was already taking off her apron as he left the porch. She said "My, I'm glad that I baked bread yesterday," adding, "and hid a few cinnamon buns." She smoothed her hair at the mirror above the washstand and instructed me further, "Get the wicker basket and put in two pints of tomato preserves and get our bonnets from the porch. It's hot."

It seemed like ages, but we were actually on the dusty road toward Rosa's house within ten minutes after Mr. Barkus told us of her broken arm. I was still in shock at the way things were working out. Almost like what people called an answer to prayer. I hoped I hadn't been responsible for Rosa's broken arm, wanting so much to see her.

Mama walked fast, carrying the basket, the tail of her bonnet flapping against her shoulders. I followed a step behind with the cinnamon buns, my thoughts entirely on Rosa. Usually, I would talk to Mama as we walked but now was silent.

She spoke, "Look, a snake has just crawled across the road. He was a big one, too."

I did think of something to say, "Mama, how far is it to Rosa's house?"

She answered, "It is three-quarters of a mile from our mailbox to the corner where we turn into her lane." She continued, "Look how thick the nightshades are growing there along the draw. They are so delicate, I can hardly believe they are as poisonous as people say they are."

I voiced another thought. "Mama, what do you think a writer and an artist woman is like? Won't she be different from people like us?" I walked faster to be beside her when she answered.

"She won't be any different from us. She broke her arm. She is just human. She needs neighbors. You wait and see, she will be delighted to have a visit."

We reached the quarter-mile corner, and Mama paused beneath a big mulberry tree. She set her basket down and told me, "Let's blow a minute before we start on down the lane." She even took off her bonnet and fanned herself.

My eyes were glued on the tar-papered shack at the end of the lane. I stood poised with the floursack bag of cinnamon buns held tightly by a knot in the sack. Suddenly, I saw a woman emerge from the front door of the shack. She wore a white dress and had some kind of queer black contraption around her neck. She took a few steps, stopped, held some part of the contraption up to her eyes, and looked down the road toward us.

I said with absolute conviction, "Mama, that's her, Rosa Paolita."

Mama agreed mildly, "I imagine it is." She put her bonnet on, picked up the basket, and we entered the lane.

The woman in white studied us a few seconds more, then did what still seems to me, after fifty-some-odd years, a most remarkable thing. She broke into a run down the lane toward us. It seems all the more remarkable because her left arm was in a cast. She kept a steady pace in the center of the lane. It was the first time I ever saw the word *graceful* in action: smooth, deliberate motions. Nothing shook or wobbled on the tall lean frame. As she approached, I burst out, "Mama, her hair is on fire," and stood stock still in the lane. Mama stopped also.

The woman was before us. She swept her good arm around Mama and kissed her warmly on the cheek. She said, "That strange bird in the mulberry tree was a good omen that something precious would happen to me today. I have searched for him with my binoculars, but he has disappeared." She turned and kissed me on the cheek under my loose bonnet, saying, "I see you have your treasure with you, a daughter."

Mama flushed slightly and said, "She is a bookworm and crazy about Jack London's stories, and she has been dying to meet you, and half-scared to, at the same time."

The woman's large green eyes pierced my soul. She said, "Take off your bonnet." I complied, and she asked a prophetic question, "You write poems sometimes, don't you?"

I nodded, unable to swallow a lump in my throat and speak.

Mama spoke for me, "She writes all her spare time, on the back of envelopes, grocery lists, any paper she can get her hands on."

The woman said "I knew it." She put her right hand on my shoulder and said, "This is actually your artistic odyssey," then she laughed like silver bells tinkling, and said, "Let's go have some tea in my tar-papered castle." She led the way down the lane.

All the fear and doubt and pain left me. I knew what writers and artists were like.

Stories from a Working-Class Childhood

Lisa Orr

Utica, New York, is a tiny upstate city, a mill town that boomed in the nineteenth century. For a while it was second only to New York City in population. By my parents' births the mills were closed, and growth was stalled, but a man, at least, could still expect to earn a living in the factories that punctuated the neighborhoods on the west side. By the time I was growing up, in the 1970s and early 1980s, the living was sketchy. Layoffs were cyclical, like the summer heat waves; few could expect to be on the same job the next year. When the layoffs struck, my father haunted the unemployment office, then drank cup after cup of coffee at the kitchen table. He was forced to be grateful for minimum-wage jobs, working for $3.35 an hour. My mother scrambled to get out of such work, teaching her fingers to recall high school typing lessons on a mechanical typewriter from the swap shop. As I was finishing high school, she secured a secretarial job at a small local college—a sure jump in status as far as we were concerned—where she taught herself computers and got library privileges for her two daughters.

I read as much as I could, because in real life I was surrounded by stories that were never softened. The library's offerings were consoling next to my grandmother's story of my Great-uncle Paul, who was hit on the head by something that fell off a two-story-high punch press and spent his few remaining years in bed, swinging a cane violently at whatever moved near him. The factory where he had worked was a block down our street; walking to the public pool in the summer, my sister and I would peer in the windows. It was dark and loud, with oil pooled dangerously on the floors and sooty-faced men with bandannas tied around their foreheads working machines that could crush a human being. In the neighborhood they called it the finger factory; pieces of countless people had been lost there. My grandfather worked there during World War II; my father worked there while I was in high school, until the morning the workers showed up to find the doors locked and plastered with bankruptcy notices. It was the middle of the week. No one outside of management had known what was coming. A man my father knew, a coworker, had just gotten married. On the strength of his and his new wife's income they had bought a modest little house. Forgivably, he had bragged a bit at work; who else, after all, owned their own home? The morning the factory doors were locked against him, this man went back to his new house, climbed to the roof, and jumped off.

I viewed the scholarship I received to a university fifty miles away as an escape route. There I was surrounded by people from one-family homes with garages and wide lawns. They had no horrible stories to tell, or if they did, middle-class strictures taught them to keep them to themselves. They didn't know how others lived, and at that point, I could not tell them. After college I ran to the prettiest place I could think of: San Diego, as white and clean as a child's dream of heaven, where I could miss my hometown without watching its decline.

What I had yet to learn was what writer Tillie Olsen instinctively knew—that the divided self must acknowledge both halves of itself. In other words, I knew too many stories to ever forget. Even as I journeyed away from the site of my childhood, even as I moved toward the middle class, part of me would never leave the working class. Olsen never romanticizes that working-class self. She speaks of it as damaged but, at the same time, shows its value as a source of connection between people. This is a link one cannot choose to ignore. Living in my homogeneous suburban San Diego neighborhood, I found myself drawn to any reminder of my former life. Instinctively, I sought out others who had seen what I had seen: the young man, who, along with his father and brothers, had fished aluminum cans out of Dumpsters for the sake of the deposits; the young woman, scarcely any older than I, who worked two jobs to support both her unemployed parents. Like aging veterans, we told one another our stories over and over.

Eventually, I returned to upstate New York, but as a graduate student, a position oddly reflective of my internal divisions. Going to graduate school is, obviously, rarely an option for young working-class women. Graduate students are notoriously "poor," yet I still make more per hour than my mother ever has. As a teaching assistant, I have some advantages: health insurance, a steady income, a pleasant apartment. No longer is the incentive to escape so pressing. At the very point when I have the time and the means to articulate what it is to be working class, I am living like a member of the middle class. This is my way of keeping a flimsy wall of resistance between myself and these stories, so that what is destructive in them will not destroy me. It gives me a space to live that self that Olsen so clearly shows crushed to brief corners of time for most of the working class. When I was a light assembly worker, operating a heat-seal machine, I had hours to think while my hands worked on automatic. But somehow the work deadened my mind in the same way that the hot die, where it touched, transformed my skin to brown paper. When my shift ended I was fit for nothing but escapism. To sit down then and write about working-class life was to continue the deadening.

To be able to journey back into that world by choice, by memory, is something entirely different. I can continue to work out, slowly, painstakingly, how the part of me which has survived can tell the story of uncles who died before I was born and the woman who worked at the next machine over, of the dirty brick factories and the bars surrounding them, of small industrial cities that are dying even as I speak of them.

"Proud to Work for the University"

Kristin Kovacic

In June 1958 Bogdan Kovacic, my father, emigrated from Zagreb, Yugoslavia, to Pittsburgh, Pennsylvania. As he likes to tell the story, he had a quarter in his pocket as the train rolled into Penn Station, and he used that to buy some crackers, hedging his bets against his next meal. He was twenty-six years old and spoke little English. He had left behind family, all of his good friends, his teammates from the professional handball team he played for. He was alone, he figured, and about to see the world.

This is part of the myth of my family, a story familiar to many Pittsburghers with immigrant roots. I am, I'm afraid, about to tell you a very old story.

Jobs, in 1958, were plentiful in Pittsburgh. Cousin Francie got him in at the plate factory. He hauled plates, dropping them now and then and making a big crash. He went to English classes at night, penciled neat meaningless sentences in a grammar book I have here—"Only a few friends are bidden to come," and, with emphasis, "You are never too old to learn." He signed his new American name, Andrew, over and over in the margins. He learned the questions he'd soon have to answer: "Are you a Bolshevik, anarchist, communist, or polygamist?" "What does Thanksgiving Day mean?" He met my mother, practiced his new words.

Trained as an electrician in Zagreb, he looked for work in his field. A friend told him he could get him in at the mill, and he went to have a look: the heat, the smoke, the filth over everything. He said no thanks; he'd have to work in hell soon enough. He found a job as an electrician at West Penn Hospital, good, clean work. He was promoted to foreman. He bought a Chevy, sky blue.

Then we were born: my brother Andy, my sister Lara, and I. This, apparently, changed everything. He started night school again, and, with an electrical degree from Allegheny Technical Institute, he landed a job at Carnegie Mellon University in 1969—two years before Richard Cyert assumed the presidency of the university. I remember the day Dad started, the new uniform my mother pressed off, and the first time the promise was made to us: you will get an education there. At that time, all Carnegie Mellon University employees were promised full undergraduate tuition for their children who were accepted there. That day, too, was the first time the challenge was set down: you will have to do well enough in school to be accepted. I was six, my brother seven, my sister was learning to crawl. It was a challenge we took very seriously; it was, we figured, our shot at seeing the world.

In those days we were required, on the first day of school, to say our names and what our fathers did for a living. One by one the kids would recite their names and then, simply, "J&L" or "Homestead" or "Duquesne Works." I would wait my turn, and then somewhat haughtily announce, "My dad is an electrician at

Carnegie Mellon University. I'm going to college there, free." I told people even when they didn't ask me.

Carnegie Mellon became our identity, the greatest part of our family myth. While the men in the mills, our neighbors, were making much more money than Dad, locked into contracts in the glory days of steel, he, at least, had *invested*, had guaranteed our futures. We got Carnegie Mellon sweatshirts, T-shirts, and notebooks for our birthdays. We cheered the buggys at carnival. When Dad worked weekends, we'd sometimes visit him on campus and ride in his little electric car, surveying what we knew would someday be ours—our library, our gymnasium, our student union. At night, passing by, we saw the beacon light in Hamerschlag Hall which Dad had installed. "That's my light," he'd say, and there it was, beckoning.

We also participated, through him, in Carnegie Mellon's road to academic glory. My dad didn't work at a factory, he worked for the university—among artists, engineers, and scientists. I didn't, for most of my early lifetime, see any fundamental difference between what my father and a professor of electrical engineering did for a living. They both worked for the university.

My father worked on experiments with monkeys and with robots. He helped harness energy from still water, bringing the physicists home for dinner after their hard day's work. Dad's work allowed Kathleen Mulcahy, the glass artist, to safely power her magnificent kiln. When he brought home the beautiful vase she made for him, my mother set it on the television set in the living room, eventually decorating the whole room around it—such colors we had never thought of bringing together. If my father was never going to see the world, Carnegie Mellon brought it closer to him and, by consequence, to us.

He was there when the computers arrived; the machines that would launch Carnegie Mellon's international star. I remember sitting at the dinner table while Dad told us about the computers, how, when we got to college, there would be a computer for every student; how we'd find a book in the library just by pushing a button; how there might not *be* any more books in the library, the computer taking over every aspect of our education. I remember being somewhat skeptical—this was long before *computer* was a household word, much less a household item. But, finally, I believed. Dad had the plans; he knew what was coming. He was the man who powered those glorious machines, who would later coordinate the installation of the "Andrew" computer network.

In 1981 I arrived and began my Carnegie Mellon education. On my first day of my first class—a core curriculum sociology course—we read about the concept of class in American society. We learned how to identify the working class from the middle class; there were just a few simple rules. The working class, my textbook said, works with its hands or, in the case of women, does clerical work like typing or filing. I did a little figuring. My mother is a secretary. My father is an electrician. His hands can get very dirty when he works, and he is scrupulous about washing them. He always carries Band-Aids in his wallet, ready for the daily cuts he gets at work, usually on his hands.

You can identify the working class, my textbook said, by the arrangement of their homes. The working class keeps its television set in the living room, for example, while the middle class keeps it in another place, like a den. I thought about our living room, Kathleen Mulcahy's vase crowning the television like a jewel. I thought, for the very first time, that I was working class. It was a genuine surprise.

I'm told that Andrew Carnegie founded Carnegie Institute of Technology for the education of the working classes of Pittsburgh. Long before I arrived, that mission had been abandoned as unprestigious and, more to the point, unprofitable. My classmates were from out of town, the daughters and sons of doctors, entrepreneurs, foreign financiers. Many of them rarely saw their parents, much less ran into them in Baker Hall, fixing a switch box. I learned the difference between an electrician and an electrical engineer. None of that bothered me; it surprised me, opening my picture of the world, and where I fit into it, much wider. Likewise, much about my life surprised my friends, whom I would bring home with me on holidays and weekends, introducing them to a genuine working-class home, television set and all. During my years in school my parents responded generously to Carnegie Mellon's requests for giving from parents, believing, in a way that other parents could not, that the money was going to the university's collective pot, whose assets were essentially our own. They also, I think, enjoyed the letters that came to the house afterward: "Dear Mr. and Mrs. Kovacic, thank you for your generous gift."

In May 1985 I graduated, valedictorian of my college. I was selected to deliver the student commencement address, and on that day, under the big tent, a number of our family dreams came together. My father was sitting, suit and tie, in the audience. My sister, who had just been accepted for admission in the fall, sat next to him, checking out *her* campus. My brother, who, after receiving his associates' degree in forestry from Penn State University, was hired by Carnegie Mellon as a gardener—following my father's path—stood on the edge of the tent in his uniform. His boss had given him special permission to attend; normally the gardeners have to stay in their shop during the ceremonies. I dedicated the speech to my father, and I used my remarks to remind my classmates about the wonder, the absolute fortune, that we were going to do our work in life with questions, theories, problems, and poems—not with our backs, not with our bleeding hands. "Very well done," President Cyert said, shaking my hand on the dais. He told the audience that he was pleased to see the daughter of a staff member be so successful at the university.

When I think about that day now, the memory is very sweet, but I am also reminded that certain dread wheels were already in motion. The university, at the time of my graduation, was about to divide the workers' union (SEIU Local 29), selling off the janitors to a management firm (ABM) and cutting them off from Carnegie Mellon benefits, including tuition benefits. Those people, many of whom were Dad's friends, no longer worked for the university. Shortly after my graduation the administration dropped *university* from its official name, suggesting that it was more like a corporation than an institution of higher education, more like a factory than a school.

Contract battles for Dad's union became increasingly difficult to win. The administration, which for years claimed that its pay scale could never compete with the steel industry's, took advantage of the labor climate in the wake of steel's collapse to demand concessions. The administration hired outside firms to "consult" on the efficiency of the physical plant. There were layoffs. One of those firms became the manager of Carnegie Mellon's building and maintenance operations, introducing suspicion among the physical plant workers—in spite of the administration's written assurances—that there would be further layoffs and that what had happened to the janitors might eventually happen to them.

In May 1990 my sister graduated with high honors, and we gathered again under the tent, to celebrate again the fulfillment of Dad's promise. President Cyert, saying his last farewells, recalled the achievements of his twenty-one years in office, the remarkable rise of Pittsburgh's Carnegie Tech to the global institution called Carnegie Mellon. My father, in the audience, could look back on those very same years, knowing that he had had a hand in all of it and that he had, in spite of all of the hard, physical work, made a very good investment in a growing institution. A steel mill might close, rust, and be razed to a clear toxic field, like the J&L South Side works he passed every day on his way to Oakland. But the university would always be there.

My sister and I were on our way. My brother was doing well in his job. Dad had three years until he could retire, and he was already planning. He would play more tennis (he is still, at sixty, a remarkable athlete). He and my mother would travel, back to Yugoslavia, where his family still lives, and to the other parts of the world they hadn't gotten around to seeing.

In June, after the tent had come down and the campus emptied out, the faculty and students returning to the cities that they come from, Dad reported to work, punched his clock. He was told not to work but to go directly through a door that closed behind him and seventeen other people, including two-thirds of all of the university's electricians, who were about to lose their jobs. They were told, for the first time, that there was a budget crisis that would require layoffs. They were told to turn in their keys and to be off the campus grounds by 10:00 A.M. They saw university police as they emerged, dazed by the blindsided blow. "Like criminals," my mother told me, through tears, over the phone. She didn't think about the cost, the financial straits this would place them in. She thought about betrayal. "They treated him like a criminal, after all those years."

My father harbored no illusions about Carnegie Mellon's benevolence. He had seen, over the years, the university's antagonism toward its union. But in 1969 he had signed what he thought was a lifetime contract—he would give them a lifetime of hard labor; they would educate his children and allow him to retire, not comfortably, but in peace. It was not an extravagant plan.

Unfortunately for him, the Carnegie Mellon that let him go was not the university that had hired him, or perhaps, sadly, it was. How could he have known that the master plan of the global university, like that of a global corporation, included the abandonment of its responsibility to the blue-collar workers in its community, not to mention its utter disregard for their intelligence and pride? At the same moment that my father and sixteen other skilled construction and

maintenance workers were shown, by an armed guard, the door, the administration announced the acceptance of a five-million-dollar gift from Paul Mellon
toward new campus construction. Who, these men and women were forced to
wonder, would be doing it? Who would design, construct, wire, and maintain the
growth for which, as Dr. Cyert so elegantly phrased it for the reporters, "Carnegie
Mellon's appetite continues to grow the larger [it] gets"? The arithmetic is tragi-
cally easy to do, even without a Carnegie Mellon education—why support loyal,
lifetime employees when you can buy contract work for less? At the same moment
that my father faced the prospect of finding, at sixty, a new job, President Cyert
eased into his retirement. The administration, as reported by the *Pittsburgh Post-
Gazette*, was then finalizing plans to purchase a $1.9 million Sewickley estate for
its new president, his wife, and their six horses.

"The emerging global company is divorced from where it produces its goods,"
Robert B. Reich, lecturer in public policy at the Harvard University Kennedy
School of Government told the *New York Times*. "It has no heart, and it has no
soul. It is a financial enterprise designed to maximize profits. Many of the people
who inhabit it may be fine, upstanding human beings, but the organization has its
own merciless logic."

It was just this merciless logic, I have to believe, that caused my father to lose
his job. Carnegie Mellon is a thriving, growing institution. It is not facing a bud-
getary crisis; it is facing a moral one—whether to cultivate the community of a
university or the elite positioning of a corporation. My family felt, with great
pride, a part of an educational community, until, without ceremony, Carnegie
Mellon abandoned its role in it. Now, like too many other working-class families
in Pittsburgh, we're left with the caution that it was foolish to have believed.

So now my father, writing in the workbook he received at his "transition" seminar, dutifully answers their questions. What do you feel is your greatest accomplishment? "My greatest accomplishment," he writes in the clipped, impossible
language he has never learned to love, "is my family." What was most satisfying
about your previous employment? "I was very proud," he says, carefully calling up
the past tense, "to work for the university."

Ruth in August

Barbara Horn

Ruth, my mother, was born August 4, 1914. Whether it was her favorite month or not, August, as I remember, distilled her strongest, most compelling traits. That was when she harvested the bulk of her flower and vegetable gardens; when she saw that abundance, in some sense, never is enough.

Like most well-tended, pampered children, I took my mother for granted, little noticing the details of *her* life, except as they pleased or fretted me. But when Ruth was in her mid-forties and I in my early teens, I watched her, really watched her, and saw the tension August brings.

Almost daily she filled containers with vibrant cockscombs and dahlias; pale cosmos and sweet peas; bright zinnias, nasturtiums, and gladioli. In August our house was a veritable garden, "too heavy with flowers," my father mildly complained. If he pulled open his dresser drawer too vigorously, a vase burdened with old-fashioned roses, ever Dad's favorite fragrance, threatened to topple into his socks. Bouquets spilled from piano top, end tables, kitchen counter, sink. They even softened the ugly metal surfaces of heating stoves. In opening our cool, dark pantry—where hundreds of jars of her home-canned produce rested—I might find clenched bunches of dandelions and marigolds, spots glowing like neon, which Mother had stuck, willy-nilly, in last year's empty jelly glasses. And when she attended a local function—such as a lodge meeting, fund-raiser, or Saturday night dance—Ruth took along containers of showy flowers "to decorate," as she called it. Every Sunday in August she rose early to pick and arrange elaborate sprays, which Dad helped her carry to our nearby Methodist church. The aroma of Ruth's stately arrangements seeped, like incense, through the sanctuary to the belfry, and met worshipers at the door. As our accompanist pounded out the staccato strains to "Love Lifted Me" and we fifty members of the congregation responded in loud voice, vases of Ruth's offerings, which crowded altar rail and organ top, shook gently, startling some and soothing other bloodshot Sabbath eyes.

The weighty ripeness of her vegetable gardens gathered even more of Ruth's attention than did her flowers. She had plowed and planted, weeded and hoed, and now the labor of spring and summer brought rewards as certain, as inescapable, as the sun's glare. Near twilight on August evenings, when rural Missouri air began to cool and dew, as slick as oil, settled on lawn and field, Ruth carried armloads of her harvest directly to our large, square kitchen. Soon bowls of sliced tomatoes, bell peppers, and muskmelons jeweled our supper table.

While my father, two brothers, and I waited hungrily, she neatly husked corn, making a quick zipping sound like the sudden tear of a garment. The effort caused Ruth's upper arms to jiggle, stretching—for the umpteenth time that day—the cap sleeves of her flowered housedress. She then immersed a dozen roasting ears in a deep pan of boiling water. In exactly ten minutes Mother fished out the corn, shaking off its excess liquid, and then onto a heavy platter she piled the feast, pyramid fashion, centering it proudly on the table. As soon as we could comfortably handle them, we gobbled up the roasting ears—all the while watching, through the steam, for Mother's next batch.

When corn on the cob, always our favorite garden crop, was at its sweetest, we had little else for lunch and supper. Slathered with butter or margarine and rolled in salt and pepper, a half-dozen pieces per child satisfied. This was meal enough. I would look at my plump brothers, their chins shiny with butter and streaked with milky corn juice, and wonder if I presented as comically worshipful, as well-fed a sight as they. Mother might also serve new potatoes simmered with snap beans or thin rounds of crookneck squash, dipped in egg and cornmeal batter, and then fried to a succulent crispness—dishes that she and my father savored—but it always was the corn that left us kids exulting.

At least twice a week during the summer our family ate poultry that Ruth and my father tended at the edge of our property. Mother had assisted during the chicks' incubation, helped feed and water the growing flock, and participated in caponizing them. But she alone slaughtered our poultry. I often watched as she performed single-handedly—right in the chicken yard—all of the messy butchering. We had no plumbing system, so Mom heated pails of water at our kitchen stove and then carried them out the back door, past flower and vegetable gardens, berry patches and grape arbor, and finally, through a gate into the fenced poultry yard. Mindful not to splash the scalding liquid, I sometimes helped her haul the steamy buckets and position her paraphernalia near a well from which we drew fresh, cold water. Our two dogs, sensing a slaying, usually followed us, and the ever ravenous flock—expecting mashed grain, vegetable parings, or chicken innards—crowded nearby, pecking at one another and vying for a spot near Mother.

Ruth grabbed a chicken by its legs and put its head under a broom handle, which she then stepped on; by yanking the animal up, she beheaded it—as quick as a squirt. Then the bird ran wildly, drunk with death. Working rapidly, Ruth sent several headless birds, flapping their wings and swooping jerkily, into what looked to me like a headlong, hapless effort to fly—an attempt to leave this earth. I could not help but draw closer to the circling action. Trickling blood, a chicken would lie still; finally dead, I would think. But then it might struggle up and flop again, its body fiercely beating the ground. After throwing a finally motionless chicken into steaming water, which made removal of its feathers an easy chore, almost like detaching blanched skin from a tomato, Ruth then disemboweled it. During a half-hour she could dress six fowls. All the time she called softly to the dogs, shooed chickens out of the way, and reminded me to pump water so she could rinse the flaccid carcasses.

To me the butcher yard was bedlam—yelping dogs, cannibalistic chickens, headless animals careening at all angles, feathers floating in steamy, blood-clotted water. Sometimes I would gag and feel my stomach pitch. Sometimes I was dazed. My eyes—never adjusting to but unable to withdraw from the appalling sight—

would blur in sadness, fascination, fear. But, as far as I could tell, Ruth never reeled from the stench of scalded feathers, warm blood, gritty gizzard. Nor did the sight of headless chickens, thrashing and zigzagging in their final, desperate dance, make her squirm or shudder.

She worked calmly, efficiently, wasting none of the carnage. Mother threw slippery entrails to the stampeding, hungry flock; chicken feet at our slobbering mongrels, who immediately cracked open this gristly treat; and cloudy butcher water, a tepid fertilizer, over the fence right onto the strawberry patch.

Because Mother was so seamless in her movements, and even capable while dressing poultry of humming a popular song, I wondered what had been crossing her mind. As she separated out the squiggly livers and tiny triangular hearts—giblets that would flavor bread stuffing and gravy—did she contemplate what bulbs to transplant come autumn? What chores to do next? What her husband was accomplishing today in his rows of wheat, corn, soybeans, and barley? Why, year after year, farming was an increasingly unreliable way to support a family? What to fix for supper?

Yes, more than likely she thought of food. While she herself found a thick onion sandwich and a plate of salted white radishes satisfying, she always fixed large, hot suppers for the family. Ruth's specialties included skillet fried chicken and milk gravy, boiled hen with homemade noodles, fowl smothered in cream sauce, and oven-roasted, stuffed capons—the latter smaller than tom turkeys but, because they were castrated, almost as full breasted and much more tender and tasty. Each summer Mother raised, in addition to two hundred fryers, over a hundred capons, which she sold as holiday fare to a fancy-poultry shipper. But she always saved a few prize birds for us to eat before fall ended. During butchering was she figuring, then, what price this year's capons might bring? How that sum would help buy groceries?

I always hoped she was planning to bake pies and cakes. Even during her most harried August days of gathering and culling, of sterilizing and canning and preserving, of killing and eviscerating and frying, Mom made glorious desserts—fresh blackberry cobbler with lattice crust, just-picked peaches and whipped cream, caramel pie glazed with meringue, and, my favorite, a towering angel food cake encased in butterscotch frosting. She used exactly eleven egg whites, from hens nesting in our poultry house, for this delicacy. Working a hand rotary beater so furiously that the kitchen table shook, Ruth spent a half-hour producing this stiff, chalk-white concoction, held up only by air. Slow baking transformed the batter into a spectacular nine-inch-high cake. After she iced it I scraped the bowl of its creamy burnt-sugar frosting, whose mellifluous name, butterscotch, merely when I pronounced it, filled my mouth with warm, smooth flavor. Some community women, Mother's peers, occasionally hired Ruth to make her celebrated angel food cake for an anniversary or birthday party. If I helped deliver it, I asked to carry this dessert and then navigated cautiously, as if I were walking on eggs.

When I think now of Mother I see her, laden with pitchers and platters and pans, bowls and vases and tubs, stepping quickly in the warm, sticky clutter of our spacious kitchen. Because we had no dining room, we took all our meals in this large, clamorous space, where she did much of her work. Countless times I watched mother stride from counter to sink to refrigerator to stove and finally, to the large rectangular table—miles of steps a day. Dad had glued red-and-black rubber tiles to the wooden table, making its top, which then resembled a floor, unattractive but easy to clean. Like most rural women's workplaces in the 1940s and 1950s, Ruth's was not a well-designed modern kitchen. Mother owned few labor-saving devices, and because the house lacked plumbing, she frequently carried in buckets of water from the well just outside her kitchen door. Mom even emptied the cumbersome, twenty-gallon slop pails when my brothers neglected this chore. And always, even in heat-choked August, Ruth boiled tubs of water for cleaning chickens, dishes, and clothes.

I sometimes helped her do laundry, which routinely took a full day. Then piles of sorted clothes covered the linoleum kitchen floor, stuttering Ruth's usual brisk stride, as she maneuvered around them and rushed back and forth into a small side room, where she had set up the electric washer and tubs for rinsing, bluing, and starching. Wash day was the only time Mother wore pants. She had ordered a Montgomery Ward pair of jeans, "for the large woman," and the stiff denim, though serviceable, made her stomach and chest more prominent than when she had on soft, faded housedresses. Elbows deep in suds, Mother used a mop stick to shepherd clothes through the wringer. I was in charge of the second-rinse water and also helped hang clothes to dry. When clothesline ran out, she told me to fasten old towels and rags to the chicken-yard fence. There, at our property's edge, near the fruit trees and ancient elm, my hands wrinkled from hours in warm water and sore from lifting and stretching, I thought of running away—all the while listening for Ruth's call from the kitchen. "Come in, Doll, and we'll rest a while," I hoped she would say.

Mother's seemingly constant motion was most evident when her family sat down to eat. Although we children helped with table clearing and dish drying, at the beginning of meals Ruth waited nonstop on us, hastily replenishing empty bowls and glasses. In the middle of the meal, however, if things were moving smoothly, she finally sat next to Dad and then visibly enjoyed her supper. She might laugh, nudge him, tell an amusing anecdote—like how, in pulling a particularly ornery stinkweed that afternoon, she fell backward, landing in a row of equally stinky turnips. "My padding saved me," she quipped. "And I didn't even hurt the turnips—much." At meals Ruth savored everything, even the lowly cabbage and the oddly named plants we kids abhorred, such as gooseberries, parsnips, and rhubarb. Truth to tell, she overate at every meal.

All of us had the hearty appetites of laborers: my father and brothers, who worked long hours in the fields and then faced heavy chores at home; mother and I, who plowed and weeded gardens, did laundry, and scrubbed floors. We ate, Dad said, like old-time threshers. None of us stopped at one serving of anything we relished. We were what Ruth called "pleasingly plump"; she herself was the most overweight. An ample size eighteen, Mother breathed heavily when she lugged buckets of chicken feed, stooped to pull weeds, or carried a dozen ears of corn to the table. At least, unlike the rest of us, she drank no sugary sodas or juices.

Instead, Ruth loved coffee and took it piping hot and black; a cup of it, even during August's most sweltering days, was always near her plate. As I watched Mother gulp the stimulant, I thought of someone hoarding an elixir. Her craving showed that mere determination to stay alert and keep working was not always adequate, even for Ruth.

In the trying heat of our midwestern August, Ruth's gait grew heavier, her face more florid. Even my adolescent eyes could see that hot weather, constant toil, and too much food had left her overweary. I was not surprised, then, that my vigorous mother, at meal's end, plopped into our kitchen rocker, which faced a window overlooking the vegetable garden. Once seated, she sighed deeply. I saw the strain and something that perplexed me—the worry and longing in her face. Cooling herself with a cheap, lightly scented fan—some promotional giveaway, undoubtedly, from a local funeral home—Mother seemed to fold up like a half-blown morning glory. Perhaps dazed by the acrid smell of spices, for it was high summer and she had pickled cucumbers, peppers, and peaches; perhaps weary to the bone from gathering and sorting, cooking and canning, filling jars with the sticky, blood red essence of tomato, raspberry, damson, and cherry; perhaps lulled by the wind in her favorite elm out by the chicken yard or the whir of a fast, westbound evening train, Mother rocked and rested. For hours she had labored, and after eating quickly and far too heavily, she suddenly lost energy.

But just before dark on some of these burdensome August days Ruth rose to gather a bushel or two of her best beefsteak tomatoes. As firm and large as my father's fists, these heavy, smooth globes were sweet enough to eat—as you would first-picked apples—right at the moment of harvest. After a shake of their vines, fruit dropped softly into Mother's stained, calloused hands. I would run along the side yard, cool dew at my feet, and watch her, a figure bending in the twilight. Quickly, she scooped tomatoes into half-bushel baskets. "Mother, look at my somersault," I might plead, but she moved on, not noticing me. At those moments she was unreachable, refusing to answer or tend to either children or husband. On such August evenings I slowly began to realize that Ruth harvested in a mysterious, single-minded way; that she was mesmerized by the smell and feel, the shape and promise of tomatoes.

By this point in the summer, Ruth had canned one hundred quarts of the crop, a year's supply, so Dad loaded the half-bushels into our Chevy, and we drove seven miles to the closest city, where a liquor store owner bought whatever "extra" produce Mother offered. There, in that town of 2,500, she sold tomatoes for only two dollars a bushel—even then, an embarrassingly small sum. But it nonetheless supplemented Dad's income. A small farmer in peril, my father could not keep a family of five solvent on field crops alone, despite good years, when corn yielded one hundred bushels an acre. In addition, then, to farming eighty acres, Dad took odd jobs in our town of 220 people. He was, by turns and sometimes all at once, Methodist Church janitor, electric meter reader, seed corn agent, country school-bus driver, and member of a railroad repair gang. Still, we bought almost everything on credit and needed more income.

Certainly, Mother's economic contribution was substantial—as the house, garden, and field work of rural women always has been—however difficult its dollar value is to calculate. Although defined as "farmer's wife," and thus officially "not gainfully employed," the more she raised and preserved, the less we had to purchase. The more she sold, even on a small scale, the less we worried about school clothes.

Some local women supplied cream, butter, and eggs to faithful customers who frequented their farms. Others occasionally bartered surplus products at one of the nearby grocery stores. But none, to my knowledge, actually delivered garden produce, as Mother did, to the customer. Her initiative, under other circumstances, could have led to a promising business. Untold thousands of farm women have sustained families with just such earnings. But that, for the most part, was decades earlier than the 1950s. Running a truck farm or fresh produce stand would not have been feasible for her, anyway—distant as Ruth was from any sizable town or well-traveled highway. Besides, most local people either had their own gardens and poultry, orchards and livestock, or else they shopped at the new attractions—large supermarkets. Mother was several years too late to truck products to Hannibal, twenty miles east on Highway 36; too late, as well, to ship eggs and capons by rail to Chicago. And, certainly, neither of the two mom-and-pop groceries in our Missouri village would have tried to sell Ruth's butterscotch pies and angel food cakes.

During the time we children became teenagers and wanted new, more durable textbooks, sports equipment, and school wardrobes, Mother and Dad experienced the crisis of American small farmers. Their soil could no longer provide.

The summer I was thirteen and Ruth forty-four, I entered a consolidated high school in the town where mother peddled tomatoes. The day school started she began her first salaried job. It was across town from my school. Both of us had freshman nerves; starting work held just as many uncertainties for her as graduating from eighth grade did for me. I had left a four-room country school with poorly trained but attentive teachers and no plumbing or gymnasium. Ruth had left the farm. The kitchen. The garden. While adapting to a comparatively large, modern building, with its bells, lockers, girls' rest room, and demanding teachers, I sometimes would pause to imagine Mother, several blocks away, learning a factory job among fifty women, all of them dressed in similar uniforms.

I remember well the new outfit Mom helped me sew for my first day of high school: a pink gingham shirt, trimmed with white lace, which matched my pink corduroy tight skirt. "You look real streamlined, Doll," she said, when I tried on the set. I wore a variation of saddle oxfords, called rock 'n' roll shoes, tied with pink laces. And Ruth's attire for her equally important starting day? I was up at 6:30 and saw her leave the house to catch a ride with a neighboring coworker. Carrying a sack lunch of onion sandwiches and hard-boiled eggs, Mother moved soundlessly, as if walking on marshmallows. She had on white oxfords with thick rubber soles, sturdy shoes in which she could stand for eight hours. Her ample body, which I always saw as soft yet strong, looked strange—stark, distant, uncomfortable. She wore a white, loose-fitting nylon uniform, like that of a nurse or waitress. Her salt-and-pepper hair she had recently dyed black, and it was held flat by an almost invisible hair net. Mother smiled nervously. "Have a good time in school, Doll, and behave," she reminded me with a hug. Her bright red lipstick only made the white largeness of her figure more remote. Government regulations required that those working in a poultry factory wear such sanitized uniforms.

Ruth's job at Henderson's Produce Company was to grade eggs and eviscerate turkeys. Among other products the plant turned out powdered eggs (for cake mixes) and premium poultry at holiday time. Although the work paid only minimum wage and was seasonal and despite the fact that Henderson's often laid off employees, Ruth had embraced the chance for paid labor, possibly as much as thirty weeks a year—enough to sustain her household.

No longer able to trim flower beds and gather vegetables as extensively as she once did, Mother asked the rest of us to help out more in the gardens. I learned that first autumn to dig potatoes, dry cockscomb, and cook lima beans. We kids even found part-time jobs; mine included selling greeting cards door-to-door and clerking at a small grocery.

Ruth tended her plants in the early evenings and on Saturdays, but as September wore on, she found little time to fill vases with asters, gladioli, and zinnias—little energy to bring in armloads of just-picked vegetables. Often she arrived home from the factory later than the school bus deposited my older brother and me on our town's main street. Dad's field work at a hiatus until soybean and corn harvest, he met the bus and drove us the rest of the way home.

We all gravitated to the kitchen, now a quiet, uncluttered room. As soon as Mother arrived, she would join us and drop wearily into the rocker. Often she told stories about other workers or complained of federal meat inspectors, and then she tackled supper. More and more, a boxed macaroni dinner or tuna noodle casserole squelched our expectations of Mom's home cooking: her fried chicken, beef stew, succotash, biscuits, and freshly made pies.

One late fall day when Dad met the bus he was angry, mumbling about how Mother too often chatted with a coworker instead of "coming right home, where she belonged." As we sat in the kitchen, Dad's mood grew darker. Where was Ruth? Where was supper? As soon as Mother entered the kitchen, an hour after our regular mealtime, saying that she had been talking to a sewing machine salesman at a coworker's place, my father's fury peaked. Calling her a "black-haired runaround," he struck his wife, not with hard fists on her face but, instead, kicking at her—blows that glanced off mother's legs and scuffed her white oxfords. Ruth folded up, crumpling softly to the floor. Dazed, I could neither run to her nor approach Dad. I saw Ruth look up, not in pain or anger but in recognition. Less startled than we kids were by Dad's behavior, she understood his raw jealousy. And then Ruth got up and said, "I'll start supper."

Death Mask

Joann Quiñones

This poem was written before the death of my grandmother, Margarita Vargas, in April 1992.

Three of your eight daughters flock around you
like fates, trying to comb your hair
so that the gray tufts won't seem so bare
on a bare, bare skull.
But you just don't care anymore about
how your hair looks,
or if your nails have been cut,
or if your eyes seem empty and stare.
A man loved you for your black hair
and married you for lively eyes,
but it dies, it dies.
And now your body is spread
like a Venus of some lost tribe. You hear
the murmur of your praying fates, calling
dead mothers to give you strength.
But you know Mary is a bad choice.
She never suffered,
had labor pains, laid in
a bed to wait for her flesh to decay.
You only know Eve,
and her punishment.
And this is the word of God.
And this is his last judgment.
And after you spewed eleven children
your flesh gives way.
Because there are only three things
a woman could be:
Mujer, Madre, Muerta
And Eve felt it in her ribs.
And Eve learned the base words.
And like Eve you shit in your bed
because leaning on your haunches
begging for someone to wipe you is too much.
Your pubic hair is dry and scattered
like the tattered dying roots of a tree.
And this is where original sin starts,

with a man taking a bite, like a serpent,
your children being spit out like apple seeds.
And this is all that is left in life,
Not even to die, but to rot with old age.
And you fade as life fades, until
death do you part by part.

For Giacomo

Edvige Giunta

He floats over a white cloud
in the photograph taken
when he was dead already.
Seven months when he died
1963   near Salerno
on a black train plunging down
to Sicily from icy Switzerland
where his parents labored.

It did not take long.
A seizure and he was gone.
They told her: don't tell
or they will take him away.

In the third-class seat she held him
for thirteen hours, as if he were
still breathing her air, still
sucking her breasts, listening
to the tick tock of her heart,
suitcase clicking with watches,
smelling of sweet chocolates.
She rocked, rocked, eyes dry,
holding the hand of her three-year-old
sitting by her wide-eyed, alive.

In the photograph his cheeks
are ruby   he almost smiles
sitting by my great grandparents'
suffering faces floating on clouds.

El olor de cansansio
(The Smell of Fatigue)

Melida Rodas

My father hangs up the phone. He puts away our colorful new kite. He puts away his smile and his Tuesday clothes as he prepares for a new battle. I watch him put on the white shirt. The checkered pants. The boots. He folds a crisp white apron and places it in the pocket of his jacket. I admire the fresh white shirt, the crisp crease that runs down his black-and-white pants. Smelling like soap and shaving cream, he returns to the restaurant where he has been slaving ever since we moved to New Jersey from Guatemala in 1979.

I see him walk slowly, tired. Another cook has left. Another dishonorable discharge, I suppose. My father is brought in to hold down the fort on his day off. The way he always does, like a respectable soldier.

Each day I see my father's hair get grayer. It won't be long before it's silver, like the buttons on a new cadet's jacket, silver like water in the sun. His hands are small. Always callused. Always pink. He holds my face like a moon before he says good-bye. "Next week," he promises, as he points to the drawer that keeps our kite. I wish that he would stay. I try to keep my eyes from telling him as he holds my face. His hands feel so strong. Strong from carrying pots of heavy soup. Strong from fighting the ambush of dinner specials, lunch specials, breakfast specials with eggs, home fries, bacon, silver dollar pancakes, California cheeseburgers, Caesar salads, BLTs, mashed potatoes, French fries with gravy, toast with marmalade, jelly, butter, cream cheese.

My father has always worked hard. Ever since the age of seven when he sold peanuts, which he carried in small bags on a cardboard box. Ever since he shared the streets with the other children who sold Chicklets and shined shoes. With the blind man who sold tickets *de lotteria* and the *viejita* who begged for money outside El Palacio National. He's worked hard ever since his toes were small and wrinkled in the rain because the leather from his shoes had finally surrendered.

Life has always been as hard as the soles of my father's feet. Like the callused hand my face melts into. He holds it like the cantaloupe before a fruit salad. Like life before America. Before it's sliced, devoured, consumed. Guatemala feels like a memory, just a memory. A humble memory that moves slowly and peacefully. It is a place not so gray with buildings. It is a landscape with green mountains, blue skies, and sweet air. It is a place where you don't fear the *Migra*. The force. The clan that comes to take you away. They search in kitchens and factories for their victims. They send them back with suitcases full of postcards of the Statue of Liberty that never got sent, subway tokens, wrinkled letters with Spanish writing decorated with exotic pressed flowers, stamped with colorful postage, smelling like perfume and crayon. Everyone who is here on borrowed time, with expired visas and false documentation, fears the *Migra*. Because it doesn't matter that you have spent all your *centavos* to buy a piece of the American pie. So what if you risked your life crossing the desert with a *coyote*, the man who guides you through the desert and river to the American border? Once you reach the line, once you dodge the bullets that the border patrol has fired at you, once you say *El Salve Maria*, you crawl to American soil. *Mojado. Indocumentado.* No visa. Your wet clothes stick to your tired back. Pictures of your children, of your family, stick to your almost empty wallet.

We come to America by bus. It takes us five days to reach *Los Estados*. We leave our colorful beautiful Guatemala for gray buildings and a promise that here we will have a better life. Here my father doesn't wear a suit and tie to work. Here there is no garden, no fruit trees, no space. Here we live in an apartment. People don't smile. People don't say hello, except for the Puerto Rican lady my mother calls Donna Ortega. She's the only one who is friendly with us when we first arrive. Americans don't want to know us. Not even the children. Patrick, who lives next door, calls me a spic. One day he spits on my face on the way home from school.

Today my father leaves our apartment for the restaurant. The awful place that fatigues him. His shoulders are small and round. His feet are heavy. The image is familiar. I realize that I've seen it before. It is the picture of a wounded soldier who returns to the battle. I feel a large *jocote* in my throat as I try to imagine the number of potatoes my father has peeled. Oh, the difficulty of surviving an infantry of dishes, a Sunday morning rush! And the heat of August days. The sweat on his brow, the napkin he wraps around his forehead to prevent it from blinding him. How do you endure the battles, such battles, Father, with pans and pots as your only allies? Vegetables, meats, oil as your weapons? When is it time to surrender the ladle, the whisk, the spoon?

My father's boots. They alone tell the story of the war. With their greasy suede and vegetable pulp trapped underneath them. When he enters our home, he

Day of the Virgin of Guadalupe,
December 1974, Guatemala

sheds the boots on the floor, as if never wanting to see them again. A reminder of the American Dream gone sour. Of times that don't get better, just get harder. Every day I've seen life take the years from my father. Years taken with unsympathetic conviction. As I walk past restaurant alleys, I remember the smell of my father's clothes when he comes home.

Sometimes the hours are so hard and so long that he asks me to take off his heavy boots. Proudly, I reach for his feet and try to give him a sense of home and gratitude. I untie the hardened laces. I dispose of the fragments of lettuce and tomato caught between them. I remove his boots like a heavy cast. His feet give off the heat of labor and *cansansio*. His socks I peel off with the delicate care of an archeologist revealing precious Mayan fossils. His pale feet wait to be freed from their torture. I squeeze fatigue away from his toes. I rejuvenate his ankles. I make his beautiful rough heels feel like they can carry him to the front line again tomorrow.

My father leaves our small apartment when the sky is still purple. He leaves when the newspapers outside the candy store are still wrapped with string and the bakery rolls are still warm in large paper bags. He leaves when the chill of Aurora glues me to a poncho my *abuelo* has sent. My father leaves when the house doesn't yet smell like tea, syrup, and eggs. When the only one who hears his footsteps is my mother, as she tries to keep the warmth he has left in their bed.

My father returns when the sky is purple again. When the first stars are saying hello. He comes home when homework is done. When you've brushed your teeth. When dishes have been used, washed, dried, and put away. My father comes home when others have taken off their ties or panty hose, have eaten dinner, paid their bills, and read their favorite book. When the day has simmered and night begins. When the enemy has ceased fire. My father comes home when you grow tired of waiting. When you surrender to the weight of your eyelids and you wish you could have told him that you made honor roll again today.

July 1986, Bayonne, New Jersey

The Pawnbroker's Window

Pat Wynne

"The Pawnbroker's Window" and "Praise the Waitresses" are lyrics set to music also written by Pat Wynne.

I grew up in the 1940s in the Bronx. I was lucky. My father had a job. He worked as a clerk in the post office. It was a government job. That meant security, a pension, and vacation pay. I don't think it meant health benefits back then because I was always taken to the local city hospital for my health care.

But my parents always told me about the Great Depression. They had been married back then. My father graduated from law school and passed the bar in 1934. He'd worked his way through college in the post office, and after he graduated he couldn't find a job better than the one he had flipping letters into slots. He stayed in the post office, never accepting a promotion, because he was a shy man who had strong political convictions. He believed that it was wrong to be a foreman or a supervisor.

Still, he felt that he was lucky, because there were many who were not employed during the depression.

Now we again are living in a time when many are unemployed, living on the streets, laid off, feeling desperate—drinking and using drugs to try to forget their demoralization.

The pawnbroker's window becomes a symbol for me of these times. I had a roommate whose family had always lived on the edge. She remembered the many times when her mother and grandmother had to pawn things from the house in order to buy food at the end of the month. The thought of people getting bargains because of other people's misfortune enraged her.

THE PAWNBROKER'S WINDOW

1. High school rings—wedding rings
    Gold and silver everythings
    Extensions of people's lives
    I couldn't buy them if I tried.
    Pocket watches, wristwatch too
    Pins and chains and dreams that died

CHORUS: We're only two paychecks away from the pawnbroker's window.

2. Here's his guitar, his sax and flute
    Her trumpet with that special mute
    No music with no instrument

How many tunes lost and silent?
A synthesizer—keyboard too
Play It Again, Sam—this swan song's for you

CHORUS: We're only two paychecks away from the pawnbroker's window.

BRIDGE: We're living in desperate times, Jack!
Don't borrow what you can't pay back
Don't look down on those who've sunk so low
We're only two paychecks from that devil's window.

3.   Here's a bargain, buy a few
No questions asked, they're good as new
A bottle of milk, some kids to feed
Maybe it fed a junkie's need.
Save a dollar, two, or three
Next one could be you or me.

CHORUS: We're only two paychecks away from the pawnbroker's window—the pawnbroker's window.

Praise the Waitresses

Pat Wynne

Living in the Bronx in the 1940s and 1950s, in a two-room walk-in apartment, sharing my bedroom with Mom, while Dad slept in the living room/dining room/kitchen, was making me crazy. Both parents were nervous and high-strung. I guess having a child was constantly demanding on Dad's salary—he was a postal clerk. I needed music lessons, school clothes, books, everything.

At Music and Art High School in New York City, I was given a small scholarship—supposedly for books and clothing. (My mother insisted on putting it in the bank, and I continued to wear hand-me-downs, anyway.) This money was given to me because I excelled in music, and I guess I looked a little shabby.

I told the dean that I needed to get away from home. She helped me to qualify for a state teachers college up in New Paltz. My folks didn't think that they could afford it. I was only sixteen and, therefore, too young to go away. Eventually, the dean convinced them, and I went away to school.

In order to afford a few extras I tried to work as a waitress in the college dining hall. It was so hard I thought I would die. I later switched to the administrative offices and did clerical work.

So many people have had to work in order to put themselves through school. They've had to stay up half the night studying in order to keep up. In the song "Praise the Waitresses," besides appreciating these hard-working women, I also wanted to salute those many people who have to work in order to do other things, such as go to school.

This song is dedicated to the hotel and restaurant workers who went on strike with Local 2 in 1984.

Praise the Waitresses

1.   When I was a little girl, little girl,
        I always wanted to be
        One of those pretty waitresses who always smiled at me.
        How could I know how hard it was?
        She always hid it well.
        'Cause she always smiled and joked with me.
        She hid her private hell.

CHORUS: Praise for the waitresses. Praise for the maids.

2.   But when I went away to school,
        I had to work at a trade;
        I finally got my dream come true,
        A waitress I became.

        But the trays they just about wore me down
        With eight to ten plates all in a row,
        I tried, but soon I saw the glamour fade;
        They let me go, I was too slow.

CHORUS: Praise for the waitresses. Praise for the maids.

3.   The jobs that women often hold, often hold,
        Like waitresses and maids,
        Are thankless and submissive jobs
        And mostly underpaid.

        So, when you're out in some hotel
        Or in some chic cafe,
        Remember the tip is part of her pay.
        Our society likes it that way.
        If they unionized, it might not happen that way.

CHORUS: Praise for the waitresses. Praise for the maids.

Faces in the Hands

Carolyn Chute

There was this party I was at recently. I was on one end of a couch . . . a teal-colored couch, I think it was. I was picking from a platter of cheeses and pickles and olives and little cupcakes. A young man in a pastel shirt and pastel pants sat beside me, and we began to chat. After only a few moments of chatting, he let it be known that he was an engineer with a company. I let my eyes give him a little quick once-over, and it was plain he didn't mean the smiling waving train engine kind. He tells me about some people employed by his company, that they have the gall to be asking for higher pay and some more benefits. They weren't like him, he assured me. They were machine operators. "Just a pair of hands," said he with a simper.

Hands body-less against space?

My eyes now did a little quickie once-over of my own hands, hands that had worked the factories. *Had* these hands been body-less, soulless against the background of the great American business? My right hand fetched a cute green-tinted cupcake and stuffed it into my mouth. What could I say to this professional who to the wide world glowed so pastel and perfect pink in his successfulness? I squinted at my hands again, dumbfounded.

My brother, a weight lifter, was Mr. Maine a while ago. During that year, a new magazine for business people hit the mails. One of its first issues featured an article on what they called "the Maine work ethic." Is the Maine work ethic really dead? Experts discussed whether or not Maine people enjoyed backbreaking, boring work as much as they used to. Even with all the "experts," the general feeling of the article was puzzlement—though an uplifting and sunshiny resolution was tacked on in the final paragraph. The magazine's glossy cover showed my brother's arm body-less against a black background. "Gosh," I marveled, reaching for a couple of olives. Is that arm truly the way the pastel–dress jacket–necktie people see the worker who makes their business possible? Is this why it's okay for so many to pay their workers wages that won't cover a month's rent? Would they pay less if they could? If it weren't for unions and the minimum wage (obscenely small as that is), would businesses pay anything at all? Is it easier to exploit people who are faceless? "Yep," I said aloud around my mouthful of olives. The engineer glanced with a startled expression at my mouth. I reached for a pickle.

Just a pair of hands. Yep. How about just a stomach? That's what I was once . . . just a stomach, body-less against space, working on the bridge of a potato harvester . . . lurching about on a windy field, a sort of gray and stormy sea . . . my stomach body-less against space on the verge of throwing up . . . hour after hour . . . day after day. And where the harvester got stuck in the mud, the potatoes were not potatoes coming your way, but a gluey, putrid, white stench. I quit. The Maine work ethic wasn't on my mind that day. Having no mind . . . just a stomach. You know, it's like that with any pain or punishment . . . impossible to get your elevated thoughts together with such distractions.

Then it was the chicken factory. Each morning it was like a knife to my heart to leave my cooking, sewing, sweeping, wash-hanging . . . my beloved home and my little daughter. At the factory the grease of the yellowy cooked meat streaked my face and gave my hair an unnatural thickness. Scaled over with grease and the roaring thrumming heat, the meat and I were one.

And so the days passed . . . identical. As the soggy golden matter chugged by on the conveyor belt and my hands flew, I would daydream of the coming weekend, which seemed a hundred years away. Or of early mornings standing at the bathroom sink brushing my daughter Joannah's hair into two ponytails, knotting green yarn bows on them to match her green dress . . . or red to match her sailor dress . . . or blue to go with jeans. Against my fingers was *not* the chicken meat but her yellow hair, an aureate braille. Hands, when they are placed on a child, are not hands in space but hands connected to your past, to your future, to eternity. It's a powerful incentive to have more babies. The less rewarding your job is, the more important children become. Children are your individual creations, singular and intricate. A child is the ultimate masterpiece.

Back at the party, the engineer on the teal-colored couch beside me is telling me more about his career. He's using one hand to gesture, and I take note that the palm and five fingers are pink and silky as lips.

Meanwhile, back at the chicken factory, I was pondering what I was going to do on payday. Times had changed, prices had swelled, but the paycheck stayed eensy. And there were more and more things our legislators, town hall authorities, school authorities, insurance companies, and neighbors said we had to have. It's the law that you and your kids and your yard and your vehicle LOOK nice, laws of one kind or another. Dress codes, building codes, mandatory liability insurance, mandatory this, mandatory that . . . lawmakers always being so quick to legislate you a new expense, so slow to raise the minimum wage . . . and neighbors with their eye on you . . . garage mechanic looking under your car . . . everybody pointing at you . . . rusty this and rusty that . . . two weeks' pay for an exhaust system, two weeks' pay for your overdue liability insurance . . . cops squinting at your car, code man squinting at your house, teachers squinting at your kids, neighbors squinting, peering, gloating, "Got a backed up septic system, huh? Better get it fixed quick!" It was hard enough being able to afford not to be an outlaw, let alone afford luxuries like house payments, health insurance, gasoline, dish detergent, propane to heat the water and cook with, doctor bills and dentist bills that insurance wouldn't cover even if you *had* insurance, lightbulbs, shoes for my girl, food, toilet paper. Maybe I could sneak a roll of toilet paper from the chicken factory ladies' room. But they got ahead of me on that. They know how to deal with outlaws and thieves. They had the tissue dispenser locked.

Now and then the bosses would stroll through the plant to check up on things. When they did this, I know they saw my face as no different from the vacant dead stare of the electrically stunned, upside-down chickens with their throats cut, dangling along toward their predestined forms: chicken spread, chicken dog food, chicken hotdogs. But behind my dead eyes my brain saw the way my kitchen looked at home, yellow cat curled in the sun on a chair, and the born and unborn children of all time flashing by, the voice that is the family trait, the nose of my father's side, the smile of my mother's side, the precise and yet ethereal possible cries of "Mumma!" and "Mumma!" and "Mumma!" while on and on my hands tore the hot chicken muscle from bones and bosses passed to the next operation, satisfied.

The Maine work ethic. What the hell is that anyway, as opposed to the Rhode Island work ethic? Consider this quote from John Poor of Andover, Massachusetts, a railroad visionary: "The capacity of the human frame for labor is found to be greater in Maine than Massachusetts or any other state, south or west of it."

Having some North Carolina blood coming in on my father's side must have been why I was getting weary of the chicken factory life. I just couldn't seem to feel that great noble surge, that "Hi-ho! Hi-ho! It's off to work we go!" frame of mind as I chugged along in my outlaw car from my outlaw home, running out of gasoline along the way, scouting for unattended-looking gas stations that might not have their toilet paper dispensers locked.

What by gorry is *any* kind of work ethic? Is it work for the sake of work? In the dictionary, the word *ethic* is described as "moral duty." Duty to whom? Wasn't it Thomas Jefferson who said an industrialized nation cannot be a true democracy?

What was it like here before industrialism? Before technology-ism, computer-ism, shopping-mall-ism, business-meeting-and-banquet-at-a-nice-hotel-ism?

When we were an agricultural people, the farm, the home, the family was the product. This was your masterpiece. You watched it grow or fail. A new season might bring renewed hope if you failed last year. Life was full of surprises. Suspense. Broken tools. Broken bones. Bad weather. Insects. Work. Work. Work. Passion. Ideas. Big ideas. Good ideas. Bad ideas. Traditions. Surprises, more surprises. Pride. The whole family . . . mother and father, teens and babies, an uncle and maybe a couple of burly aunts, everybody together battling away at the godly and ungodly forces that trickled out food, water, heat. Family with one goal in common . . . the finish line, the home plate . . . the harvest, the woodpile, the *home*.

Of course, not everybody liked farming. But in those days if you got caught out behind the barn with a book, you might get the strap. Reading a book was goofing off. Funny how fashion goes, isn't it? Who is it that decides these things?

Family units. Life in common. Work in common. Misery in common.

Families are not necessary to industry. But work for the sake of work is necessary to industry.

If we, Maine, we, America, are going to have a *true* free enterprise system in the future, we're going to have to think seriously of why the work ethic is dying and if there ever was one.

And "family." Are we going to see the extinction of *that* "system"?

Will we someday be little more than individual ants with one great corporate queen-ant biz dictating from the top?

Another cupcake . . . chocolate with white nonpareils. And the voice from the other side of the couch chatting away about his latest project. But what is there for me to reply to this person who will not really ever know me, he a person who cannot understand anything but the academic A plus? My thoughts must remain my own this evening.

So whose babies *are* the mills? *Somebody* must love them. The owners, of course. The owners love their mills, dream of them all night. They feel a thrill over mills. Passion. Joy. Consternation. Challenge. Surprises. Incentive. Pride. They have a *great* sense of the work ethic. They bounce out of bed each morning to work on that baby, to make it grow and to keenly dwell on that margin of profit and to ask, "What's the matter with the workers? How come they don't work harder? And harder and harder? What's all this complaining about wanting more pay? How come they don't love my mill, my masterpiece, my baby?"

I quit that chicken-picking job, too. I do not have enough Maine work ethic. I am not a good person. I am not a good American. I went on welfare, which is even worse. Welfare people are lazy no-counts living off the dole, they say.

Years later, on the teal-colored couch, checking out more pickles, sweet and dill, one of each, I am wondering, What about businesses that quit the people? Especially the ones that move somewhere else to find cheaper and cheaper, more desperate help. Leaving the state. Leaving the country. Where's *their* moral duty? *Their* patriotism?

And what about these big businesses that get the dole?

Why does the obligation, the duty, always wind up in the lap of the individual, the worker, and never, NEVER the big guys? And how come comfy Joe and Jane America, the ones who are themselves workers but somewhat better paid workers, are always so quick to blame higher prices, higher taxes, job shortages, and what-all on the lower paid worker or the out-of-work worker and sometimes the better paid union worker . . . but never do they blame the boss, the owner, Mr. Biz?

"Joe and Jane are worried," I mutter around a dill pickle. "Yep, that's it. They are worried sick by the terrible power of the great punishing Dad . . . Dad who is America, God, and Wealth . . . especially Wealth, for if you don't pray to it enough and honor and obey it, it won't trickle down. If you question its holiness, things might get seriously worse for you."

"Excuse me?" wonders the man in pastel on the couch beside me, looking with narrowed, bewildered eyes at my mouth. Was I thinking aloud again? I reach for a little embossed napkin and wipe the pickle juice from my fingers.

Our neighbor Glen stops by for tea sometimes. Stepping out of his truck, he always has that same embarrassed look most Mainers have these days having to drive around with VACATIONLAND and red lobsters on both front and back bumpers. Glen is a carpenter and does some work in the woods, logs and pulp, firewood. He is building his own house, a farm, he tells us . . . the slow old-fashioned few-boards-at-a-time way, the no-bank-loan way, the you-don't-get-it-all-at-once way. He is independent, thoughtful. With a tea mug in one hand, he gives his mustache a few deep-thought pulls with the other. He says he's been thinking about why workers in some places, like those plants in the Midwest that make cars, are never happy with their paychecks and benefits, even when they have pretty good paychecks, at least by the standards we Maine workers know. He says he thinks the reason is because no matter how much they make, they have this unexpressed knowing that they are possessed, owned. Body and soul. They know what they'll be doing tomorrow. They know what they'll be doing next week. Next year. They can see their lives stretching out before them unvaried, flat, and uniform. They have already lived their future. They are the living dead. Carcasses, if not slaves. What price would you put on your life? The price is never good enough.

And yet what does the business owner vow to you? That plant can shut you out tomorrow, leave you fifty-five years old and jobless.

Something moves. Gives me a start. It's the young engineer on the couch beside me, reaching for a pink cupcake. He turns it in his long fingers and asks, "What do *you* do?"

"Blipe," I say around a big bite of very sunshiny yellow cupcake. And another olive. I chew thoughtfully, nodding, smiling, stalling. I'm wondering if the engineer has children. But of course. It's his privilege. It's the low-pay people who aren't supposed to have kids. You hear it time and time again: "And there they were in that dumpy place with all those kids. Argh!" or "After a person *that* poor has more kids than she can afford, you start taking the kids away."

How come nobody threatens to take away the kids of the employer who pays his people too little? Why don't *those* types stop having kids? Look at what their kind has made this world into? Look at their high-pay, high-profit waste. They are smashing the world.

I am remembering Reuben. Am I enraged by his death? Or content? I want to tell you about Reuben, but first I have to tell you about his people, my people.

One of the things I admire most about my husband, Michael, is his hands. I remember when I met him in a darkish lakeside barroom, even while falling in love with his voice and eyes, his beard, his lanky, sinewy height, my eyes scrutinized those hands. I remember thinking, yes, those are the hands, the hands of my people.

My people. Memories filled with hands. My grandfather died when I was eighteen. I was terrified of the "viewing room," where you stand around the open casket. I stayed out in the anteroom with my cousin Jane. Jane's father was my grandfather's brother, Jim. Jim had died young. Jim dug bait worms for a living in Belfast. When we went to Belfast to visit, I remember my aunt's hands breaking open clams in the slate sink. Jim took us kids to the shed. I'll never forget him unbolting the shed door and there, living in wet hay, was the prize, the longest stinging bait worm he'd ever dug. It looked like a red snake with legs. I was impressed.

Jim was dying even then. Later he spent most of his time in a chair in the kitchen. His black, black hair was long because he was too sick to have it cut, our aunt told us apologetically on one of our last visits before he died. But I thought that hair was the most beautiful thing, back in those days when you never saw anybody's true hair, back in those days of buzzers and crew cuts. I remember holding my eyes on him, dazzled. He was part Indian, death in his eyes, his hands in his lap.

After my grandfather's funeral, on the ride home, my mother said, "You were right, Carolyn, not to want to see him. It didn't look like him at all." She sighed. "Except his hands . . . his beautiful hands." I could see clearly the short fingers, one with a "claw," and his wedding ring . . . how he always bragged he had never taken that ring off since it was put there. Not ever. By the time he died, the ring was as thin as a yellow hair.

My husband, Michael, wears green workshirts and green workpants. His eyes are brown, hair black, a little long. My mother says he looks like our uncle Jim. Michael is respectful of and dazzled by all life. He has magic in his hands. I've seen him carry a spider to safety. Another time a mouse. I have a photograph of Michael with a butterfly calmly settled on one of his thumbs. He has a volunteer job these days. He takes meals around to old folks. Some days he goes back and spends afternoons with them. He feeds their pets for them. The old guys and Michael shoot the breeze. They cover woods, weather, guns, and other country stuff. Michael can only write his first and last name, not his middle name. He can't read my name at all. His pay job these days is mowing graves. Makes $1,000 a year thereabouts.

Back in school Michael was called dumb by a lot of his teachers. Some called him a troublemaker. One of them put him out in the hall every day in third grade. Later he went to a fate worse than the hallway. SPECIAL ED, OR "RETARD ED," as some of the kids called it. Just because of dyslexia, because words scrambled on the page before his eyes, he was scolded, jeered, punished, stigmatized.

Back then, even then, Michael loved old people, had a way with them . . .
aunt, uncle, grandmother, gramp were what life was about to Michael. But public
school doesn't give you a grade in OLD PEOPLE. That's not ACADEMIC enough. It's
not a thing you can do at your desk. And now in adulthood, Michael finds his
greatest gift is still not valued. Helping old people is not a product. It's not a thing
rich people can buy shares in. So his talents will never earn him a paycheck. In
the eyes of America, Michael is still a failure.

We had mixed feelings back when we discovered I was pregnant with Reuben.
The world was not exactly waiting for Reuben with open arms. But I studied the
prenatal pamphlets showing fetuses at all stages of growth, trying to imagine
Reuben's face, cell by cell, our masterpiece.

If I slammed the door of our old truck or dropped a kettle lid, Reuben would
startle inside me, jerking back his hands and feet. Other times he would yearn up
toward his father's spread hand.

It was in the days when President Ronald Reagan was riding his horse and
talking softly into the microphone and many people were mesmerized. "He will
cut those lazy types off without a dime!" good-pay Americans cheered. "And then
those lazy bums will have to get themselves REAL jobs."

I overheard a neighbor snorting, "The president will clean up the garbage" and
rolled his eyes toward my pregnant belly.

People who heard I was on welfare, people who had good-pay jobs, said, "Why
doesn't Mike get a better job? Why doesn't he get two jobs? Three jobs? When I
was young, I worked twelve hours a day, six days a week for fifteen dollars a week,
and I didn't complain, I didn't ask for welfare." Sometimes they said, "Why
doesn't Mike get his high school diploma? You can't amount to anything without
that."

Once, when someone said this, Michael's hands tightened in rage. He went to
the bureau drawer, found his high school diploma, gave it a toss into the wood-
stove, and said gravely, "I've wanted to do that for a long time."

The unborn baby grew big. On both sides of the family, nice big babies were
the usual.

Meanwhile, Michael was at the dairy farm or the orchard, pruning apple trees,
harvesting potatoes, or splitting other people's firewood . . . moving from job to
job . . . salvage yard, gardening, cold storage work, jobs that didn't require him to
read and write . . . jobs that didn't depend on self-esteem. Jobs that paid minimum wage or less.

Meanwhile, President Reagan was riding his horse and tipping his hat, and the
good-pay Americans were cheering as he cut money to the states and as the state
of Maine took away my medical card, which was giving me and my baby medical
care that Michael's check wouldn't cover.

Meanwhile, industries were leaving Maine, the great conveyor belts silenced,
the truck bays and loading docks empty . . . chicken . . . shoes . . . textiles. Gone.
Everybody scrambling to grab up what was left of the jobs.

The governor said not to worry. New jobs were on the way. Tourism was coming. You'll have lots of jobs soon. We tried to grin and bear the VACATIONLAND red lobster license plates. Some tried to grin and bear the new tourist-related jobs that were always part-time jobs and that offered low pay and no benefits. People even grinned through seeing the tourists who decided to STAY and live in Maine where *life is as it ought to be* . . . tourists whose willingness to pay *any* price sky-rocketed the price of a home . . . a price low-pay working people could not afford and better-pay working people *thought* they *could* afford, going into debt neck-deep.

Everybody was grinning.

They told Michael, "Go get a job at McDonalds."

"Raise your aspirations," said others. Educators especially. They love that word. ASPIRATIONS. All over the state you can hear that long word rolling off their tongues. It's something the low-income people don't have enough of, they say.

Aspirations???

Where are the little farms? A person with learning disabilities who wasn't born to be a pastel-shirt person could get by with his own little farm . . . could be *inter*dependent . . . could practice Yankee ingenuity and good Yankee sense. The farm . . . the farm . . . just a fading whisper . . . gone.

And now the mills. Going.

The governor says what we need is more tourist-related jobs. We should bring in more tourists. But then sometimes the governor says tourist-related jobs are bad. What's the matter with you people? Can't you raise your aspirations? The governor tells the schools to give the kids more homework and longer school days to help them raise their aspirations and get them out of those dead-end tourist jobs.

Somebody tells Michael, "Raise your aspirations! Computers are the thing."

Everything's getting fast, faster. Keep up or keep out. "That's life," the politi-cians say. "If you can't keep up, you fall by the wayside. Fact of life."

Meanwhile, with no welfare medical card, I lost my private doctor. The pre-natal clinic I went to was crammed with those fallen by the wayside of the presi-dent's and the governor's cuts. The hospital was crammed . . . so crammed that I was in labor with a breech birth baby for two weeks and a temperature of 104 degrees before the hospital would let me in.

His name was Reuben. Thick auburn hair. Narrow-shouldered. Dehydrated. Starved. He is buried here in these hills among his ancestors going back 150 years, the farmers of small farms and their great independence and pride. When I visit his grave, I am content. I tell him I'm glad he's dead. Safe. Spared. I say, "Dear, dear Reuben . . . dear gentle person. What if you were born?"

Well, there he goes again. The governor is on the radio talking higher aspira-tions for us all . . . more homework, more school hours, more, more, more! That'll cure the problem, he assures us. Doesn't he realize that the higher the white-shirt pastel-people raise their aspirations for us who are already failing *their* idea of success, the more we lose sight of our own true aspirations and the deeper into complete failure they leave us?

Reuben, dear gentle person, maybe you inherited the learning disabilities of your father and me. Maybe your talents would have been unmarketable. Maybe you would have had to take time and care with everything you would do. Schools and jobs have no patience. Maybe by the time you were a man, you couldn't feel like a man. You'd break one of their laws. And soon there are going to be A LOT MORE LAWS . . . school classrooms packed like cattle pens, prisons full of people standing shoulder-to-shoulder, more capital punishment, capital punishment for lesser crimes to make room, more drugs, lots more drugs, more disease, less help from doctors, people getting mad, people in mobs . . . everybody falling by the wayside . . . no place for the gentle, old-fashioned people . . . room only for the high-aspirations people. "Better people!" Better, smarter, cleaner, spotless, odor-less, hair that doesn't seem like hair, skin that doesn't smell like skin, hands and fingernails that are silky as lips, humanity with no trace of mammalhood but uni-formly glib with accent-free voices. Such creatures! Polymerized, preserved, freed of flaw, soaring up, up, up, and away . . . the ultimate win.

Something shifts on the couch beside me. I see the pastel-shirt pastel-pants fellow is still admiring his pink cupcake, but he doesn't eat it. He is telling me about something "incredible" he has just read in the *New York Times* this week.

Meanwhile, at the Blaine House (fancy mansion the governor lives in), the gov-ernor is probably helping himself to a snack before the maids bring supper. With his right hand he reaches for a cracker, applies soft cheese with a knife, leans back into his chair, and nibbles. His hands brush crumbs from his pastel dress pants. Governors everywhere reaching. And the president. Not the one on the horse; now it's the one with the big gas-guzzling boat. He is perhaps in his office this evening, leaning back in his big groaning chair with wheels, reaching, munching. President munching. Governors munching. Hands brushing crumbs to the rug.

You hear it these days . . . a lot of talk about choices . . . good choices, bad choices. You are shepherds of your own destiny, they say. There are how-to books on making the right choices. There are high-price counselors you can go sit with to help you pick the right life.

Doesn't luck play into this game somewhere? Like having the great big good luck of having what you are naturally good at be marketable, highly paid, highly respected.

But the idea of luck might take away the moral aspect of things, the idea that good people make the right choices, bad people make bad choices, and people get what they deserve.

Work hard, you win. Goof off, you lose. This is the belief.

The words of yesteryear's Maine were WORKING TOGETHER. The word today is COMPETITION. Like sports. Like school spirit. Whose baby is reading first? Whose school has the better team of better babies? Whose SAT scores are higher? Whose school puts out more professional types, fewer flunk-outs? Whose country does? Are we beating the Russians with more smart, more knowledgeable, more high-drive graduates? Beating the Japanese? Whose country has, if not more work ethic, bigger tanks, bombs, rockets, nuke subs, cruise missiles, and various other winged monstrosities . . . in case the smarter, better, faster babies of other countries get too smart or just too big and pushy, too crowded, too used up in resources, or too greedy, too "crazy"?

Our leaders and experts are always saying about the low-pay people, "They've got to break the cycle." As if the low-pay people are the ones totally in control of the situation here. What about the leaders' and experts' cycles of greed and waste? And ignorance? Especially ignorance. Gosh, how *little* they know!

"Low-income people have got to escape," they say. Escape what? Do they mean *leave home*? Leave town? Like they did? Do they mean escape that life we have here in Maine with our family ties and hometown ties and go to . . . to . . . to Harvard or Yale, like they did? Live in a faraway city? Be a yuppie? Is that the only acceptable choice? Why was it so easy for *them* to leave *their* homes, these leaders, these experts, these professionals? Were their homes dysfunctional in a way social workers aren't trained to recognize?

And besides, I thought Maine was *where life is as it should be*.

Maybe by "escape" they mean something along the lines of . . . get out of the way. Like a long time ago when they gave the Maine natives reservations to live on. What do they have in mind for us this time? Cement block public housing?

Back then, were they telling the Maine folks (the Passamaquoddies and Penobscots), "You have choices. You are the shepherds of your own destinies. The reservation or Harvard—take your pick."

Down at the pub for pizzas, Michael and I see some of the box shop guys who have been laid off . . . some woolen mill folks . . . and those who work in the woods . . . talking weather, sports, war, and the god-awful price of a can of Spam. The light from the table lamps on these men's hands is yellow and fuzzy and forgiving. Their hands, like their faces, are expressing glee or rage. One of them has a short finger. One of them has a couple of short fingers and a fingernail like a claw. I look across the table at my husband's hands and at his dark green workshirt buttoned in a formal way at his throat. His hands on the table are empty. But to me and to many, he is the axis of the earth.

Meanwhile, the governors unfold their cloth napkins and pick up pretty forks. The open newspaper tells of some of the doings of the low-pay people OUT THERE . . . the trials and tribulations they cause, their peculiarities, their discontent . . . distant . . . distant beings . . . as distant as if on a small blue planet in the black firmament. "What the hell is going on with these low-income types?" the president wonders. "What are we going to do about the mess they cause?" And the governors scratch their heads. In their respective mansions, they reach for the crusty bread.

I turn. The engineer is waiting for me to say something. Here's my chance. Should I explain, "Dear young fellow, in the hands of the working people, I've seen life, death, patience, enduring patience, surrender, miracles, and mistakes. Working people are as human as you are. They need to eat and sleep and stay warm and have a doctor when they need one, just like you do." Or should I say, "If the queen bee were alone, she'd die. All of us humans working together are a perfect thing, a human network of needs and gifts. Boss and worker, each is a gift to the other."

No, the truth is that there are too many people today . . . indeed . . . too many. In each other's way. Grabbing. Clawing. Overlapping. War and disease are ready to do nature's task . . . to cut us down. And as in employment, so in war and disease, the working people and out-of-work people, not the A-plus people, will bear most of the blows. Survival of the fittest is still the great law of the land. *The Capitalist creed.*

The truth is, I'm not looking at the young engineer's face. "You seen one yuppie, you seen 'em all," some say. I want to close my eyes to the fear and hate that rises in me. There is nothing he and I have to say to each other. Diplomatic talks only take place between two powers. Not one power and one powerless. And maybe he's not all that powerful anyway, just one small-time yuppie . . . just a guy trying to get through another party, another day.

I narrow my eyes on his right hand. It's not the future I see in this man's hands. It's just a pink cupcake.

Recovering Working-Class Autobiography and Oral History

'We Did Change Some Attitudes'

Maida Springer-Kemp and the International Ladies' Garment Workers' Union

Compiled and edited by Brigid O'Farrell and Joyce L. Kornbluh

In 1955, Maida Springer, a forty-five-year-old factory worker and union activist from the garment district of New York City, was one of the first African American women to travel to Africa on behalf of the American Federation of Labor and Congress of Industrial Organizations (AFL-CIO). An international labor pioneer, she has worked for fifty years with trade union leaders from many countries, including Kenya, Nigeria, Tanzania, Ghana, and South Africa, establishing education and training programs and acting as a critical link between the labor leaders on both continents.

Interwoven with her work in Africa are activities in the International Ladies' Garment Workers' Union (ILGWU), which she describes as "one of the most exciting unions in the world." After joining Local 22 of the ILGWU during the depression, she became very active on several committees. Several years later, she became a local union education director, and one of the union's first African American business agents. In 1945, she was chosen by the American Federation of Labor (AFL) to represent them on a goodwill mission to England for the Office of War Information. It was there that she first met some of the emerging young African leaders and became committed to their need for training, education, and independence. That same year she was named one of the Women of the Year by the National Council of Negro Women.

In the 1960s, Maida became an international representative for the AFL-CIO International Affairs Department and then worked with the affiliated African-American Labor Center and the Asian American Free Labor Institute. She also worked as a general organizer for the ILGWU in the South and as a Mid-west director of the A. Philip Randolph Institute, and served as vice-president of the National Council of Negro Women. Increasingly, she focused on the needs of women trade unionists in the United States, as well as in Africa, Indonesia, and Turkey.

While recognizing problems of racism and sexism within unions, Maida continues to see the labor movement as a major force for improving the lives of working women and men. Today, she lives in Pittsburgh, near her son and his family. She continues to travel to Africa, and her home remains a meeting place for visitors from around the world.

Drawing on oral histories, interviews, and papers, we offer some of Maida's remarkable story, as told in her own words, supplemented with some historical notes to help the reader.[1]

School and Community

*During the 1920s, the Harlem Renaissance embodied the strong African American cul-
ture in New York City, embracing music and literature, as well as intellectual and civil
rights movements. Maida Stewart grew up in this atmosphere with her mother, Adina
Stewart. Maida was born in the Republic of Panama in 1910. Her father had come
from the West Indies to work on the Panama Canal; her mother was born in Panama.
After her younger sister died at age three, they immigrated to New York, arriving at Ellis
Island in August 1917. They lived at first with relatives in Harlem, and then her parents
separated. Maida says little about her father, but describes Adina as intelligent, viva-
cious, and "always young." Her mother worked first as a domestic and then as a cook
and beautician, eventually opening her own beauty shop. Family and church played
important roles in Maida's youth, but she was also strongly influenced by the African
American leaders of that time. Her mother was a follower of Marcus Garvey (1887–
1940), founder of the Universal Negro Improvement Association. Maida attended high
school at the Bordentown Manual Training and Industrial School for Colored Youth, a
private boarding school in New Jersey, where she heard speakers like W. E. B. Du Bois
(1868–1963), a leading intellectual and one of the founders of the National Association
for the Advancement of Colored People (NAACP), and Paul Robeson (1898–1976),
a great actor and Civil Rights activist.*

The first school I ever went to was in the United States. But I could read and
write when I came here. The public schools in New York City—that was something else! I was enrolled in St. Mark's, the Catholic school near our home. Then
I went to a black boarding school in New Jersey. This was a black industrial
school for boys and girls. They had football and tennis and all of these things, but
it was an industrial school. It wasn't a "hoity-toity" school. They attempted to set
a standard. They gave you the best that they could offer.

The teachers were excellent men and women who had very superior education. Miss Grant taught English literature. She spent the summer in Europe, and
every September she came back and opened up a whole new world. Poetry had
meaning. Medieval architecture had meaning. Rome, Switzerland, Africa—all
had meaning. One of the professors there was William H. Hastie, later Judge
Hastie. He taught me science. My history professor was a Harvard graduate. His
father had been a janitor at Harvard. And seeing him stand there and talk about
the *ex post facto* law. . . . These were great awakenings. To see Paul Robeson
standing on the platform in our assembly at the school. He was then at Rutgers.
He was great. These were the images I had. Dr. Du Bois talking over our heads
because he was always the elegant aristocrat and giving you a worldview. These
were the role models of men and women of intellect and men and women who
talked about what a social system should be.

In terms of identity, the Garvey Movement was another great influence on my
life. We came to the United States at the point that Garvey, the burly black
Jamaican, was really at the top of the mark. My mother, of course, immediately
joined the Universal Negro Improvement Association. I listened to men and

women of the day passionately speaking a language that most black Americans were not speaking. These were passionate men and women, envisioned Americans, West Indians, and a few Latins, and they were talking about a society in which men and women, regardless of color or race, should share. There should be a caring, and then . . . the challenges: don't buy where you can't work, develop your own industry, develop your own initiative in the community, own buildings. We were one of the early stockholders in the Terry Holding Association, which was a building society.

My mother marched as a Black Cross nurse in the Garvey Movement, and she had this child by the hand. I went to the meetings because there were no baby-sitters. We were not sophisticated enough for that in those days—so wherever she went, I went. And so I listened to all of this. In our home, people from our part of the world, from the Caribbean Islands—many of them congregated in our house. My mother was a marvelous cook and a joyous woman, so there was always a coterie of people, and there was singing, and there was talking, and beyond that, a realization of a role we had to play in this society.

It didn't matter whether on Monday morning you were scrubbing floors or were a porter someplace, or whether you were doing the most menial job. This was all the society would permit to be open to you. Many doctors and lawyers in that early period were people who had worked at menial jobs, and worked on the shifts in order to continue their studies. It was only a very small percentage of black Americans whose families could support a fine education.

FACTORY WORK

Like the lives of most young women of her day, Maida's life was dramatically affected by the Great Depression. While in high school, she got a job in a garment factory, one of the few places hiring young black women, where she learned to use a pinking machine "to cut the jagged edges on the garments." After graduation, in 1927, she worked as a receptionist until she married Owen Springer, a West Indian from Barbados. Their son, Eric, was born in 1929. Owen had a good job in a dental equipment firm and expected his wife to stay at home, but when the depression started, he had to take a large cut in salary and Maida went back to work in a garment factory.

In 1932, I went to work in a garment shop, first as a hand sewer and later as a power machine operator. In those days I had a lot of family in-laws. My sister-in-law lived on one floor and she had seven children. I lived on the top floor. I never had a baby-sitter, never needed one. When I moved away from 142nd Street, if Owen and I were going out someplace, one of the older girls came and spent the night. That was the family.

The industry was in a chaotic condition. The union was very weak. People came in very early in the morning, didn't have their lunch hour, and all sorts of things. If the manufacturer of the garment thought something was wrong with it, you fixed it for nothing. Oh, it's hard to describe.

I kept threatening that I was going to the union. The cutter and I became very friendly. It was unusual in those days to see a Negro man a cutter, but he was excellent, and since they paid him next to nothing, and it was nonunion, he was able to hold the job. Most shops were nonunion shops. But I knew something about unions. I had heard A. Philip Randolph speak in Harlem and had some positive views about unions. I joined the Dressmakers' Union, Local 22, of the International Ladies' Garment Workers' Union in May 1933. I went in and told them what was happening at work because it was just getting under my skin. The fee to join the union was $2.50 and dues were $0.35 a month.

UNION ACTIVISM

The unions in New York's garment industry were largely dominated by European immigrants with strong ties to socialist and communist organizations. Communist influence started to decline in the ILGWU beginning in 1926, with a disastrous five-month strike led by the communist trade unionists. In 1933, the National Industrial Recovery Act first gave workers the right to organize unions. Under the leadership of David Dubinsky, elected president of the union in 1932, the ILGWU's New York Joint Dress Board called a general strike. On 16 August 1933, 60,000 workers, mostly women, marched to the strike halls in New York, New Jersey, and Connecticut. The strike was brief, but the union won increased wages and better working conditions, and union membership rose from 50,000 in 1933 to 200,000 in 1934. The number of black women dressmakers in ILGWU Local 22 increased from 600 to nearly 4,000.[2] Maida began a lifelong career as a strong union activist, and the Springer family's way of life was forever changed.

We were part of a social revolution. You see, the garment industry was built by European immigrants, most of whom were victims of oppression in their native lands. Their political opinions ranged from anarchism to Zionism, but communists made up the largest group. Charles "Sasha" Zimmerman, the manager of my own Local 22, had been an ardent communist. After the 1926 strike, which nearly destroyed the union, he turned against their ideology and became their most bitter foe and target. The worst of it was over by 1933, but you still had lots of problems after that. In the big local unions, you had challenge and conflict. I was involved in all of that because the communists constituted the opposition to the union leadership. The communists were not concerned with the domestic life of the worker in America. They had a political ideology that was destructive to improving workers' conditions.

When the strike was settled, industrywide, then we had to begin to build the union. Oh, just hundreds and thousands of workers were enrolled into the garment workers' union and this was a great excitement. My own Local 22 was one of the bigger locals. Everyone who was not Italian belonged to Local 22, the dressmakers. We had thirty-two nationalities. We prided ourselves on this. We immediately began focusing on educational work because we had all of these raw recruits. So they began all kinds of classes—English for the non-English-speaking, classes on parliamentary procedure, classes of all kinds to provide a very simple, basic understanding of the union agreement. It was really the first important agreement that we had. I began on that level as an activist.

You still had the Italian workers belonging to Local 89, which was the Italian-language local—they spoke Italian. You think of Luigi Antonini, with his flowing black tie, who looked like a great opera impresario. He brought to the garment workers a kind of cultural content, because any celebration meant going to the opera or bringing the greatest of the opera stars to the garment workers. When we had our celebration in Madison Square Garden after we won the general strike, everybody from the Met was there to sing for the workers. You had the great freedom song of the Italian workers, *"Pane y rosa,"* "Bread and Roses." That's why I say that, for me, the trade union movement was always a great love affair and a great excitement.[3]

I'm a member; I work in the shop. I go and work in the shop every day from 1933 until 1941 or 1942. But I'm active, very active, chairman of the education committee in my local during one period. I took all the courses that were required of me. Those early courses were for activists to be more intelligent and to be more informed. For those who were, I suppose, more aggressive than I, they looked forward to becoming an officer. But, on my life, this was not my concern. I could not be a member of the Committee on Prices in my local union if I did not know what I was talking about. I could not represent the shops. So I took the courses I did on the advice of my business agent so that I could be a better union member.

I was an executive board member of Local 22 and represented the union on all kinds of committees. A bread-and-butter committee, when I worked in the shop, was to settle prices. Our wages were based on the settlement of the piece-rate price: what a worker would be paid for each piece completed. I was on one of the first committees of the local and I was to represent workers in structuring our base, how we settled the garment, what we were to be paid. I was elected by my shop to be their representative on the jobber's premises, the manufacturer's premises, to argue for what we would be paid for making the garment. It was complicated to learn. At first, it was most frightening, but you had the guidance of your union representative, you had training, and you and other workers who represented other shops, you met together. But the employer tried to intimidate you. This was a brand-new experience.

The union changed our way of life. I'd go off to training programs on weekends and Owen would not go. I wanted him to understand what I was trying to do in this country. I would say, "Eric needs the best chance we can give him. We only have one child, and the union has made it possible for women to be involved, to expand my opportunity." I think he resented it, which made life difficult for all of us, but he was a wonderful human being, a wonderful father. By the time Eric was ten years old, he had all kinds of involvement in activities after school, and his father came straight home from work, or my mother was always close.

THE NEW DEAL

The early 1930s ushered in the Roosevelt administration and its far-reaching labor and social legislative agenda. In 1935 the National Labor Relations Act ensured the right to organize and bargain collectively, and in 1938, the Fair Labor Standards Act provided the first national minimum wage. The ILGWU was a very progressive union, proud of its early policies against segregated locals and pay differences based on race. Maida learned to lobby and work with people in the Roosevelt administration. In 1942, she ran unsuccessfully as a candidate for the American Labor Party (ALP) for the New York State Assembly from the Twenty-first District in Harlem.[4]

We were fighting for legislation, for all of the things that went on in the Roosevelt administration in which labor was so closely identified. My first lobbying experience was on minimum wage. The minimum wage was thirty-seven cents an hour. I think we were asking for something like fifty cents. Well, the way those senators and congressmen talked about it, you would have thought we all had tails. This was my first exposure to government. I was so incensed for years because here I am, a proud citizen, and these people talking to us as though we're scum. One senator, he read a statement about mother love and how changing the wage structure would destroy mother love and the family. Now, what mother love had to do with wages, I don't know. Women would still have to work.

The labor movement was just beginning to be recognized. There were friends of the labor movement working for legislation to strengthen unions, like the National Labor Relations Act. After Roosevelt was elected, it became a reality. When I went to work in the garment industry it was chaotic; we did not have a strong union. In those early days, people did a lot of work at home, so that after a worker spent twelve hours in the factory, she then took work home, often to a Lower East Side apartment heated with a coal stove. It was a sweated industry indeed! But by 1935, we were considered the wild ones because President Dubinsky demanded and negotiated and got a thirty-five-hour workweek. This was unheard-of! Only the union printers had a thirty-five-hour workweek. They said it would drive all the manufacturers out of business. It didn't, of course. Most of the manufacturers only got richer.

Innovative things were done by the trade unions in terms of health, in terms of leisure. Unity House, for example. Where could a worker go with a limited income and no money for a vacation? Unity House is a resort in the Pocono Mountains run by the ILGWU where union membership made it possible for you to go away the way a wealthy person might go. The Amalgamated Clothing Workers Union pioneered in housing and banking, establishing cooperative housing projects and banks that were available to union members. You had men of great genius and innovation who saw that union leaders had to create the climate of change and fight for housing, health care, and recreation, in addition to wages.

I would be called out of the shop, for example, to go to a meeting at lunch to represent the union. On one occasion, it was a luncheon meeting at the Waldorf-

Astoria. This was a great honor. I came to work that morning in my moccasins and working clothes, you know, a heavy coat. I was a size ten then. The whole shop got involved. I was loaned somebody's pocketbook; a dress was taken off of the dress form and fitted on me, and somebody else gave me a better-looking coat than the one I had on, and I marched off to the luncheon dressed to the nines. Three women who were there, Madame Chiang Kai-Shek, Madame Litvinov, and Mrs. Roosevelt—and there I was, representing my local union, representing the ILGWU in solidarity.

I went back to the shop and stitched my dresses and at six o'clock, I went to the union board meeting in my moccasins and my old coat and my tam-o'-shanter. There was a great howl because a few hours earlier I had been so dolled up. This was the kind of political and social atmosphere of that whole period.

EDUCATION DIRECTOR, LOCAL 132

One of the effects of World War II was a change in the workforce as young men went off to war. In 1942, this change became a major challenge for Maida. To prepare her for going on the union staff, Sasha Zimmerman, general manager of the New York Dress Joint Board and a good friend and mentor, arranged for her to become education director of Local 132, the Plastic Button and Novelty Workers Union. According to Maida, the membership was 70 percent male, 30 percent female, working in metals, plastics, and materials like acetone. The union lost about 40 percent of its young male members to the war, and the new members, many more of them women, came from very diverse ethnic and racial backgrounds. Maida saw education as a key to effective interracial unionism, based on her own experiences at programs like the Harlem Labor Center and the Hudson Shore Labor School.[5] During this time, Owen went into war work and commuted during the week to a shipyard in Baltimore, where the men made good money, but shared very crowded living conditions.

I became, in 1942, the educational director of the Plastic Button and Novelty Workers Union, which was one of the accessory locals of ILGWU. It included all kinds of nationalities: Poles, Germans, Swedes, and Italians. While they hated one another sometimes, they jointly hated anything black. All these new people were coming in: the poor devils who had escaped the gas chambers of Hitler; the Negroes who had just come up from the South, who had never had a working experience in an industrial setting, in a factory; women who were strange to mass employment, housewives who were just coming to work—and a part of the training was to make all of these people understand something about the union.

So we had classes, which I initiated, two or three sessions. We had lecturers who came down and talked about the union and the contract and the union constitution and the rest of it. Well, the first thing you do is start out by indicating that they have one common bond. You didn't have to love one another, we would tell them, but you wanted decent wages, hours, conditions of work. You wanted those safety measures to affect everyone, and every worker to have a sense of responsibility to the other workers—because there were some highly dangerous materials that you worked on—the plastics and acetone and poisons and the rest of it, so that you had to be responsible for the other worker. You used some heavy machines. You could stamp off a man's hand or stamp off a woman's fingers. Also, the introduction had to include good trade unionism. For people coming from a racial community where they had never been exposed to anyone that did not look just like them, this required some doing.

For example, I would organize a weekend institute. You would have marshmallow roasting, frankfurters, and after you had pumped trade unionism and workers' education and the history of the labor movement over a weekend, each evening you tried to do some of the social things people did there—country dances and the rest of it. A couple of young women came to me and desperately wanted to go, but the brothers in the family said that if "niggers" were going to be there, particularly men, they could not go.

So how could I persuade their brothers? I started with the mothers. I developed some allies. Most of the mothers I won over. It had to do with a belief that I was one Negro that maybe they thought met their standards. Their standards were much lower than mine in most instances, but, again, these are the prejudices you had to deal with.

This was my first paid union responsibility. But it was a lasting experience since it was a small local union—5,000 members, in contrast to Local 22, for example, which had 25,000 members—and the staff was a small staff. As the educational director, I went to the plant doors at four or five o'clock in the morning and issued leaflets when the shifts changed. The union staff did all sorts of things together. An interesting by-product of this, with the war on, was that we developed a labor newspaper. It brought families together. Brothers who were in the same army found one another when they got this little union magazine, *The Voice of Local 132*. We were all very patriotic. The Red Cross had a blood bank, but I refused to give blood for the reason that they segregated the blood, even though Dr. Charles Drew, a black doctor, perfected the plasma technique so useful during World War II. It was a union staff of five or six people. We knew every shop steward. We knew every committee, and *we did change some attitudes*.

CIVIL RIGHTS

In 1932, before becoming a union member, Maida went to hear a speech by A. Philip Randolph, a well-known leader in the African American community, president of the Brotherhood of Sleeping Car Porters, and later vice-president of the AFL-CIO. Randolph "really turned my head around at that meeting," she reported, "talking about the rights of workers and the dilemma of black workers and white workers who could be easily misused and abused . . . that there must be a joining."[6] Randolph became a mentor and close family friend who would have a lasting influence on Maida's interconnected commitments to the labor movement and the Civil Rights movement in both the United States and Africa. While committed to helping women, she believed "the first barrier is always race." In 1941, due in large part to Randolph's efforts on behalf of African American workers, President Roosevelt signed Executive Order 8802, prohibiting job discrimination on the basis of race, creed, color, or national origin in government and the defense industry. Mass rallies were held around the country to support establishing a permanent Fair Employment Practices Committee (FEPC) after the war ended. A major effort was a rally in Madison Square Garden in 1946, and Maida became executive secretary.[7]

We were involved in staging a Madison Square Garden rally to establish a permanent FEPC. Mr. Randolph called Sasha Zimmerman and President Dubinsky, and said, "We would appreciate it if you would allow Maida to help us put this rally together." I was terrified at the idea. The only people who could fill the Garden in those days were the communists. In addition, I did not think I had the administrative qualifications and the fund-raising abilities to do it. You know, there were some things I was modest about.

So, to everyone he sent to me, I said, "No, I would not do it." Then Brother Randolph called and asked me to come see him. I walked in, and he said, "Now, Maida dear, the cause of social justice is at stake. We had, as you know, Executive Order 8802." Since I was prepared to march about that, I said, "Yes, sir," and he said, "Now, our colleagues in the Congress, and so and so, and Mrs. Roosevelt is going to lend her support and she will talk with Franklin." You know, I walked out of there with my head bowed and a check for a $3,000 down payment on Madison Square Garden. Billy Bowe, an officer of the Brotherhood, escorted me to the Garden to make the transaction official. The Garden in those days cost $6,000 empty.

You had to raise money and then on and on. We had good fortune. Helen Hayes, Orson Welles, and a host of others—they did the dramatic part of the program. But the building of such a program, I can't tell you. I was twenty pounds lighter and years younger, and terrified. You knew you were going to get help, but how do you stage all this, and how do you keep the momentum going as you raise money and as you do the drudgery? There was strong support from groups like the NAACP, the Urban League, people in the arts, and the churches. Max Delson, a prominent socialist lawyer in New York, did a lot of work to limit our mistakes. You got the support of trade unionists and young people from colleges. Then you were busy calling all over the country and you were busy with promoters. In terms of raising the money, I had to carry the stick for this project. Union leaders used to say to me, "Well, Springer, how much is this conversation with you going to cost?" But with a dedicated staff of people to work with, it got so that you learned in the doing.

We filled Madison Square Garden with 25,000 people, and we had a five-hundred-voice choir that no one believed was possible. I used to hang my head because they would say, "What do you mean, a five-hundred-voice choir, whoever heard of such a thing?" There was a woman who was trained, a gospel singer, choir leader. I heard about her, so I hotfooted to meet her. She liked me, and I liked her, and she said, "Yes," and we began to work. She did not have five hundred voices but she began building and building around it. The Garden was the backdrop. These men and women, the women all in their dark skirts and white blouses, and the men with their black suits and white shirts, were . . . a dramatic presence. A lot of these women worked as domestics. On the night of this rally, most of their employers were there to see them perform.

It was impressive. All of the people who came to contribute and share in that occasion were extraordinary, so it was quite an experience. If someone has faith in you, and asks you as Brother Randolph did, you try. If he had told me to walk the water, I would have tried. I tell you, I would have tried. Especially with my own union backing me up, and saying, "Yes, we want you to do this." They paid my salary for the period. The trade union movement was superb, and this was AF of L and CIO. They worked at making the rally a success. This was the meeting for the forward thrust on legislation for a permanent Fair Employment Practices Committee, the catalyst of these laws around the United States.

BUSINESS AGENT, LOCAL 22

The heart of the garment industry, and thus a major focus of the union, was the piece-work system. How the work was assigned and the price paid for each piece determined wages and working conditions. Maida knew the system as a worker, a union activist, and local union education director. The next step in learning the roles and responsibilities of local union leadership was mastering the complaint process from the staff side. In 1945, she returned to Local 22 to learn the internal mechanics of the complaint department; to settle complaints about wages and grievances about working conditions, and to deal with all of the regulations that have to do with contract negotiations. In 1947, she went on the staff as a business agent, the second African American business agent for Local 22 and the first to be responsible for a district.[8]

Well, going from an activist in the shop, when you thought you knew what you were doing, to a business agent is quite a jump, because as an activist, you think you know the instruments of the union. You walk up to the window at the complaint department office and you tell them you want this, you want that. You get a lot of action. But as a business agent, you were then the responsible person and the person who had to resolve the complaints or they would complain about *you*.

As a business agent, I had fifty-eight shops. The shops were small. The section of the industry which I was given some responsibility for was called the Better Makers because you began with the wholesale price of $10.75, which was higher-priced. You had a wide range to cover and you had to overcome the suspicion of the very talented and wise men and women who were the craftsmen in the industry. Now they had to respect you, to believe that you could resolve their grievances, and stand up to the employer and be able to defend them.

A business agent's responsibility is to see that the shop functions, and to see that the worker is treated fairly by the employer and to see that the union committees function properly. Because it's a piecework system, you had to see that the slow worker had an advantage as well as the fast worker, because the employer's tendency would be to give all of the big bundles to the fast workers and all of the rags and tags and single garments to the slower worker. He would naturally lean to what would be more profitable to him. It's a horrible system. It dehumanizes you, but I don't know what the answer is. It's a system that we grew up with and it's now expanded because the needle trade has become a multinational corporation.

Every garment shop was a small government. You had to be cognizant of the personalities that you were dealing with. After you got over the suspicion that you didn't know what you were doing and you were black and you were a woman . . . after you had overcome that, then you had to overcome the suspicion that you were probably selling the workers out to the employer. Now this had nothing to do with color or race. This just meant that you were authority and you were suspect.

You made sure that you did certain things when you walked into a shop. You greeted your unpaid elected union officers. The chairlady or chairman worked there every day and if there was a grievance, you got the chairlady and a union committee to work with you on solving it. Then you went in and sat down with the employer, but under no circumstances do you go into the employer's office in a hurry. In your anxiety to get the job done quickly, since you have a long list of shops to service, you may do that. When you walk out, the assumption might be that you have made some deal to the workers' disadvantage. You walked into a shop and sometimes by the time you're through, you've created a riot. You had to know the union contract. Your business is policing the union agreement. I did that for thirteen years. Your responsibility to the union members was every hour of your life.

You don't just start as a needle worker, a garment worker, without a good deal of discipline, and a good deal of disappointment, and a lot of inconvenience in your personal life. I've had discrimination; I've had a lot of discrimination. I've had a lot of problems. I have been rejected. There were racial hostilities in the union. I would be an awful liar if I said that there were not. We tried harder, but we suffered from all of the prejudices and disabilities of our society. Within the union there were sufficient men and women who were concerned, who tried. But there were officers of the union who really could never see the black worker or the Spanish worker moving straight across the board. You had that to fight.

On the job there could be discrimination. It was a piece-rate system. The bulk of the workers, maybe operators in the dressmakers' union, got paid for what they made, but there were certain lines. With the cheaper line, you could get a job where you just work and work and work and kill yourself to make it. With the better line, you had to be more skilled and make the whole garment. A case could be made, and was made, that people were excluded. Black people or Spanish people were excluded from the better lines. There were jobs that the men just said to themselves, "These jobs are not for women." The employer and the workers agreed that we will not let women be the tailors. There were many subtle ways it could be done. Both race and sex discrimination existed.

When I was made a member of the union staff, the manufacturers' association said that their officers would not be seen with me. I was the first black business agent. Sometimes you get sick of being the first of this and the first of that and the first of the other. But my own union leader, Zimmerman, said, "All right, nobody

will function. You don't want her—you won't see her—you won't see any of us.
She's an officer of our union." We won and he never told me. I found out months
later that the association had officially protested. This is what always creates my
constant affection and love for what a workers' organization has done to raise the
sights and the sense of respect for the working men and women in the United
States—which industry on its own would not do.

ROLE MODELS

*While Maida was profoundly influenced by several prominent men, such as Du Bois,
Randolph, Dubinsky, and Zimmerman, she also attributes much of her commitment to
the labor movement and women's rights to a number of strong women activists. Among
them, Mary McLeod Bethune (1875–1955), founder of the National Council of Negro
Women, offered guidance and support. Her close friendship with Pauli Murray (1910–
1985)—feminist, lawyer, minister—was reflected in Murray's autobiography,* Song in
a Weary Throat, *which is dedicated to "Maida, incomparable companion, critic, and
guide on the pilgrimage."[9] Maida worked closely with women in the Amalgamated Clothing
Workers Union (ACWU), such as Esther Peterson and Dolly Lowther Robinson, but
perhaps most important to her development in the union were the role models from her
own ILGWU, especially Pauline Newman and Fannia Cohen.[10]*

I think part of the feeling I have had, my own constant passion about the labor
movement with all of its bumps and warts, is because I came up at a time when
there were so many role models. Pauline Newman, who was then directing one
section of the health department of the ILG, this woman had been in the
Triangle Shirtwaist Company fire. She was one of the giants, determined, articulate, volatile about workers' dignity and the pursuit of excellence, wherever you
are. Rose Schneiderman, who headed the Women's Trade Union League, brought
the women of wealth and prominence to understand the concerns, the problems of working women. Fannia Cohen was at ILGWU national headquarters in
the education department. I respected her.

Fannia Cohen, Pauline Newman, and a host of others were among the
rambunctious, tenacious women who made themselves heard. Talk about the
Uprising of the Twenty Thousand. When the men in the unions wanted to settle
for less, these women garment workers were prepared to stay on strike and be
hungry and to march in the winter. The men had families and other responsibilities, and felt that they ought to make the compromise, but the women felt that
they had reached the point of no return, and they could do no worse. I think
sometimes our madness is part of our survival. All of these women touched my
life and mind, and so I did come up at a time of great transition.

In the garment workers' union, where the majority of the membership are
women, deep down below I imagine there are people with those prejudices that
women do not stay in the union and therefore it's harder to get them into leadership. But the majority of the members of the union, most of them women like
myself, were members for twenty-five and thirty years. Even though a woman has

been a member and attended meetings and done all these things and brought up a family, there is the myth that she thinks like a woman, that she's going to be away from the meetings, from serious contract negotiation—which, in fact, is not so. It's a block one has to get over, but the doors are more open now, out of pure necessity and some intelligent leadership.

INTERNATIONAL BACKGROUND

Men like Sidney Hillman, president of the ACWU, joined the Roosevelt administration to help coordinate the war production effort.[11] Part of this effort was an exchange of workers to share experiences and ideas. Maida's first international experience began in 1945, when the AFL and the CIO were asked by the Office of War Information exchange, to send four women workers to represent the American labor movement and share wartime experiences during several weeks in England. The AFL nominated Maida and Julia O'Connor Parker from the International Brotherhood of Electrical Workers. Maida's appointment, as the first African American woman to represent labor abroad, was a history-making event documented in the New York Times.[12] *While in England, she also made her first contact with a group of young African trade unionists and the pan-African movement dedicated to ending colonialism and establishing independent African nations.*

I remember standing up on a table in a huge factory in England and after saying whatever I was going to say, asking them to join me in a trade union song. The factory owner, you know, 2,000 workers, everybody stopped, and people were waving their hands and singing. Some of their women were among the strong militants in their unions, as were women in the United States. But insofar as being in the top leadership of the trade union movement, the British Trades Union Congress was a male organization, just as the AF of L and CIO were male organizations.

An opportunity to meet the Queen of England was, of course, very exciting. We had some interesting moments, because the ladies-in-waiting had to tell you how to behave and we had to argue among ourselves the night before about who was going to curtsey and who would shake hands. We were very strong about the democratic way of doing things. But Queen Elizabeth was so utterly charming that she just put us at ease.

My colleagues—they had problems. The CIO thought that it was the egalitarian organization of the world, and that the AF of L was the reactionary organization of the world. The CIO was considered more progressive. Here you are with this black woman representing the AF of L. The CIO ladies were horrified that the CIO had been upstaged. My partner, Julia O'Connor Parker from the Telephone Workers Union, had sat with Samuel Gompers in the discussions for the International Labor Organization after World War I. She was horrified at first at the idea of having to share responsibility with this Negro woman, but we developed mutual trust and respect. We were a good working team. We were the conservatives. I had never considered myself a conservative until that time.

But when doing any of our public discussions, the larger issue was the trade union movement as a social and economic force; what it represented to millions and millions of working people. This was the goal, and how do you get a government and the employers to see that the worker is not just a pair of hands, that the worker has a mind, the worker has a home, has a family, and needs to be treated with respect, to have wages commensurate with what he or she is doing, to have a decent standard of living. If this was our goal, we had no problems.

My unofficial introduction into the politics of black Britain began at a press conference in London. George Padmore, a reporter, asked to see me. He was both an author and one of the leaders of the Pan-African Congress that had just concluded a conference in Manchester which W. E. B. Du Bois had chaired. I met Jomo Kenyatta, later president of Kenya, who asked, "Young lady, what does the American working class know about the struggle against Colonialism?" I accepted this as a challenge.

OXFORD AND AFRICA

In 1951, Maida received a scholarship from the American Scandinavian Foundation to study workers' education in Denmark and Sweden for three months. She then spent the academic year as an Urban League Fellow at Ruskin Labor College, Oxford University, England, where she made strong and lasting ties to the labor leaders of Africa also studying there. She made her first trip to Africa, on loan to the AFL, as a delegate to the first seminar in Africa of the newly formed International Confederation of Free Trade Unions (ICFTU).[13] She worked closely with Randolph and George Meany (1894–1980), who became president of the AFL-CIO. By this time Eric was at Oakwood, a Quaker boarding school in Poughkeepsie, New York. Owen had become one of the first black workers to secure a job in the New York transit system after the war. He was a member of the union, but was never active and never encouraged Maida in her union activities. They bought a house in Brooklyn and Maida's mother lived with them, but, by that time, Maida said, Owen would not discuss the yearlong trip with her. They divorced in 1955.

In London, at Ruskin College, I worked with African students, and some of these men were senior labor officers. They were down at Oxford and I was at Ruskin, but I attended some of the international lectures at Rhodes House because I was interested in international affairs. So I had contact with all of these men and women from Africa—mostly men; there were very few African women in the colleges in England at the time. Many of the men were revolutionaries who, while they had a facade of accepting the status quo, were busily working at changing the status quo. We sat up at nights discussing the future of Africa.

My first trip to Africa was as a representative of the American Federation of Labor. The international labor movement, the International Confederation of Free Trade Unions, of which the AF of L and CIO were members, invited the American unions to send as observers two delegates to the first ICFTU meeting in Africa. This seminar in Africa was for about three weeks, and trade unionists from all over the continent who were able to come—many of them had been in jail. The emphasis was on an exchange of views, and they were talking about agriculture, mining, wages, hours, conditions of service, workers' education, the prospects of independence, and the role of labor in that world that was to come.

You must remember, this is early 1955. Ghana was the country that was preparing for independence, even though its leader, Dr. Nkrumah, had been jailed. It was very interesting that the man who jailed him, the governor general, was the man who was at the prison gates to welcome him out to form a government. These were very exciting times. There were two delegates from the United States, one prominent officer from the United Auto Workers and myself, and there was a delegate from Canada. I was the only woman. It was a time of very serious work.

After this conference, of course, there were resolutions and a program. I came back to the United States and made some recommendations; reported to the AF of L; reported to the ILG, because I was an officer of that union simply on loan to the AF of L. One of the problems that the AF of L-CIO had was that we felt some of the decisions taken were very good on paper, but they took so long to implement. A. Philip Randolph, as a vice-president of the AF of L-CIO and president of the Brotherhood of Sleeping Car Porters, was one of the strong forces in the executive council of the AF of L-CIO. He championed actions which would more rapidly move programs to help the trade unionists be a social force for good, as we recognized and saw the transition in Africa toward independence. He made some of the most stirring addresses and worked within the AF of L-CIO Council for Change.

He was kind of the catalyst, a standard for the young Africans as they attended international seminars and saw him within the leadership of the AF of L-CIO in the international labor movement. He gave a sense of dignity, courage, and intellect. He was speaking on behalf of workers who had had the least, because the Brotherhood of Sleeping Car Porters had a long and bitter struggle. He was a great example and I was fortunate to have been able to serve in some capacities as a result of Brother Randolph's help in saying that "this young woman, I believe, can share constructively."

One of the myths that I would like to lay to rest is many Americans looked at President Meany as the conservative who only saw the status quo. He was concerned with what was good for workers and what was good for the citizen, and I don't think he's ever deviated from that. But he was an absolute optimist, and a challenger and a supporter when it came to working toward faster change in Africa. There is not a program with which I was associated subsequently, when I was on the staff of the AF of L-CIO in the Department of International Affairs, that President Meany did not actively support; he put his weight behind any proposition that he felt would give the worker a fairer chance on the continent of Africa.

I could tell you intimately about the differences between President Meany and President Randolph. They had very different approaches, and I do not pretend that Mr. Meany saw the need for the rapidity with which things had to change. They had a difference in method, and Mr. Meany had a fine Irish temper. But these two men had mutual respect and other people were angry that Mr. Meany and Mr. Randolph were not angry with each other. They disagreed on method, and Mr. Randolph felt that unions should be aggressive in combatting racial discrimination or thrown out of the AF of L-CIO and the rest of it. Mr. Meany was not going to go that round. But on Africa, they had no differences. Mr. Randolph's voice on colonialism was the voice that President Meany concurred with. We were being asked by the trade unions in Africa to help them.

AFL-CIO International Representative

In 1955 the AFL and the CIO merged into one federation, consolidating their international activities. After the merger, the international department intensified its work with unions in the rest of the world. This included developing labor education programs and job training centers in Africa.[14] *While there were many political and ideological reasons for labor's involvement in Africa, Maida's main concern "was to develop a cadre of trained African trade unionists who would be prepared to participate in the development of their independent countries."*[15] *She developed lasting friendships with men such as Tom Mboya, who became general secretary of the Kenya Federation of Labor. She was influential in interpreting their goals to the American labor movement and focusing the AFL-CIO's attention on the problems in their countries.*[16] *During this time, Maida remained very involved with ILGWU Local 22. In 1960, however, she joined the international staff of the AFL-CIO, and devoted her energies full time to Africa.*[17]

One of my experimental projects was based on a discussion with some African leaders, one from Rhodesia and one from Nigeria. I developed a program for trade union leaders in the African needle trades or related industries. Some of us had been thinking for years that while you taught the rudiments of trade union representation and the functioning of an organization that has to function with officers and representation and writing letters properly and learning how to deal with management, there was a second phase, which I was particularly interested in. That was training workers in employment.

So, beginning in 1956, these trade unionists, these garment workers, talked to me and said, "You are our sister in the needle trades; you see the need. We need to upgrade and we need to teach ourselves. Could you help us?" Well, I tried for years and we were getting nowhere with it. I did a memorandum. This was roughly 1961–62. President Meany said, "Well, if you can put together the arrangement, this based on the request of the trade union movement in Africa, the AF of L-CIO will be supportive in the ways that we need to be. You just go and work it out with President Dubinsky."

I always knew that when President Dubinsky raved and stormed, if I kept quiet, I had won. He said, "Springer, you always come with your unilateral ideas," and I said, "No, this is not a unilateral idea, it's a recommendation. I've gone to President Meany with this, and he's approved it. You have the school and I have come to ask you. . . . there are workers in our industry in Africa who need to improve the standard of their representation, as well as their knowledgeability of our standard of work." Finally, he said, "Go ahead and act," and so it came to pass.

I have been singularly fortunate because the leadership of the American labor movement has always given me the kind of leeway for what was unorthodox. Well, the school is now fourteen years old. This was nation building; this was looking toward independence and looking toward a way that the trade union movement could work with the independence movement.

I worked at this with the commercial workers in Africa; worked with the motor drivers to set up a school in Nigeria. I saw the training of workers in industrial competence as a priority second to their knowledgeability on dealing with the employer and understanding the union contract and the legislation in their country.

Tom Mboya, General Secretary of the Kenyan Labor Federation, on his first trip to the United States in the 1950s, was here under the auspices of the American Committee on Africa. The organization had very little money and I always offered help in my small way—a room. We had an old house in Brooklyn, a typewriter, a telephone, and food. We didn't have money, but these were the things we shared with dozens of young Africans who were in the United States for various purposes. He was twenty-three years old when I met him in 1955. He and my son were peers in age—I don't know who was a few years younger—and so I always thought that Tom was my second son. He was probably forty-six in terms of his sense of the fitness of things, his keen perception, his composure, and his rapid mind. He was a very rare human being. He never lost his sense of humor.

In the mid-1950s, preventive detention was still the way of life in Kenya under British rule, and Africans had to be off the street by nine o'clock at night unless you had a pass. Unless you had some reason—that you were working somewhere or you were doing something—you could be arrested summarily. I have been threatened with arrest because as I walked down the street it was assumed that I was an African woman being on the street without a permit or some reason for being on the street. I've attended many meetings of local trade unions in Kenya and was careful to protect the leadership from breaking curfews and other laws that put them in jail. When it got to be nearly nine o'clock, Tom had already organized the ways in which everyone could get back home, to ensure that they were not arrested.

So Tom and I worked on many projects. I suppose the one that stands as a memorial to our work is Solidarity House, the trade union center in Nairobi; the William Green Fund contributed the first $35,000 for the building. Vice-President Randolph presented the check to the Kenya Federation of Labor. In the planning process, we had gone around to the then colonial government with a simple statement of fact. The idea was that the workers in Kenya would do something like buy a brick as their involvement and contribution to it. And so we tried to state this. We were suspect, of course, by the colonial government, but since we had nothing to hide, we gave the Kenya Federation of Labor rationale and its American counterpart supporting it, which subsequently became international support, through the International Confederation of Free Trade Unions. In July 1978, there was a seminar for women workers and the opening ceremony was held at Solidarity House. The tradition, the history, of this workers' center continues.

THE WOMEN'S MOVEMENT

Throughout her long career, Maida expanded opportunities for women workers and fought discrimination on the basis of sex as well as race within both the workplace and the labor movement. She fought for women garment workers across the United States. In 1959, she advocated for a vocational school for African women and in the 1960s helped to establish the Institute for Tailoring and Cutting for women and men in the garment industry in Kenya. In 1970, she became vice-president of the National Council of Negro Women. In 1980, as a consultant to the Asian American Free Labor Institute, she helped establish the women's bureau of the Turkish Federation of Labor. Her concerns with race, women workers, and international affairs came together at the World Conference of the United Nations Decade for Women in Mexico City, in 1975. She also came to recognize the limits of her special status. While helping with organizing drives in the South, she noted in a letter to Dubinsky that "Negro workers are aware of their need of a strong trade union movement, but we need also to believe that the trade union movement has moved from the concept of a few chosen for their high visibility to an inclusiveness which makes unionism meaningful to all the workers in industry and at all levels."[18]

I am a supporter of the women's movement. In the same way that I think the labor movement is very often misunderstood, I think that the women's movement is misunderstood. The women's movement should be here to stay. It's simply another step in our development. I am a retired member of the Coalition of Labor Union Women (CLUW). There was a need for such an organization. The National Organization for Women has settled down. Both NOW and CLUW are training grounds for building self-assurance and for participating in constructive ways.

The IWY, International Women's Year, the meeting in Mexico City, was a turning point in the historical development of the role of women. The press emphasized the conflict because that's what sells. I was in Mexico City as a part of the program of the National Council of Negro Women. I was then a vice-president of the National Council of Negro Women. We had within the conference our own program of meetings with women from Africa, the Caribbean, and Latin America. Dr. Dorothy Height, President of the National Council of Negro Women, then hosted twenty-seven of these women, who traveled with us after Mexico City, because this was part of the International Memorial Year for Mary McLeod Bethune, the beloved African American educator and Civil Rights reformer, and we were celebrating Mrs. Bethune's 100th birthday. These women went to Mississippi with us to look at rural development, at the kinds of programs that are very related to the kinds of programs there are in Africa, in the Caribbean, and in Latin America.

International Women's Year, as far as I'm concerned, was a very constructive way of reaching across the world to women. There was much that was substantive and what many people forget is that we are not talking about International Women's Year, and, thank you very much, it's finished. We are talking about

International Women's Decade, which is a ten-year period. There are meetings going on all around the United States, regional meetings, and there are meetings going on in many countries. There are programs as a result that are being structured.

Anything that's underfinanced is vulnerable. A women's program is almost always taken tongue-in-cheek and the assumption is "Let's get on with it and perhaps we can forget about it after." But the problem is that the women are not going to let anyone forget about it after, because every nation in the world subscribed to the document of International Women's Year and International Women's Decade. Now the fact that programmatically there has to be a great deal of effort made and funds provided for continuity, therein lies the tale. I don't think we will get 100 percent of our objective, but then nothing ever does. Oh, I'm enormously pleased and fortunate that I was one of the minor participants in the International Women's Year.

WORK AND FAMILY

Long before commuter marriages, blended families, and caring for elderly parents were the subject of research, popular articles, and policy debates, Maida was living these issues. During her years working in Africa she remained based in the United States because she was the head of a household that included her son, her elderly grandmother, who moved from Panama when she was ninety-four, her mother, and her elderly step-father. In 1965, Maida resigned from the international department of the AFL-CIO and returned to the ILGWU for a combination of work and family reasons. She explained that there were increasing tensions between her trade union worlds in Africa and the United States, as many African leaders focused increasingly on nation building and absorbed the labor unions, limiting the workers' freedom of association. That same year she married James Kemp, a lawyer, who was president of Local 189 of the Building Service Employees Union from 1946 to 1983. He was an active leader in the Chicago Federation of Labor and the Chicago NAACP, sharing Maida's commitment to both labor and the black community, and he very much wanted Maida to return to work in the United States. Although she and Kemp separated several years later, they stayed in contact until his death in 1983. Maida reflects on the importance of family and work in her life.

My son grew up in a period when there were still very limited opportunities for the young black intellectual. The advice I gave him was, "Pursue excellence, but be the best you know how to be. Then, whatever the context of your capabilities, always remember that you give a helping hand to someone who is striving, because there but for the grace of God, there you go. You are always one step removed from a mother who was a factory worker and from a grandmother who eventually owned a beauty parlor but before that worked as a domestic in this country. Never forget that."

I think the best contribution I have made is to have set an example for my son, who is a lawyer, but who has never forgotten that his responsibility is not only to himself and his family, but that he has a social responsibility to give back something to the society that helped to fashion his life. And to see his children now growing up with a sense of history. They have parents who are teaching them that they have a commitment—that's my best contribution.

The next is a privilege that in the labor movement I have been able to learn and learn enough to make me humble, and always know I've got to pay back something. I'm an industrial worker and I have had some of the best training and best experience in the world. I come out of a factory. While I have attended a variety of schools, I always try to learn things. I've none of the snob labels; I've never taken myself seriously.

I haven't told you about my failures. You have a lot of those, too. You make bad judgments. I had learned early on: you have a disappointment, you get up, you wipe the blood away and go on to the next thing. Don't dwell on it. I've had my share of bloody experiences. I usually recover very quickly. As I look back on it, the bad spots were my being too highly motivated, too highly emotional about what I was doing. Very often I didn't see it from the outside, but I was so involved in what I was doing that I was blind to the motivations of others and my trust was misplaced. This happens to everybody. We wipe the blood off our noses and keep going.

In whatever field, pursue excellence; learn as much as you can about your field; do not wear your ability across your chest. If you have it, you do not need to flaunt it. Have a sense of history and do not believe that you created the wheel, because you will always learn that there were wheels there long before you came along, and that what you are doing is building. Have a sense of community identity. Give something back to society; give something back to your forebears. Never be so single-minded that you think there is only one way to live and only one choice. Learn not to be bitter about defeats and not to be arrogant about successes; each can limit you. Life is a combination of things: family, sharing, a personal relationship, which does not rob you of your self-respect and your own identity.

Always remember that the person who has done something against you—or the society, the people in that society—they are the lesser human beings than you are, or else they would not have to resort to denying you the right to opportunity. They are smaller people than you are, because in order for them to be superior they must teach you to be inferior. Never let anyone do that to you. Always remember, if bruised, you hurt; if bruised, they hurt. If cut, you bleed; if cut, they bleed. They have an Almighty that they go to in their end, as you do, and if one can get a perspective on all of this, even though you're temporarily humiliated, look at the source from which it comes, and never stop respecting yourself.

SISTER MAIDA

In 1965, Dubinsky offered Maida a vice-presidency in the ILGWU, but without a membership base in the union, she declined and instead became a general organizer in the South. As a troubleshooter, she was involved in organizing drives in North and

South Carolina, Georgia, and Florida. In 1969, she focused her attention more on the Chicago area as Mid-west Director of the A. Philip Randolph Institute, an organization Randolph established to work on issues of race, workers, and unions. She continued to travel to Africa on behalf of unions, African Americans, and women workers. In 1973, she returned to Africa, first joining the staff and later acting as a consultant to the AFL-CIO affiliate, the African-American Labor Center (AALC). In 1985, she attended the World Conference on the United Nations Decade for Women in Kenya. In 1991, she spent the winter traveling in East Africa with her family and also had an opportunity to visit old friends. Today, she lives in Pittsburgh, Pennsylvania, near her son, who is a lawyer, and his family. She continues to travel and welcome visitors to her home.[19]

Maida Springer-Kemp is a remarkable woman. Some years ago, Dr. Julius Nyerere, president of Tanzania, wrote to Randolph that "in Tanganyika she is 'Sister Maida' in more than a conventional sense. She is one of them. She is equally at home in Kenya. She has already worked a near miracle in Uganda where she helped to reunite a labour movement which was being fragmented."[20] Today, for many women and men on several continents, she remains Sister Maida in more than a conventional sense.

NOTES

1. The first interview documenting Springer-Kemp's labor career was conducted in 1977, by oral historian Elizabeth Balanoff for the four-year nationwide oral history project "The Twentieth-Century Trade Union Woman: Vehicle for Social Change," sponsored by the Labor Studies Center at the University of Michigan, funded by a seed grant from the Rockefeller Family Foundation, and directed by Joyce L. Kornbluh, head of the Labor Studies Center Program on Women and Work. This project taped and transcribed over eighty interviews with women rank-and-file, elected leaders, and staff of trade unions in the United States and Puerto Rico. Transcripts of all the interviews are deposited at the Bentley Library at the University of Michigan. Selected transcripts, including Springer-Kemp's, are also deposited at the George Meany Labor Archives; Schlesinger Library, Radcliffe College; and the Walter P. Reuther Archives on Urban and Labor Affairs, Wayne State University. Excerpts from the Balanoff interview are found in the Black Women's Oral History Project published by K. G. Saur, Schlesinger Library, Radcliffe College, Cambridge, Mass. The Twentieth-Century Trade Union Woman project also published Working Women's Roots: An Oral History Primer (Ann Arbor: 1979) and conducted workshops on oral history techniques for local union activists.

In 1994, an additional interview with Springer-Kemp was conducted by Brigid O'Farrell in preparation for her and Joyce Kornbluh's Rocking the Boat: Union Women's Voices 1915–1975 (New Brunswick, N.J.: Rutgers University Press, 1996). Related articles include African-American Labor Center, AALC Reporter 27, no. 4 (1992); 28, no. 1 (1993); ILGWU, Justice (Feb. 1986). The interview quotes in this article are edited from these oral history interviews and articles. Springer-Kemp's papers are available at the Schlesinger Library and the Amistad Center, Tulane University.

In 1994 Yevette Richards, at the University of Pittsburgh, completed a doctoral dissertation on Springer-Kemp, which she graciously shared with us. Her historical data, insights, and analyses have been enormously helpful. "'My Passionate Feeling About Africa': Maida Springer-Kemp and the American Labor Movement" (Ph.D. diss., Yale University, 1994) provides over 900 pages on Springer-Kemp's life, with seven chapters of background and analyses alternating with seven chapters of Richards's in-depth interviews with Springer-Kemp. She provides rich detail on each of the topics in this article, plus many other important topics not covered here. For example, there is an entire chapter on South Africa. Richards concludes, "This biography enriches the scholarship on pan-African, labor, and women's histories and demonstrates the ways in which international labor relations, pan-Africanism, African independence movements, the United States Civil Rights movement, and Cold War politics are intertwined. . . . This collaborative work demonstrates the power of her oral testimony to reshape our understanding of the past" (22, 891).

We acknowledge, with appreciation, the contributions of Elizabeth Balanoff, Mary Anne Forbes, Lucile DiGirolamo, and Caitlin O'Farrell. We sincerely thank Yevette Richards for sharing her manuscript and for reviewing this article. Most importantly, we would like to thank Maida Springer-Kemp for sharing her life story with all of us. Maida Springer-Kemp's life story is available in Yvette Richards, *Maida Springer: Pan-Africanist and International Labor Leader* (Pittsburgh: University of Pittsburgh Press, 2000).

2. The garment industry in New York, the growth of the ILGWU, and the relationship to the Communist Party is described by Philip Foner in *Women and the American Labor Movement from World War I to the Present* (New York: The Free Press, 1980).

3. Zimmerman immigrated to the United States in 1913. A member of the Communist Party, he was expelled from the ILGWU in 1925. He was reinstated in the union in 1931, and served as a vice-president of the union and general manager of the New York Dress Joint Board from 1934 until he retired in 1972. Antonini (1883–1968) was general secretary of Local 89 and vice-president of the union from 1934 to 1967. See Gary Fink, *The Biographical Dictionary of American Labor Leaders* (Westport, Conn.: Greenwood Press, 1974).

4. The ALP was formed in 1937 by the leaders of the ILGWU and the Amalgamated Clothing Workers Union to help unite progressive people in support of Franklin D. Roosevelt. Although Springer-Kemp did not seriously want to run for office, she became the first trade union member nominated from a Harlem district and won the primary on the ALP ticket. See Richards, "'My Passionate Feeling,'" chapter 3; "Maida Springer Represents New Type Leader Harlem Could Use," *New York Amsterdam News*, 1942 (Maida Springer-Kemp Papers, box 1, folder 8, Schlesinger Library, Radcliffe College; hereafter cited as Springer-Kemp Papers).

5. Richards, "'My Passionate Feeling,'" provides a detailed history of the African American labor movement in Harlem. Chapter 2 deals with "the strong connections between the ILGWU leadership and the anticommunist black civil rights and trade union leadership" (173). In 1935, 110 AFL delegates, including blacks and whites, organized the Negro Labor Committee, which offered organizing and education programs for the black community at their headquarters, the Harlem Labor Center. Competing programs were offered by the Garveyite Harlem Labor Union, the Father Divine Movement, and the communist-run Negro Labor Victory Assembly. The Hudson Shore Labor School was an interracial workers' education institution established by Hilda Worthington Smith in 1935 as a continuation of her work as director of the Bryn Mawr Summer School for Women Workers, started in 1921.

6. Richards, "'My Passionate Feeling,'" 247.

7. For additional information on A. Philip Randolph and the rally, although not Springer-Kemp's role, see Jervis Anderson, A. *Philip Randolph: A Biographical Portrait* (New York: Harcourt Brace Jovanovich, Inc., 1972). The complicated fight by Randolph and the black community to end discrimination and achieve equality in employment in gov-

ernment, the military, and the private sector during World War II is also described by Doris Kearns Goodwin, *No Ordinary Time: Franklin and Eleanor Roosevelt: The Home Front in World War II* (New York: Simon and Schuster, 1994).

8. According to Richards, Springer-Kemp was the second black business agent for Local 22 and the first to be responsible for a district. Edith Ransome was the first black business agent and the first black staff member of Local 22. She settled prices for finishers, but was not responsible for a district ("'My Passionate Feeling,'" 259).

9. Richards, "'My Passionate Feeling,'" 1.

10. Peterson was a workers' educator and lobbyist for the ACWU, director of the U.S. Department of Labor Women's Bureau, and advisor to presidents Kennedy, Johnson, and Carter. Robinson was an activist laundry worker with ACWU, who later served with Peterson at the Women's Bureau, was active with Springer-Kemp at the National Council of Negro Women, and went on to receive a law degree and teach. Newman (1891–1986) was one of 20,000 shirtwaist workers in New York City who went on strike in the winter of 1909–1910, an event referred to as the Uprising of 20,000. She also survived the Triangle Shirtwaist Company fire in 1911, in which 146 workers, mostly women, were killed ("Twentieth-Century Trade Union Woman," interview). Cohen (1885–1962) was the first female vice-president of the Women's Trade Union League from 1926 until it disbanded in 1950. See "Twentieth-Century Trade Union Woman" oral history project, for interviews with Peterson, Robinson, and Newman.

11. For an analysis of labor and the Roosevelt administration, see Steven Fraser, *Labor Will Rule: Sidney Hillman and the Rise of American Labor* (New York: The Free Press, 1991).

12. The importance of this event and the luncheon are described in "Women Labor Leaders Are Going to England in Good-Will Exchange With 4 From There," *New York Times*, 10 January 1945; as well as the *New York Amsterdam News*, February 1945 (Springer-Kemp Papers).

13. The ICFTU was established in 1949 in London, when many democratic unions left the communist-dominated World Federation of Trade Unions.

14. A review of the labor movement's long, complicated, and sometimes controversial history in the international arena is beyond the scope of this article. It is clear, however, that members of the Communist Party were forced out of the unions after World War II and that during the Cold War the AFL-CIO's international initiatives were guided by a strong anticommunist policy that coincided with the foreign policy of the U.S. government. Springer-Kemp had rejected the communists organizing in Harlem during the 1930s, worked closely with the leadership of the ILGWU, and supported the AFL-CIO policies during the Cold War.

15. Springer-Kemp, as quoted in Richards, "'My Passionate Feeling,'" 14.

16. Mboya became the General Secretary of the Kenya Federation of Labor in 1953. He was assassinated on 5 July 1969, leaving Jomo Kenyatta, whom Springer-Kemp had met in 1945, the undisputed leader of Kenya. See David Goldsworthy, *Tom Mboya: The Man Kenya Wanted to Forget* (New York: Africana Publishing Company, 1982); and Springer-Kemp, "Tom Mboya: In Memoriam," *AFL-CIO Free Trade Union News*, August 1969 (in Richards, "'My Passionate Feeling,'" 682).

17. During a 1958 strike, for example, she was described as a "militant Black woman" who told the strikers, "Our union will tolerate no gunka-munka business in the enforcement of future contracts!" Gunka-munka, described by Dubinsky as a blend of dillydallying and monkey business by chiselers on the employer side, became the strike slogan of the 105,000 striking dressmakers. See Tracy Sugarman, "Echoes on Paper, Reflections on My Garment Workers Sketchbook, 1958," *Labor's Heritage* (winter 1993): 35.

18. Springer-Kemp, 23 November 1965 letter to Dubinsky (Richards, "'My Passionate Feeling,'" 850).

19. Richards also traveled to Africa with Springer-Kemp and interviewed several people familiar with Springer-Kemp's life and work. For analyses of union policy and South Africa, see "The AALC Comes to South Africa," in Richards, "'My Passionate Feeling,'" chapter 6.

20. As quoted in Richards, "'My Passionate Feeling,'" 518.

Maida Springer-Kemp (far right), International Ladies' Garment Workers' Union, AFL, was one of four women who went to England through the U.S. Office of War Information Exchange to share wartime experiences in 1945. She was the first African-American woman to represent labor abroad. Other members of the delegation were (from left to right): Grace Blackett, United Automobile Workers, CIO; Anne Murcovich, American Federation of Hosiery Workers, CIO; and Julia O'Connor Parker, International Brotherhood of Electrical Workers, AFL. Photo courtesy of George Meany Center for Labor Studies, the George Meany Memorial Archive.

Autobiography and Reconstructing Subjectivity at the Bryn Mawr Summer School for Women Workers, 1921–1938

Karyn L. Hollis

"Bryn Mawr has given me a new definition of internationalism and a new feeling for the word 'tolerant,' " writes . . . a cigar worker from a southern mill. "At first I thought my mother would have a fit if she knew I was going around with the cotton mill girls. Now I see that they are just as nice girls as anyone else, and I am trying to get them to come to our club [YWCA Industrial Club]. I got acquainted too with a lot of the Russian girls, and learned a lot from them."

—Hilda Worthington Smith, *Women Workers at the Bryn Mawr Summer School*

When I first read the narratives written by students at the Bryn Mawr Summer School for Women Workers, I was moved by the growth in intellect, self-confidence, and political awareness found in the texts before me. Clearly, these working women benefited greatly from the eight-week immersion in liberal arts and labor economics, offered on a beautiful suburban college campus where, in the words of a student, "the scent of the honey suckles made us feel that we were in heaven" (Smith, *Women Workers*, 18). The Bryn Mawr Summer School was the first of four resident workers' schools for women established in the 1920s and 1930s, and students were offered some of the advantages and luxuries their more elite counterparts enjoyed during the fall and spring terms. They were taken on field trips to local museums and factories, honored with teas and luncheons, taught to swim and play tennis, and treated to guest lectures by W. E. B. Du Bois, Margaret Sanger, Norman Thomas, Francis Perkins, Harold Laski, Walter Reuther, Eleanor Roosevelt, as well as many other renowned labor, political, academic, and feminist leaders. This extraordinary pedagogical experiment also stands as one of the few moments in U.S. women's history of successful cross-class alliance among upper-, middle-, and working-class women from a variety of ethnic, religious, and geographic backgrounds.

The more I learned about the summer school, the more convinced I was of its relevance to teachers and scholars interested in improving women's lives. As women recover their history, the individuals, organizations, commitments, and struggles unveiled all provide valuable examples that lend strength and understanding to our current endeavors. The Bryn Mawr Summer School for Women Workers offers an important antecedent to the feminist and progressive pedagogies we strive to develop today.

Although I am now at work on a book that considers the different forms of writing done at the school, in this essay, I focus on autobiographical narratives.[1] The women wrote copiously, at the urging of the predominantly female faculty, whose student-centered pedagogy helped transform these women's untold dreams, desires, and fears into expressed demands for social justice. In their textual self-(re)presentations these working women developed critical and powerful voices, reworking the speech and text they encountered in their daily lives for their own, often collective, ends. My analysis of this discursive subjectivity—the writing of the self—will be informed by literary autobiographical criticism and linked to the current composition research on gender and autobiography.

A SCHOOL FOR WOMEN WORKERS

The Bryn Mawr Summer School for Women Workers was an indirect response to the favorable climate for women's rights and worker education that prevailed during the Progressive Era. Its actual founding, however, was more directly due to the efforts of the National Women's Trade Union League, which in 1916 called on the women's colleges to do more to educate working women, and to two feminist educators connected to Bryn Mawr: M. Carey Thomas, suffragette and president of the college for thirty-five years, and Hilda Worthington Smith, Bryn Mawr graduate, dean, and director of the summer school for thirteen years. During its seventeen-year history approximately fifteen hundred working women, eighty to one hundred each summer, attended the school. Appointed by Thomas to head the school, Smith attracted the upper- and middle-class Bryn Mawr alumnae to the cause of worker education through a flood of promotional publications and presentations.[2] While alumnae committees did the bulk of recruiting and fund-raising, the school was also assisted by the Industrial Department of the Young Women's Christian Association (YWCA), the National Women's Trade Union League, labor unions, churches, corporate and private benefactors, and former summer school student alumnae groups. The school very consciously aimed for and achieved diversity in its student body, with the largest number of working women coming from the needle trades of the Northeast. Many were fairly recent immigrants from Russia or Eastern Europe. The school required an eighth-grade education and recruited women eighteen to thirty-five years old, with the average age being twenty-five.

As years passed, students and faculty pushed for a stronger alliance with progressive elements of organized labor. By 1938 the connection to labor had alienated a great many Bryn Mawr trustees and alumnae. After an incident in which the school was falsely accused of supporting a strike (forbidden in the administrative agreement with the college), it was asked to leave the Bryn Mawr campus. The school then moved to the Smith family estate in Upstate New York and continued there as the coeducational Hudson Shore Labor College. The college closed its doors in 1952, as workers turned to short-term classes offered by unions, university residential and nonresidential courses, and university labor education programs to meet their needs.

Developing a Pedagogy: Faculty and Students Together

Based on their own accounts, faculty considered it an honor to be asked to teach at the summer school. Included among the faculty were distinguished professors from colleges and universities across the nation, many of whom gave up their summer research opportunities to come to the Bryn Mawr campus; others were high school teachers or YWCA Industrial Department administrators; still others had eschewed traditional educational careers to devote themselves year-round to worker instruction. The majority were women with a strong commitment to women's education. They formed a close-knit, cooperative academic community, drawing on one another for disciplinary knowledge, teaching techniques, and administrative skills.

Democratic participation in administrative and curricular matters by faculty and students alike was a cornerstone of the workers' education movement much promoted by Smith, and students were given an equal vote on all governing committees.[3] The policy-making Joint Administration Committee adopted the mission statement of the summer school in 1923, according to which, the school was to provide

> young women in industry opportunities to study liberal subjects and to train themselves in clear thinking; to stimulate an active and continued interest in the problems of our economic order; to develop a desire for study as a means of understanding and of enjoyment in life. The School is not committed to any theory or dogma. The teaching is carried on by instructors who have an understanding of the students' practical experience in industry and of the labor movement. It is conducted in a spirit of impartial inquiry, with freedom of discussion and teaching. It is expected that thus the students will gain a truer insight into the problems of industry, and feel a more vital responsibility for their solution. (Smith, *Women Workers* 7)

In attempting to carry out these aims, the faculty developed a pedagogy derived from several sources: worker and adult education movements in the United States and abroad, Deweyan educational philosophy, leftist and liberal social thought, and, to a certain extent, feminist principles. Faculty often worked individually with the women, and undergraduate assistants from eastern women's colleges participated in various capacities, from tutors to typists.

Curriculum committees met almost daily during the summer session and frequently during the year to work on instruction methods and curriculum. The curriculum was critiqued and amended in response to student suggestions and criticisms and faculty perceptions of what worked and didn't work. One basic principle, however, remained constant: workers' own experiences should be central to their education. Regarding the importance of using workers' own lives as a starting point for intellectual inquiry, Smith and her coauthor Jean Carter wrote that "it may seem like an illogical arrangement of material," but "learning is strangely illogical. . . . It is only teaching which aims to be logical and in so doing it often misses the necessary contact which results in learning. The contact must be with the experience of the worker and the starting point—logical or illogical—must be there" (Carter and Smith 25). Smith and other faculty believed workers had a right to an education that revealed their personal role in economic production and would help them improve their daily lives.

WOMEN WORKERS AND THE AUTOBIOGRAPHICAL ASSIGNMENT

Since personal experience was to play such a key role in the course of instruction at the summer school, it is not surprising that writing an autobiography was one of the first tasks the women were assigned in their English composition class (Heller, "Blue Collar" 119). Indeed, former instructor Alice Hansen Cook emphasized the importance the faculty gave to the autobiography assignment and stressed that the assignment "was something that we all did" (interview).

Today some feminist and poststructuralist critics express a certain distrust of autobiography, and as I will discuss, some scholars of composition studies have warned of the patiarchal cast of traditional autobiography.[4] In A Poetics of Women's Autobiography, Sidonie Smith maintains that, "during the past five hundred years, autobiography has assumed a central position in the personal and literary life of the West precisely because it serves as one of those generic contracts that reproduces the patrilineage and its ideologies of gender" (44). In other words, autobiographical subjectivity is compromised by androcentric illusions of a unified, autonomous self that "valorizes individual integrity and separateness and devalues personal and communal interdependency" (39).

Although faculty working at the summer school in the 1920s and 1930s would not have expressed their understanding of subjectivity in contemporary poststructuralist terms, they were not uncritical of bourgeois subjectivity. Judging from the assignments, faculty saw autobiography as a way to represent the reconstruction of a subjectivity that was both self-critical and critical of the status quo. Perhaps because of their close association with their working-class students, faculty came to understand the needs and perspectives of these "Others." In fact, the faculty also seemed aware of how their own, more privileged class backgrounds imposed on their ability to know their students. In her coauthored book on worker education, Hilda Worthington Smith wrote "the first concern of the teacher should be to discover the special interests and the occupational backgrounds of his students. . . . Without this background of detailed knowledge . . . the teacher may plan instruction which is remote from any real significance in their daily lives" (Carter and Smith 25). Smith and her faculty thus regarded the student autobiographies as a source of information crucial to classroom success. Another benefit of the autobiographical assignment, therefore, was that it helped the faculty understand whom they were teaching.

In her relevant essay on Victorian working-class autobiography, Regina

Gagnier has shown the unfortunate results that can occur when working-class autobiographical subjects, both male and female, do not move beyond prevailing autobiographical conventions. Those working-class subjects who attempted to construct a subjectivity in terms of bourgeois norms—including close family upbringing, lengthy schooling, romantic love and marriage, and a progressively successful career—often experienced narrative and psychological breakdown because of the disparity between what happened to them and what they believe should have happened to them according to bourgeois ideology. Gagnier finds that a happier outcome occurs when the working-class writer recognizes the difficulty, if not the impossibility, of embourgeoisement and critiques the inequities of class structures, gaining strength by calling on collective subjectivity (114).

Typical of the English composition instructors at the summer school was long-time faculty member Ellen Kennan. Teaching at the school from 1925 to 1938, she began all her classes with an autobiographical assignment, which was modified over the years to account for her students' life experiences and to produce increasingly more critical responses. The two versions of the assignment that follow reflect Kennan's growing awareness that workers' lives did not mirror the ideal bourgeois life pattern of familial nurturing, uninterrupted schooling, romantic love, and career development but, instead, likely involved truncated schooling and economically strained family relationships.[5]

Ellen Kennan's 1926 Autobiography Assignment

The first assignment is to write an essay about yourself. The following questions are not designed as a kind of third degree. They are suggestions merely. Please answer as many of them as you will and add anything in your life which seems to you to have influenced you.

- What is your age?
- Where were you born?
- How far did you go in school?
- What studying have you done since you left school?
- What work do you do now?
- At what age did you begin?
- How did you happen to take up that kind of work?
- Do you like it?
- What work would you like to do if you had your choice and the training for it? What would be your second choice?
- How did you happen to come to this school?
- What do you want to get from the school?
- Name the three books which you have read which you enjoyed the most.
- What amusements are you fond of?
- What things in your training (either from your parents or teachers) are you beginning to feel doubtful about? (Autobiography n.p.)

Even in this early version of the assignment Kennan clearly wanted her students to take a critical perspective on their lives. "Do you like it [your work]?" she prompts, and "What work would you like to do if you had your choice and the training for it?" With a final question on doubt, she avoids encouraging received opinions about how her students' lives should be unfolding.

Ellen Kennan's 1934 Autobiography Assignment

First Composition
I. Family and Background
II. Childhood
   What is the first thing that you can remember?
   What do you remember that you wish you could forget?
   Did you have a grandmother?
   What thing in your childhood are you glad about?
III. Education
   What schools did you go to?
   What did you get outside of schools?
   What did you fail to get?
   What did you get that you later found untrue?
   What friends did you have? Were they lasting ones?
IV. Work
   Did you choose it?
   Do you like it?
   What work would you do if you had your choice?
V. What do you do for fun?
   (Do you read, for example? What sort of books? Do you go to plays? Do you enjoy games, music, dancing?)
Note: Don't take any of these questions as commands. Answer what you please. Tell everything about yourself that you will and can.

If you do not wish to write an autobiography, the following questions may suggest a different kind of composition:
I. What kind of life would you live if you could arrange your life just as you wished—if you could do as you wish and be what you wish?
II. What beliefs and ideas that you have grown up in are you beginning to question? What ones have you cast aside entirely? What first caused you to question accepted ideas? Do you now challenge some things that you formerly considered sacred?
III. If there is a particular subject that you have in mind and wish to write upon, you may do it, regardless of the other suggestions. (Autobiography n.p.)

By 1934 Kennan has expanded the original assignment and divided it into five parts. Even though the categories may reflect bourgeois life patterns, the questions asked encourage a critical examination of these patterns. Omitted from the 1934 assignment are the specific inquiries about age and birthplace, perhaps because this information was easily obtained from the lengthy application forms available on each student or perhaps because such facts were not pertinent to the work ahead. We see that Kennan now invites her students to write on family and background as well as childhood. Perhaps she wanted to help students understand how these culturally derived constructs or discourses shaped the selves or subjectivities they were representing in their autobiographies. One can only speculate, but perhaps Kennan may have found that workers tended to neglect these categories if their experiences hadn't been as "happy" as prevailing ideology required. And, true to her critical aims, Kennan also asks, "What do you remember [about your childhood] that you wish you could forget?" Similarly, Kennan wants a critical perspective on education. She prompts: "What did you get *outside* of schools?" "What did you *fail* to get?" "What did you get that you later found untrue?" Under "Childhood," the question about having a grandmother (as opposed to a grandfather) may reveal Kennan's hope for a more woman-centered investigation of family ancestry. Finally, Kennan conveys a distrust of autobiographical subjectivity as she recommends that students: "Tell everything that you *will and can*."

WOMEN WORKERS WRITING AUTOBIOGRAPHICAL NARRATIVES

The narratives that follow appeared in *Shop and School*, the student magazine published during every summer school term. *Shop and School* contained prose, poetry, humor, and labor drama. I examined 163 narratives appearing in the last ten issues of *Shop and School* and dating from 1928 to 1938,[6] the period when the students and faculty were organized into the effective, interdisciplinary groups. Because many teachers at the school assigned autobiographies, I have not been able to determine these students' teachers. But while I cannot say for certain that the texts I examined were written for Kennan, the narratives they tell fall readily into the categories set up by her assignments.[7]

By far the most popular topic among the students concerned some aspect of their work lives. More than half of the pieces I examined were of this type. Titles include "Waste in My Shop," "My Start in Industry," "A Working Girl Speaks," "An Incident in My Shop," "Piece Work System," "The Long Arm of the Job," and "My First Experience as an Organizer." As the economic hardships and labor struggles of the 1930s increased, the titles begin to reflect more conflict, as well as the resultant difficulties in workers' lives: "A Day Searching for a Job," "The New York Elevator Strike," "My First Arrest," "On the Picket Line," "The 1931 Hosiery Strike in Philadelphia," "An Experience with a Sweatshop Boss," and "The Effect of Unemployment on One's Health."

The next most popular topic was education. About 16 percent of the narratives dealt with this topic, whether stressing the value of the Bryn Mawr experience, the need for more workers' education projects, or a critique of earlier educational experiences. Another 15 percent of the pieces addressed family and background. Many of these narratives told how the economic conditions of the times had led to extreme deprivations. Typical titles include "A Mining Village," "Motherless,"

"Homeless in Russia," and "My Childhood during the War." As the depression wore on, workers wrote less about their early childhood experiences and family backgrounds and more about their current economic difficulties in the context of the family—for example, "The Pressure of High Rent" and "The Effect of Unemployment on My Family."

The remaining narratives could be placed for the most part into Kennan's second group of topics. Some students wrote utopian descriptions of lives they would like to lead; others criticized forms of organized religion they had begun to doubt or wrote of a recently acquired sympathy for Southerners, Northerners, African Americans, Jews, or immigrant women they had met at the summer school; while others wrote about how they had begun to think of themselves as public speakers or activists. Still others described such things as the funeral of Nicola Sacco and Bartolomeo Vanzetti, a speech made to the Pennsylvania House of Representatives, a racist incident in a restaurant, or the Pennsylvania Amish. Incidentally, the "fun" category was hardly ever chosen. Smith comments that many workers had to be taught recreation while at the school, never having had the opportunity for it before (*Women Workers* 164).

Narratives on Family and Childhood

The narratives on family, background, and childhood often reveal an important shift in consciousness from an isolated, powerless "I" who writes, to a more forceful "we" who act. Beulah Parrish, a student at the summer school in 1930, wrote this brief narrative about life in a southern mill town. A white student from Durham, North Carolina, Parrish's application revealed that she was twenty-one years old when she attended the school. She had never voted and was not a union member, but she was a leader in her church and the YWCA Industrial Club. She left school at age thirteen to work in a hosiery mill.

Those Mill Villages
by Beulah Parrish, 1930

For three years I lived in a southern mill village. I found it very unpleasant. An employer may shout "Cheap Rent" all he wants to, but what do we get for our cheap rent?

The streets of the village are usually narrow and muddy. Sometimes they are poorly lighted. Most of the houses are small and have no bathtubs. In the village where I lived we were not allowed to have telephones. Our lights were turned off at certain hour every night. They were turned on again early in the morning, and then turned off at daylight. The lights were turned on for one day each week so that we could do our ironing.

It seems as though there were always more children in a mill village than anywhere else. Many of the mothers have to work in the mill. Their children, having no one to take care of them, roam about the streets wherever they please.

People are inclined to look down on the people who live in a mill village. The employer seems to think he more or less has control over the people. We workers do not want our employers to give us community houses and cheap rent, with lights and water free. We want wages that will enable us to live in better houses on better streets and to pay for our own amusements. We should feel much more independent—and that is how everybody wants to feel.

Notice how Parrish first represents her subjectivity: "*I* lived in a southern mill village. *I* found it very unpleasant." This first-person singular narration is the conventional narrative device for autobiographies. Sidonie Smith argues that this "narrated I" typically presents a singular, unitary consciousness—the bourgeois subjectivity—which reflects on a painful past to be vanquished as the narrative progresses (*A Poetics*, 78). As Parrish's example and others' show, however, this pattern is not typical of the autobiographical narratives written at the summer school. Parrish turns over her narrative to a narrating *we*, a narrator of participation, a much stronger and more confident collective subject, which, as noted earlier, Gagnier has found to be beneficial to working-class writers. "*We* workers do not want our employers to give us community houses and cheap rent," writes Parrish. "*We* want wages that will enable us to live in better houses on better streets." As is typical of this discursive move, the shift in person is often accompanied by a shift in tense. Thus, the exploited *I* is left in the past, while the *we* becomes an active subject of the present or future and plays a public, adversarial role on behalf of all mill village workers. As is also typical, the *we* carries the more resistant stance of the narration. The narrated I is critical of her surroundings, but the narrated we offers solutions to the exploitation. While *I* generally belongs in the private sphere, *we* ventures into the public domain. This shift in person, tense, and discursive domain occurred in three-fourths of the narratives I examined, and there is no evidence that such shifts were prompted by the assignment.

As is typical of many of these working women, Parrish does not seem to have been exposed to a feminist critique of her work or home life, or if exposed to such a critique, she chose not to highlight this in her narrative. She does not denounce the fact that the female workers she describes probably earned less than the men or that the women most likely returned from mill work to do a shift of housework. Although women's issues of home and family predominate in her narrative, they are intended to be read against middle-class standards. For example, Victorian domestic discourse of woman as nurturer and homemaker when compared with the realities of the mill village, where children roam the dirty streets while their mothers work, helps legitimize Parrish's claim for improved living conditions. In another discursive appropriation she uses the androcentric discourse of worker empowerment to achieve a strengthened collective voice. This melding of discourses in her text, and in others that follow, offer examples of Mikhail Bakhtin's "heteroglossia," amalgams of various social discourses in dialogic interaction. That the women use and exploit various discourses for their own ends, incorporating them with personal discourses connected to their needs of work and family life, corresponds to the notion of constructed knowledge. In *Women's Ways of Knowing*, Mary Field Belenky and her colleagues argue that women attain constructed knowledge when they welcome, rather than feel threatened by, the thoughts of others, integrating these thoughts into a personally meaningful set of beliefs.

The next narrative was written by an African American student.

Looking Back
by Eloise Fickland, 1933

If it were possible for me to turn and look back along the years of some six generations, I'd see my mother's maternal and paternal ancestors in this America.

My mother's mother was a slave. Four generations of these slaves had served four generations of one family. My mother is the result of the joining of the two families. We never knew my father's people. We never saw them and heard very little, for he died before we were old enough to be interested and to ask questions.

My maternal grandmother told many tales of the slave life, and *The War*. Some of these stories were very sad.

From the time I was able to sit on the floor and hold my sister I have had the responsibility of "the children." I was the one to whom each child came with all cares from a scratch to a fight; all secrets I kept, notes from teachers even; all kinds of trouble.

Well do I remember, once, when my next oldest sister and I had to act Santa. My father was away, and my mother was too ill to help. We had just finished trimming the tree, putting around the presents, and filling the stockings when we had to hide as my brother and next sister came down to take a look around. It was a narrow escape.

We were a happy group of youngsters. A group that was so sheltered that it has proven a handicap to some of us.

It is nearly nineteen years now since my father died. Ah! the awful change that death made. My oldest brother had just married. Yes, there was a little insurance. A Methodist minister, how can he pay for a large policy with nine children to support?

Depression! The depression started nineteen years ago with us.

Fickland's autobiographical piece highlights many themes and emphases that scholars have identified with black autobiography. Margo Culley writes that, "for most black women, as for most black men, the foundational category [of being] is race" (8). Thus, Fickland begins her narrative by emphasizing her lengthy roots in this country and identifying herself as a descendant of slaves, an African American. She probably knew that few, if any, among her predominantly white schoolmates could claim to have had family in the United States for six generations, and this gave her a birthright and legitimacy that may have surprised some of her classmates.

In an important essay, "In Search of the Black Female Self," Regina Blackburn locates three interrelated themes informing most black women's autobiographies: the first is defining the black self; the second is valuing that self; and the third is achieving an awareness of the double bind that being black and female imposes (136). True to the first of these points, Fickland defines herself matrilineally, through her African American female ancestors, inheriting character and strength that her narrated I values greatly. Elizabeth Fox-Genovese has found that black female autobiographers make frequent reference to the love "felt for and felt from their female elders: mothers, aunts, grandmothers" (71). William L. Andrews has traced this tradition back to nineteenth-century female slave narratives. "In general, nineteenth-century black autobiographers single out their mothers, sisters and grandmothers for special praise," he writes (227). He continues, however, noting that because these autobiographers wanted "to reconcile an absolute moral standard for womanly virtue prescribed by white culture with the actual circumstances of a slave woman's complex lived experience," a certain ambivalence is found in their narratives (230). Perhaps a similar ambivalence motivated Fickland's rather oblique reference to her mother's conception as "the result of the joining of the two families."

Like Parrish, Fickland addresses concerns that are traditionally within women's domain—the home, mothering, children. Both use, as a backdrop, the conventions of Victorian domesticity to help register their points. Fickland appropriates this domestic discourse as she presents a self that others come to for solace and comfort. She derives a great deal of self-esteem and self-respect from this role. Fickland offers her experiences, and those of her forebears, as evidence of her authenticity as a woman, partly legitimizing herself—as Fox-Genovese notes many black women are compelled to do—in terms of "bourgeois women's domestic discourse" (83). Neither Parrish nor Fickland explicitly critique this discourse of womanhood, but each uses it as a means to point out what she has been denied—material comfort, respect, and justice. Fickland, because she is black, must reassure her readers that she approximates the white feminine ideal. Parrish, because she is white, can, in this instance, take her gender for granted and directly protest the injustice of not having middle-class independence and comfort.

Fickland, however, has had to go well beyond the bounds of the white bourgeois or working-class mother and temporarily assume a role traditionally reserved for men. At Christmastime she has played Santa, the mythical male provider, implying what others have stated more explicitly: that black women's status as women has not shielded them from "man's" work. Thus, Blackburn's third theme is present in an emergent form here. Not unlike the other female African American autobiographers Blackburn studied, Fickland shows an awareness of the double oppression that being both black and female imposes.

Her narration then slips into "we," but not the androcentric, narrating we of Parrish, which collectively confronts an oppressive situation in the present. Fickland's we is familial, woven in and out of her narrative, firmly connected to her past I by close ties of kinship. "We were a happy group of youngsters" she writes, perhaps too "sheltered" to confront successfully the racism of white culture. Suffering has long been a part of this family's collective experience: always present under the surface, it forces its way out in the narrative's ending. Severe deprivation didn't begin with the depression, as it may have in the white culture. For her family "the depression started nineteen years ago," with the death of her father and the "loss" of her older brother to marriage.

Perhaps Fickland does not use the collective, masculinist voice of worker empowerment because, as the daughter of a minister, she considered herself middle class, or perhaps she had never been exposed to this rhetoric, or perhaps she rejected it. Perhaps Fickland's purpose here was to paint a familial portrait in African-American terms. Since racial discrimination was the overriding historical factor contributing to Fickland's oppression, any discourse that did not give race prime consideration would not likely be adopted by her. Fox-Genovese argues that "the tension at the heart of black women's autobiography derives in large part from the chasm between an autobiographer's intuitive sense of herself and her attitude toward her probable readers" (74). We feel this tension in Fickland's references to her mother's conception, her having to play Santa, her overly sheltered family, and her last overly controlled statement.

Narratives of Work and Union

In her study of contemporary working-class women's writing Janet Zandy finds that reference to historical events can trigger narrative response (11). She mentions that several contemporary women poets have written about the Triangle fire of 1911. Similarly, one of the women at Bryn Mawr wrote about when—as a young woman working near the Manhattan factory—she first learned of the fire.

Sacrifice
by Rose Greenstein, 1930

The most panic-stricken moment of my life was at the time of the Triangle fire in 1912 [sic], when I saw one hundred and fifty-four of my fellow-workers burned to death in a non-union dress shop. But it is not of my own sick horror that I want to tell you. It is of the revelation that that fire brought to all workers, everywhere.

The Triangle Waist and Dress Company was one of the largest of its kind at that time. The firm employed about three hundred people, mostly girls. During the historic strike of the Ladies Waist and Dressmakers' Union of 1909, we did not succeed in organizing that shop, though the workers put up one of the most heroic fights in the history of the trade. They were out on the streets twenty-six long and bitter weeks, and, finally, broken down by the brutality of the place, they gave up, but with an unbroken spirit. They decided to go back to work, but only to prepare themselves for a renewed struggle, in which they, and not the employers, should be victorious. To the sorrow of the working class, they did not live to see that day.

After the rest of the workers in the garment industry had won for themselves a fifty-hour week, and were working on Saturdays only until one o'clock, the Triangle factory still worked fifty-nine hours. And so it happened that one Saturday a crowd of us, going home at one o'clock from our shop across the street, called up to them a cheerful good-bye. It had become almost a tradition with us to cry out to them: "So long, until the victory is yours!"

But that Saturday was the last time we called. Nor did we ever see those glorious fighters again, for that very day, before five o'clock, they were smothered to death in a blaze that did barely any damage to the building or to the employers. Later, definite proof was brought forward that the doors had been bolted to keep out inspectors and interfering union members, and it was revealed that those who were not actually burned were found huddled together on the floor against locked doors. They had died of suffocation.

Since then, you are sure to find, on the third Sunday in March of every year, a group of workers from the Dressmakers' Union gathered around a grave in Brooklyn. They are honoring twenty-four unidentified victims, who fell in the workers' cause.

In his pioneering essay on working-class women's writing Paul Lauter has pointed to the "instrumental" nature of much working-class women's writing, which, unlike bourgeois autobiography, does not reflect on the path to success followed by an individual but, instead, shows how a collectivity has struggled, and must continue to struggle, for a better life. Lauter also points out that a rich intertextuality links working-class women's narratives to other popular cultural forms and artifacts such as songs, workplace narratives, broadsides, political fables, union banners (18), and, I might add, the Bible and political theory. "Sacrifice" is an example of such a richly intertextual and multivocal construction. Again, Bakhtin's notion of heteroglossia is helpful here, as we notice the various discourses that assist the writer in telling her story.

From her first horrific statement concerning the burned women workers, Greenstein leaves the narrated I, or unitary subject, behind. She forcefully refuses to reflect on her self or on her unique response to this event: "It is not of my own sick horror that I want to tell you. It is of the revelation that that fire brought to all workers, everywhere." The author then records the history of a working-class struggle for fair wages from the inside, as one worker among many. Her first two paragraphs set the background for the tragedy in terms that reveal a familiarity with organizing tactics and collective, worker-centered interpretations of labor history. "During the historic strike of the Ladies Waist and Dressmakers' Union of 1909, we did not succeed in organizing that shop, though the workers put up one of the most heroic fights in the history of the trade." Greenstein's slightly unidiomatic "Until the victory is yours!" marks her as a recent immigrant, carrying the sociolinguistic strains of an experience steeped in European leftist ideology. Greenstein's phrasing also reveals her familiarity with left-wing rhetoric of worker empowerment: "all workers, everywhere," "to the sorrow of the working class," the "renewed struggle in which they . . . should be victorious." An allusion to messianic revelation and sacrifice is also found in the text. Greenstein says her narrative is about the "*revelation* that that fire brought to all workers, everywhere"; "It was revealed that those who were not actually burned were found huddled together on the floor against the locked doors." Thus, these young women workers died together as they worked together, collectively to the bitter end, giving their lives in the fight for workers' rights.

Greenstein shifts to a collective voice similar to Parrish's: "A crowd of us . . . called up to them a cheerful good-bye" and later, "Nor did we ever see those glorious fighters again." This is the narrative *we* of worker empowerment, a discourse the writer was familiar with through union and political work. The narrative's inclusiveness continues with a direct address to the reader, "Since then,

you are sure to find. . . ." And she ends with a tribute to the twenty-four unidentified victims—the nameless, or Others—who fell for the still deferred "workers'
cause." Again, it is the narrating *we* that participates in an example of active public resistance.

The next narrative offers one of the few critiques I found of sexism in unions.
The writer, Sarah Gordon, was a Jewish immigrant with family in Russia and
Poland. She was thirty-nine years old and had been in the United States for
twenty years when she wrote this piece. She spoke Yiddish, Russian, and English.
She worked as a hat trimmer and was a member of the Cap and Millinery
Workers Union. She had already lost one job and had been blacklisted after a
very successful organizing drive among women workers in the glove trade. She
had taken courses in literature and economics at the Rand School of Social
Science and reports that she read "various daily papers" and "some magazines."
Where she acquired her feminism is not evident; perhaps it was from her teachers
at the Rand School. Or perhaps some feminism had been instilled in her union by
organizers with ties to leftist political parties. For, although rife with sexism themselves, these parties did at least address "the Woman Question" (Coiner 164).

A Typical Day in My Life
by Sarah Gordon, 1929

What does a day in the life of a working girl mean? It seems so insignificant and yet it
means so much. I have a habit of saying when I start out in the morning that I am going to
war, for war it is for a worker, in an unorganized trade especially. We must always be on the
defensive because we never can tell how our day will end; it depends on the mood of our
employer. I will however try and describe one of the average days in my life.

I start the day wondering why the car company was allowed to raise the fare and was not
made to add one or two cars so that the early morning passengers should at least have a seat.
But I have found that there is an advantage in hanging on a strap shaking to and fro; it gives
me an opportunity to observe my fellow passengers.

I love to observe people's faces; it is almost like reading books. I always wonder what is
going on beyond their calm exteriors. I also like to observe what people are reading, for
almost everybody is reading in the train. I have learned to classify people by their reading.

In the morning paper the average girl is reading the novel first, the young man the
sports page, the middle-aged business man turns to the stock exchange news, and the
elderly, tired-looking man tries to solve the crossword puzzle, probably as a means of relax-
ation, but very few people read the editorials, or the news of the day unless there is a big
headline about a murder, a scandal, or a society wedding.

But I? I read all these people. Out of the train I come up to my shop, full of impressions.
I would be glad if I were given work and were allowed to work my day through peacefully.
But no!

Just one look at the boss who always wears a grouch on his face, another look at the boy
who deals out the work, and at the girls who have come before me, and I instantly feel that
there is trouble in the air. I do not question immediately but wait for developments.

In the meantime I have a feeling as though I were sitting on a slumbering volcano, I can never tell on which side the lava will break out. I do not have to wait very long before it comes. The boss cannot forgive the girls for making him pay three or five cents more on a hat. He begins picking at the work; he accuses them of unfairness, the girls defending themselves; there is general confusion.

A little later a heated argument among the girls about the unequal distribution of work, endless talk, some bitter words, general resentment, but who is to blame? The system, the struggle for existence.

Lunch hour—I eat my lunch in a hurry, and go out to the "corner" that is the "labor market" of the trade. There I meet the girls from other shops, also some union officials. We discuss conditions in the trade; we get some information as to what is happening in different places, but the most heated discussions are about the split in the organization. This is now the most vital question of the day.

I come back to work usually under the impression of the argument started on the street and am compelled to continue it, because half of the workers of our shop, that is, the men workers, belong to the opposition and are responsible for the break in our organization. These arguments take on very violent and in many cases dangerous forms. It is a very difficult life for us girls in these days; we have to fight our boss on one side, our union that should otherwise protect us on the other, and we are crushed between the two.

Under such physical and mental strain I finish my day's work.

And then the evening! That much desired evening! I straighten up my shoulders, walk out on the street, sniff some fresh air, and go to eat in a place where I can meet friends. We eat and talk about current events, and then we go to a lecture or a meeting or to see some good play, or to the Symphony Concert according to the day. This the anti-toxin which must counteract the poisonous effects of the day in the shop.

As in the other autobiographical narratives, Gordon makes use of a narrative we, in the present tense and the public domain. But this time the *we* represents women's collective voice: "We have to fight our boss on one side, our union that should otherwise protect us on the other." Another salient characteristic of this piece is the frequent reference to physical violence, with an emphasis on bodily harm. In Gordon's narrative men are the source of this violence, and it is directed at women. She compares a working girl's life with "war." She sits on a "slumbering volcano" in fear of vitriolic eruptions from her boss as "he begins picking at their work . . . accus[ing] them of unfairness." Arguments with men in her union take on "violent" and "dangerous" forms. The women are "crushed" between their union and the boss. Sidonie Smith maintains that in bourgeois, androcentric autobiography—whether written by men or women—woman's sexuality, woman's body, her desire, is written out of the text, erased. When female autobiographers begin to address this lack, Smith asserts that a new type of subjectivity may be created. In other words, this emphasis on the physicality of woman's experience in autobiography is a resistant, counterhegemonic move, a way to subvert the "metaphysical self" of disembodied, androcentric autobiography ("Resisting" 77). Smith speculates that "with that new subjectivity may come a new system of values, a new kind of language and narrative form, perhaps even a new discourse, an alternative to the prevailing ideology of gender" (*Poetics* 59). While we are now beginning to see that new discourse in the writing of French feminist critics and others, here we see a similar attempt by an American working-class woman as she inserts a language of woman's desire into the previously male-centered discourse of worker collectivity. In her final comment we sense the important regenerative power she experiences when meeting both physical and intellectual needs.

The final self-(re)presentation is by an African American woman whose experience at the summer school seems to have changed her life quite dramatically.

It Set Me Thinking
by Marion Jackson, 1937

When first I learned of Bryn Mawr's Summer School for Women Workers in Industry, immediately I decided I would like to attend. I never once took into consideration the true purpose of the school. I have always had a craving for knowledge, but I have never had time or money enough to complete my education; so, when at a YWCA conference I found out about this school, I thought, "Oh, how nice! Now, here's a chance for me to learn a little something. Who knows? Someday it may come in handy."

I have always felt one should learn all one can at every possible opportunity. I am terribly ashamed to say that I thought only of my own selfish gain. I was thinking of a possible chance of getting a better job, and I believe that foremost in my mind was money.

I am a piece-worker in a dress factory. My work is seasonal. It is not a very comfortable feeling when you realize that the end of the season is nigh, and soon your income will cease while your obligations will go on. For that reason I have always hoped for a steady job with steady pay, or, shall I say, secure employment.

I knew that this school was neither a trade nor a vocational one, but I believed that it gave one prestige to attend the school and meant much in one's favor when seeking employment. I therefore set out to gain admittance to Bryn Mawr.

On Monday, June 15, at the official opening exercises, I listened with profound interest to President Park. She related the origin of the school. It was a vision of former president M. Carey Thomas that led her to create a place where women working in industry might go to prepare themselves to meet any problems that might confront them in their field.

Dr. Susan Kingsbury in her address very clearly pointed out that any woman receiving this training should, when she has returned to her home, feel it her duty to render a service to fellow workers through leadership or individual service. There were many more interesting and important facts brought out through these and other speakers—far too numerous for me to mention.

This meeting to me was really an awakening! The true purpose of the school was unfolded.

It set me thinking. I have been asking myself, "What can I, in my small way, do to contribute to labor or humanity? I am only one little insignificant person among a multitude."

At such a time one has a feeling of inferiority, realizing the lack of training and experience; obviously one feels hopeless.

I come from the large and prosperous city of Philadelphia. There we have our trade unions, workers' education, adult education, peace conferences, youth congress groups, churches, and other civic organizations all seemingly well organized and fairly advanced in their movements, and so I still wondered what then could I do?

I was walking through the hall in Denbigh on Tuesday afternoon when the girl in room 13 called to me. She wanted to know what I could tell her about the Scottsboro case and about Angelo Herndon, the Negro organizer. I am a Negro; still I was forced to confess that there was very little I could tell her. Many of us feel that the Negro problem is a tremendous one and we feel so helpless in regard to it that we take the easiest way out and shut our eyes to much of the real suffering of our people. Of course, we know that this is the wrong way to look upon the matter; but then too we often feel that we are only one tenth of the population, and that is a very small minority. Then the girl in room 13 reminded me of the fact that nearly 90 percent of the Negro population were workers, and the workers are the masses. Therefore we need only to unite our forces and we will bring about a betterment of conditions for all. Through unity of forces we can break down race discrimination and class discrimination.

I am glad my sister student called me into her room that day. She set me thinking in an entirely different direction. I no longer think in terms of dollars and cents. I think in terms of what I can do for my class and my race. I feel that I too can do my part, be it ever so small. I feel that I will have accomplished a great deal if I am able to convince other Negroes that we as a race must stop sitting down and taking it on the chin, so to speak.

We must stop looking for the path of easiness, for we must face facts and learn truths—know the cause in order to find a cure.

I intend therefore on returning home to connect myself with the National Negro Congress and to learn Negro history, since what education I do have I have received in the public schools and any favorable facts pertaining to the Negro were very intentionally omitted.

I have then to thank Bryn Mawr for putting me on the right track.

I have Bryn Mawr to thank for making me race and class conscious.

Similar to Fickland, Jackson concentrates on the tasks of defining and assigning value to a black self in her narrative. Details of the interactions between the writer, college administrators, and a student illustrate Jackson's awakening and growth from self-interested individualism to racial pride and working-class solidarity. Although Jackson mentions no ties to left-wing political organizations, this type of "working-class success story," as Mary Jo Maynes points out, was common among European socialist autobiographers in the early 1900s ("Gender and Narrative" 110). Jackson admits that her first reason for coming to Bryn Mawr was the desire to complete her education for "selfish gain." Motivated by bourgeois values, Jackson's narrated I believed "that it gave one prestige to attend the school and meant much in one's favor when seeking employment." It wasn't until the opening exercises that she learned from President Park the true purpose of the school: "to render service to fellow workers through leadership or individual service." Park and other speakers motivated the narrated I to a certain extent, and Jackson came away committed to seeking change for "labor [and] humanity." At that point, she still felt, however, that she was "only one little insignificant person among a multitude." In Gagnier's study of the ways white Victorian working-class autobiographies differed from those written by members of the white middle class, she describes the "social atom" phenomenon, in which, for a variety of reasons, the narrative begins with a "statement of the author's ordinariness." This is not the case for the conventional bourgeois autobiographer, who frequently begins with family lineage or a birth date (103).

Continuing to describe her past subjectivity, Jackson creates a narrated we that begins to identify with many of the Philadelphia movements for civic and worker improvement. "There we have our trade unions, workers' education, adult education, peace conferences." But this collective we is not an empowered one. Jackson "still wonder[s] what then could I do?" Up to this point in the narrative Jackson has not yet dealt with her blackness. Perhaps the source of her powerlessness lies in the fact that her we is still racially unaware. Blackburn has written that "most African-American female autobiographers confess to one incident in their early years that awakened them to their color; this recognition scene evoke[s] an awareness of their blackness and of its significance, and it had a lasting influence on their lives" (134). The incident involving the "girl in room 13" serves this purpose for Jackson. Although the girl subsumes the black cause within the larger struggle, she reminds Jackson "of the fact that nearly 90 percent of the Negro population were workers, and the workers are the masses," powerful in their numbers. For Jackson there is no assimilating the black cause in the white one. She separates the issues of race and class. Although she is willing to join forces with white workers, she keeps racial equality a separate and distinct goal. Like Fickland, Jackson's subjectivity slips back and forth between I and we. On returning home, I intends to join the "National Negro Congress and to learn Negro history." Thus, with consciousness raised, Jackson is motivated to act, as an African American in a larger workers' movement.

Similar to most of her counterparts in the school, Jackson does not discuss her problems from a gendered perspective. Many reasons have been given for American working-class women's lack of a feminist consciousness. The women's movement of the early twentieth century and beyond has been criticized for its mainly upper- and middle-class constituency. Working women, in general, had little access to feminist rhetoric as such, and the Bryn Mawr Summer School experience proved to be no exception. When interviewed by Marion W. Roydhouse on the issue, Hilda Worthington Smith said that "at the Bryn Mawr Summer School [we] never talked directly of women's problems because these were women, and we knew they were women, and we knew what they'd come for." Roydhouse nevertheless argues that "the Summer Schools were certainly feminist in the early years," because the students and faculty did discuss disparities in wage scales or the difficulties faced by married women in the work force, "but they viewed these issues within the context of needed change in the industrial system, rather than as problems resulting from a male-dominated society" (203).[8] Roydhouse further maintains that the feminism of the summer schools was based on "an idealistic belief in women's potential for fuller participation in society, rather than in the kind of commitment that led to the introduction of the ERA during the same period" (203). Scholars have termed this approach social feminist.[9] At any rate it seems clear that the feminism operating at the school was one of equality, not difference.

Other scholars have argued that gender may not be so decisive a factor in working-class women's lives as it is for the middle class. In her analysis of gender and class in early twentieth-century German working women's autobiography, Maynes concludes that

> Gender oppression was not regarded as primary by any of the female autobiographers. Whether socialist or apolitical, whether writing for a working-class audience or a middle-class one, whether positing collective or individual solutions to their problems, or no solution at all, these autobiographers all seem to agree that it is mostly because they are poor and reliant on their labor that they suffer. . . . While their identity as women is certainly central to their accounts of their life courses, they do not regard solidarity with women, across class lines, as a possible or desirable tactic for improvement. ("Gender and Class" 243–44)

It may be that, because these working-class women were well aware of the brutality of working-class men's lives, as Parrish indicates, they did not aspire to equality with them but, instead, to a more humanized world for everyone—men included.

In the context of the Bryn Mawr Summer School the autobiographical assignment was often successful in encouraging the women workers to represent empowered, collective subject positions through their narratives and, occasionally, to take up feminist positions. Through their autobiographies the working women were offered the opportunity to represent newly acquired versions of more powerful selves. Although these ideas of empowered selfhood were usually derived from androcentric configurations offered to workers in their Bryn Mawr classroom, as well as in institutions of working-class culture, the women often used this rhetoric to win better working conditions and more respect on the job for female workers. Follow-up studies of alumnae also attest to the fact that many went back to their communities and became civic, church, and union leaders. These accomplishments were remarkable indeed.

WOMEN AND AUTOBIOGRAPHY: WORKERS AND STUDENTS, PAST AND PRESENT

Important implications for writing instructors can be drawn from comparisons among the Bryn Mawr autobiographers, literary autobiographers, and studies of today's student autobiographers. The research on autobiography by literary critics and composition theorists alike finds that women focus on human relationships in their writing to a greater extent than men. This finding tends to hold true across race and class—at least in the United States. For example, in her groundbreaking study of female autobiographers, Estelle C. Jelinek found that these writers concentrate on "personal lives—domestic details, family difficulties, close

friends, and especially people who influenced them" (8). Elizabeth Flynn reports
that the narratives of her female college students are "stories of interaction, of
connection, or of frustrated connection" (428). Similarly, Linda H. Peterson
notes that "the topics that women students choose are almost always 'relational'—i.e., they focus on the relationship of the writer with some other person
or group" (173). The same focus on relationships is present in the Bryn Mawr
narratives by both black and white women and in Zandy's anthology of contemporary working-class women writers.

In explaining women's greater concern with human interactions, researchers
in both scholarly groups tend to rely on social constructivist readings of Nancy
Chodorow's theories and/or Carol Gilligan's extension of them. In "Women's
Autobiographical Selves," Susan Stanford Friedman asserts that applying
Chodorow's theories of selfhood (as well as those of Sheila Rowbotham) "to
women's autobiographical texts—particularly those by women who also belong
to racial, ethnic, sexual and religious minorities"—helps expand the autobiographical canon by de-emphasizing the androcentric or conventional focus on
the individual self (35). Quoting Chodorow, Friedman asserts that "we can antic-
ipate finding in women's texts a consciousness of self in which 'the individual
does not oppose herself to all others,' nor 'feel herself to exist outside of others,
but very much with others in an interdependent existence' " (41). Since many
women have been found to write in this manner, their focus on relationship and
their de-emphasis of the individual ego need not—indeed, must not—be devalued in academic writing. As Peterson cautions, "Evaluation of personal essays
should not privilege certain gender-specific modes of self-representation, nor
penalize others" (175).

Another point shared by both composition theorists writing about autobiography and literary critics of autobiography is their emphasis on the poststructuralist
notion of a discursive or textual construction of subjectivity. They argue that gender is a social construction, shaped by cultural beliefs, values, and attitudes—all
"texts," in their language-constitutive nature. These texts motivate the behaviors
marking gender. For example, Sidonie Smith writes that the tropes an autobiographer uses in self-(re)presentation "are always cast in language and are always
motivated by cultural expectations, habits and systems of interpretation pressing
on her at the scene of writing" (*Poetics* 47). Similarly, Geoffrey Sirc argues that
"any occasion for the actual production of written discourse is going to reflect the
way that the writer (as well as the text) has been inscribed into the forms of gender's discourse" (4). Since, in our culture, conventional discourses of gender, race,
and class are not equal in the opportunities they provide individuals, the activity
of reconstructing subjectivity through autobiography for more powerful self-
(re)presentation is a valuable assignment in a writing class whose aim is, among
other things, to build self-confidence and social equality.

It also seems clear from research by composition theorists and from the evidence provided by the summer school autobiographies that certain textual and
extratextual conditions for autobiographical writing produce more empowered
subjectivities than others. Sirc's assignment—to "re-create . . . in words a single

incident in which you were involved or which you witnessed"—provides a good example of disempowering textual conditions (5). This topic did not result, for the most part, in self-(re)presentations of strength for his female students. Sirc reports that most of their written responses did, indeed, include scenarios of nurturing or of providing care (7); he also found, however, that the female students "were more likely to picture themselves as confused and out of control" than his male writers (8). When women's traditional focus on others is accompanied by an autobiographical subjectivity that is devalued, subservient, or exploited, instructors who are teaching for the empowerment of women need to reevaulate their assignments and provide textual contexts (readings, assignments, discussions) that are conducive to personal growth. As Sidonie Smith maintains, "To write an autobiography from that speaking posture [oppressed] does not . . . liberate woman from the fictions that bind her; indeed, it may embed her even more deeply in them since it promotes identification with the very essentialist ideology that renders woman's story a story of silence, powerlessness, self-effacement" (*Poetics* 53). Sirc (8), Flynn (434), and Peterson (173) voice a similar concern.

That the texts written by the women workers are so strikingly different from Sirc's further underscores this point. There were almost no voices of confusion or disorientation among the Bryn Mawr narratives I examined, and I maintain that one reason for their strength lies in the textual context for writing encountered at the Bryn Mawr Summer School, as well as the unions, the YWCA, and progressive churches in which these women came into contact with empowering discourses. Also, as we have seen, the Kennan assignment asked for a critical appraisal of the workers' life situations. Thus, the Bryn Mawr project teaches the importance of exposing students to an array of empowering voices so that they are better able to meld those voices with their own. Several feminist scholars support this contention. Chris Weedon argues that to reconstruct more appropriate subjectivities for themselves "women need access to the different subject positions offered in imaginative alternatives to the present, in humorous critiques and even by positive heroines" (172). Peterson recommends that "the readings suggested as models for the [autobiographical] assignment should include examples by and about both masculine and feminine subjects" (175). And Patricia Bizzell has advocated a pedagogy for the composition class which will "generate egalitarian social power relations" (55). She urges composition teachers to offer readings "that are not simply pluralistic, but politically engaged in a variety of ways; and . . . to try to get students into these texts even if they initially seem very uncongenial" (67). Of course, as Bizzell implies, our focus need not solely be on women. Members of the working class and minorities can benefit from reading discourse about collective strength and control.

The use of a collective subjectivity (*we*) marks the most significant difference between the student autobiographical writing reported on by composition teachers and that of the Bryn Mawr writers. The crucial factor that produced this striking stylistic feature was likely the extratextual context in which the working women were writing. In "Literacy Theory, Teaching Composition and Feminist Response," I argue for the importance of the wider social, economic, and political

context in producing critical literacy. Both text and subjectivity have a dialecti-
cal relationship with material conditions, such as the economy in which they
occur, and both respond to and influence these conditions in the culture at large.
As Weedon writes, "discursive practices are embedded in material power relations which also require transformation for change to be realized," yet these
"material power relations constitute and inhere within discursive practices"
(106). When people believe that better lives are possible through writing, their
writing will reflect this expectation. The theories and practices of worker empowerment offered at Bryn Mawr and in other collective movements of the time may
have led the women workers to believe that their lives could be improved
through school and writing, organizing and protesting. Such worker texts did in
turn influence the social, economic, and political context of the period. The shift
in the Bryn Mawr narratives from the private *I* to the more public *we* likely arose
from this more public arena for the students' collective writing and actions.

Writing about working women in the early 1900s, Gagnier concludes that
"contrary to the claims on behalf of a room of one's own, workers' autobiographies
suggest that writing women were those whose work took them out of the home"
(100). This supports findings by social historians that "the process of 'self discovery' and emergence of a group consciousness for early 20th century women
depended on employment outside the home" (Eisenstein 9). This group consciousness is indeed very crucial to women's empowerment, but I would add that
history also shows us that, unless women and other oppressed groups are provided
with the discourse of collective experience, protest, and power, they will likely
remain in a weakened, individualist frame of mind. In the manner of the Bryn
Mawr educators I think we need to study our students through their autobiographies and other means and strive to create textual and even extratextual contexts
that lead them to greater self- and group confidence. Occasionally, requiring students to write in a collective voice might change their perceptions of themselves
as isolated individuals with disparate problems to a powerful collectivity with
legitimate rights and demands. If students learn to write as *we*, instructors may find
them better able to appreciate the benefits of collective endeavor. We may even
reencounter the raised consciousness and liberating discourse that characterized
the students at the Bryn Mawr Summer School back in the 1920s and 1930s.

NOTES

1. My book will be published by Southern Illinois University Press in 2002.

2. Much of my background information comes from Smith's 1929 book describing the
school's early success, *Women Workers*. My account is also based on records of the school's
various administrative and curricular activities, which Smith and subsequent directors
carefully preserved. These records, as well as student publications, application forms,
course syllabi, and committee minutes, are found in archival collections located at Bryn
Mawr, Rutgers University, Cornell University, and the University of Wisconsin. In addition, I received much inspiration and information from Rita Heller's definitive dissertation, as well as the film she produced, *Women of Summer*, which depicts the history of the
school and a moving 1984 reunion of many of the summer school faculty and students. I

also obtained information from interviews with eighty-nine-year-old Alice Hansen Cook, former summer school faculty member, and two summer school students, Garineh Narzakian and Mary Scafidi, now well into their seventies, who live in the Philadelphia area. Full citations for these and all subsequent sources can be found in the bibliography.

3. See Smith, "Student and Teacher"; and *Women Workers* (41); and Carter and Smith, *Education*.

4. See Rose, "Reading Representative Anecdotes", Flynn, "Composing"; Sirc, "Gender"; and Peterson, "Gender and the Autobiographical Essay."

5. Kennan's syllabi and assignments are located in a set of files containing business records, correspondence, publications, course materials, curricula, student works, and photographs donated by Smith to the Institute of Management and Labor Relations, Rutgers University.

6. Because of a dispute with the Bryn Mawr College Board of Directors, the summer school was not on the Bryn Mawr campus in 1935. I have not been able to obtain an issue of *Shop and School* for that year.

7. Similar assignments were found in Dorothy Weil's English syllabus of 1927 and William Card's syllabus of 1936, both of which can be found in the Bryn Mawr Summer School archives at the Institute of Management and Labor Relations, Rutgers University.

8. In fact, economist Amy Hewes and her students published several pamphlets on such issues. Published in the U.S. Department of Labor's *Bulletin of the Women's Bureau,* they include "Women Workers and Family Support: A Study Made by Students in the Economics Course at the Bryn Mawr Summer School" (1925); "The Industrial Experience of Women Workers at the Summer Schools, 1928–1930" (1931); and "Women Workers in the Third Year of the Depression" (1933).

9. Roydhouse cites Stanley Lemon, *The Woman Citizen,* for more on the issue of social feminism.

BIBLIOGRAPHY

Andrews, William L. "The Changing Moral Discourse of Nineteenth-Century African American Women's Autobiography: Harriet Jacobs and Elizabeth Keckley." In *De/Colonizing the Subject,* edited by Sidonie Smith and Julia Watson. Minneapolis: University of Minnesota Press, 1992.

Bakhtin, Mikhail. *The Dialogic Imagination: Four Essays by M. M. Bakhtin.* Translated by Caryl Emerson and Michael Holquist. Austin: University of Texas Press, 1981.

Belenky, Mary Field, Blythe McVicker Clinchy, Nancy Rule Goldberger, and Jill Mattuck Tarule, eds. *Women's Ways of Knowing: The Development of Self, Voice and Mind.* New York: Basic Books, 1986.

Bizzell, Patricia. "Power, Authority, and Critical Pedagogy." *Journal of Basic Writing* 1, no. 2 (1991): 54–70.

Blackburn, Regina. "In Search of the Black Female Self: African-American Women's Autobiographies and Ethnicity." In *Women's Autobiography: Essays in Criticism,* edited by Estelle C. Jelinek, 133–48. Bloomington: Indiana University Press, 1980.

Carter, Jean, and Hilda W. Smith. *Education and the Worker-Student.* New York: Affiliated Schools for Workers, 1934.

Coiner, Constance. "Literature of Resistance: The Intersection of Feminism and the Communist Left in Meridel Le Sueur and Tillie Olsen." In *Left Politics and the Literary Profession,* edited by Leonard J. Davis and M. Bella Mirabella, 162–85. New York: Columbia University Press, 1990.

Cook, Alice Hansen. Interview by author. Ithaca, N.Y., 16 June 1992.

Culley, Margo, ed. *American Women's Autobiography: Fea(s)ts of Memory*. Madison: University of Wisconsin Press, 1992.

Eisenstein, Sarah. *Give Us Bread but Give Us Roses: Working Women's Consciousness in the United States, 1890 to the First World War*. London: Routledge and Kegan Paul, 1983.

Fickland, Eloise. "Looking Back." *Shop and School* (1933): 32.

Flynn, Elizabeth A. "Composing as a Woman." *College Composition and Communication* 39 (1988): 423–35.

Fox-Genovese, Elizabeth. "My Statue, My Self: Autobiographical Writings of Afro-American Women." In *The Private Self: Theory and Practice of Women's Autobiographical Writings*, edited by Shari Benstock, 64–89. Chapel Hill: University of North Carolina Press, 1988.

Friedman, Susan Stanford. "Women's Autobiographical Selves: Theory and Practice." In *The Private Self: Theory and Practice of Women's Autobiographical Writings*, edited by Shari Benstock, 34–63. Chapel Hill: University of North Carolina Press, 1988.

Gagnier, Regina. "The Literary Standard, Working-Class Autobiography, and Gender." In *Revealing Lives: Autobiography, Biography and Gender*, edited by Susan Groag Bell and Marilyn Yalom, 93–114. Albany: State University of New York Press, 1990.

Gordon, Sarah. "A Typical Day in My Life." *Shop and School* (1929): 27–28.

Greenstein, Rose. "Sacrifice." *Shop and School* (1930): 30–31.

Heller, Rita. "Blue Collars and Blue Stockings: The Bryn Mawr School for Women Workers, 1921–1938." In *Sisterhood and Solidarity: Workers' Education for Women, 1914–1984*, edited by Joyce L. Kornbluh and Mary Frederickson, 110–45. Philadelphia: Temple University Press, 1984.

———. "The Women of Summer: The Bryn Mawr Summer School for Women Workers, 1921–1938." Ph.D. diss., State University of New Jersey, 1986.

———. *The Women of Summer*. Film. National Endowment for the Humanities, Washington, D.C., 1985.

Hollis, Karyn L. "Literacy Theory, Teaching Composition and Feminist Response." *Pre-Text* (spring 1993): 103–16.

Jackson, Marion. "It Set Me Thinking." *Shop and School* (1936): 9–10.

Jelinek, Estelle C. *The Tradition of Women's Autobiography: From Antiquity to the Present*. Boston: Twayne Publishers, 1986

Kennan, Ellen. Autobiography assignment, 1926 and 1934. English syllabi, Bryn Mawr Summer School for Women Workers. Papers donated by Hilda Worthington Smith, Bryn Mawr Summer School Archives, Institute of Management and Labor Relations, Rutgers University, N.J.

Lauter, Paul. "Working-Class Women's Literature: An Introduction to Study." *Radical Teacher* (March 1980): 16–26.

Lemon, Stanley. *The Woman Citizen: Social Feminism in the 1920s*. Urbana: University of Illinois Press, 1973.

Maynes, Mary Jo. "Gender and Class in Working-Class Women's Autobiographies." In *German Women in the Eighteenth and Nineteenth Centuries: A Social and Literary History*, edited by Ruth-Ellen B. Joeres and Mary Jo Maynes, 230–46. Bloomington: Indiana University Press, 1986.

———. "Gender and Narrative Form in French and German Working-Class Narratives." In *Interpreting Lives: Feminist Theory and Personal Narratives*, edited by Personal Narratives Group, 103–17. Bloomington: Indiana University Press, 1989.

Parrish, Beulah. "Those Mill Villages." *Shop and School* (1930): 6.

Peterson, Linda H. "Gender and the Autobiographical Essay: Research Perspectives, Pedagogical Practices." *College Composition and Communication* 42 (May 1991):171–83.

Rose, Shirley K. "Reading Representative Anecdotes of Literacy Practice; Or 'See Dick and Jane Read and Write!'" *Rhetoric Review* 8 (spring 1990): 244–59.

Rowbotham, Sheila. *Woman's Consciousness, Man's World.* London: Penguin, 1973.

Roydhouse, Marion W. "Partners in Progress: The Affiliated Schools for Women Workers, 1928–1939." In *Sisterhood and Solidarity: Workers' Education for Women, 1914–1984,* edited by Joyce L. Kornbluh and Mary Frederickson, 189–221. Philadelphia: Temple University Press, 1984.

Sirc, Geoffrey. "Gender and 'Writing Formations' in First-Year Narratives." *Freshman English News* 18 (fall 1989):4–11.

Smith, Hilda Worthington. "The Student and Teacher in Workers' Education." In *Workers' Education in the United States,* edited by Theodore Brameld, 181–202. New York: Harper and Brothers, 1941.

———. *Women Workers at the Bryn Mawr Summer School.* New York: Affiliated Summer Schools for Women Workers in Industry and American Association for Adult Education, 1929.

Smith, Sidonie. *A Poetics of Women's Autobiography: Marginality and the Fictions of Self-Representation.* Bloomington: Indiana University Press, 1987.

———. "Resisting the Gaze of Embodiment: Women's Autobiography in the Nineteenth Century." In *American Women's Autobiography: Fea(s)ts of Memory,* edited by Margo Culley, 75–110. Madison: University of Wisconsin Press, 1992.

Weedon, Chris. *Feminist Practice and Poststructuralist Theory.* Oxford: Basil Blackwell, 1987.

Zandy, Janet, ed. *Calling Home: Working-Class Women's Writings—An Anthology.* New Brunswick, N.J.: Rutgers University Press, 1990.

Working Class Consciousness in Jo Sinclair's *The Seasons*

Florence Howe

I want first to explain the impulse behind this essay. As publisher of more than one hundred books over the past twenty-two years, I have only twice before been moved to write a critical paper. Janet Zandy asked me to reflect on this fact, as though to move from experience to theorizing working-class literature. The subjects, each time I was moved to write, were working-class books—Agnes Smedley's *Daughter of Earth*, an autobiographical novel, and Maimie Pinzer's *The Maimie Papers*, a collection of correspondence that can be read as memoir.[1] Both are rarities in form and substance. Jo Sinclair's memoir, *The Seasons: Death and Transfiguration*, joins them and, in terms of form and substance, takes another leap.[2] Like Smedley's fiction and Pinzer's correspondence, Sinclair's memoir tries to make sense of a would-be writer's life.[3]

And not one life only: the immediate impulse for Sinclair's book is the death of her beloved Helen Buchman, the person who rescued the twenty-five-year-old, part-time working-class writer and who, for the next twenty-five years, provided a middle-class family setting—a room of Jo's own—and comforts for a full-time writing life. It is the story of what Jo calls "levels," a word she uses to suggest moving from her working-class place into a middle-class life and which she then uses to mean carrying the sense of the past in the present, and especially feeling the present pain in the memory of the pleasures of the past.

Although I did not see the manuscript of *The Seasons* until the late 1980s, the memoir reads as though it was written in 1969, thus "covering" the thirty-one years between then and 1938, when Jo and Helen first met. The memoir is divided into three unequal chronological periods: first, the twenty-five-year "Journal of Life," Jo's second quarter of a century, from age twenty-five to fifty—the joy with which she credits Helen for transforming the "tough ghetto kid" who wore her hair unusually clipped, walked funny, and even talked funny, into the successful writer who lived for more than twenty years with Helen Buchman, her husband, Mort, and their two children, in three different houses, two in Cleveland and one thirteen miles into the countryside. Second, the "Journal of Death," the final nine months of Helen's life, in which Jo becomes the strong, life-giving person, and Helen the frightened, sick one. And third, the six years after Helen's death, when Jo must struggle alone to reclaim the will to live and to write.

The form of the book (and much of its substance) comes organically from the tool that wise Helen knew would bring spiritual health to Jo and great pleasure to both of them and many others: the garden. This is not your ordinary small city or suburban plot: by the time they move into their third house, the "garden" is a small farm, the fruits, vegetables, and flowers sufficient for many families. Partly with the aid of two found journals, the memoir moves through *the seasons* of growing, from spring to winter, three times: first, with respect to the life of twenty-five years together; second, with respect to the death—Helen's first stroke occurs in the spring of 1963, the fifth at the end of December that same year; and, third, with respect to the six years following Helen's death.

So the book is at once the story of a twenty-five-year daily relationship, the story of an early death (Helen was fifty-four in 1963), and the story of loss and recovery. In it, of course, Sinclair tells us much about herself, even glimpses of the twenty-five years without Helen in her life, and it is that young, class-bound Jo who reappears after Helen's death. Sinclair has to fulfill two purposes: she wants us to know this person who made such a difference in her life, and she wants us to know the dimensions of the difference. That last purpose means she needs to weave into the chapters of life and loss the making of herself as writer, for, as Jo sees it, Helen's belief in Jo's ability was essential to the production of Jo's novels, stories, and plays. We hear Helen's refrain, even after her death, "Ruthie, go write me a book." Thus, into key positions within the book's narrative of the death, as well as the life, Sinclair places flashbacks that testify to Helen's belief in Jo (or Ruth or Ruthie, as Helen calls her) as a writer and to her own need, as a writer, of Helen's supportive presence. These flashbacks, present in the "Journal of Death," serve especially to prolong and to make more poignant the loss of Helen, who seems to have become not only Jo's friend, mentor, beloved intimate but, symbiotically, also her alter ego. Helen's physical death is Jo's "creative death," only to be released when written out through the pain.

To accomplish both of these purposes Jo Sinclair *works* class consciousness into her text, in three different ways, which I want to outline here. First, Helen is Jo's "teacher" and, in fact, for two years, the person Jo calls her "green thumb psychiatrist." During that period, before Jo moves into the house, she sees Helen daily for "therapy" and lunch. Not surprisingly, the lists of "she taught me" are, at first, dominated by material goods: linen napkins, napkin rings, foods the ghetto kid had never eaten—"shrimp salad on Bibb and watercress, Southern biscuits in a basket—wrapped in a huge damask dinner napkin to keep them hot" (50). Then she offered culture: music, art—Käthe Kollwitz and Vincent Van Gogh become her favorites—and writers outside the United States—"I read all about Oscar Wilde in prison, and knew all over again how confused and ignorant and fearful my psyche had been before Helen" (52). Later in the volume, during the partial recovery after the first stroke, there is this dialogue:

> ME: "Do you realize that I had never heard of a counter-tenor before I met you?"
> HELEN: "Do you realize that I had never heard of a bagel or a potato knish before you?"

Yes, Helen is Jewish, as is Mort, but they are so very different from Jews I could recognize that Jo had to correct my assumption that they were Christian, thus demonstrating the significance of class.

At least as important as food and culture, Helen teaches Jo that it's all right, even lovely, to express affection through touching, kissing, even language, though only Helen uses the tender endearments. For example, she calls Jo "*toi*," the familiar French pronoun reserved for intimates and perhaps reminiscent of Jo the "tough kid," the "toughie." Helen extends the lessons to Jo's mother, her sisters: "My little mother—who ever kissed her in Russia, or in rotten Brooklyn, or all the years in Cleveland? Helen and the kids are really kissers! And Ma kind of pushes at them, but she loves it" (115).

Second, Jo emphasizes the contrasting moods in which the two begin their relationship, seeming at first to define thereby their social class: the earthbound pessimist Jo; the stargazing dreamer of an optimist Helen. Jo expects defeat when her first novel is declined by a publisher; Helen sends *Wasteland* off again, and it wins the $10,000 Harper prize. Honest Jo would not leave the portrait uncomplicated by reality; she reminds us that her sister Fannie is also an optimist, a joyous, happy person, though someone without Jo's aspirations. I would theorize that the mood difference sharpens when a working-class person is either crossing the boundary of her class or understands enough about class to want to do so. How do I know this? I know it from my own experience. Here is a brief example: at age twenty, living in my first middle-class setting, an elegant mansion housing twenty-eight graduate students at Smith College in 1950, I was told by the housemother that I was "clearly an unhappy person," that I would be "depressed" all my life. I thought she was magical to know how I felt, but, of course, both she and I were blind to class differences. I was the only working-class person in the house.

I cannot review in detail the class-bound fights about money that occur with some regularity in *The Seasons* or the varying reactions to Helen's medical treatment. In general, however, Jo's response is fury, often mingled with suspicion. The key word, and feeling, so familiar to my own working-class emotions, is *unfair*. It is unfair that Helen be cursed with so wounded a body; it is unfair that she did not have superior, really knowledgeable medical treatment that might have saved her life.

Third, and most important, is the tool for all the rest, the language in which Jo and Helen speak to each other over a twenty-five-year period: their voices, their diction and metaphor, are class bound. I should say at once that *The Seasons* is filled with dialogue. In one place Jo describes Helen as a voice teacher: "Well, a person is a kind of instrument, too. And whatever voice or song lies within is dependent, so often, on a teacher." Not in imitation. Jo continues: "And of course, the person-instrument is always different. What fashioned this particular one?—or who? Where was it created?" And the final question, for Jo in the volume and for us as readers of Jo Sinclair today, "How can an instrument go mute again, after so many years of singing? Her kind of teacher should have left permanence in an ardent student like me."

And, of course, I must at least mention the idea of "permanence," so important to the fifty-year-old Jo mourning the friend who first gave her the sense of even the possibility of permanence. And we both understand the significance of class here: as a working-class person, my whole body vibrated to that desire for permanence and for the keeping of Helen's promise, that she would not leave Jo. Dying, of course, breaks her promise.

For dozens of pages early in the volume Jo distinguishes between her vocabulary and Helen's, often in language invented for their shared experience of gardening/farming. And these words are often class bound: Jo's "chiselings," for example, for plants borrowed or taken from other places; Helen's "Johnny" for the woodchuck, named after a character in a children's book Jo had "never even herd of." But, then, the recognition: "Oh, Christ, our vocabularies are one language, so often" (22). Perhaps the single best example can be found in another of the volume's refrains: Jo's description of herself "touring the joint," meaning a long walk through several gardens that surround the house down to and around the pond, to note not only the growth of plants and bloomings of trees and shrubs but also the life of animals and birds. And, of course, to report all of this—once Helen is ill and bed- or house-ridden—in detail to Helen.

To conclude I must return the question of how I knew what I did about this book: how I read what was suggested under the surface, how it was that I could theorize about working-class language and sensibility, how I knew especially about the need for affirmation, the lack of confidence as a given. I used to think that my own lack of confidence stemmed chiefly from gender, but I know otherwise now, and perhaps that is why *The Seasons* spoke so deeply to me. The need for support and affirmation may be doubled by gender, but the dimensions particular to Jo Sinclair (and to me) are rooted in class. I am theorizing now: the need Jo has for support, assurance, belief, affirmation, formed during the first twenty-five years of her life, does not disappear, but simply retreats from dominance during the second twenty-five years of her life. And then it returns. To state the idea somewhat differently, without a single Helen Buchman, one would continue to need many versions of Helen. I never even tried to write, never even believed enough in myself to try, until, by accident, I wrote a long piece about Mississippi's Freedom Summer, which, also by accident, was published to small acclaim. That was 1965. Even today, I am "surprised" when some different "Helen" declares my work (which is, in fact, the way I refer to my writing) to be worthwhile. So, I understand—from the inside—Jo's need for affirmation, though that is only half the story: the loss of twenty-five years of sustained love and friendship warrants its own kind of mourning. Beyond mourning this book ultimately affirms Jo Sinclair's ability to capture and inscribe the memoir with her unmistakable literary working-class hand and voice. We are grateful to her (and thus to Helen) for a text that honestly evokes, neither exalting nor diminishing, the making of a working-class writer.

NOTES

This essay was first read as part of a panel on working-class literature, chaired by Janet Zandy, at the Modern Language Association's meeting in December 1992. I am grateful to Janet Zandy for her generous encouragement and her insightful criticism.

1. Smedley, *Daughter of Earth* (1929; reprint, with a foreword by Alice Walker and an afterword by Nancy Hoffman, New York: The Feminist Press, 1987); Pinzer [pseudo.], *The*

Maimie Papers: Letters from an Ex-Prostitute, ed. Ruth Rosen and Sue Davidson (New York: The Feminist Press, 1977).

2. Sinclair, *The Seasons: Death and Transfiguration* (New York: The Feminist Press, 1993); page numbers for all quotations are given in the text.

3. The memoir also takes on writing and silence—explaining why, although Sinclair wrote and published four novels between 1940 and 1960, there were no more after that. The novels were *Wasteland* (1946); *Sing at My Wake* (1952); *The Changelings* (1955); and *Anna Teller* (1960). The latter two books have been republished by The Feminist Press.

The Writing on the Wall, Or Where Did That Dead Head Come From?

Cy-Thea Sand

The dragon slayer looks up, alerted by a subtle shift of energy. Something has changed here as the day's light dims into darkness. She looks beyond her shield and gasps with disgust. The monster suddenly has another head, and it is dangling obscenely from Dragon-Lady's thick neck. Depression. The face of Depression. A Dead Head, yellowish brown with scorched and shriveled scales. Its tongue distends from a cavernous mouth, thick and ugly, and its eyes are vacuous and remote. Old ideas and loss of spirit register here as lethargy. The eyes weep pus. The dragon slayer's angry protest against Anxiety's fiery dictates falters, tripped up by fatigue. The Dead Head invites the dragon slayer to read the writing on the wall as Despair.

I have worried over the years that I would lose my mind from the stress of Dead Head's oppressive tactics against me. I once asked friends with whom I shared a communal home to sign a statement promising that they would never let me be taken to a psychiatric ward. Several years ago I wrote that I hesitate to call myself a writer in part because "I identify with the millions of women rocking back and forth, shuffling down hallways or staring out of windows. Scrapes of last night's supper have crusted on the housecoats they pull closer to themselves. Few of them speak. The ones who do usually shout or force the odd syllable from drug-swollen tongues."[1] In my imagination these women are fat and poor and hate themselves just like me. We are all driven mad by a self-rejection that is so deeply inscribed that its origins are erased. The Dead Head has colonized our bodies and minds, and we are too tired to break free.

Brick by brick, brick by brick, the writing on the wall gets writ.

The Dead Head of Depression invites me to classify, measure, compare, differentiate, judge, and qualify myself, in short, to back myself up against a wall of constructed madness and impoverished ideas that gnaw at the beauty and splendidness of my life. Its tongue is swollen with lies, with old, bloated, useless ideas about me. Its eyes are shut, blind to my resourcefulness and my power to overcome the passivity it embodies.

I narrowly escape confinement in the Allan Memorial Hospital in Montreal, where Dr. Ewen Cameron conducted his horrific, de-patterning experiments on people suffering under the influence of Anxiety and Depression. While I am entering my adolescent years in the Verdun district of Montreal, several women and a few men are subjected to Cameron's "concentration camp techniques" of brainwashing. The Allan Memorial is housed in a cold, stone mansion once known as Ravenscrag on Mount Royal. Ravenscrag used to be the family mansion of shipbuilding millionaires, near the district of Westmount, where my great-aunt and my father's sisters worked as domestic servants in the 1930s. As I grow into womanhood, a half-hour bus ride away, a Gothic house of horrors muffles the screams of patients tortured by prolonged drugged sleep, LSD, and electroshock "treatments." A son of one of Cameron's victims has written that Ravenscrag was "once a place of elegant parties, of the English elite in a French city, now for us, it was a mansion of despair."[2] Cameron once kept a woman—who was under the influence of the Dead Head of Depression—in a sealed room for thirty-five days, her eyes blindfolded, her ears blocked, her hands and feet padded.[3] Isolation and sensory deprivation were Cameron's cure for psychic pain.

Raven scrag. *Scrag* is a slang word in Verdun for an ugly girl. As I grow up in its cement and brick world of sweltering summers and arctic winters, I grow up in the landscape of an urban consciousness saturated with ideas about how working-class women should look and act and be. Ewen Cameron performed those operations on the mind and psyches of imprisoned women while I am growing into adolescence, just miles from the horror. I see myself standing in the schoolyard of Verdun High School, chatting with my best friend, tense with self-consciousness and worry. It is the early 1960s. The Dead Head of Depression has stalked me since I was about eight years old: I am frightened by the despair of the people around me, especially my father's. I feel helpless and powerless over his chronic irritability, sullenness, and worries about money.

In 1963, while I am chatting with my girlfriend in the schoolyard, I already have years of experience with feelings of despair, hopelessness, and immobility. I look like a cool teenager, but I already know a monster of tremendous power exists. It seems to feed on the unhappiness in my family. I don't understand it. I just know it's there, and I live in fear of it. I look up at the Verdun Aqueduct, a canal that links Lachine and Verdun with the city of Montreal. The water drifts along in the direction of the horror house of Ravenscrag. I am a working-class girl in deep psychic pain because I can read the writing on the wall: girls aren't as important as boys, and they just grow up and get married and have kids—my value is in direct proportion to my looks because I am just a girl, and I am supposed to find a man with a good job and get married and have kids. That man can't be French or black though. And that man can't be a woman. The writing also says that people who work for others never get ahead and are always worried about money, and *that* never changes. You do the best you can and drink when you're not working. I know how bad the world can get, how hate can mani-fest, because I read books about the Holocaust. I know there's no hope because, when I talk to my parents about my concern, they always say the same thing: "It's human nature, and you can't change it. Notions about change are ridicu-lous."

The writing on the wall is penned with the indelible ink of dread. I am not in command of my feelings: anger, shame, and frustration eat me up as I shut down deep within myself. I feel shy and unconfident. I am terrified of the world beyond my family, but I am dying to escape the borders of the existence I see here in Verdun. Feelings overwhelm me and begin writing the story I have lived within until very recently, the story that I am tense, nervous, and deeply morose. Depressed. When I swallow a bottle of pills at eighteen, too frightened to face an audience and speak, my doctor and family send me to a psychiatrist. Dr. Gray or Grayson, I can't remember. But I like how his name sums up the color of the experience for me. I am so terrified of him and his huge, dark, wood-paneled, uptown office that I cannot speak. He calls my mother into his office and recommends that I be put in the hospital right away. But I refuse to go. I recruit my rage into effective action and vow to finish my undergraduate degree. "Fuck him, I'm going to finish my courses," I told my brother in a dragon slayer–like protest against Gray's pathologizing the effects of gender, class, and familial oppression on me.

While I am growing up female and working-class in a world that worships maleness and money, "the godfather of Canadian psychiatry"[4] is dreaming up ways to erase impressions, memories, and insights that cause his patients suffering. A few years later, when Dr. Gray wants to send me off to Ravenscrag, Dr. Ewen Cameron is two years dead, but his dangerous ideas are alive and well in psychiatric circles. I guess I was a dragon slayer in training back then because I defied my worried parents and an imposing medical authority. I knew Dr. Gray's drugs would imprison me as effectively, if not more than, the brick and wood and concrete I'd be kept in. I could read the writing on the wall. I knew that commitment to a mental hospital would devastate my already precarious self-esteem. I knew that suppressing the feelings that were overwhelming me was not the way to liberation. The dragon slayer in me intuits that Freedom's door cannot be opened by silenced and controlled pain.

The idea behind the book I'm writing, *Magic in a Metaphor,* is that I have deconstructed my emotional life and liberated myself from the devastating problems of Anxiety and Depression by using a therapeutic technique informed by postmodern thought. The idea behind this book is that ideas are powerful and really do have a life of their own. I have always loved ideas. Big ideas like socialism and feminism and the belief that human consciousness is evolving more and more toward liberation. Maybe it was time for me to use radical concepts and perspectives to transform my own inner world so I could write again and in order for my passion to dare to wake up. What I want to celebrate with you is that the narrative approach to therapy is a big wonderful grand idea in my life. It is a therapy of metaphor and respect. It is a way of working with problems and with language that invites me to flaunt my success all over these pages.

With this narrative about the narrative, this story of a therapeutic approach to the forces that threatened to annihilate my spirit, I am creating a story around my ideas of what feminism, class analysis, and a narrative approach to therapy mean to the resurrection of my creativity, to my "awesome lust for life," to my "hunger growing and growing inside the earth for centuries on end!" to honor Anne Hebert's description of women's relentless persistence about life and freedom. Here I interview myself and make public my private story with the passion of a poet, the clarity of a critic, and the curiosity of an investigative journalist. I have accepted Nicole Brossard's invitation to become my own mistress, and with this offering I play in a place of experiment and dare to take a risk. To my own story I apply a few of the skills expected in the literary world, such as the ability to research; interview; define concept and structure, narrative and dialogue, voice and stance. I also develop a skill expected in the academic world—that is, to take information and notes from various sources and then synthesize this study into a coherent whole or thesis. The idea, as I understand it, is to add to a *body* of knowledge with original conclusions or analyses. In other words, a student must read all the authorities on a given subject and then produce something new, a piece of work that builds on the ideas and perspectives of other thinkers.

With this rhetorical pastiche, this postmodern auto*body*graphy, I visualize theory into a narrative of expertise about the meaning of *my own experience*. In it I play with postmodern ideas and alter the text of my life. I consult myself as source in an exploration of the effects of class and gender oppression on my body, on my voice, and on my stance in the world. Writer and critic Susan Crean encouraged me to write a book about class during the summer of 1988, when she was my instructor in a creative documentary course at a women's writing retreat here in Vancouver, British Columbia. Susan suggested that I gather together all the material I had been exploring over the years I wrote about class as an issue in feminist political theory and in women's literary production. This is the book I must birth first. In this text I disrupt my old fixed identity, the old story of domination. I play with the script. I learn to perform my own meaning as I become my own referent and a sovereign with many subjects. This is the project that breathes life into the possibility of others.

In 1992 I was invited by narrative therapy practitioners to consider that Anxiety and Depression could be understood as *external* forces that were *subjugating me*. An Australian therapist explains the basis of narrative therapeutic thought in this way:

> The body of ideas known as postmodern or constructivist thought presents a perspective on the construction of our reality that allows us to see how we have been recruited into particular ways of being that may or may not be useful or helpful. The possibility of developing new ways of being, that are more in line with what we would prefer, is opened up. We give meaning to our lives by interpreting the experiences we have in the light of the beliefs that we have about ourselves, and we largely dismiss those experiences which do not fit these beliefs. But these beliefs can be changed, they are not fixed or based on any essential truth about human nature.[5]

In other words, each of us can write a preferred story of who we are in opposition to ideas about ourselves which oppress or limit us—ideas that undermine the delicious text of our existence, what theologian Matthew Fox calls the original blessing of our lives. In her novel *Borderlines* Janette Turner Hospital writes that the past is a capricious and discontinuous narrative and the present an infinite number of fictions. The narrative therapeutic idea thrives in this realm of the imagination, in the rich, playful realm of possibilities. The heart of the narrative idea is political; it's about power and possibility. It's about the idea, the passionate idea, that I can separate my life and my relationships from ideas about myself that hurt and oppress me. As a person, I am distinct from my problems. I am a person, and a problem is a problem.

Narrative therapeutic practice is based on the belief that reality is cocreated within a cultural discourse and that problems can be deconstructed *away from a person's identity* or sense of who they are. People and problems are two separate entities. The narrative is about *externalizing* the problems. This has turned out to be a transformative technique for me. This is the big idea that has birthed my emotional freedom. The problem does not reside in me. The problem is the problem, or, more specifically, the *effects* of the problem are the problem. I am invited to resist notions of determinism and the paralyzing impact of pathologizing that informs the medical model of dis-ease in this culture. The narrative approach to human struggles invites me to resist the idea that somehow to be anxious and depressed are part of my essential self or part of an indelible problem-saturated story of my life. I am invited to resist the domination of Anxiety and Depression and to have more of a say in the direction my life is going.

The magic in the metaphor began for me when I was able to see Anxiety outside of me in the shape of a fire-breathing dragon that kept threatening to incinerate me. The panic attacks I suffered felt like I was burning alive, and, as the metaphor became more and more real to me, I was able to gradually separate myself from its domineering influence and to name it Dragon-Lady. My life gradually and sometimes dramatically transformed, and I began to write again after several years of silence. Then one day the dragon appeared as a *two*-headed monster, and the Dead Head manifested in my imagination. The tongue on the second head hung from a cracked-lipped mouth, a putrid profusion of passivity. I knew what that swollen tongue was silencing. Working on this piece, my chapter about Depression, had become a struggle. I gazed at the Dead Head of Depression before me, and I knew it was *its* voice telling me that I am too tired to handle the stress of looking for work *and* the focus and discipline needed to write this story. "How can you write the second chapter of a book?" Dead Head laughs at me, opening its mouth just wide enough to expel its venom. "I will tire you out!"

Dead Head dangles loosely from the dragon's thick neck, its eyes closed, a putrid, swollen tongue dominates its flaccid mouth. William Styron describes the word *depression* as slivering "innocuously through the language like a slug, leaving little trace of its intrinsic malevolence."[6] But Depression's malevolence and deadly grip are clearly manifested in my imagination at this moment, and I know I have externalized the problem of Depression in proportion to its dominance in my life. It is not just a scale on Dragon-Lady's tail as I had previously thought. It is not just doing a bit part in the old story. It is not just a syllable in the problem-saturated discourse of femininity. It is its language system, its life-support system. It is a big problem, a big life-threatening problem.

Women describe its effects on their lives as overpowering; it fosters a feeling of helplessness and loss of control over one's life. People under the influence of Depression have six times more marital failures, three times more serious problems in school, and are more likely to be alcoholics than the general population.

They suffer two to three times more heart attacks and are significantly more likely to die of cancer or suicide.[7] Furthermore, women receive shock treatment twice as often as men do and are prescribed 72 percent of all mental health–related medications.[8]

Dragon-Lady's attacks on me are an immediate challenge, an adrenaline rush that forces me to move, to act to save myself. But the Dead Head of Depression is a weightier matter. I feel breathless in its bloated presence. It makes me tired and tricks me into thinking I need to sleep or eat. What's the point of writing or studying or taking photographs, anyway? Who cares? What difference does it make? It interrogates me with life-draining questions over and over, over and over. My Muse, my Maenad, my creative inner child, who loves to play with words and images, suffers a broken heart, and my days and nights are submerged in passivity and powerlessness. How I look is not good enough, what I do or think is not good enough, and the sparkle and magic of existence are extinguished. I drag myself from chore to chore, forgetting to laugh, oblivious to the kaleidoscope of color outside my kitchen window. I don't care if the purple finches come or not.

Dead Head is Dragon-Lady's twisted twin. Dragon-Lady's tongue spits fire, and the Dead Head spews news and views that gag me, that cut off my breath, that leave me too breathless to speak or write. (Don't be too creative, too passionate, too intelligent.) Depression is the consequence of Anxiety: I feel trapped, victimized, and paralyzed by the toll fear and tension extract from my spirit and from my body. I wake up in the middle of the night; my stomach is nervous, and I am tired out. I want to hide from the challenge of living and breathing. My turbulent history of fear and nervousness has me rocking back and forth on the bed, enveloped by a quilt and the cold cruelty of despair. I am afraid of being publicly shamed if I voice these thoughts.

Depression used to be a wail of a tale in my mind's eye, but no more. This scale carries too much weight. Its ideas continue to oppress me and keep me in my place by comparing me to others and torturing me with repetitious nonsense, with stories of failure and loss. Brick by brick, brick by brick, the writing on the wall gets writ. (If my own father appears to hate me, how can I possibly matter? Don't relax, don't trust, don't be happy, don't poke out the eye of the ever-watchful double-headed monster.) Dead Head disentitles me to a life of my own, sculpted by care and compassion. It demands allegiance to passivity and people pleasing. The importance of my voice and my life fade away. I feel lost in a fog of fatigue, and I can't seem to make it matter.

Maybe Dead Head appears between the need to belong and the demands of conformity. Maybe Dead Head lives in the distance between dreams and possibilities. After all, a 1978 British study theorized that working-class women were four times more likely to become depressed than women from middle-class homes.[9] Lack of money leads to fewer ways to cope with stress and that old helpless feeling. Poverty devours hope in this story much like Dragon-Lady devoured my energy, focus, and vision. And another study argues that, as a society, we cannot improve women's mental health until we improve their status.[10]

I grew up in Verdun, roller-skating, skipping rope, walking fences. The red and gray brick of Verdun cemented my options: stay, marry, or work as a clerk or secretary and help your folks out. The wall of my childhood was a place referred to in the sociological jargon of the 1930s as an immigrant colony or catch-basin of poor and working-class people. My father's parents immigrated from Scotland in 1929 and settled here in Verdun, a district of Montreal in the province of Quebec. (Brick by brick, brick by brick, the writing on the wall gets writ.) The black iron railings of Verdun extend like tentacles along the quarter-mile of brick flats, side by side, creating a density, a closed atmosphere, a containment. Poverty and hardship are main characters in this scene.

I remember my Great-aunt Nan stooped over, an exhausted expression on her tiny-featured face, her neatly styled hair, her eyes small, blue, intense. She works as a cook in the wealthy district of Westmount, Quebec. When she can leave her employer's kitchen, my mother's simple meals soothe and nourish her like the brown vinyl hassock under her aching legs.

Nan sits in her favorite armchair, slightly bent over and intent on her television program. She is enjoying her half-day off from live-in domestic service, relaxing in our living room. Thursdays and Sundays were her rest times, according to my mother, who welcomes her husband's aunt into our tiny Verdun flat. My mother baby-sits neighbors' children, my father works as a supply clerk, the two paternal aunts who live with us work in the same company: one is a factory worker; the other spends her days upstairs in the office working for an erratic boss who is under the influence of alcohol most of the time. My aunt makes many crucial decisions for her boss that her paycheck never reflects. During the evenings our pet budgie pulls bobby pins out of my aunts' hair, as they set their hair in 1950s fashion and laugh as the budgie dips his beak in the glass of water beside the pins.

The outside world for my family is one of bosses and landlords, us and them, the privileged ones and our family, who work for *them* as a matter of course, as a matter of fact, as a matter of history. American archivist and activist Joan Nestle argues that the feminist dictate that the personal is political can be expanded to embrace the notion that the more personal is, in fact, historical. In the preface to her book *A Restricted Country*, Nestle writes that the more personal demands attention be paid to how we fill our days and our nights, as we participate in any given economic system. This idea reflects what the British working-class sociologist Carolyn Steedman calls the drama of class, the process of working-class autobiography. I approach history as Tillie Olsen defines it as both a personal past, which gives one a continuous identity, and a social legacy, which links generations. My tension comes from knowing that history's paradigms do not include servants, factory or office workers, or the private world of domesticity. Charlotte Perkins Gilman noted that all the distinctive lines of human progress lie outside this private realm of household management.

In 1987 I traveled to Montreal on a Canada Council grant to interview my aunts, who all worked as domestic servants in Montreal during the 1930s and 1940s, before getting better work in factory, sales, or office jobs (except Aunt

Nan, who worked in service all her life). As I travel from Westmount to Verdun in a taxi, I feel the geography of class in my bones, as sharp and persistent as fatigue. As I drive into Verdun's density of brick row housing far away from the Westmount spaciousness my aunts served, I feel disquiet. Steedman writes that "accounts of working class life are told by tension and ambiguity out on the borderlands,"[11] and her words gnaw at my insides: Will my aunts remember enough details for me to build a narrative? Will I be able to sift through the family silences to catch a glimpse of my aunts as young immigrant workers? The inherent/ inherited maid-in-me feels awkward riding in a taxi from Westmount to Verdun, the fare paid from Canada Council coffers. Aunt Nan rode the bus, after all.

How did I begin this work, this story of my aunts as workers? It began in my academic voice, the voice that approached the Canada Council for an explorations grant to search for radical Canadian women writers of the 1920s and 1930s, using a feminist cultural framework informed by both a class and historical perspective on writing by women. I wrote that I wanted to search for the Canadian equivalents of Tillie Olsen and Meridel Le Sueur, as well as for evidence of the lives of female domestic servants in Montreal during the 1920s and 1930s. I wanted to know if any records were left of their lives and whether or not any of them wrote. I wanted to understand what limited these women's creative expression. I could not accept Canadian poet Sharon Stevenson's perspective that "the working class works, and the owning class directs the affairs of the country. The class in between writes."[12]

But Sharon was right, of course. And I think the main reason I had such a need to search out evidence specifically of domestic workers who wrote is the memory of my Aunt Nan. She loved literature and used to recite the classics to me, like Samuel Taylor Coleridge's "The Rime of the Ancient Mariner," her voice soft, her face etched with the exhaustion of working long and hard hours for the luxury of others. But her crinkled, lined countenance seemed to soften as the sounds of the words echoed around our tiny bedroom.

Nan had access to the tremendous libraries of her wealthy employers in Westmount and brought their books home to Verdun with her when she came to rest on her days off or for longer periods, when she was on holiday. Often when I left for school in the morning I would notice where she was in her book and be amazed, when I returned home for lunch, by just how much she had read. A half-read novel on my aunt's lap cheered me somehow: the world seemed less dreary, less limited by the demands of the laboring life I witnessed everyday in the eyes and gestures of my family members. I imagined Nan retreating to her room in her employer's large house with a book of prose or poetry in her hand, and somehow this idea comforted me.

I even embellished this story because I liked it so much. I dared to wonder if my aunt ever wanted to write. Did she resist her role as servant at all in her imagination? Did she feel excluded from the dominant culture of the white men who produced the fine literary work she read so lovingly? One (female) professor was outraged at my questions when she read them in my funding application. She insisted that they denoted "a subjective phenomenological thrust that is antipolitical, possibly dangerously so. Whatever her subjectivity, and despite her subjectivity, your aunt was excluded, she was not capable of writing in the discourse that has been defined culturally as 'literature,' she was defined for her employers and their friends and on government documents as a servant. People like your aunt are exploited whether they think so or not."

I let this response silence me for a while—a long while. Haunted by my own misgivings about the value of my nonmainstream work, I let this reasoned statement of the nature of reality undermine my confidence. I forgot that academics can be dangerous. Ideas and musings seldom are. I felt directionless. I felt dominated by Shame. I felt silly about wondering if Aunt Nan ever thought of writing. Still, I think it was these questions that coached me to fill out a Canada Council application form in the first place and to declare boldly that "I am committed to a full-length study of Canadian women's literary production from both a materialist and feminist viewpoint and am interested in what critics Wendy Frost and Michelle Valiquette call the 'specificity of women's writing'—the social, cultural, historical, and economic contexts in which it is produced." If my aunt and other well-read domestic servants like her left evidence of their writing, perhaps in their work, I could find a kind of tradition to sustain me in my tortuous ambivalence about academe: I love ideas but am repulsed by academe's inaccessibility, its language and arrogant assumptions about what is worth considering, about whose lives and ideas are worthy of attention and care.

My Aunt Nan was the closest I got to the power of the word, the power of language to transport me out of the economic, social, and emotional confines of being a girl in a working-class family. My Uncle Steve loved literature, too, but the slaughter and chaos of World War II left its topography on him: he recited poetry in the frenetic language of skid-row despair.

Imagining my aunt in a library of her own may be a way I ask for permission to write. Imagining my aunt away from the culinary details of someone else's kitchen may be my way of asking for clues, for comfort, for support—a kind of reaching into my family's history for permission to write, for permission to even consider myself someone with public authority. With this narrative I escort my family into the public domain of what is considered to be history.

The Dead Head of Depression appears at night and writes nightmares on garage walls and the sides of buildings in Verdun. I read them each morning as I board the bus from Verdun to a downtown university with a language all its own.

But this is a postcolonial text. To externalize Depression as an effect of oppression that is informed by subjugating ideas about gender and class *and* to witness its manifestation as a moribund protrusion of a metaphoric monster are salvific and fun. With it I oppose the Dead Head's subjugation of my imagination. I awaken from its hypnotic chant of inadequacy. I cut out its tongue with my pen as mighty as the sword, and I speak against its impoverishing ideas. If I believe that Depression is a part of me—a biochemical quirk or disorder or an emotional tendency—*I* become the problem to be controlled and fixed. If I believe that Depression is not me, I am invited to separate myself from its strategies and sneaky, insidious ways. I am invited to defy it. The most powerful element of this radical conversation is the not-me aspect of externalizing. To fully understand that Depression is *not-me*, that I am not a depressed person, is a tactic against Depression. I may have been immobilized by the spirit-stealing grip of Depression for most of my life. Dead Head may still try to take over my imagination at times, but *I* am not depressed.

In the light of all this, it's my royal duty now to end Dead Head's occupation of my mind, to tear down the walls, brick by brick. The subject of my life can no longer be contained. I have taken charge of the meaning of my suffering. I have taken charge with a pen/sword, and I now cut off the Dead Head whenever I need to. It's my mind, it's my imagination, and the sharp effectiveness of rewriting my life script pleases this duchess.

I like to live in the heart of lightheartedness. Did I mention that I am a duchess as well as a dragon slayer? The Duchess of Verdun, a friend humorously named me a few years ago as we hiked through the woods and I marveled aloud at the comforts that the money I long for could buy. My friend saw how I love luxury and long for elegance. But I grew up in the working-class district of Montreal, where my people sat on porches to drink beer and tea so they could wake up the next morning to work for others. Poverty has stalked the duchess most of her life. But now I am the subject and sovereign of my life.[13] I love pleasure. I take delight in my own skin. There is a friendly takeover in progress. I have suffered long enough with the cellular memories of occupation, of severe takeovers of my self. I am in charge of my realm now, my body, my mind. The light is on, and I'm at home with myself. I can no longer leave my life to the double-headed dragon of Anxiety and Depression. I can no longer leave my body to suffer the *effects* of oppression on it. I prefer to intervene on my own behalf and have more of a say in the direction my life is going in. I reclaim my imagination as my own playground which thrives at a safe distance from ideas that want to incarcerate it.

NOTES

This piece is an excerpt from the second chapter of a book-in-progress by Cy-Thea Sand. Her working title is *Magic in a Metaphor: A Dragon-Slayin' Tale about Narrative Therapy.* The first chapter describes how she became a dragon slayer and defeated Anxiety. It was published in *White Rock Journal of Family Therapy* 1 (November 1993): 19–23. The segment included here tells a story about the Dead Head of Depression and how it began to stalk Cy-Thea from the very beginnings of her life as a working-class woman.

Cy-Thea's lyrical documentary prose explores the theory and practice of deconstruction and its application to a form of therapy known as the narrative. Its power lies in the fact that Cy-Thea has liberated herself from Anxiety and Depression after suffering under their abusive power for most of her life. She has become a dragon slayer extraordinaire. To become conscious of the forces operating against her was the beginning of her ability to speak on her own behalf, to argue for her preferred story. Cy-Thea believes that she could not give effective, transformative voice to her opposition—to the forces of Anxiety and Depression—until there *was* an opposition, a double description, of dragon slayer and dragon.

1. Cy-Thea Sand, "A Question of Identity," *Fireweed* 25 (July 1987): 59.

2. Harvey Weinstein, *A Father, a Son and the CIA* (Toronto: James Lorimer, 1988), 5.

3. *Vancouver Sun*, 17 January 1984.

4. Ibid.

5. Maggie Carey, "Perspectives on the Men's Movement," *Dulwich Centre Newsletter*, nos. 3–4 (1992): 71.

6. William Styron, *Darkness Visible: A Memoir of Madness* (New York: Vintage Books, 1992) 37.

7. Pat Leidl, "Poor Job Prospects Linked to Older Women's Depression," *Vancouver Sun*, 26 September 1988.

8. Jane O'Hara, "The Agony of Depression," *McLeans' Magazine*, 19 March 1994.

9. As quoted in O'Hara, "Agony of Depression."

10. Leidl, "Poor Job Prospects."

11. Carolyn Steedman, *Landscape for a Good Woman: A Story of Two Lives*, (London: Virago Press, 1986) 22.

12. Sharon Stevenson committed suicide. In the introduction to Stevenson's book of poetry, *Gold Earrings* (Vancouver: Pulp Press, 1984), Robin Endres writes that the contradictions Stevenson experienced as a working-class woman and a writer invited her to meet these contradictions with both strength and self-assertion and paralyzing self-denial.

13. I have photographs to prove I'm the Duchess of Verdun. Kathleen Symmons, who calls herself the Baroness of Burnaby, is my dear friend, and is an anti-Anxiety activist as well as an artist. She took photographs of my duchess persona for a project for one of her classes at the Emily Carr School of Art and Design here in Vancouver. Kathleen calls her project *Frame of Mind* and it includes photographs of four working-class women, including herself, her mother, her roommate at the time, and yours truly, the Duchess of Verdun. Kathleen describes her work "as a project to empower *us*, in a sense to deconstruct the dominant story based on gender and class issues or play with the dominant story to externalize this story and see what our gender, our class/cultural beliefs and family of origin assign to us and how this dictates our position, place, and power. This project plays with my belief in the horizontal connectedness of all people and demystifies and disempowers the existing vertical hierarchy of the patriarchy."

Autobiographies by American Working-Class Women

A Bibliography

Cheryl Cline

I believe that the study of women's autobiographical writings—of our lives—is better served by an elastic definition of autobiography *than by one too narrowly defined. The writing of working-class women, in particular, too often finds itself on the wrong side of the border used to separate autobiography from other literary forms; the writing often violates the rules set down to define* autobiography *as an expression of the self—that is, an expression of oneself, written by oneself. In truth, much of women's autobiography is oral history, taken down from women who may be illiterate or at least not of a literary bent. Women may also, as often as not, write their autobiographies into collective histories, whether it be labor struggles, regional culture, the history of their own ethnic group in and/or outside of the United States, or family history. This bibliography, therefore, includes not only formal autobiographies but also memoirs, diaries, oral histories, and interviews. It includes "as told to" autobiographies by celebrities and common working women alike: country singers and cotton mill girls, actors and labor leaders. I have also included a number of experimental autobiographies, ones that weave together fiction and fact, as well as collections in which it is difficult to draw lines among personal narrative, political writing, and poetry. I have also included a few texts that are as much documentary as autobiography but which serve to ground the writer's experience in her culture.*

ANTHOLOGIES, ORAL HISTORIES, AND DOCUMENTARY HISTORIES

Andrews, William L., ed. *Sisters of the Spirit: Three Black Women's Autobiographies of the Nineteenth Century.* Bloomington: Indiana University Press, 1986. Includes, with footnotes and commentary, *The Life and Religious Experience of Jarena Lee* (1836), *A Brand Plucked from the Fire,* by Julia Foote (1879), and *The Memoirs of the Life, Religious Experience, Ministerial Travels and Labours of Mrs. Zilpa Elaw* (1846). 245 pp.

Anzaldúa, Gloria, ed. *Making Face, Making Soul/Haciendo Caras. Creative and Critical Perspectives by Women of Color.* San Francisco: Aunt Lute, 1990. 402 pp.

Buss, Frances Leeper, comp. *Dignity: Lower Income Women Tell of Their Lives and Struggles.* With an introduction by Susan Contratto. Ann Arbor: University of Michigan Press, 1985. Oral histories. 290 pp.

Byerly, Victoria, ed. *Hard Times Cotton Mill Girls: Personal Histories of Women and Poverty in the South.* As told to Victoria Byerly. With an introduction by Cletus F. Daniel. Ithaca: Cornell University Press, 1986. 223 pp.

Coltelli, Laura, ed. *Winged Words: American Indian Writers Speak.* Lincoln: University of Nebraska Press, Bison Press, 1990. 209 pp.

Delacosta, Frédérique, and Priscilla Alexander, eds. *Sex Work: Writings by Women in the Sex Industry.* San Francisco: Cleis Press, 1987. 349 pp.

Dublin, Thomas, ed. *Farm to Factory: Women's Letters, 1830–1860*. New York: Columbia University Press, 1981. 191 pp.

Hourwich, Andria Taylor, and Gladys L. Palmer, eds. *I Am a Woman Worker: A Scrapbook of Autobiographies*. New York: Affiliated School for Workers, 1936. Facsimile reprint, New York: Arno Press, 1974. 152 pp.

Kahn, Kathy, ed. *Hillbilly Women*. With photographs by Al Clayton and Franck Blechman, Jr. New York: Doubleday, 1973. 230 pp.

Lynd, Alice, and Staughton Lynd, eds. *Rank and File: Personal Histories by Working-Class Organizers*. Boston: Beacon Press, 1973. Reprint with illustrations, Princeton, N.J.: Princeton University Press, 1981. 296 pp., illustrated.

———. *The New Rank and File*. Ithaca: Cornell University Press, 2000. Updated and expanded version of the 1973 edition. 288 pp.

Martin, Molly, ed. *Hard-Hatted Women: Stories of Struggles and Success in the Trades*. Seattle: Seal Press, 1988. 265 pp.

Moraga, Cherríe, and Gloria Anzaldúa, eds. *This Bridge Called My Back: Writings by Radical Women of Color*. With an introduction by Toni Cade Bambara. Watertown, Mass.: Persephone Press, 1981. Reprint, Latham, N.Y.: Kitchen Table/Women of Color Press, 1984. 261 pp.

Myerhoff, Barbara, ed. *Number Our Days*. New York: E. P. Dutton, 1978. Reprint, New York: Simon and Schuster, Touchstone, 1980. A study of aging based on and including oral histories of elderly Jewish immigrants living in Southern California. 306 pp.

Penelope, Julia, ed. *Out of the Class Closet: Lesbians Speak*. Freedom, Calif.: The Crossing Press, 1994. 481 pp.

Seifer, Nancy, ed. *Nobody Speaks for Me! Self-Portraits of American Working-Class Women*. New York: Simon and Schuster, 1976. 477 pp.

Seller, Maxine Schwartz, ed. *Immigrant Women*. Philadelphia: Temple University Press, 1981. An anthology of memoirs, oral histories, diaries, and fiction. 347 pp.

Sheth, Jagdish, and David A. Heffner, eds. *Voice with a Smile: True Stories from American Telephone Operators*. Barrington, Ill.: PERQ Publications, 1993.

Sternsher, Bernard, and Judith Sealander, eds. *Women of Valor: The Struggle Against the Great Depression as Told in Their Own Life Stories*. Chicago: Ivan R. Dee, 1990. 312 pp.

Swann, Brian, and Arnold Krupat, eds. *I Tell You Now: Autobiographical Essays by Native American Writers*. Lincoln: University of Nebraska Press, Bison Press, 1987. 283 pp.

Thomas, Sherry, ed. *We Didn't Have Much, but We Sure Had Plenty: Stories of Rural Women*. New York: Doubleday Anchor, 1981. The second edition (1989) was published with the subtitle *Rural Women in Their Own Words*. 185 pp.

Tokarczyk, Michelle M., and Elizabeth A. Fay, eds. *Working- Class Women in the Academy: Laborers in the Knowledge Factory*. Amherst: University of Massachusetts Press, 1993. 335 pp.

Tucker, Susan, comp. *Telling Memories Among Southern Women: Domestic Workers and Their Employers in the Segregated South*. Baton Rouge: Louisiana State University Press, 1988. Paperback edition, New York: Schocken Books; Toronto: Random House of Canada, 1988. 278 pp.

Wetherby, Terry, ed. *Conversations: Working Women Talk About Doing a "Man's" Job*. Millbrae, Calif.: Les Femmes, 1977. 269 pp.

Zandy, Janet, ed. *Calling Home: Working-Class Women's Writings*. New Brunswick, N.J.: Rutgers University Press, 1990. 366 pp.

———. *Liberating Memory: Our Work and Our Working-Class Consciousness*. New Brunswick, N.J.: Rutgers University Press, 1995. 366 pp.

Individual Works

Abbott, Shirley. *The Bookmaker's Daughter: A Memory Unbound*. New York: Ticknor and
  Fields, 1991. 290 pp.
———. *Womenfolks: Growing Up Down South*. New York: Ticknor and Fields, 1983. 210 pp.
Ahern, Nell Giles. *Punch In, Susie! A Woman's War Factory Diary*. With drawings by Alan
  Dunn. New York: Harper Bros., 1943. 143 pp.
Allison, Dorothy. *Skin: Talking About Sex, Class and Literature*. Ithaca, N.Y.: Firebrand
  Books, 1994. 261 pp.
———. *Two or Three Things I Know for Sure*. New York: Dutton, 1995. 94 pp.
Anderson, Mary. *Women at Work: The Autobiography of Mary Anderson*. As told to Mary
  Winslow. Minneapolis: University of Minnesota, 1951. 266 pp.
Angelou, Maya. *I Know Why the Caged Bird Sings*. New York: Random House, 1969. 281
  pp.
———. *Gather Together in My Name*. New York: Random House, 1974. 214 pp.
———. *Singin' and Swingin' and Gettin' Merry Like Christmas*. New York: Random House,
  1976. 269 pp.
———. *The Heart of a Woman*. New York: Random House, 1981. 272 pp.
———. *All God's Children Need Traveling Shoes*. New York: Random House, 1986. 210 pp.
Anzaldúa, Gloria. *Borderlands/La Frontera: The New Mestiza*. San Francisco:
  Spinsters/Aunt Lute, 1987. 203 pp.
Barber, Olive. *The Lady and the Lumberjack*. With an introduction by Stewart H.
  Holbrook. New York: Crowell, 1952. 250 pp.
Barnes, Kim. *In the Wilderness: Coming of Age in Unknown Country*. New York: Doubleday,
  1996. 257 pp.
———. *Hungry for the World: A Memoir*. New York: Villard Books, 2000. 241 pp.
Barr, Roseanne. *Roseanne: My Life as a Woman*. New York: Harper and Row, 1989. 202 pp.
Baxter, Freddie Mae. *The Seventh Child: A Lucky Life*. Edited by Gloria Bley Miller. New
  York: Alfred A. Knopf, 1999. 223 pp.
Bloor, Ella. *We Are Many: An Autobiography*. New York: International Publishers, 1940.
  319 pp.
Bolton, Ruthie. *Gal: A True Life*. New York: Harcourt Brace, 1994. 275 pp.
Box-Car Bertha. *Sister of the Road: The Autobiography of Box-Car Bertha*. As told to Dr. Ben
  L. Reitman. New York: Sheridan House, 1937. Reprint, New York: Harper and Row,
  1975, 314 pp. Reprint, with an introduction by Kathy Acker and an afterword by Roger
  Bruns, New York: AMOK Press, 1988. 285 pp.
Brant, Beth [Degonwadonti]. *Mohawk Trail*. Ithaca, N.Y.: Firebrand, 1985. 94 pp.
Burrow, Brunettie. *Angels in White*. San Antonio, Tex.: Naylor, 1959. 132 pp.
———. *I Lay Down My Cap*. San Antonio, Tex.: Naylor, 1961. 96 pp.
Caldwell, Taylor. *On Growing Up Tough*. Old Greenwich, Conn.: Devin-Adair Co., 1971.
  159 pp.
Campbell, Janet Hale. *Bloodlines: Odyssey of a Native Daughter*. New York: Random House,
  1993. 187 pp.
Carpenter, Arie. *Aunt Arie: A Foxfire Portrait*. Edited by Linda Garland Page and Eliot
  Wigginton. New York: E. P. Dutton, 1983. 216 pp.
Caudill, Rebecca. *My Appalachia: A Reminiscence*. New York: Holt, Rinehart and
  Winston, 1966. 90 pp.
Cavalleri, Rosa. *The Life of an Italian Immigrant*. Edited by Marie Hall Ets. With a foreword
  by Rudolph J. Vecoli. Minneapolis: University of Minnesota Press, 1970. 254 pp.

Cochran, Jacqueline. *The Stars at Noon*. Boston: Little, Brown, 1954. 274 pp.

Cuero, Delfina. *The Autobiography of Delfina Cuero, a Diegueno Indian*. As told to Florence C. Shipek. Los Angeles: Dawson's Book Shop, 1968. 67 pp.

Cunningham, Laura. *Sleeping Arrangements: A Memoir*. New York: Alfred A. Knopf, 1989. 195 pp.

Davis, Alice Pauline. *Bayou Boats*. New York: New Voices Publishing Co., 1950. 143 pp.

Davis, Skeeter. *Bus Fare to Kentucky: The Autobiography of Skeeter Davis*. New York: Birch Lane Press, 1993. 338 pp.

Day, Dorothy. *The Long Loneliness: An Autobiography*. Illustrated by Fritz Eichenberg. New York: Harper and Row, 1952. Reprint, with an introduction by Daniel Berrigan, New York: Harper and Row, 1981. 288 pp.

Day, Helen Caldwell. *Color, Ebony*. New York: Sheed and Ward, 1951. 182 pp.

DeForest, Elsie Davis. *Out of My Cabin*. Boston: Christopher, 1956. 186 pp.

DeRosier, Linda Scott. *Creeker: A Woman's Journey*. Lexington: University Press of Kentucky, 1999. 228 pp.

DeSalvo, Louise. *Vertigo: A Memoir*. New York: E. P. Dutton, 1996. 263 pp.

Dickerson, Debra J. *An American Story*. New York: Pantheon Books, 2000. 285 pp.

Dodge, Helen Carmichael. *My Childhood in the Canadian Wilderness*. New York: Vantage, 1961. 77 pp.

Durbin, Marina. *Lima Beans and City Chicken: A Memoir of the Open Hearth*. New York: E. P. Dutton, 1989. 172 pp.

East, Lorecia. *The Boomers: The Autobiography of a Roughneck's Wife*. Baton Rouge, La.: Legacy Publishing Co., 1976. 63 pp.

Ellis, Anne. *The Life of an Ordinary Woman*. With an introduction by Lucy Fitch Perkins. Boston: Houghton Mifflin Co., 1929. Reprint, New York: Arno Press, 1974. Reprint, with a foreword by Elliott West, Lincoln: University of Nebraska Press, 1980. 300 pp.

―――. *Plain Anne Ellis: More About the Life of an Ordinary Woman*. Boston and New York: Houghton Mifflin Co., 1931. Reprint, Lincoln: University of Nebraska Press, 1984. 264 pp.

―――. *Sunshine Preferred: The Philosophy of an Ordinary Woman*. Boston and New York: Houghton Mifflin Co., 1934. Reprint, Lincoln: University of Nebraska Press, 1984. 248 pp.

Emerson, Irma Lee, with Jean Muir. *The Woods Were Full of Men*. New York: David McKay Co., 1963. 242 pp.

Engle, Ada M. *It Happened at 1001*. New York: Vantage Press, 1959. 80 pp. Engle ran a Philadelphia hardware store with her husband; the book is a portrait of the working-class community there.

Erickson, Gail [pseud.]. *The Whole Works: The Autobiography of a Young American Couple*. By Bruce and Gail Erickson, as recorded by Starry Krueger. New York: Random House, 1973. 205 pp.

Erwin, Carol, with Floyd Miller. *The Orderly Disorderly House*. Garden City, N.Y.: Doubleday, 1960. 284 pp.

Evert, Gertrude S. *My 28 Years as an Army Nurse*. New York: Exposition Press, 1959. 84 pp.

Ferris, Louanne [pseud.]. *I'm Done Crying*. As told to Beth Day. New York: M. Evans, 1969. 275 pp.

Flynn, Elizabeth Gurley. *I Speak My Own Piece: Autobiography of "The Rebel Girl."* New York: Masses and Mainstream, 1955. 326 pp. Revised edition, published as *The Rebel*

Girl: An Autobiography. My First Life (1906–1926), New York: International Publishers, 1973. 351 pp.

Four Years in the Underbrush: Adventures as a Working Girl in New York. New York: Charles Scribner's Sons, 1921. Published anonymously. 315 pp.

French, Emily. *Emily, The Diary of a Hard-Worked Woman*. Edited by Janet Lecompte. Lincoln: University of Nebraska Press, 1987. 166 pp.

Gazaway, Rena. *The Longest Mile*. Garden City, N.Y.: Doubleday, 1969. 348 pp.

Gerken, Mabel R. *Ladies in Pants: A Home Front Diary*. New York: Exposition Press, 1949. 96 pp.

Giles, Janice Holt. *Forty Acres and No Mule*. Philadelphia: The Westminster Press, 1952. 215 pp. Second edition, with a new prologue by the author, Boston: Houghton Mifflin, 1967. 239 pp.

Gilfillan, Lauren [Harriet Woodbridge Gilfillan]. *I Went to Pit College*. New York: Viking Press, 1934. 288 pp.

Golden, Marita. *Migrations of the Heart: An Autobiography*. Garden City, N.Y.: Doubleday, Anchor Press, 1983. 234 pp.

———. *Long Distance Life*. Garden City, N.Y.: Doubleday, 1989. 321 pp.

Goldman, Emma. *Living My Life*. 2 vols. New York: Alfred A. Knopf, 1931. Reprint, with an introduction by Sheila Rowbotham, London: Pluto Press, 1986.

Goodwin, Ruby Berkley. *It's Good to Be Black*. Garden City, N.Y.: Doubleday, 1953. 256 pp.

Gornick, Vivian. *Fierce Attachments: A Memoir*. New York: Farrar, Straus and Giroux, 1987. 204 pp.

Guffy, Ossie. *Ossie: The Autobiography of a Black Woman*. As told to Caryl Ledner. New York: W. W. Norton, 1971. 224 pp.

Guillory, "Queen" Ida, with Naomi Wise. *Cookin' with Queen Ida: "Bon Temps" Creole Recipes (and Stories) from the Queen of Zydeco Music*. With interviews by Michael Goodwin and Irene Namkung. Rocklin, Calif.: Prima Publishing, 1990. 240 pp.

Hart, Elva Treviño. *Barefoot Heart: Stories of a Migrant Child*. Tempe, Ariz.: Bilingual Press/Editorial Bilingüe, 1999. 236 pp.

Hasanovitz, Elizabeth. *One of Them: Chapters from a Passionate Autobiography*. Boston: Houghton Mifflin, 1918. 33 pp.

hooks, bell. *Talking Back: Thinking Feminist/Thinking Black*. Boston: South End Press, 1989. 184 pp.

———. *Bone Black: Memories of Girlhood*. New York: Henry Holt and Co., 1996. 183 pp.

———. *Wounds of Passion: A Writing Life*. New York: Henry Holt and Co. 1997. 260 pp.

Hurston, Zora Neale. *Dust Tracks on a Road*. Boston: J. B. Lippincott, 1942. Reprint, with an introduction by Larry Neal, Boston: J. B. Lippincott, 1971. New edition, edited and with an introduction by Robert Hemenway, Urbana: University of Illinois Press, 1971, 1984. Reprint, with a new foreword by Maya Angelou, New York: Harper Perennial, 1991. 278 pp.

Huttman, Barbara. *Code Blue: A Nurse's True Life Story*. New York: William Morrow, 1982. 280 pp.

Jackson, Nannie Stillwell. *Vinegar Pie and Chicken Bread: A Woman's Diary of Life in the Rural South, 1890–1891*. Edited and with an introduction by Margaret Jones Bolsterli. Fayetteville: University of Arkansas Press, 1982. 108 pp.

Jacobs, Harriet A. *Incidents in the Life of a Slave Girl. Written by Herself. . . .* Edited by L. Maria Child. Boston: published for the author, 1861. Reprint, with an introduction by Valerie Smith, New York: Oxford University Press, 1988. New edition, edited and with an introduction by Jean Fagan Yellin, Cambridge: Harvard University Press, 1987. 306 pp.

Jordan, June. *Soldier: A Poet's Childhood*. New York: Basic Civitas Books, Perseus, 2000. 261 pp.

Karr, Mary. *The Liar's Club: A Memoir*. New York: Viking Penguin, 1995. 320 pp.

———. *Cherry*. New York: Viking, 2000. 276 pp.

Kaufman, Regina. *Sketches of a Working Woman*. Los Angeles: self-published, 1980. 178 pp.

Keckley, Elizabeth Hobbs. *Behind the Scenes, or, Thirty Years a Slave, and Four Years in the White House*. New York: G. W. Carleton and Co., 1868. 371 pp. Reprinted, New York: Oxford University Press, 1988. The Oxford edition is in The Schomburg Library of Nineteenth-Century Black Women Writers series. 371 pp.

King, Coretta Scott. *My Life with Martin Luther King Jr*. New York: Holt, Rinehart and Winston, 1969. 372 pp.

Kingston, Maxine Hong. *Woman Warrior*. New York: Alfred A. Knopf, 1976. 209 pp.

———. *China Men*. New York: Alfred A. Knopf, 1980. 308 pp.

Kunkler, Anita. *Hardscrabble: A Narrative of the California Hill Country*. Edited, with commentaries and notes, by Wilbur S. Shepperson. Reno: University of Nevada Press, 1975. 252 pp.

Larcom, Lucy. *Letters of Lucy Larcom to the Whittiers*. Edited by Grace F. Shepard. Baltimore: The Southworth Press, 1930. First published in the *New England Quarterly* 3:3 (1930). 20 pp.

———. *Lucy Larcom: Her Life, Letters and Diary*. Edited by Daniel Dulany Addison. Boston and New York: Houghton Mifflin Co.; Cambridge, U.K.: Riverside Press, 1894. 295 pp.

———. *A New England Girlhood, Outlined from Memory*. Boston and New York: Houghton Mifflin, 1889. Facsimile reprint, New York: Arno Press, 1974. Reprint, with a foreword by Nancy Cott, Boston: Northeastern University Press, 1986. 274 pp.

Le Sueur, Meridel. *Ripening: Selected Work, 1927–1980*. Edited and with an introduction by Elaine Hedges. Old Westbury, N.Y.: The Feminist Press, 1982. Second edition, with a new afterword by Meridel LeSueur, New York: The Feminist Press, 1990. 295 pp.

Logan, Onnie Lee. *Motherwit: An Alabama Midwife's Story*. As told to Katherine Clark. New York: Dutton, 1989. Reprint, New York: Plume, 1991. 177 pp.

Lorde, Audre. *The Cancer Journals*. Argyle, N.Y.: Spinsters' Ink, 1980. 77 pp.

———. *Zami, A New Spelling of My Name: A Biomythography by Audre Lorde*. Freedom, Calif.: Crossing Press, 1982. 256 pp.

Lucas, María Elena. *Forged Under the Sun/Forjada Bajo el Sol: The Life of María Elena Lucas*. Edited and with an introduction by Fran Leeper Buss. Ann Arbor: University of Michigan Press, 1993. 314 pp.

Lynn, Loretta, with George Vecsey. *Coal Miner's Daughter*. Chicago: Regnery, 1976. Reprint, New York: Warner Books, 1980. 269 pp.

Mason, Bobbie Ann. *Clear Springs: A Memoir*. New York: Random House, 1999. 298 pp.

McConnell, Roberta. *Never Marry a Ranger*. New York: Prentice- Hall, 1950. 261 pp.

McGarvey, Lois. *Along Alaska Trails*. New York: Vantage Press, 1960. 200 pp.

McNatt, Rosemary Bray. *Unafraid of the Dark: A Memoir*. New York: Random House, 1998. 304 pp.

Mitchell, Dorothea. *Lady Lumberjack*. Vancouver: Mitchell Press, 1967. 135 pp.

Moody, Ann. *Coming of Age in Mississippi*. New York: The Dial Press, 1968. 348 pp.

Mora, Pat. *House of Houses*. Boston: Beacon Press, 1997. 296 pp.

Moraga, Cherríe. *Loving in the War Years: Lo que Nunca Pasó sus Labios*. Boston: South End Press, 1983. 152 pp.

Moss, Barbara Robinette. *Change Me into Zeus's Daughter: A Memoir*. New York: Charles Scribner's Sons, 2000. 319 pp.

Mother Jones. *The Autobiography of Mother Jones*. Edited by Mary Field Parton. With an introduction by Clarence Darrow. Chicago: C. H. Kerr, 1925. Reprint, New York: Arno Press, 1969. Reprint, with an introduction and bibliography by Fred Thompson, Chicago: Published for the Illinois Labor History Society by C. H. Kerr Publishing Company, 1972. 242 pp.

———. *Mother Jones Speaks: Collected Writings and Speeches*. Edited by Philip S. Foner. New York: Monad Press (distributed by Pathfinder Press), 1983. 724 pp.

Murray, Pauli. *Proud Shoes: The Story of an American Family*. New York: Harper, 1956. 276 pp.

Nestor, Agnes. *Woman's Labor Leader: An Autobiography*. Rockford, Ill.: Bellevue Books, 1954. 307 pp.

Nieman, Linda. *Boomer: Railroad Memoirs*. Berkeley: University of California Press, 1990. 252 pp.

Ortiz Cofer, Judith. *Silent Dancing: A Partial Remembrance of a Puerto Rican Childhood*. Houston: Arte Público Press, 1990. 158 pp.

Padow, Mollie Potter. *A Saga of Eighty Years of Living*. Philadelphia: Dorrance, 1971. 228 pp.

Parker, Sybil Rosa. *Working Stewardess to Captain's Lady: My Life on the Luxury Liners*. Los Alamitos, Calif.: Hwong Publishing Co., 1979. 195 pp.

Parton, Dolly. *Dolly: My Life and Other Unfinished Business*. New York: HarperCollins, 1994. 338 pp.

Peacock, Molly. *Paradise, Piece by Piece*. New York: Riverhead Books, Penguin Putnam, 1998. 337 pp.

Pesotta, Rose. *Bread upon the Waters*. Edited by John Nicholas Beffel. New York: Dodd, Mead and Co., 1944. Reprint, with a new introduction by Ann Schofield, Ithaca, N.Y.: ILR Press, 1987. 435 pp.

———. *Days of Our Lives*. Boston: Excelsior, 1958. 262 pp.

Pinzer, Maimie [pseud.]. *The Maimie Papers: Letters from an Ex-Prostitute*. Edited by Ruth Rosen and Sue Davidson. With an Introduction by Ruth Rosen. Old Westbury, N.Y.: The Feminist Press, 1977. Reprinted, with a new afterword by Ruth Rosen and a literary afterword by Florence Howe, New York: The Feminist Press, 1996. 439 pp.

Ponce, Mary Helen. *Hoyt Street: Memories of a Chicana Childhood*. New York: Anchor Press, 1993. Reprint, under the title *Hoyt Street: An Autobiography*, Albuquerque: University of New Mexico Press, 1993. 338 pp.

Ray, Janisse. *Ecology of a Cracker Childhood*. Minneapolis, Minn.: Milkweed Editions, 1999. 285 pp.

Red Shirt, Delphine. *Bead on an Anthill: A Lakota Childhood*. Lincoln: University of Nebraska Press, 1999. 146 pp.

Rich, Kim. *Johnny's Girl: A Daughter's Memoir of Growing Up in Alaska's Underworld*. New York: William Morrow, 1993. 302 pp.

Ritchie, Jean. *Singing Family of the Cumberlands*. Illustrated by Maurice Sendak. 1955. Reprint, New York: Oak Publications, 1963. Includes words and music for forty-two songs. 258 pp.

Rodriguez, Rosalie. *Oh! For the Life of a Stewardess*. New York: Comet Press, 1953. 123 pp.

Ruby, Edna R. *Shorthand with Champagne*. Cleveland: World, 1965. 246 pp.

Rutland, Eva. *The Trouble with Being a Mama*. New York: Abingdon, 1964. 143 pp.

Santiago, Esmeralda. *When I Was Puerto Rican*. Reading, Mass.: Addison-Wesley, 1993. 274 pp.

————. *Almost a Woman*. Reading, Mass.: Perseus Books, 1998. 313 pp.

Scarborough, Mary Grossman. *Whirlwinds of Danger: The Memoirs of Mary Grossman Scarborough*. With a foreword by William McAdoo. New York: David Walker Press, 1990. 187 pp.

Schneiderman, Rose, with Lucy Goldwaite. *All for One*. New York: Paul S. Ericksson, 1967. 264 pp.

Scully, Julia. *Outside Passage: A Memoir of an Alaskan Childhood*. New York: Random House, 1998. 219 pp.

Shear, Claudia. *Blown Sideways Through Life*. New York: The Dial Press, 1995. 116 pp.

Sinclair, Jo. *The Seasons: Death and Transfiguration*. New York: The Feminist Press, 1993. 279 pp.

Smedley, Agnes. *Daughter of Earth*. 1929. Reprint, with a foreword by Alice Walker and an afterword by Nancy Hoffman, New York: The Feminist Press, 1987. 432 pp.

Spewack, Bella. *Streets: A Memoir of the Lower East Side*. With an introduction by Ruth Limmer and an afterword by Lois Elias. New York: The Feminist Press, 1987. 180 pp.

Strainchamps, Ethel Reed. *Don't Never Say Cain't*. Garden City, N.Y.: Doubleday, 1965. 168 pp.

Stewart, Elinore Pruitt. *Letters of a Woman Homesteader*. Boston and New York: Houghton Mifflin Co., 1914. Reprint, with a foreword by Jessamyn West, Lincoln: University of Nebraska Press, 1961. 282 pp.

Stokes, Rose Pastor. *I Belong to the Working Class: The Unfinished Autobiography of Rose Pastor Stokes*. Edited by Herbert Shapiro and David L. Sterling. Athens: University of Georgia Press, 1992. 173 pp.

Tam, Augusta. *By Dim and Flaring Lamps*. Transcribed by Katherine Boies McCallen. New York: Vantage Press, 1964. 143 pp.

Tarbell, Ida Minerva. *All in the Day's Work: An Autobiography*. New York: Macmillan, 1939. 412 pp.

Terrell, Mary Church. *A Colored Woman in a White World*. Washington, D.C.: Ransdell, 1940. Reprint, Washington, D.C.: National Association of Colored Women's Clubs, 1968. Facsimile reprint, New York: Arno Press, 1980. Reprint, Salem, N.H.: Ayer, 1986. 436 pp.

Tywoniak, Frances Esquibel, with Mario T. García. *Migrant Daughter: Coming of Age as a Mexican American Woman*. Berkeley: University of California Press, 2000. 237 pp.

Van Vorst, Mrs. John, and Marie Van Vorst. *The Woman Who Toils. Being the Experience of Two Gentlewomen as Factory Girls*. New York: Doubleday, Page, 1903. 303 pp.

Vorse, Mary Heaton. *The Autobiography of an Elderly Woman*. Boston and New York: Houghton Mifflin Co., 1911. Reprinted, New York: Arno Press, 1974. 269 pp.

————. *Footnote to Folly: Reminiscences of Mary Heaton Vorse*. New York: Farrar and Rinehart, 1934. Reprint, New York: Arno Press, 1980. 407 pp.

Walker, Alice. *In Search of Our Mother's Gardens: Womanist Prose*. San Diego: Harcourt Brace Jovanovich, 1983. 397 pp.

Walker, Margaret. *How I Wrote Jubilee*. Chicago: Third World Press, 1972. 36 pp. Reprinted in *How I Wrote Jubilee and Other Essays on Life and Literature*. Edited by Maryemma Graham. New York: The Feminist Press, 1990. 157 pp.

Waterman, Sherry. *From Another Island: Adventures and Misadventures of an Airline Stewardess*. Philadelphia: Chilton Books, 1962. 206 pp.

Weisbord, Vera Buch. *A Radical Life*. Bloomington: Indiana University Press, 1977. 384 pp.

Williamson, Anne A. *Fifty Years in Starch*. Culver City, Calif.: Murray and Gee, 1948. A nurse's story. 245 pp.

Yamauchi, Wakako. *Songs My Mother Taught Me: Stories, Plays and Memoir*. Edited and with an introduction by Garrett Hongo. With an afterword by Valerie Miner. New York: The Feminist Press, 1994. 257 pp.

Yezierska, Anzia. *Red Ribbon on a White Horse*. With an introduction by W. H. Auden. New York: Scribner's, 1950. Reprint, with a new introduction by Louise Levitas Henriksen, London: Virago, 1987. 220 pp.

Practicing Working-Class Studies

Reclaiming Our Working-Class Identities

Teaching Working-Class Studies in a Blue-Collar Community

Linda Strom

> *We struggle to live.*
> *We strive for more.*
> *We struggle for more.*
> *To begin where we started.*
> *We start at the bottom.*
> *To work our way up.*
> *When things fall apart,*
> *We move on*
> *and start*
> *at the bottom*
> *again.*
>
> W. Kay W., *"The Cycle"*[1]

The cycle the writer describes in this epigraph was once a familiar one to me. Before entering college at the age of thirty, I worked a string of low-paying pink-collar jobs that left me frustrated and struggling from paycheck to paycheck to make ends meet. I longed for meaningful work that would be valued by me and by others. Education seemed like the way to break the cycle and to find work that mattered.

In the beginning the strong work ethic instilled in me by my parents and the years of working an eight-hour day translated well into the academic world. I approached school like a job, putting in a day's work and finding myself rewarded with praise and good grades. Soon, however, I discovered that the longer I stayed in school, the more separated I felt from the first thirty years of my life. The signs of separation were all around me. I now had two distinct groups of friends—those I had made while working and those I had made while in school—and, like my two lives, these two groups of friends never mixed. My family, while supportive, also began to feel like I was growing away from them. My father and brother once told my mother that they thought that, because of my education, we no longer had anything in common.[2]

I began to notice, too, a growing anxiety in myself. I did not know what world I belonged in anymore.[3] The turning point for me occurred while I was attending the 1990 National Women's Studies Association Conference in Akron. Janet Zandy was chairing a panel made up of contributors to her anthology of working-class women writers entitled *Calling Home*.[4] Zandy and Victoria Byerly, the author of *Hard Time Cotton Mill Girls*, discussed their struggle to reclaim and to integrate their working-class backgrounds with their present academic lives.[5] When Zandy opened up the discussion and invited us all to join in, I was amazed to find myself in a room full of women who shared a similar feeling of pride and shame in their working-class roots. Hearing their stories and hearing myself speak, for the first time, about my two separate lives made me realize that much of the experience and the story of working-class people has been, until recently, invisible in the academic world.

Recent scholars such as Zandy, Paul Lauter, Deborah Rosenfelt, and Tillie Olsen, who have helped make visible the forgotten or silenced literary history of the working class, can be seen as the pioneers in defining the field of working-class studies. With the publication of *Yonnondio: From the Thirties* and *Silences*, Olsen not only rekindled an interest in writers of the 1930s but also an interest in working-class fiction.[6] Rosenfelt's essay entitled "From the Thirties: Tillie Olsen and the Radical Tradition" reconnected Olsen's *Yonnondio* with the literary and cultural history that produced the text.[7] Until that essay the importance of Olsen's early political work in the Communist Party and her working-class background had not been sufficiently acknowledged.[8] In 1980 Lauter's essay "Working-Class Women's Literature: An Introduction to Study" provided a much needed bibliography, one which sketched out the beginnings of a literary history of working-class women writers.[9] Zandy's *Calling Home* continued that history by showing us the themes and issues that concern twentieth-century working-class women writers. The notion of reclaiming and legitimizing our working-class past—illustrated by the work of Olsen, Rosenfelt, Lauter, and Zandy—became the focus of a class I teach, Working-Class Women Writers.

My primary concern when I was designing the course was to connect the themes and issues of the various works by women with the students' own personal experiences and backgrounds. I teach at Youngstown State University, where the majority of students come from blue-collar families. The university is surrounded by deserted steel mills—mills that, when they were in full production, according to Terry F. Buss and F. Stevens Redburn "made Youngstown's steelworkers one of the most productive, best-paid, and seemingly secure industrial labor forces in the world." When the mills began closing in 1977, Youngstown went from what Buss and Redburn describe as "the prototypical industrial city" to "the prototypical city in economic crisis." In less than three years over ten thousand jobs were permanently eliminated within the metropolitan area.[10] In response to the crisis the local union, the rank and file, and the people in the Youngstown community organized the Ecumenical Coalition of Mahoning Valley and attempted to buy back one of the mills and make it an employee-run operation.[11] The plan failed, but it is only one example in a long history of the community's labor struggle. As Staughton Lynd, a labor lawyer and a political activist, writes, "[Youngstown] is a strong union town."[12]

Although it seems at times that the shutdown of the mills has overshadowed the powerful history of Youngstown's working class, in the course that I teach students begin to make connections between their current struggle to work, in some cases full time, and to attend school with the struggle of past laborers within the community—laborers who are often their parents, grandparents, or relatives. As the course progresses, we begin to construct a communal history that is woven together with the history of working-class people represented in *Calling Home*, which is the main text for the course.[13]

To help the students make the connection between their personal histories and the larger political history of working-class people, I frame the course with the students' own writing, asking them to keep a journal and, at the end of the term, to submit a creative piece of writing—an essay, a poem, or a short story—that reflects the themes discussed throughout the term. These writings are then gathered together into a class book, which is edited and assembled by the students. Ideas for the final creative piece often take shape in the first journal assignment, in which I ask the students to write the story of their work histories. To get them started I begin class the same way I began this essay—by describing my family background, my work history, and my experiences in college. By writing their own and their family's work histories, the students feel empowered by their working-class experiences and begin to take pride in their class background.

During the second class session the students read their autobiographies aloud. The stories are amazing. They tell of men and women who organize unions, go on strike and walk picket lines, file charges against employers who have sexually harassed them, go to work as teenagers to help support the family, and struggle to make life better for themselves and their families. Individually or collectively, they create an impressive story of working-class life within the community. Writing and hearing the stories helps students identify themselves as members of the same socioeconomic class while also showing them how differences such as race, gender, sexual preference, and income level can complicate that identity. Their differences inflect their autobiographies, their readings, and their final creative projects.

As we begin discussing the readings in *Calling Home*, I encourage the students to write their own experiences into their analyses of the readings. I want their voices to interrupt and to intersect with the voices in the text, thus providing a continual link with the issues and themes of other working-class people. For most of the students the extreme poverty and the oppressive home and working conditions that shaped many of the women's lives in *Calling Home* fall outside their perceptions of growing up in a working-class home. Although, as one woman put it, while she personally had not experienced the pain and suffering documented in the readings, every reading made her remember someone in her life who had.

The final, collaborative class book becomes an important step for collecting memories of family, of childhood, and of work experiences. Everyone is asked to submit a piece of writing for the book, and the last two weeks are spent editing the submissions, writing the introduction, and deciding how to organize the writing into sections of shared themes. The students are often inspired by a piece they read in *Calling Home* and go on to write about a similar experience.

For example, after reading Donna Langston's poem "Down on the Strike Line with My Children," Laura Kollat recalls the time her mother packed up all the children and took them down to join their father on the picket line.[14] Kollat writes about the importance of this memory in an essay entitled "My Mother Is a Working Woman":

> I remember my mom in the traditional role of mother and wife, care-taker and nurturer. I remember her cleaning the house, helping with the homework, making dinner, and doing laundry. There was a time, how-ever, when she was much more to our family—a time I sometimes forget.
>
> It was almost winter, and I was only seven years old the first time my father went out on strike with his union. I didn't understand what it meant, I only knew that mother got a job and became a member of the "working society."[15]

Her mother "found work at Montgomery Ward's, a department store on the other side of town," working "long days and even longer nights, taking as many hours as the management would give her." In her mother's absence Kollat learned "to clip coupons" and "make soup from left-over chicken bones." All throughout this family crisis Kollat is impressed with her mother's resourcefulness: "My mother was a wonder at making what little money we had stretch far beyond what it should. Yet, despite all her worries about not having enough, she never let my brother and me know just how much of a financial bind we were in."

The hard work and sacrifice of mothers is a constant theme in the students' writing. In "Second Helpings" Tracy Coleman writes that, as a child, she used to complain to her mother "that [she] was sick and tired of being poor." Her mother never told her how much her complaining hurt her until Coleman was an adult: "She says that back then, I may have been sick and tired of being poor, but she was just plain sick and tired—and she didn't have the time or energy to explain or to make me understand that a single woman with three children couldn't work any harder."[16] In her poem "Image of My Mother" Sherry T. celebrates her mother's years of laboring in other people's houses to support Sherry and her sister and, as in Kollat's essay, her mother's resourcefulness:

> Glancing downward I look at my mother's hands,
> how they toiled to make dollars too few . . .
> Cleaning houses for others, and ironing clothes,
> accepting hand-me-downs; making them look new.[17]

Along with celebrating the hard work and the sacrifices of their mothers, the students also acknowledge their own struggles. They write about the tedious jobs they must hold to support themselves and to pay for their schooling. For example, in her poem entitled "The Line" W. Kay W. writes about what it's like to work on an assembly line day after day:

> I punch in at the clock
> on my way to the line.
> I pick up an order

and the top one is mine.
I follow the order
one thing at a time.
Place it all in the box—
send it on down the line.
I return to the bin
and again from the top
I repeat the whole process
which seems never to stop.[18]

Denise Bowell, in her poem entitled "Everyday," describes a similar kind of daily monotony:

Everyday she walks into the same
workplace, punches in the same timecard,
works the same job, and sees the same
people.

Everyday while she works, she wonders to
herself, "Am I working to live, or
am I living to work?"[19]

While the students' writings describe the daily struggle to work and go to school, these writings also reveal a determination not to let work destroy spirit. Sherry Buzzard writes in her poem "They Don't Have Me!" that, while her employers "may have 9 hrs of my day / They don't have me!" She ends the poem by claiming her power: "The will never take away / my dignity or my will to do better in life![20]

In the introduction to *Calling Home* Zandy writes that working-class "lives are obscured and erased; their work is barely visible. And their writing is not read in literature classes."[21] As the field of working-class studies grows, the experiences and literary history of working-class people and culture begin to come into focus. Reclaiming the past is an important first step not only for the students, teachers, and scholars who work in the field but also for those of us who come from working-class backgrounds. Our pasts have taught us that we must have what Pam Limbert describes in the introduction to *Our Voyage Toward Life* as "searching eyes—eyes that delved back to where it all began for each, and enabled each to stretch forward to see, to discover, what lies beyond what each thought possible."[22]

NOTES

1. This poem is taken from *Hidden Treasures: The Discovery of Working-Class Identities*, a work written and edited and then, in March 1994, self-published by the students enrolled in Working-Class Women Writers, a course I teach at Youngstown State University. Later in this essay I draw from another student-produced publication that flowed from the course, *Our Voyage Toward Light* (May 1994). I am grateful to my students for allowing me to reprint the work included here.

2. Richard Rodriguez describes a similar feeling of alienation from his family in his essay entitled "The Achievement of Desire," in *Hunger of Memory: The Education of Richard Rodriguez* (Boston: Godine, 1981). See also Michelle M. Tokarczyk and Elizabeth A. Fay, introduction to their edited collection *Working-Class Women in the Academy: Laborers in the Knowledge Factory* (Amherst: University of Massachusetts Press, 1993), 3–24, for a description of that feeling in working-class women academics.

3. My anxiety took the form of what Tokarczyk and Fay, *Women in the Academy*, describe as the "imposter complex": "As outsiders in academia, many [working-class women academics] have an imposter complex; they fear they've scammed others into giving them doctorates and academic positions" (17).

4. Zandy, ed., *Calling Home: Working-Class Women's Writing—An Anthology* (New Brunswick, N.J.: Rutgers University Press, 1990).

5. Byerly, *Hard Times Cotton Mill Girls* (Ithaca: Cornell University Press, 1986).

6. Olsen, *Yonnondio: From the Thirties* (New York: Dell, 1975); and *Silences* (New York: Dell, 1978).

7. Rosenfelt, "From the Thirties: Tillie Olsen and the Radical Tradition," *Feminist Studies* 7 (1981): 371–406.

8. See, for instance, Selma Burkom and Margaret Williams, "De-Riddling Tillie Olsen's Writings," *San Jose Studies* 2 (1976): 64–83, who refer to Olsen as a humanist.

9. Lauter, "Working-Class Women's Literature: An Introduction to Study," *Radical Teacher* 15 (1980):16–26.

10. Buss and Redburn, *Shutdown at Youngstown: Public Policy for Mass Employment* (Albany: State University of New York Press, 1983), 2, 1.

11. For a more complete history of the community's response to the closing of the steel mills, see Staughton Lynd, *The Fight Against Shutdowns: Youngstown's Steel Mill Closing* (San Pedro: Singlejack Hooks, 1982). Lynd was the attorney for the coalition. See also Thomas G. Fuechtmann, *Steeples and Stacks: Religion and Steel Crisis in Youngstown* (New York: Cambridge University Press, 1989).

12. Lynd, *Fight Against Shutdowns*, 5.

13. Along with Zandy, *Calling Home*, I also use Sandra Martz, ed., *If I Had a Hammer: Women's Work in Poetry, Fiction, and Photographs* (Watsonville, Calif.: Papier-Mache Press, 1990); and either Agnes Smedley, *Daughter of Earth* (New York: The Feminist Press, 1976); or Dorothy Allison, *Bastard out of Carolina* (New York: Plume, 1993).

14. Langston, "Down on the Strike Line with My Children," in Zandy, *Calling Home*, 281.

15. Kollat, "My Mother Is a Working Woman," in *Our Voyage*. In the list of contributors Kollat describes herself as "coming from a great family, trying to create a great family, so that there may be a great family to come."

16. Coleman, "Second Helpings," in *Our Voyage*.

17. Sherry T., "Image of My Mother," in *Our Voyage*. Sherry T. describes herself in the list of contributors as "a full-time student, with a full-time job, a mother and a grandmother attempting to educate, hoping to elevate and praying her efforts will not be in vain."

18. W. Kay W., "The Line," in *Hidden Treasures*. W. Kay W. writes in the list of contributors that she "has had many different jobs, all blue-collar or minimum wage, the longest lasting of which was working on a warehouse line." She claims to have learned a lot from her job experience, mainly what she does not want to do forever: "run a cash register, sell food, work in meat packing, work in a nursing home, or work in a warehouse for the next forty years."

19. Bowell, "Everyday," in *Hidden Treasures*. Bowell writes in the list of contributors that she "began work at sixteen and has been working since."

20. Buzzard, "They Don't Have Me," in *Our Voyage*.

21. Zandy, *Calling Home*, 5.

22. In the list of contributors Limbert writes that she is "daughter, sister, wife, Mother, teacher, student, volunteer, Citizen of the Universe."

APPENDIX: SYLLABI FOR TWO COURSES

WORKING-CLASS WOMEN WRITERS
Required Texts

Allison, Dorothy. *Bastard out of Carolina*. New York: Plume, 1973.
Zandy, Janet, ed. *Calling Home: Working-Class Women's Writing*. New Brunswick, N.J.: Rutgers University Press, 1990.

Course Description

Through our discussion of our own personal and work histories we will create a framework for reading and analyzing works written by or about working-class women. Implicit in our discussion will be the effects of socioeconomic class on women's lives and the conflict women feel when they move from one class to another. The format of the course will be discussion, group presentations, and a final collaborative project.

Course Requirements

Journal. This is a place for you to respond to the readings and the class discussions. There should be a journal entry for every reading assignment and another entry after we have discussed the readings. There will also be specific journal assignments. Use the journal to note insights, to raise questions and concerns, and to suggest issues that you feel are important and that perhaps we overlooked in our initial discussion. Bring your journal to every class meeting. Your grade will be based on the quality of your responses.

Group Presentations. Each student will participate in a group presentation. On the day of your presentation you and your group will be responsible for leading class discussion. Creative approaches are encouraged.

Two Midterm Exams. There will be two open-book exams: the first one is on *Calling Home*, and the second one is on *Bastard out of Carolina*. Questions for these exams will be taken from our class discussions.

Creative Project. This final project is meant to be enjoyable and personally rewarding. After reading about other women's personal and work experiences, you will have the opportunity to express your feelings and attitudes about working-class life in a poem, a short story, a play, a drawing, a photograph, a short autobiography, or an essay. It is also possible to write about someone else whose personal history or experience has influenced or had an impact on your life.

Collaborative Class Book. During the eighth week of class we will work together in groups to put together a collection of our creative projects. For collaboration to be successful everyone must show up and do their part; consequently, any student who misses class during this time will lose credit for that portion of the grade.

WORKING-CLASS EXPERIENCES IN AMERICAN FICTION

One characteristic of working-class writing is that we often pile up many events within a small amount of space rather than detailing the many implications of one or two events. This means that our lives are chock full of action and also that we are bursting with stories which haven't been printed, made into novels, dictionaries, philosophies.

—Judy Graham, *The Work of a Common Woman*

Required Works

Arnow, Harriette. *The Dollmaker.* 1954. Reprint, New York: Avon, 1972.

Bulosan, Carlos. *America Is in the Heart.* New York: Harcourt Brace, 1946.

Hansberry, Lorraine. *A Raisin in the Sun.* New York: Modern Library, 1995.

Lynd, Alice, and Staughton Lynd, eds. *Rank and File: Personal Histories by Working-Class Organizers.* New York, Monthly Review Press, 1988.

Odets, Clifford. *Six Plays by Clifford Odets.* New York, Grove Press, 1979.

Olsen, Tillie. *Yonnondio: From the Thirties.* New York: Dell, 1975.

Course Description

This class is meant to introduce you to the lives of the working class in American literature. Its purpose is to acquaint you with working-class literature written in this century and to increase your skill in reading and interpreting poems, novels, plays, films, and personal histories. Your thorough preparation and active participation are crucial to the success of the class.

Course Requirements

Two Critical Papers. Topics will be generated from the class discussion. Rough drafts of these two papers will be presented to a small group, for help with revisions. These essays should be approximately five pages.

Weekly Position Papers. These brief papers will give you a chance to try out ideas for the two critical papers and will be shared with a small group. Some of these papers will be written in class, and some will be written out of class.

Group Presentation. Each student will participate in a group presentation. On the day of your presentation your group will be responsible for leading the class discussion of a text. The purpose of the presentation is to enhance our understanding of the text. Creative approaches are encouraged. I will pass out a sign-up sheet the second week of class, and we will discuss possible ideas for presentation at that time.

Reading and Attendance. Because this is a discussion class, it is important that you keep up with the reading, attend class, and contribute to discussions. For each class for which we have a reading assignment, I will ask you to write two thought-provoking questions for discussion. These questions will be collected at the beginning of the class period and will be used to generate class discussion.

Course Schedule

Week 1. Odets, "Waiting for Lefty," and "Awake and Sing!"
Week 2. Olsen, *Yonnondio*
Week 3. Poets of the 1930s.
Week 4. Modern Times; rough draft workshop on the first essay
Week 5. Bulosan, *America*
Week 6. Arnow, *The Dollmaker*
Week 7. Hansberry, *Raisin*
Week 8. Selections from Lynd and Lynd, *Rank and File*
Week 9. Selected Writing: Judy Grahn, Philip Levine, James Wright, and selections from *Calling Home*
Week 10. Last Exit to Brooklyn; rough draft workshop on the final essay

A Wealth of Possibilities

Workers, Texts, and the English Department

Laura Hapke

> *Every human being . . . is a millionaire in emotions.*
>
> —Isaac Bashevis Singer

Since the early 1970s, when I was a graduate assistant at a campus of the City University of New York, I have always found a streetwise student body receptive to the rebellious literary naturalism and so-called lower depths subject matter of Theodore Dreiser, Frank Norris, and Stephen Crane. (Of course, these authors, though fascinated by labor-class themes, were not worker-writers: I had yet to discover Agnes Smedley and Anzia Yezierska, Jack Conroy and Meridel Le Sueur.) Even in my part-time teaching days my syllabi clung tenaciously to *Sister Carrie* (1900), Dreiser's unfashionable, poignant ode to the urban down-and-out. To other skeptical graduate students I defended *McTeague* (1899), Norris's forgotten tale of simple people destroyed by nature, nurture, and social indifference. And, in halting conversations with those unmoved movers, my graduate professors, I inserted allusions to the not-yet-resurrected Crane (praised then, only occasionally, for *Red Badge of Courage* [1895]) and his experimental melodrama of blue-collar womanhood, *Maggie: A Girl of the Streets* (1893).

But it was only when I was strapped into tenure and a professorship, above desire and beyond reproach, that I turned my department's suggested syllabi into rejected ones. I offered, instead, a series of courses about labor fiction in general and proletarian literature in particular, whose titles included Classics of Working-Class Literature and Blue Collar: The Worker in City Fiction from the Civil War to the Present. (When, by no choice of my own, the course had a less defiant label such as Introduction to Writing, I used my own titles as subheadings.)

Repeatedly, I found that the students seated so passively at semester's opening—as if with the same compliance I had so recently abandoned—were completely unfamiliar with the literary imagination of manual and industrial labor.[1] Yet soon they became interested and, in some cases, intrigued. I found that my colleagues, seated politely at my brief department talk on teaching working-class literature, were familiar—at least in passing—with this body of fiction, though largely uninterested. Or, in the way of academics wary of a new approach, their collective response reminded me of my old thesis advisor's rejoinder to my request for a bibliography: "It doesn't matter what books we read as long as we read the same books."

Clearly, the subjects of my departmental talk—Chicago-based Jack Conroy's Bottom Dogs saga of heavy industry, *The Disinherited* (1933); Smedley's passionately autobiographical *Daughter of Earth* (1928), the radical coming of age of a

Colorado mining town girl; and *Love on the Dole* (1933), Walter Greenwood's classic of British mill town unemployment—were not on that list. Was not, my colleagues inquired, the 1930s radical novel, or any leftist fiction for that matter, "lacking in playfulness"? Were there any "real" writers among the cohorts of proletarian author Mike Gold (not to mention that ur-Communist Party [CP] member, Gold himself)? In today's United States, was there even a working class about which literature could now be produced? And who cared about texts that were not high art, anyway?

Two days later my talk received a final, belated response—a short, ambivalent note from one of my most scholarly colleagues. He wrote that I was probably right about the value of labor texts, which the department should assign if it was "capable."

The *Encyclopedia of the American Left* reminds us that "intellectual disfavor of radical literature became the norm in universities when . . . English professors adopted a 'New Criticism' that devalued writing that was politically committed."[2] Furthermore, particularly at a business-oriented university like mine, post-HUAC (House Un-American Activities Committee) fallout remains, while the Stalinism (and Nazi-Soviet "pactism"), which Mike Gold embraced philosophically, is wrongly conflated with the radicalism of his thinking on literature.[3] But the careful frostiness that greeted my apologia for working-class texts may have a deeper cause. Literary theories superseding New Criticism and empowering feminist, black, and multicultural literatures are now in place, while working-class literary studies are still in their infancy. Perhaps the task of assigning fictive texts that pay compassionate attention to the factory worker denied his or her right to strike or the plight of the urban transient involves too drastic a shift from the aesthetic to the humanistic, or a relocation of the aesthetic in what Janet Zandy aptly terms the "collective sensibility."[4] Nor—partially excepting the brief spurt of late-nineteenth-century American literary naturalism—if that lone colleague who was fitfully considering my new classroom agenda had really wished to survey labor fiction from the American Revolution onward, would he have found in classic literature prior to the 1930s any balanced or even extended descriptions of the laboring experience. Although with the rise of the novel, American authors of the magnitude of Herman Melville and Henry James did not simply relegate the working class to the status of Shakespeare's "rude mechanicals," neither did they pay much, or respectful, attention to the subject. Indeed, from Melville's "Bartelby the Scrivener" (1853) and "Paradise of Bachelors" (1855), to James's *Princess Casamassima* (1886) and *The American* (1877), portrayals of the clerking, shopgirl, servant, and garment trades classes resonate with the prejudices of bourgeois literary production. The lower orders, laboring or otherwise, are variously comic, eccentric, vulgar, manic, or, worst of all, awash in Dickensian sentiment.

Thus, as the departmental silence on my topic suggested, it is not surprising that modern critic-teachers, already little motivated to hunt out less stereotyped portrayals, often choose to omit the blue-collar classes and their importance to noncanonical world literature from inquiry and reading lists for the undergraduate classroom. Even a text billed by its publisher, the Modern Language Association

(MLA), as a "groundbreaking volume," the newly published collection *Redrawing the Boundaries: The Transformation of English and American Literary Studies* (1992), includes essays on gender and African American criticism but nothing on labor studies.

The flowering of labor studies among the new social historians, the proposed establishment of a permanent MLA section on working-class literature, and the publication of works such as *Canons and Contexts*, by Paul Lauter (1991) and *Left Politics and the Literary Profession*, edited by Lennard J. Davis and M. Bella Mirabella (1990), all broaden the somewhat weary definition of "the humanities" to include neglected, lost, and maligned texts of the laboring life.

To join this still modest revolution, I offer here some proposals for curricular change. They are based on a transformation of my own university's Introductory Literature and Basic Composition courses with their devotion to traditional readings, into courses centered on the crucial social and literary questions such readings inspire. In creating these courses, I selected classics of labor fiction and, to provide a historical context, of social documentary nonfiction. By their very nature these courses challenge the goals of the new consumer-oriented urban university, whose largely first-generation college students, for good or ill, perceive education as vocational training. I found it not as difficult as I had thought to balance the college/student agendas with my need to awaken my captive audience to the realities of class difference, the underside of the American Dream, and the democratic eloquence of working-class fiction. By appealing to the fundamental sense of fairness in young people whose own parents' ascension to lower-middle-class security was recent enough, any instructor can interest students in the unofficial history of the United States—that of the laboring classes—and in so doing help awaken in them a compassion for those at the bottom of the socioeconomic barrel.

In a 1979 account of his Boston University course on the history of work in modern America, Marc Miller wrote that he hoped to convey why the struggle of workers to create unions was an important one. To his disappointment he found students in the main "hostile to the concept of organized labor," even though some of them worked at jobs not far removed from the hardships or monotonies of mass-production work. Miller implied that, while his course did much to prod students to examine the industrial job site beyond what might be termed the "local color" side of work life, there was a general "failure to go beyond description to analysis."[5] My aims were less ambitious. As my university, though it includes a School of Arts and Sciences, is for the most part business oriented, with the majority of students pursuing careers in accounting, finance, and computer science (preferably of the information systems variety so suited to today's banking houses), I did not expect indignation to greet Conroy's novelistic accounts of the hellish stench of the Mid-west rubber factory or management's attempts to plant spies or workers' attempts to found a company union. What I did hope for was an increased awareness that, then as now, big business exploits the working stiff and causes economic suffering, and that to care about the protagonist of a novel by a Conroy is in some way to care about a whole class of people.

Though my students could recite the latest rock tunes and speak volubly of cast changes in *Roseanne* (which they considered a "real-life blue-collar sitcom"), they hadn't heard about the thousands, some out of a job for a year or more, who stood in the predawn Chicago cold for some crummy hotel jobs a year or so ago. News to them too was the Southern chicken processing plant fire, a sad reprise of the Triangle Shirtwaist Factory debacle of 1911. Nor did they know of the failed Midwest Caterpillar strike, in which, despite a powerful international United Auto Workers (UAW) union, longtime workers had to watch scabs take their work, sometimes permanently. And when I asked what they thought the title of the 1930s song "Brother, Can You Spare a Dime?" meant, they laughed knowingly and said it was written by someone panhandling on the subways.

To generate some enthusiasm about novels that challenge rather than celebrate upward mobility in a classroom filled with devotees of such ascension, I devised a three-stage syllabus. The first part of the semester was spent demystifying what turn-of-the-century tenement crusader Jacob Riis, with both telling accuracy and unconscious condescension, called "the other half": the working and workless poor, the homeless, and the vast criminal population of the stale beer dives and bottle-alleys of New York. Though not a worker-writer, Riis was a good choice, for the ideological transformation of the "poor" into the "working classes" was a recent one, and Riis was halfway between the two ideologies: on the one hand, castigating the immorality of the impoverished and, on the other, lauding honest toil.

To usher Riis in, we began with a recent *New York Times* piece on the city's roving hordes of transients, moved to the stunning Lower East Side poverty photos and somewhat elitist descriptive/reformist essays of Riis's *How the Other Half Lives* (1901), and generally dwelt in a climate receptive to what one student called the realization that the other half might be "equal to the half that I thought I lived in."

In stage two of the term's work, a novel from the depression era, when the largest number of literary texts on labor unrest were produced, was a crux for discussions about mass production, job site injustice, and the hero who can only, in Conroy's words, "rise with his class."[6] In the course's final stage, the research component, students tied Conroy's realistic fiction to events such as the Akron Rubber Strike of 1936 or the use of black strikebreakers in the coal industry; surveyed other "proletarian authors" such as Le Sueur or Nelson Algren, as well as what their period critics—and bitter foes—thought of them; or took more modern occasions such as the controversy raging about the mental stability of New York City's homeless or the place of women in the construction trades as their subjects of inquiry.

Because, whether in basic or advanced courses, virtually all of my students needed solid writing instruction, a brief sampling of a *New York Times* article—in this case a 1991 one on a derelict collecting return-deposit bottles, scrutinizing the depiction of the homeless man—combined well with reviewing the principles of essay construction. Had the bylined article advanced a thesis? Provided detailed support through idea and example? Moved logically from one part of the argument to the other? Concluded clearly and thoughtfully? And so on. After a few assignments requiring students to write their own descriptions of "subway people," neighborhood barflies, etc., and some dissection of the *Times*'s brand of temperate muckraking—including discussion of "liberal" bias in reportage about the poor—it seemed proper to turn to a more complicated text and series of writing assignments: Riis's other half

The Riis text is, of course, a compelling social document. But, as recent revisionists have pointed out, it is also a middle-class one. Given the tension between the egalitarian and elitist Riis, asking students to compare the poignant photos with the rather stiff essays damning female "dishonor" and freely using terms like "*Jewtown*" is a valuable exercise. It proved particularly useful to analyze the structure of a classic *Other Half* essay, "The Working Girls of New York," again from the dual perspective of structure and content.

After some prodding, students discovered that the celebrated news reporter delayed his thesis (which was confusing), offered a disorganized argument, and circled back needlessly to the obsessively reiterated idea of the working girl's need for purity. Riis's very emphases led to new insights. Why were working women judged on their virtue when the men were not? Why, if the women, as Riis pointed out, did the same garment trades jobs as men but were paid less, did he not voice moral outrage about that? And why, although he alluded to prostitution as an evil road for starving seamstresses, could he not bring himself to use the word?

Having analyzed the bourgeois Riis, we turned to his less moralistic, more brilliant side. In a series of comparison essays using Riis's photos, we came face to face—"as if you were there without looking at the pictures," as one student put it—with the emotional toll of poverty: sad-faced child-rearing girls, mothers to slightly younger brothers; shivering urchins, sleeping on top of grates; pinched sweatshop women, breathing the lint-filled air of the contractor's apartment-factory; maddened-looking Police Lodging House alcoholics, female and male. All of these subjects produced a level of eloquence in my students' responses which I had never seen when I assigned a Shakespeare play or a William Carlos Williams poem. "In Jacob Riis's *How the Other Half Lives*," wrote one of my students, "although the children in the pictures 'Prayer-time in the Nursery' and 'Street Arabs in Sleeping Quarters (Areaway, Mulberry Street)' are both young, the youngsters in the first photo have a place to sleep, unlike the boys in the second, who have none." She had not produced anything like this relative stylistic sophistication in responding to the department's rather dry placement test question regarding New York City Mayor Dinkins's fiscal management. With her (single) mother she had recently moved from one rather unsafe apartment in the Bronx to another, and most days she arrived late and flustered; I wondered to what extent she identified with the two sets of hapless children Riis had immortalized.

Other students, more emotionally and financially serene, began the semester freely using the word *bum* to describe the subway mendicant. They too produced sensitive descriptions of Riis's classic "Didn't Live Nowhere," a medium close-up of two barefoot street boys who stare exhausted into the camera, otherwise disclosing nothing. In the best of the student papers subject and viewer seemed almost to fuse, as writers replaced Riis's emotionally distant narrative voice with their own, newly gentle ones.

Riis's text was a "landmark in the annals of American social reform,"[7] and Riis was instrumental in the kind of tenement house reform that brought open spaces, parks, and playgrounds to a dangerously overcrowded Lower East Side. Nevertheless, his proselytizing brand of philanthropic benevolence placed him on the side of those whom Jack Conroy (who incorporated his own experience as a factory hand and sometime hobo into his novel of the 1930s) satirized as do-gooder intruders. Conroy's newly reissued 1933 novel *The Disinherited*—like reprints of Le Sueur's *The Girl*, Daniel Fuchs's *Summer in Williamsburg*, Smedley's *Daughter of Earth*, and Tillie Olsen's *Yonnondio*—wrests verbal control of work from the bourgeois reformer. The Conroy text—an account of mining camp youth Larry Donovan's travels through the worlds of coal workers' families; railway car, steel, and rubber factory toil; strikes, organizing marches, and Hoovervilles—was, like the others, a text on which the working-class writer stamped his or her personality.

Used in stage two of my courses, sometimes in tandem with Farm Security Administration photographs or women's writing from the 1930s, *The Disinherited* contains scenes to which students, building on their own experiences, are particularly responsive. In one key chapter a Christian committee comes to take away the children of the newly widowed Mrs. Donovan to foster care. Her husband has just been killed in a mining accident, and the committee's presumption is that middle-class parents can give the Donovan brood the gentility they require to be civilized. The whole vignette, complete with comic references to the pretentious visitors, is written from the insider's perspective, albeit an insider who has taught himself to write a somewhat stilted prose: "One day a group of church workers came to see us. They sat decorously in the front room, their inquisitive eyes ferreting into every crevice" (82). Despite students' reluctance to read such ponderous stuff—much less look up the vocabulary used in such sentences—they liked the man who had written the description. Conroy, after all, had frequently redeemed himself with passages on young Larry's humiliations by the flaxen-haired farmer's daughter, who considered him "camp trash" (44). If they themselves had not endured quite such abuse, many of my students knew what it was to be humiliated in minimum-wage jobs or chance meetings with Ivy Leaguers.

Using my colleagues' "but is it art?" objections to the worker novel of the 1930s, I asked the students to consider why so many of the Conroy chapters seemed episodic, fragmented. A number of them, pressed to define why they considered that structure "realistic," pointed out that events are depicted as if they are happening, not recalled later. I asked why Larry and his creator were so earnest, humorless, intense, and why he/they needed to strew big words in front of the reader. Some students noted—admittedly, after many generous hints from the instructor—that he saw the lives of workers as deadly serious, that he was proving his ability to compete with the "educated" authors of classic fiction. I inquired, too, why Larry renounces white-collar ambitions, in a (beautiful) passage such as this:

> I no longer felt shame at being seen at such work as I would have once,
> and I knew that the only way for me to rise to something approximating
> the grandiose ambitions of my youth would be to rise with my class, with
> the disinherited: the brick-setters, the flivver tramps, boomers, and out-
> casts pounding their ears in flophouses. (265)

There the responses were more negative. Students were skeptical whether a
1990s Larry would have to make such a decision. A few of them termed the
novel's final passage—in which Larry rides off in a secondhand auto, cold wind in
his face, to become an organizer—"corny."

Certainly any teacher who employs the polemical novel favored by leftist writers, from Conroy to Le Sueur, Gold to Olsen, early James T. Farrell to Smedley,
will have to prepare careful responses to this kind of objection. For my part I
asked my classes to consider what today's unemployed blue-collar man or woman,
or the nation's vast homeless population, had to look forward to without a group
allegiance. And I wondered aloud whether the class knew if companies they
wished or planned to work for had any unions or, instead, trumpeted their "generosity" to employees.

Finally, in their thinking about Conroy, the more introspective not only found
Larry's decision understandable but even made allowances for the racist language
that cropped up so often in the text. In the semester's last phase, in which students prepared their research essays, some of the African American students,
justly angered at the racial ignorance of so many white workers in the Conroy
novel, were sufficiently interested to hunt down information on blacks in actual
1930s unions and labor upheavals. Most of the students flinched at any mention
of Larry's potential work as an organizer for the CP and were soothed when told
Conroy soon broke with the CP. They saw the reasonableness of labor strikes,
remembering the smallest details for an in-class essay on that theme. And several
constructed admirable essays on the ideological contradictions between empowering all people and consigning women to being helpmeets rather than comrades
in the 1930s worker novel, at least the masculine version.

If there were time, some semesters I shifted to a reconsideration of classic
American texts from a revisionist viewpoint. Conventionally considered on a
loftily (and conveniently?) symbolic level, the 1853 Melville story of a lawyer
who carts off his clerk who will not work to the Tombs Prison, "Bartelby the
Scrivener," raises crucial questions about the kind and quality of monotonous
modern work. Why, I asked, are the clerical workers Turkey, Nippers, and Ginger
Nut cast so comically? With whose interests do they identify, those of their mar-
ginally white-collar class or of the employer? Why are they so hostile to Bartleby?
Is it solely the result of his refusal to shoulder his work burden? Or, given their
loyalty to the narrator-lawyer, do they refuse to see their connection to another
ill-paid member of clerkdom? When the worker-characters speak, are they permitted lengthy speeches? Do their voices sound real? Or does it seem that
Melville and the narrator distort them? And so on.

In searching out the literary criticism of American work as depicted in canonical texts, most instructors are on their own. In researching a book on images of breadwinning women in late-nineteenth- and early-twentieth-century fiction, I was surprised at the dearth of studies on the work experience in American fiction. Still, in courses combining the literature survey and the composition requirement, a scrutiny of works such as James's *The Princess Casamassima*—with its lively, censoriously viewed shopgirl, Millicent Henning—from a labor-class perspective can illuminate how these texts exemplify period fears about social revolution and the dangerous classes, uncover the injustice in their creators' ideology of "the deserving poor," and locate idées fixes about the immorality of the female breadwinner. While such a perspective need not replace the traditional "masters of literature" one, it is essential for deepening it.

When it came to stage three of my courses, library research (a department mandate), as a springboard to further labor studies, it seemed to me that the depression era cried out to be investigated. Students with a literary critical bent could scour *Writers in Revolt: The Anvil Anthology*, edited by Jack Conroy and Curt Johnson (1973), to mine the rich field of short proletarian fiction. Those with historical interests could research the 1935 National Labor Relations (Wagner) Act, the Akron Rubber Strike of 1936–37, the Flint sit-down strike of 1937. Others, usually a minority, could compare the supposed solution to the social problem of the economically disenfranchised or exploited in our time with the New Deal's—or else the Communist Party's—programs. And students sophisticated enough to summarize literary critical controversies could chart the culture wars of the Left and take a stand on Conroy's merit, perhaps citing Gold or post-Party sympathizer Farrell.[8] While many instructors wishing to introduce their classes to working-class studies may prefer more timely topics, it does well to remember that alienated students can feel as empowered rediscovering an obscured past as in mastering a modern social problem.

In these acts of resurrection a good number of my students came to care about long-dead labor organizers, the militant rank and file (presented, perhaps, as overly violent by their accounting or finance professors), and the hostilities against black workers that constitute the underside of the labor movement. One wrote enthusiastically about Margaret Cowl and the Women's Commission. Another went to Schomburg Center, the New York Public Library's jewel in the black studies crown, to look at back issues of the Harlem-based journals *Crisis* and *Opportunity*. And another secured a copy of the Wagner Act from the university's law library. All students had the opportunity to acquaint themselves with the new bibliographies on (or with large sections devoted to) the working class: (Maurice F. Neufeld, ed.) *American Working-Class History: A Representative Bibliography* (1983); (Martha Jane Soltow and Mary K. Wery, eds.) *American Women and the Labor Movement, 1825–1974* (1976); (Nancy Ann Sahli, ed.) *Women and Sexuality in America: A Bibliography* (1984); (Janet L. Sims-Wood, comp.) *The Progress of Afro-American Women: A Select Bibliography* (1980). Significantly, none of these sources is listed among the standard handbooks of research technique, which pelt students with *The Reader's Guide to Periodical Literature* and *The Encyclopedia of Banking and Finance*, both certainly no less specialized than those about labor studies.[9]

In terms of dictionaries and encyclopedias all college students, whether fasci‐
nated by the Flint sit‐down strike of 1937 or contemporary rulings on abortion
that impact on lower‐class and poor women, should know of Gary Fink's *Labor in
Conflict: An Encyclopedia* (1990); Gary Fink's *Biographical Dictionary of American
Labor Leaders* (1974); and Angela Howard Zophy and Frances M. Kavenik's
Handbook of American Women's History (1990). For students of labor literature,
surveys such as Fay M. Blake's *The Strike in the American Novel* (1972); Walter
Rideout's *The Radical Novel in the United States, 1900–1954* (1956); and, in the
women's studies category, Janet Zandy's anthology *Calling Home: Working‐Class
Women's Writings* (1990); and my own *Tales of the Working Girl: Wage‐Earning
Women in American Literature, 1890–1925* (1992) are contributions to a still
under‐researched field.

To conclude: A reexamination of a neglected classic of labor life such as Jack
Conroy's depression‐era novel *The Disinherited* uncovers aspects of the human
experience erased from or presented condescendingly by canonical texts and
thereby provides excellent occasions for composition and literature assignments.
Corollary texts from the social history of muckraking—Riis's *How the Other Half
Lives*, to name a prime example—are rich sources of exercises in the classroom,
stimulating students to challenge the trope of the American Dream, to make new
connections between the arresting photography of Riis and their own immigrant
backgrounds and/or experiences of economic dislocation. Students find they are
able to forge their own eloquence about the miseries of the underclass, all the
while practicing the traditional rhetorical forms of classification, definition, argu‐
ment, and comparison. Above all, these new pedagogical strategies, by expanding
the canon (or the black, ethnic, and feminist anticanons) to include texts by and
about the working classes, enable students, particularly college entrants from
modest circumstances, to revisit an idea that threatens to fade away entirely in
our materialistic time: the dignity of labor.

NOTES

1. Although I avoid the term *proletarian fiction* for its too rigid association with the
1930s—save for isolated exceptions, themselves largely the products of "undercover" eye‐
witness historians (Dorothy Richardson's *The Long Day* [1905]) or former workers
ascended socially (Theresa Malkiel's *Diary of a Shirtwaist Striker* [1910])—the worker‐
writer's literary visioning of labor under capitalism does not mark the American scene
until the Great Depression. Precursors such as the muckraking factory fiction of Rebecca
Harding Davis and Elizabeth Stuart Phelps, not to mention the rabidly antistrike novels of
John Hay, were produced by solidly middle‐class authors. Comments Nancy Armstrong in
"Introduction: Literature as Women's History" (*Genre* 19 [winter 1986]: 347–69), "Middle‐
class practitioners of the novel located the cause of working‐class misery in the improperly
socialized working‐class individual and not in the violent conflicts and crashing changes of
a society that was undergoing rapid industrialization" (353). I agree with Paul Lauter in
"Working‐Class Women's Literature—An Introduction to Study" (*Radical Teacher* 15
[March 1980]: 16–26) that working‐class literature may be about or by working‐class
people, but note that the former is more likely to include works "ignorant of or hostile to"
workers (16).

2. Dan Georgakas and Ernie Brill, "Proletarian and Radical Writers—1930s and 1940s," in *The Encyclopedia of the American Left*, ed. Mari Jo Buhle, Paul Buhle, and Dan Georgakas (New York: Garland, 1990), 605.

3. See James D. Bloom, *Left Letters: The Culture Wars of Mike Gold and Joseph Freeman* (New York: Columbia University Press, 1992).

4. Zandy introduction to *Calling Home: Working-Class Women's Writings—An Anthology*, ed. Janet Zandy (New Brunswick, N.J.: Rutgers University Press, 1990), 10. This is not to contend that feminist or multicultural texts do not require an equally radical pedagogical shift, particularly to the extent that class intersects race, ethnicity, and gender. But it is to suggest that American working-class texts inevitably raise the issue of leftist orientation in a way that a lost suffrage novel or an African American slave narrative need not.

5. Miller, "Teaching the History of Work," *Radical Teacher* 12 (May 1979): 27, 30.

6. Conroy, *The Disinherited: A Novel of the 1930s* (1933; reprint, Columbia: University of Missouri Press, 1991), 265; hereafter cited in text.

7. Charles A. Madison, preface to *How the Other Half Lives*, photographs and text by Jacob Riis (1901; reprint, New York: Dover, 1971), vii. Less adulatory discussions occur in Carol Shloss, *In Visible Light: Photography and American Writers, 1840–1940* (New York: Oxford University Press, 1987), chap. 3; and Maren Stange, *Symbols of Ideal Life: Social Documentary Photography at the Turn of the Century* (Cambridge: Cambridge University Press, 1989), chap. 1. Stange points out that not only did Riis often "rehearse . . . imagery familiar to any reader of illustrated periodicals" but that his photographs often borrowed from his fellow Bowery watcher Richard Hoe Lawrence (11).

8. Gold, "A Letter to the Author of a First Book," *New Masses* 9 (9 January 1934): 25; Farrell, "A Working-Class Novel," *Nation* 137 (20 December 1933): 714.

9. See, for instance, *The Prentice-Hall Handbook for Writers* or *The Bedford Handbook for Writers*. Oh for the day that the handbooks also include sources such as Jayne Loader, "Women in the Left: A Bibliography of Primary Resources," *Michigan Papers in Women's Studies* 2 (September 1975): 9–82; (Marianne A. Ferber) *Women and Work, Paid and Unpaid: A Selected, Annotated Bibliography* (New York: Garland, 1987); Mari Jo Buhle's classic work *Women and the American Left* (Boston: G. K. Hall, 1983); and Virginia Prestridge, *The Worker in American Fiction: An Annotated Bibliography* (Champaign: University of Illinois Institute of Industrial and Labor Relations, 1954).

A Community of Workers

Marilyn Anderson

The images and text on these pages are from an ongoing project to document and interpret the range and diversity of work performed in a single community—Rochester, New York. In 1990 Jon Garlock, a writer, historian, and active unionist, and I, as photographer, began to collaborate on this project. Thus far we have visited over fifty work sites, photographing and interviewing hundreds of industrial, building trades, service and public sector, and transportation and communications workers. To date we have shared extensively with the community the images and texts edited from these photo shoots; through an exhibit we have traveled to schools, union halls, galleries, and public events.

Because our project is sponsored by the local labor council each shoot is initiated through calls to one of the affiliated unions. Whenever we go to a workplace we arrive under the auspices of a union and with the approval and cooperation of management. One simply can't gain access to many work sites without such support—which is probably one reason one finds so few pictures of workers.

Generally, the workers are pleased to see us. In some cases they have discussed the shoot and decided what operations should be documented. In other cases, especially at construction sites, the activities photographed and the workers interviewed are determined by what is happening at the moment. Workers like to tell us about what they do, whether it is giving a detailed description of work processes or expressing pride in their skill. Or they may note how younger workers lack skills or how new work processes require less skill. Or they may talk about how people don't understand or appreciate what they do:

> I've shown thousands and thousands of miles of film, enough to go from here to the moon and back; people who come to the movies don't even know we exist.

> I've tried to explain what I do and it's very hard. A friend of mine asked me, "So what is it you do there?" I go, "Oh, well, I run a lathe." He says, "Oh, a lathe. What does a lathe do?"

As we go around a work site, we hand out printed brochures that have my photographs of workers, interview text, and information about the educational purpose of our documentation project. Most of the workers are positive about the project and want to participate, especially when they recognize that it will be used to help kids to understand what work is about.

We find that teachers appreciate being able to use the exhibit, often in conjunction with career education. Teachers and guidance counselors are able to show students a wide range of occupations within their own communities. Not infrequently, students recognize family or friends in the photographs or have family members who work at the job sites documented in the show. This immediacy helps them to relate to issues raised by the exhibit's images and text, especially workers' feelings about their jobs, working conditions and issues of job security, the social significance of their labor, and changes in work resulting from global competition or the introduction of new technology.

During Career Exploration Night at a local high school the exhibit provoked as much discussion with parents as with youth, including many parents who were as concerned with keeping their own jobs as finding work for their kids after graduation.

Because the exhibit touches on many aspects of work, it offers teachers an opportunity to discuss work-related issues with their students, rather than introducing the topic of work uncritically, as a range of employment opportunities. A workshop we did, Teaching Work, revealed that some teachers were willing to have students examine the arrangements and question the assumptions underlying employment in capitalist society.

Because all the workers in the exhibit belong to unions (as do many of the teachers themselves), the exhibit can also be used to stimulate consideration of the role of unions in providing job protections through contracts.

Teachers of social studies, English, art and photography, business and economics, and other subjects have developed assignments and exercises based on the exhibit. Students have conducted research, interviewed family members about work, reflected on their own summer and part-time work experience, and even photographed and interviewed workers.

Doing the Community of Workers project, we have been privileged to enter factories, schools, garages, hospitals, construction sites (including a sewer tunnel being dug *beneath* the Genesee River), and other work sites rarely visited except by workers themselves. My partner and I have been moved by the language people use to describe their work and by their insights into their situations. In our document we try to avoid romanticizing either workers or their labor: our project, as Studs Terkel writes in his book *Working*, "being about work, is, by its very nature, about violence—to the spirit as well as to the body." At the same time, we cannot report only the casualties of class warfare as it is waged daily in the workplace. To do so would be to ignore the humor, to strip away the dignity, and to distort the humanity of these women and men.

It is our hope to extend this project to the point that it truly documents a community of workers. More than a collection of images and words from myriad distinct trades and occupations, more than an exhibit or curriculum supplement, such a document will connect these tasks and these workers, demonstrate their common unity, and corroborate Walt Whitman's insight:

> The hourly routine of your own or any man's life, the shop, yard, store,
>   or factory,
> In them the development good—in them all themes, hints, possibilities.
>   "A Song for Occupations"

Laborers Local 435/Perini

Laborers Local 435

I like working outdoors.
I did secretarial work before this
And that was a hard job, you know.
I worked in a real estate office—
You've got telephones, you've got
    people.
At least now I get fresh air and sun-
    shine.
I really like it.

IUE 509/Delco

It's a very essential part of the car,
    what we do.
The transmission for the wiper—
Every car's got to have a wiper
    transmission.

UAW 1097

Electronic, Electrical, Salaried Machine & Furniture Workers International Union (IUE) Local 323

PEF Local 283/Rochester Psychiatric Center
We do have quite a few people
That are homeless,
That don't have relatives
And can't take care of themselves
And are actually walking around on
     the streets very ill.
They find their way here,
And it's very important
That they have something, someone,
To help take care of them.

We're here as that support for them.

ACTWU Local 14/Hickey Freeman (UNITE)
It's a tradition.
They don't want to sew the button-
     holes by machine.
It's very cheap.
All the buttonholes are done by hand.
But it's very hard to learn how to make
     a buttonhole.
It's one of the skilledest jobs in the
     building.

ACTWU Local 14/Hickey Freeman (UNITE)

NYSUT 2969

I check passes. I do so much. I show
    students to classes
If they don't know where they are. I do
    some study halls.
I run any kind of errands the school
    needs help with—
I might bring something to the main
    office for a teacher.
We work in the office, the library.
Sometimes we put labels on envelopes
    for large mailings.
    Break up fights.
We monitor in the lunchroom. We
    talk to students a lot.
They really confide in us a lot—their
    personal problems.
They borrow money when they forget
    their lunch money.
It's just like being a housewife, you
    know:
Do everything but nobody pays any
    attention to you.

Automobile, Aerospace, & Agricultural Implement Workers of America, International Union (UAW) 1097

Amalgamated Clothing & Textile Workers Union (ACTWU) Local 3-T

Here and Now Local 466/Rochester Convention Center

All right, listen up.
Tonight we're going to have cocktail
    servers at the tables.
They've got about five tables per
    server.
So if anyone turns to you and asks for a
    cocktail,
Just take a look at the board where
    your station is,
And they'll be able to handle the
    drinks.
Seven-fifteen are doors
And then they're going to have the
    welcome and the prayer.
About seven-forty we'll have the
    dinner.

Here and Now Local 466/Wesley-on-East

I was a nurse here for thirty years.
Well, it went by fast. Left me in good
    shape.
So it didn't hurt me. They called me a
    couple of times,
Wanted to know if I could come back
And just help them out.
I come in and work a couple of days
And I'm happy—you know—
Because the most important thing is
    being happy.
I have to keep it in my mind that I'm
    retired.
Things now, nothing is going to come
    to me.
I've got to go to it,
I've got to go to things.

We have different levels of environ-
    mental service workers.
Level 1 is laundry—cleaning resident
    areas.
Level 2 is fresh linen:
They pull the carts back and forth
    with clean linen and so forth.
Level 3 is the heavy equipment level.
All of us in environmental services
    just say "Housekeeping."

Here and Now Local 466/Wesley-on-East

United Food & Commercial Workers District Union Local 1

'Women Have Always Sewed'

The Production of Clothing and the Work of Women

Janet Zandy

One characteristic of working-class studies is an attentiveness to those seemingly mundane tasks and things that are either invisible or generally ignored. This attention to material existence is not from the ubiquitous business perspective of salable commodities, but, rather, it is with the intent of seeing the human labor relationships embedded inside finished products. This brief outline of clothing production is intended to historicize and localize textile work for students. This factual world of labor history can be expanded to include novels, photographs, music, films, oral history, and fieldwork. Foregrounded are the human hands—usually women's—which produce the jeans, shirts, and socks we buy today and the shirtwaists and overalls purchased by earlier generations.

As Alice Kessler-Harris and others have documented, women have always worked. They have also always sewed, providing their families with clothing and household linens, bedding and quilts. Technological change and the accumulation of capital shifted the site of clothing production from the home to the factory. The invention of the cotton gin heightened the efficiency of producing cotton, as it accelerated the technology of slavery. The industrial revolution produced huge quantities of material goods and a technology of work. *Technology* is not just hardware; it was and is also a technique or system of human labor. If we look at what's behind the shirt we buy, we see a confluence of gender and race ideologies embedded in textile production. Styles may change, but patterns of labor relationships have a stubborn continuity. From Lowell to the global assembly line, the women who make the garments worn by the consumers of the world are caught inside intersecting technologies of gender and capital. These are techniques that involve gender-specific systems of work production. The sites of clothing production have frequently been contested. Women workers have struggled for better wages, safe and sanitary working conditions, and more control over their own labor. They have asserted their humanity and refused to be turned into *its*—that is, *things*—mere adjuncts to their sewing machines. Perhaps it is in the recognition and development of that resistance that new trade union models can be forged in solidarity with other workers, political activists, and cultural workers.

> Needle, running in and out,
> In and out, in and out,
> Do you know what you're about,
> In and out, in and out?

(Hall, "Puzzled Stitches")

I want you women up north to know
how those dainty children's dresses you buy
at macy's wannamakers, gimbels, marshall fields,
are dyed in blood, are stitched in wasting flesh,
down in San Antonio, "where sunshine spends the winter."

(Olsen, "I Want You Women Up North to Know")

WORKS CITED

Hall, Hazel. "Puzzled Stitches." In *May Days: An Anthology of Verse from Masses-Liberator*, edited by Genevieve Taggard. New York: Boni and Liveright, 1925.

Kessler-Harris, Alice. *Women Have Always Worked: A Historical Overview*. Old Westbury, N.Y.: The Feminist Press, 1981.

Olsen, Tillie. "I Want You Women Up North to Know." In *Calling Home: Working-Class Women's Writings—An Anthology*, edited by Janet Zandy. New Brunswick, N.J.: Rutgers University Press, 1990. First published in *The Partisan* 1 (March 1934).

A WORKING OUTLINE

I. "The Lowell Girls": New England mill women (1840–54)
   A. Francis Cabot Lowell; the stolen power loom design; and the construction of Lowell, Massachusetts, the first planned industrial city
      1. Starting in 1822, the mills expanded to nineteen five-story mills
      2. A departure from the family mills system
      3. The expanding market for raw cotton in the North increased cotton production in the South, and expanded slavery
   B. The Lowell mill system employed New England farm girls: the intersection of economic and social systems
      1. Seventy-five percent of the Lowell employees were young, farm-raised, highly literate New England women
      2. Lowell perfected a form of corporate paternalism in its construction of boardinghouses for the factory workers; every aspect of daily life was regulated
      3. Despite the boardinghouse system of surveillance and moral policing, the "girls" resisted a degradation in their working conditions in the Ten-Hour Movement in the 1840s and exercised a kind of literary release in the publication of their writing, collected in *The Lowell Offering*
   C. Of seven thousand operatives in 1836, fewer than 4 percent were immigrants; by 1860, 61.8 percent were immigrants, mostly Irish

SOURCES AND PARALLEL READINGS

Atwood, Margaret. *The Handmaid's Tale*. New York: Fawcett Crest, 1987. An interesting fictional contrast to Lowell.

Dublin, Thomas. *Women at Work: The Transformation of Work and Community in Lowell, Massachusetts, 1826–1860*. New York: Columbia University Press, 1979.

Eisler, Benita, ed. *The Lowell Offering: Writings by New England Mill Women (1840–1845)*. New York: Harper and Row, 1977.

II. The East: The sweatshop—from the loom to the finished goods
    A. The Shirtwaist: the Gibson Girl and the labor of immigrants
    B. The Uprising of the 20,000 (1909–10)
    C. The Triangle fire, 25 March 1911—146 workers died because of locked doors and unsafe working conditions
    D. The movement of the clothing business
        1. In the 1950s New York lost jobs to low-wage domestic areas in Pennsylvania, where wives of unemployed miners were eager for work
        2. Manufacturers moved to the antiunion South
        3. With further breakdowns of work into low-skill operations and improvements in cargo transport, garment manufacturers turned to Southeast Asia; as a result, imported clothes sold at wholesale prices 20 percent below domestic goods
    E. More recent sweatshops: garment workers in New York City in the 1980s are frequently Chinese or Central or South American immigrants who face a two-tiered industry: a legitimate sector, in which workers earn about $5.00 an hour (in the mid-1980s), and an illegitimate, under-the-table system, in which workers earn considerably less. In both cases female workers sew pieces of a garment, have no opportunities for advancement, and work long hours under stressful, unhealthy conditions
        1. Seventy percent of garment workers work in outside, contract shops. These jobs compare unfavorably to welfare and so are filled by undocumented immigrant women
        2. Men are still cutters, women sewers
        3. Unlike the Lowell girls, many of the female garment workers are mothers who must settle for piecework at home or bring their children to work if relatives cannot care for them
        4. The unions: membership in the International Ladies' Garment Workers' Union (ILGWU) is 90 percent female, but the leadership is still all male

SOURCES
Jensen, Joan, and Sue Davidson, eds. *A Needle, Bobbin, Strike*. Philadelphia: Temple University Press, 1984.

Llewellyn, Chris. *Fragments from the Fire: The Triangle Shirtwaist Company Fire of March 25, 1911*. New York: Viking Penguin, 1987.

Stein, Leon. *The Triangle Fire*. (1962). Reprint, New York: Carrol and Graf/Quicksilver, 1986.

Weiner, Elizabeth, and Hardy Green. "A Stitch in Our Time: New York's Hispanic Garment Workers in the 1980s." In Jensen and Davidson, *A Needle, Bobbin, Strike*.

III. Textiles and the South
    A. The South had industrial workers since the colonial period, but large-scale

textile production did not develop until after the Civil War and the construction of textile mills in the 1880s

1. Mills depended heavily on the labor of women and children
2. Textile work served as the main conduit into industrial-waged labor for families unable to make a living as tenant farmers
3. The South had greater blending of farm and mill, with textile mills dotting the Piedmont region down to the Carolinas and into Georgia and Alabama
4. The mills were racially segregated, and mill work was reserved for "whites"; women were supervised more closely than men
5. As in Lowell, corporate paternalism declined as the numbers of desperate workers increased. In 1975 the average textile wage was only 61 percent of the national average, or $1.30 less

B. The South frequently had absentee corporate owners living in the Northeast, producing what Herbert Gutman describes as a "colonial economy"

1. The Gastonia strike—the largest and most famous of a series of walkouts in textile mills across the Carolinas and Tennessee in 1929
2. Oneita Knitting Mills—a runaway shop from Utica, New York, moved to Andrews, South Carolina. In 1963 the company decided to break the union (ILGWU). In 1964 the Civil Rights Act forced Oneita to hire black workers. The Textile Workers Union began organizing workers in 1971 and took advantage of the racial mix of workers. In 1973 Oneita workers walked off their jobs. The workers held the line against the company in a bitter six-month strike and finally won a contract
3. Greenville, South Carolina: the "most relentlessly antiunion city in the nation"

SOURCES

Byerley, Victoria. *Hard Times Cotton Mill Girls*. Ithaca: Cornell University Press, 1986.

Gutman, Herbert G. *Power and Culture: Essays on the American Working Class*. New York: Pantheon, 1987.

Hall, Jacquelyn Dowd. "Disorderly Women: Gender and Labor Militancy in the Appalachian South." In *Unequal Sisters: A Multicultural Reader in U.S. Women's History*, edited by Ellen Carol DuBois and Vicki L. Ruiz. New York: Routledge, 1990.

Miller, Marc S. *Working Lives: The Southern Exposure History of Labor in the South*. New York: Pantheon, 1980.

IV. The Southwest border: El Paso and the two-year strike at Farah Manufacturing Company in El Paso, Texas

A. A typical labor story: the owner, Willie Farah, claimed he'd rather be "dead than union." The workers had low wages, unsafe conditions, and, frequently, speedups. The local power structure harassed the strikers with police dogs and antipicket ordinances. The strikers had the support of the Amalgamated Clothing Workers of America, which mustered a boycott of Farah pants. After two years the strike ended with a weak union contract

B. The Farah strikers were virtually all Chicanas

C. The Farah strike illustrates the difficulty of unionization in the garment trade and in the face of the mobility of capital and the abundance of needy workers

D. Border cities like El Paso have been able to take advantage of documented and undocumented laborers from Mexico

SOURCE
Coyle, Laurie, Gail Hershatter, and Emily Honig. "Women at Farah: An Unfinished Story." In Jensen and Davidson, *Needle, Bobbin, Strike*.

V. Global restructuring and female workers in transnational settings

A. The emergence of the global assembly line, in which research and management are controlled by the developed countries and assembly line work is relegated to peripheral nations

1. Overlapping of the formal and informal sectors of women's work

2. Growth in the informal sector

3. The name of this old game is to move capital to the cheapest labor site

B. Life for women workers in Transnational Corporations (TNCs)

1. The "assurance" of patriarchal stability—women move from the control of their families to industrial settings, with male managers and systems to ensure control

2. Female garment workers (according to a 1984 study) earn $.16 an hour in China, $.57 cents an hour in Taiwan, and $1.00 an hour in Hong Kong. Many women remit most of their earnings to their families. In some cases (e.g., a case study of female workers in Java), families subsidize their female workers

3. In the short run TNCs offer some new economic opportunities; in the long run female workers face lack of mobility, hazardous working conditions, and low wages

C. The informal sector of the global assembly line, in which women do both production and domestic work at home, is a highly problematic "solution" to the contradictions between women's patriarchally defined domestic roles and the demand for cheap female labor

D. Situated along the Mexico-U.S. border, more than one hundred assembly plants, or *maquiladoras*, have sprung up in Ciudad Juarez, across the border from El Paso, Texas

1. Eighty-five percent of the workers are women

2. As in Lowell, plant managers like to employ women who have been recommended by current, reliable workers

3. Sexual harassment is especially blatant. Women are blamed; fears of loss of female virtue blend with fears of female independence

4. The mobility of capital, the competition for available jobs, and the fragmentation of work make organizing workers on the global assembly line a formidable task

E. Resistance of female workers: in addition to forming unions and striking, women have used innovative strategies to resist their work exploitation. Some of these "oblique strategies" include "hormone breaks," baby showers, and possession by religious spirits

1. Noncapitalist imaginations speaks to alienating class relationships (Ong)

2. The social construction of work is comparable to earlier patterns—absentee (Japanese) corporate owners, families dependent on young women's wages, segregated work sites, frequent turnover, no mobility, gender hierarchy, paternalistic mystification; moral concerns translate into economic and social control

F. Transnational worker solidarity: in March 1992 sixty demonstrators picketed the Van Heusen Factory Outlet store in Penfield, New York (a suburb of Rochester), owned by Phillips-Van Heusen (PVH), this country's leading seller of men's shirts, in support of shirt workers employed by PVH in Guatemala, who earn only two to three dollars a day and are trying to form their own union in the face of frequent physical abuse and even death threats

SOURCES

Fernandez-Kelly, Maria Patricia. "Maquiladoras: The View from the Inside." In *My Troubles Are Going to Have Trouble with Me: Everyday Trials and Triumphs of Women Workers*, edited by Karen Brodkin Sacks and Dorothy Remy. New Brunswick, N.J.: Rutgers University Press, 1984.

Ong, Aihwa. "Japanese Factories, Malay Workers: Class and Sexual Metaphors in West Malaysia." In *Power and Difference: Gender in Island Southeast Asia*, edited by Jane Monnig Atkinson and Shelly Errington. Stanford, Calif.: Stanford University Press, 1990.

Ward, Kathryn, ed. *Women Workers and Global Restructuring*. Ithaca: Cornell University Press, 1990.

The Fire Poems

On March 25, 1911, a fire at the Triangle Shirtwaist Company took the lives of 146 workers, mostly young Jewish and Italian immigrant women. Located near Washington Square Park in New York City, Triangle was one of the largest manufacturers of the sheer blouse known as a shirtwaist—emblem of a freer, more independent, and, of course, class-privileged American woman. Triangle employed hundreds of female workers under an insider contracting system. The workers were hired by a factory middle man, who negotiated with the boss. The payroll listed only the contractors and not the female workers. The women who produced the shirtwaists were both figuratively and literally invisible to the owners who profited from them.

The famous strike of 1909–10, called the Uprising of the 20,000 (some historians estimate 30,000), actually began at the Triangle factory. The strike lasted five months, as one by one the factory owners settled, but the workers at the Triangle factory had to return to work without a union contract. They lost their fight for a shorter workweek and safer and more sanitary working conditions. Rose Safran, one of the Triangle strikers, said, "If the union had won, we would have been safe, but the bosses defeated us . . . and so our friends are dead" (Stein 168).

It was spring, a late Saturday afternoon. The workers had already received their pay. The Triangle factory occupied the eighth, ninth, and tenth floors of a building that was considered technically fireproof. There was no sprinkler system; heavy metal doors opened inward and one was kept locked, and the one narrow fire escape reached only to the second floor and collapsed under the weight of escaping workers. The fire spread rapidly; workers on the ninth floor had no warning and were trapped. People along busy Washington Place heard the muffled explosion. Someone noticed "a bale of dark dress goods" come out of a window (Stein 14). He thought it was an attempt to save expensive cloth. Then another bale came down, and another. One caught the wind and opened. It was not a bale of goods; it was a young woman.

I have always felt a visceral reaction to the knowledge of this fire—a deep sense of injustice. I thought this feeling was just my own until I began researching and collecting material for an anthology of working-class women's writings and I received a number of poems about the fire from contemporary writers. One writer said, "I know that everybody writes about this fire, here's my version." I realized that I am not alone in my private interest in this fire. Others have taken it personally, too. Others have been compelled to read the old newspaper accounts, look at the photographs, actually go to the site of the fire and imagine that terrible moment of choice—fire or sky.

Working-class writers have historical and literary references that come out of lived experiences, handed-down accounts of bad and risky jobs, old newspapers, songs, family lore. They often draw on these as a set of literary antecedents—noncanonical texts that trace a history that is rarely learned in school. The Triangle fire seems to tap a collective memory of class oppression and injustice, especially for women. What is distinctive about the "fire poetry" is that most of the contemporary writers do not work in the garment trade, nor are they from New York City nor of the same race or ethnicity as the workers. What the writers have in common is gender and class, a connection to other female workers, and a call to tell the story so that it won't be forgotten. The subject of these poems is not the personal angst of the poet but, rather, the muted and silenced voices of the 146 women who died. This event—because it was a profound tragedy inflicted on common people—becomes through memory and language and history a catalyst for breaking silence and recovering working-class identity. The communal quality of the Triangle fire poetry allows the reader and the writer to engage in a ceremony of mourning, remembrance, and continual struggle.

Carol Tarlen's "Sisters in the Flames" and Safiya Henderson-Holmes's "Rituals of Spring" are fine examples of this fire poetry.

Janet Zandy

REFERENCES

Stein, Leon. *The Triangle Fire*. 1962. Reprint, New York: Carrol and Graf/Quicksilver, 1986.

Zandy, Janet. "Fire Poetry on the Triangle Shirtwaist Company Fire of March 25, 1911." *College Literature* 24 (October 1997): 33–54.

Sisters in the Flames

Carol Tarlen

for Leah

> *Spectators saw again and again pitiable companionships formed in the instant of death—girls who placed their arms around each other as they leaped. In many cases their clothing was flaming or their hair flaring as they fell.*

—"The Triangle Fire," *New York World*, 26 March 1911

Greenhorn
bent over the machine
your hair a mess of red curls
like flames I said
my words extinguished
by the wailing motors
we never spoke
together we sewed
fine linen shirtwaists
for fine ladies we worked
in our coarse gowns
and muslin aprons twelve hours
in the dank rooms
nine floors above the street
our fingers worked
the soft cloth
our coarse hands
fed the machines

Stranger
I saw you once in the elevator
going down going home
your eyes laughed
when I whispered too loud
strands of red hair falling
over your cheek and neck I
touched your red rough hand
my shoulders ached
my pay envelope tucked
in my coat pocket
for Papa for Mama

for the rent I need
a new skirt I need
a day in the sun
I need to unlock the doors
of this factory
I'm still young
I whispered and you laughed
because of course
we all were young

Sister
of the flames
take my hand
I will hold you in the cradle
of my billowing skirt
in the ache of my shoulders
the center of my palm
our sisters already dance
on the sidewalk nine
floors below the fire
is leaping through my hair
Sister I will hold you
the air will lick our thighs
grab my hand
together now fly
the sky is an unlocked door
and the machines are burning

rituals of spring

(for the 78th anniversary of the shirtwaist factory fire)

Safiya Henderson-Holmes

from bareness to fullness flowers do bloom
whenever, however spring enters a room
oh, whenever, however spring enters a room

march 25th, 1911
at the triangle shirtwaist factory
a fire claimed the lives of 146 people, mostly women,
mostly children in the plume of their lives,
in the room of their lives
begging for spring, toiling and begging for spring

and in my head
as i read the history, afraid to touch the pictures
i imagine the room, i imagine the women
dressed in pale blues and pinks,
some without heads or arms—sitting
some without legs or waist—hovering
hundreds of flowering girls tucking spring into sleeves,
tucking and tugging at spring to stay alive

and so a shirtwaist for spring
a dress with a mannish collar, blousing over breast,
blousing over sweat, tapering to fit a female waist,
tapering to fit a female breath
sheer silk, cotton, linen
hand-done pleats, hands done in by pleats
hands done in by darts and lace

colors of spring
pale blues, pale pinks, yellows, magentas, lavender, peach

secret thoughts of spring
falling in love under a full moon, forever young
with money enough to buy a flower or two,
time enough to smell it
yes, from bareness to fullness a flower will bloom
anytime, everytime spring enters a room

and here, near these machines, hundreds of flowering
girls

shirtwaist factory room 1911
crowded, hard, fast, too fast, closed windows,
locked doors, smell of piss, of sweat,
of wishes being cut to bits,
needle stabs, electric shocks, miscarriages over silk,
fading paisley, fading magenta,
falling in love will get you fired, forever old,
never fast enough, buying flowers is wasteful
so hurry, hurry, grind your teeth and soul
six dollars a week send to grandfather,
four dollars a week send to aunt ruth, sleep over the
machine and you're done for, way before you open your
eyes ma'm, madam, miss, mrs., mother, girlie
hundreds of flowering green spring girls in rows
waiting with needles in hands for spring to show

women workers
from ireland, poland, germany, france,
england, grenada, mississippi
thin clothes, thinner hopes, months full of why,
of how, of when
answers always less than their pay
but the sewing machines grew like weeds,
thick snake roots strangling the flowers everyday
strangling the roses, daises, lilies everyday
hundreds of blooming girls
hundreds of blooming, spring girls

the shirtwaist building 1911
135-feet-high, wooden, cold, three floors,
not enough stairs,
one fire escape ending in midair,
ending in the spring midair
a tender room of hundreds of blooming bright girls
hundreds of daisy bud girls who pray for spring
to enter their world,
who pray and sweat for spring to enter their world

the strike the year before
and they shouted; open the doors,
unwire the windows, more air,
more stairs, more quiet time, more fire escapes

and to the ground damn you,
and more toilets, more time to be sick,
more time to be well,
and remove the fear and slow it down,
for god's sake, slow it all time, it's spring

they shouted
hundreds of flowering girls,
hundreds of flowering girls shouted
for spring to hurry, hurry and enter their world

and
triangle won a half-day
but the doors remained locked,
windows remained wired, no extra air,
no extra quiet time, or sick time, the fear stayed,
nothing slowed
and god watched hundreds of flowering girls twirl
hundreds of flowering girls willow and twirl

march 25th 1911 at triangle
a worker is expendable
a sewing needle is not
a worker is bendable
a sewing needle is not
a worker can be sent straight to hell
a sewing needle is heaven sent
and must be protected well
a sewing needle is the finger of god
and must be protected well
over hundreds of flowering girls,
hundreds of flowering sweet dandelion girls

march 25th, smoke
smoke, stopping the machines
run to wired windows, run to locked doors,
run to the one and only fire escape,
everyone run to the air
hundreds of flowering girls

smoke
stopping eyes, stopping hearts, stopping worlds
elevator move faster, elevator you are a machine
managed by a human being move faster, c'mon faster

carry all the flowering girls, carry all the sweet,
sweet orchid girls

fire
catching bouquets of girls in a corner, tall, long
stemmed lilies on fire in a corner,
from bloom to ashes in a corner, smell
them in the rain hundreds of tulip girls

on a window ledge
pliés for life, on a window ledge lovely, ribboned young
ladies on their tiptoes twirling, twirling
an arabesque for life
hundreds of flowering girls
smell them in the rain
hundreds of jasmine girls

the ladders were too short
the hoses were too short
the men holding the nets were not gods, only men
who were never trained to catch falling bodies, or
falling stars, or hundreds of flowering girls, hundreds
of carnation bud girls

and the girls
were girls not angels jumping,
not goddesses flying or hovering
they smashed, they broke into
large pieces, smell them in the rain

and the sidewalks
opened in shame to meet the flowering girls
the sidewalks opened in such horrible shame to cradle
the remains of violets
and the gutters
bled for hours, choking on bones, shoes, buttons,
ribbons, holy sewing needles
the gutters bled for hours all the colors of spring
the cool magenta of delicate spring

and the fire ate
the locked doors and the wired windows,
ate the fast machines
in their narrow rooms, ate the lace and hand-done pleats,
the silk, the cotton, the linen,

the crisp six dollars a week, the
eternal buzz of someone else's dreams
nightmares and screams of quiet girls,
loud skull-cracking noises from shy girls
smell them in the rain, the lilacs, daffodils
in the rain

spring, 78 years later
triangle is now part of a university, with offices
and polished intellect, arched unwired windows,
hydraulically controlled and unlocked doors,
air conditioning, swivel chairs, marble walls and fire
alarms

but oh, hundreds of flowering girls still roam
hundreds of blushing spring girls still roam
78 years later in the paint, in the chrome
in the swivel of the chairs
hundreds of blossoms twirling in the air
daring to descend if ever, oh ever the fire comes again

yes, like lead they will drop
if ever, oh ever the fire comes again
to hundreds of flowering girls
smell them in the rain, iris, peonies, magnolias,
bending for the rain

Working-Class Texts and Theory

Readerly/Writerly Relations and Social Change

The Maimie Papers as Literature

Carole Anne Taylor

A symposium on race and ethnicity in the United States views the documentary film *Who Killed Vincent Chin?* and watches spellbound as violent destruction of Japanese cars creates the context for the beating death of Vincent Chin. Afterward the discussion does not center on how General Motors encouraged the exercise of destruction or who stood to gain from scapegoating the Japanese. Rather, it focuses on the shocking brutality of the workers and their terrible ignorance of racist stereotypes. Student discussions of Frank Norris's *The Octopus* or Rebecca Harding Davis's *Life in the Iron Mills* acknowledge the pathos of poor characters, but focus primarily on the problematics of art depicting "deprived" social conditions, or students reading Maimie Pinzer's *The Maimie Papers* foreground her self-repudiating anti-Semitism and her "manipulation" of her benefactors even as they sentimentalize how the correspondence with the patrician Fanny Howe "allowed her to grow." All such instances attest to a trying pedagogical problem in teaching working-class materials to either largely middle-class students or students who have internalized middle-class values (and therefore, to at least some degree, perhaps most students): the sensibilities they find in the voices of those talking about lived experience often seem less insightful, less artful, less complex in their understanding of social relations than do the writerly sensibilities of more privileged writers, theorists, or observers who analyze or portray the experiences of both working and nonworking poor.

Here I describe experience in teaching and understanding *The Maimie Papers* as a work of literature, one with a provocative relation-in-difference to the genre of autobiography and the modes of realism and naturalism. I want to suggest that finely argued positions about who is or is not a working-class writer, or exactly what the parameters of definition for a working class might be, may matter less to pedagogy than does close attention to the positioning of both readers and writers in relation to what a writer describes. Rather than pursuing some calculus with which to determine the class positioning of readers, writers, or texts, one might more fruitfully ask about how the world of writing relates to lived experience and why it matters. Although classes specifically on working-class literature or traditions of dissent might well use more self-consciously theoretical approaches to how class intersects with other social categories, my approach presumes a survey class that reads Harriet Jacobs's slave narrative alongside Herman Melville's "Benito Cereno," Pinzer alongside William Dean Howells or Henry James or Norris, and Meridel Le Sueur alongside John Dos Passos or John Steinbeck. Here the primary task involves framing work with texts in ways that provoke seeing a writer's representation of life struggles as part of a specifically literary complexity, different from what they recognize in the overt "literariness" of James or William Faulkner, but no less interesting or artful. Insisting that students engage Maimie Pinzer *as a writer*, rather than as victim or anomaly, can provoke engaged discussion about the character of writerly lives that are not synonymous with social privilege. Concomitantly, focusing on how *The Maimie Papers* engages its readers in readerly/writerly relations intersects several important theoretical discussions about class and resistance, most notably, the contemporary idea that resistance always participates to some degree in what it resists (an idea applicable to both readers and writers).[1]

Maimie Pinzer's letters represent for readers problems of editing and evaluation not conventional to most literature classes. Yet, because she wrote outside her own understanding of received literary genres, she provides a provocative enactment of writing that becomes literary in the act of negotiating tensions between real and written experience. Although it makes pedagogical sense for my students of twentieth-century American literature to read Norris's 1900 novel, *The Octopus*, first and then refer comparatively back to this earlier text when reading *The Maimie Papers* (written 1910–22), I want here to foreground work on Maimie Pinzer's life story in letters, referring back to *The Octopus*—as we do in class—when its relation-in-difference as a privileged, canonical text helps to differentiate how texts may embody conflicts they do not overtly represent. Such a reading under the influence of pedagogy intends to address many concerns common to anyone reading or teaching working-class literature, but readers should understand my narrative past tense as putting a great deal of pedagogical trial and error under happy erasure, emerging instead with a combinatory, idealized version of how the teaching works when it does, yet not losing sight entirely, I hope, of what it costs to teach in ways that chafe away at students' habitual ways of thinking about texts and about themselves.[2]

My primarily middle-class students tend to take at face value the implied readerly/writerly relations of Maimie's letters, as though eavesdropping on a private correspondence that has no very sustained or artful development.[3] Because so many of her letters serve clearly instrumental purposes—justifying money spent or choices made and rehearsing the hardships of her daily struggle for subsistence—they may seem "unliterary," especially when they overtly plead for approval from her addressee-benefactors. When asked about what characterizes artful or literary texts, students generally respond that literary texts show complex developments in theme, structure, and style, developments that reach some kind of climax in which all the parts, usually through indirection, in some way show forth their connections. This, they often argue, implies that the writer has explicit aesthetic control over the genre or genres in which she writes, a kind of aesthetic self-consciousness they see nowhere in *The Maimie Papers*. Thus, the sequential tasks I ask them to work on with the text address both the nature of developmental complexity in the letters and the relation-in-difference to the representation of social change in a writer such as Norris, with both realist and naturalist novels before him as fictional models. If presented before close reading, classes tend to resist the argument that though Maimie's letters may embody tensions not explicitly resolved by her, this does not differentiate her from those writers writing firmly within specifically literary modes or generic conventions. The resistance resembles, I think, that experienced by those in social science disciplines trying to teach that those with power and privilege also possess ideologies, that white folks also have race, heterosexuals a stylized self-presentation, and so on.

Among initial responses many complain that the chronic suffering recounted in *The Maimie Papers* wears them down as readers and that the verisimilitude of daily, recurrent hardship has a relentless sameness rather than cumulative power. Classes as a whole may fall into a felt superiority to Maimie's anti-Semitic repudiation of her own Jewishness, her manipulations of her benefactors, and her own class consciousness. And they may chide her for a cloying subservience, even while acknowledging the conditions that produce it. Over the years I have tried (often unsuccessfully, when acts of repression are at stake) to respond to aesthetic judgments grounded in social distance not with contrary judgments, but, rather, with specific analytical tasks designed to lead to revisionary reading—and, if not to that, then at least to framing responses in ways more aware of the social tensions implicit within aesthetic judgments. After initial responses I ask students to form groups in which they look for evidence of changes in Maimie's concerns or departures from the terms of these early self-repudiations. Depending on prior discussion, they may choose to divide the tasks according to Maimie's developing social views on class, Jewishness, education, prostitution, and philanthropy or according to literary categories (developments in theme, structure, style, tonality). In either case what the groups discover tends toward mutual and overlapping insights about precisely the correspondences and interrelations they have formerly designated as without art.

In describing developmental changes, students sometimes initially presume that changes in Maimie's ideas and self-representations occur because of the good influence of Fanny Howe, and in this case their explanations of those changes range from "Mrs. Howe gave her self-esteem" to "the correspondence with Mrs. Howe allows Maimie to develop." But when asked to find passages in which Maimie herself either identifies changes in her own frame of reference or evinces such change, Mrs. Howe fades from the center of discussion. Without diminishing the value of Mrs. Howe's encouragement and material support, the focus on Maimie's changes—both in her concerns and in her self-representations—show little evidence that Maimie moves beyond either her anti-Semitism or her social pride because of contact with Fanny Howe. Rather, her own experience of discrimination and sexism in trying to make a living in business and her engagements in the lives of needy young women spur her to more intense personal reflection on social conditioning and injustice, reflection that shapes her relation to her correspondence.

Students variously trace how Maimie's early self-repudiations alter as her social vision develops. They note that Maimie, like any of us, cannot entirely reject the constructions that mold her early values, and yet she progressively supplants judgments based on those values with judgments based on social action. In the value she places on Bennie, her loyal and socially progressive husband, Mr. and Mrs. Goldstein, and others, she largely overcomes earlier stereotypical associations of Jewishness with loudness, fatness, acrimoniousness, and so on, even though her descriptions may still betray vestiges of those associations. Similarly, early emphasis on the lack of manners and crudity in language or gesture gives way to concern for the exigencies and constraints of others' lives, even though she may still note who appears clean or neat or well-spoken. Students work out that, as her social vision of a home for "unfortunates" matures into fruition, she increasingly treats character as shaped by possibility—i.e., as nurtured or distorted by social conditioning rather than somehow deserved or earned. They note, too, that just as she much less often refers to bad character or habits as essential traits, so she tends increasingly to identify her own life with the lives of those she helps. Stories from her own past, once told to illustrate her mother's or brother's failures in sympathy, become stories told to illustrate the commonality of young girls' desires. She even comes full circle: whereas she once differentiated herself because of superior education or manners from other women fallen into prostitution, she now identifies fully:

> And somehow—Stella is Maimie. Do you get the idea?
> I am afraid I am not able enough to describe how I mean this. But I know every heartache and longing "Maimie" had. And instead of running true to form—which is, that being older and not desiring the same pleasures, one must condemn them in a younger person—I foresee what will make this girl's lot easier and relieve that terrible pressure that everyone condemns her—and love her instead. (274)

The "pleasures," of course, refer to material and not bodily pleasures (sometimes misread), but the issue of prostitution itself represents a significant pedagogical quagmire. One could devote a full semester to dealing with many students' feelings that only starvation could force *them* to such a thing; they often have little sense of prostitution as a necessary consequence of differentials in gender and power relations and even less of the way in which, by an extension that is not just figurative, constructions of sexuality imply an economic or market context as present in marriage contracts as on street corners. They do engage readily, however, in thinking about how "who pays for what" affects all gender relations, and, having at least introduced the terms of an argument that none of us escape those connections, I try to get students to focus, instead, on how what Maimie feels she can and cannot write about her life matters to the writing. How does the process of writing for an audience change as the letters progress, and how does she conceive of literary genres and her own relation to them?

Perceptive students note that passages some formerly described as "manipulative" seem to struggle to accord with the unacknowledged rules of what her correspondents expect from her and what she might expect from them. (Judith Butler puts this well when she describes how "the production of the *un*symbolizable, the unspeakable, the illegible is also always a strategy of social abjection" [190].) The early letters talk much of the financial hardship of a "clean" life, and adopt the locutions of the society in referring to her attempts to "live right." Thus, forays into the temptations beyond the "life of prayer" recommended by Mr. Welch usually acknowledge that their articulation belongs to a forbidden realm. Even with Fanny Howe, Maimie resorts to frequent circumlocution and makes frequent reference to the impossibility of total honesty, as in: "Now I believe I told you all, and it is off my conscience; for I believe though I try to be absolutely honest with you, I can't help but let some deceit creep out. I know I wrote you that I did not need anything—and it is because it is galling that I do. I don't mind the sordidness of it all as much as the thought that I can't help myself" (15). That this letter ends with an appeal for information of a very different kind marks the felt assymetry of the correspondents' roles: "Will you write me something about your home? If you have a dog and what kind—or something I can place around you, as I only can think of you now in that chair with your hat on, and that sort of awes me" (18). In fact, Maimie's early repudiations of other prostitutes and the pains she takes to differentiate herself from them occur frequently in defensive assurances to Fanny Howe that she would never embarrass her, as in her protestation that "you need never fear that I would get into some public place; I don't have to do that. I never did that before, never did anything even one-tenth as low, and consider that the last gasp. I never associated with low women—I don't think I ever met, to talk to the second time, a woman who was publicly known to live other than she should. I shun such people" (77).

In Maimie's early epistolary personae, students find all kinds of textual evidence that she understands as such both her acts of self-justification and even the contrition her correspondent's role demands, and that she makes fine distinctions between how she writes to Mr. Welch and how she writes to Fanny Howe. She explains to the latter, for example, the self-consciously "therapeutic" role adopted by the "father" in Mr. Welch, when even in writing about a time of severe depression, she begins with an extrapolation on his role as evaluator:

> Mr. Welch . . . when I first began to correspond with him, would send back my letters if there were any grammatical errors in them: he made just three corrections altogether, and then ceased. I never forgot the corrections, and never made the mistake again. So lately, in a recent letter, I asked him if he would not do as he did in the beginning—that is, tell me of my errors. And he answered that he certainly should have corrected errors had there been any, but there had not been *one*. But—he would suggest that I adopt "brevity of style"! (121)

Above all, she senses a need to reinforce her correspondents by showing improvement, or at least being hopeful, often putting off writing because, as she once put it, "I have no excuse except that I hated to write to complain and I have wanted to do nothing else" (125).

Structurally, students begin to relate self-repudiating tonalities to felt abjection, and they begin to understand the logic of why Maimie does not tell the story of her own prison experience or describe bodily suffering from venereal disease until much later. Later tonalities have more assertive resonance, as when, at the end of a paragraph pleading with Fanny Howe not to continue to suggest that she perform her social work in an institutional setting, she insists that "prisons and institutions for reform should not be tolerated by Christian people" (257). A self-referential layering attends her description of the difference in Stella's voice on her return from a horrific experience in a public ward for venereal disease: "Though her appearance has changed considerably, her general mental condition has changed more. I mean by that, that she asserts herself. Prior to this, since the time I first knew her, she was absolutely without opinion or desire, and it would be hard to imagine any one more acquiescent and 'ductile' (I just learned this word). While she is not aggressive now, nor disputatious, still there is a change; and it is one for the better" (300).

As Maimie's stories of others acquire more self-referential layering, they also undertake acts of transformation as she herself moves from subservience to passionate explication and from viewing her own life as exceptional to viewing it as representative. Such transformation mitigates against mere chronology because—far from depending on editorial selection or the letters' dates for coherence, the only kinds of "made" coherence initially felt relevant—they cumulatively order personal experience in designs that develop self-reflective themes, weave others' stories into her own, and use flashbacks, foreshadowings, and levels of irony to elaborate a more and more replete social vision. True, the letters present a loosely episodic structure in which links between events and moods have an often brutal chronicity. But students speculate that, as Maimie works out for herself what forms unpatronizing and noncondescending help to others might take, she also revises how she thinks about writing and what she values in storytelling. They find accumulating evidence of resistance to the "insincerity" the writing demands, especially that of the later accounting to benefactors beyond the former inner circle.

Increasingly, Maimie establishes the habit of writing letters that go beyond obligatory reportage, and, increasingly, she testifies to being drawn into narrative art, even when describing incidents in her own life. Understandably, such narration may lose its sense of a specific epistolary address: "I did not think to tell you this story so thoroughly; but I felt, when I began, I just wanted you to know: then, as I wrote, it seemed to be as though I was writing the story of that particularly ugly part of my life as though it was a narrative. Somehow, I feel now as though perhaps I wrote you this before" (197). Students find changes evinced in style as well as narrative tonality, as Maimie moves from that vaguely artificial, even occasionally sickly-sweet style of the Brownie and Poke episodes to the much more colloquial, earthy, assertive mode in which she describes her social work with "errant" young women. In 1912, after hearing of a pet by the name of Brownie in the Howe household, Maimie tells a story about the "tragic" end of a different Brownie, framing it formally with, "Perhaps you could tell the children about this little Brownie," at the beginning and closing with: "I hope I haven't bored you with this tale about Brownie. I feel you and the children might some-

times think of your Brownie as our Brownie on earth again for another lease of
life" (120). What might have been a pithy story about battling a neighbor who
poisoned dogs becomes a somewhat cloyingly sentimental one about dogs who
eat with refinement, press noses against the glass "crying to get in," and end in
pathos. Framed as though in a genteel tradition highlighting fine feminine feeling, as though a set-piece for a "literary" magazine of the kind sent to her by
Fanny Howe, the story has little of the stark expressivity of later stories about her
own life and those of her "girls." Increasingly concerned more with agency than
with pathos, she confines sentimentality to tales of her dog Poke, who gradually
diminishes in importance as her emotional engagements turn to young women in
need and danger. With an imaginative range that draws from her own past, from
the pasts of those whose stories she tells, and from her own social and philosophical reflections, she increasingly moves toward narration and storytelling with not
one whit of sentimentality (such as the story about her being imprisoned on the
evidence of her mother and sexually abusive uncle as a punishment for running
away from home). And in so many episodes, what she has always prized as a well-
educated, literary life reveals itself as limited in its social vision (as in her meeting
with Mary Antin, for example, whose "conceited" self-promotion and rudely
insensitive treatment of those who have come to admire her convinces Maimie of
the social boorishness that may accompany a genteel, writerly existence).[4]

Toward the end of the letters students discover that Maimie evinces much
more overt resistance to matching epistolary tonalities to rhetorical goals; by the
time she observes to Fanny Howe that she has had to tell her mother that "I am
obliged to write in fine detail of my expenses," the observation has a critical edge.
She makes almost purposefully dry, formal reports on what Mr. Welch has insisted
on calling "The Montreal Christ's Mission for Friendless Girls," despite her conviction that coming to a "mission for friendless girls" would be tantamount to
admitting defeat. After nearly two pages on the harmful implications of calling
her home "a mission for friendless girls," Maimie only *seems* to follow Mr. Welch's
request that she ask Fanny Howe for her advice, making the very question part of
the explanation: "Mr. Welch . . . thinks you far more capable of knowing what is
better than he does, and in this matter *and in all matters* . . . [writes that] I should
follow any advice you'd be kind enough to give. Therefore I ask you what you
think of making this mission a 'different kind' in more ways than one—as, for
instance, leaving it nameless?" (344). Still conscious of Howe or Welch as
audience, she nevertheless prioritizes her understanding that the girls need relationships, stories to tell, in order to enhance their own changes. With the impossibility of interactive relationships across the correspondences she undertakes
before her, she questions Mrs. Howe about how to write another donor:

> Shall I disillusion her and lose the possible benefits? Shall I write as if to
> compel her attention, and thus reap the benefits? . . . I am capable of
> doing either but is it sincere?
>
> What shall I do? I hate to write knowing it isn't sincere. I hate to
> accept her benefits knowing they are given under false pretenses. And

yet, aren't most charitable things fostered under the same conditions—
and should I sit down my personal feelings and be insincere for the girls,
who are at present in greater need than ever . . . ? (385)

Maimie's increasing emphasis on the therapeutic intimacy of exchanged life
stories gradually eclipses any mention of autobiography, and students find particularly remarkable the correspondence between changes in personal aspiration and the function of storytelling. Throughout, Fanny Howe has encouraged
Maimie to work on an autobiography, but neither she nor Maimie herself conceived of her letter writing as relevant to the project. Even at the height of her
epistolary output, Maimie bemoans having no time to write anything of literary
value:

> I had wanted to write about the possibility of writing my autobiography,
> as you suggested, but as I couldn't seem to feel sure of my own opinions
> on the subject, I didn't write. There seems so many reasons why I could
> not do it. For instance, the little time—even if it only took fifteen min-
> utes a day—is so hard to spare. There are so many tasks—stockings
> always to be darned, letters to write, sometimes work for the office—that
> I don't feel I could accomplish much, if I did start. I really feel I could
> write it—if I could only write a bit at a time. And maybe I will try it; and
> if it goes easy, keep on with it. (199)

"Letters to write" takes its place among darning and office work as a duty keeping
her from autobiography, even the kind that might be done "a bit at a time"! Later,
with a replete social philosophy intact, Maimie uses her own life story to make
others at ease and to encourage their own tellings, wearing down their resistance
to her status as "social worker" with frank and empathic self-revelation. Now she
tells the stories of her "girls" as they themselves tell it, if not directly quoting
them, then as a second-order telling imitating their own narrations. The work
she seeks for her charges prioritizes self-worth and a cooperative context and thus
corresponds to the value of a storytelling outside the context of writing as production. An interactive intimacy foregrounds the human context and function of
storytelling art, rather than demonstrating the virtuosity of a writerly art. Quite
opposite to a cult of individual genius, Maimie regards this storytelling as belonging not just to herself but to many; its place in her own development, cultural and
otherwise, stands available to any of those entering her home.

Relatedly, Maimie's social philosophy informs her critical appreciation of literature, enabling her to contrast the sincerity and self-revelatory quality of Oscar
Wilde's writing in prison with the letters and poems of an anonymous prisoner
published in *Harper's Monthly* under the name of X107. Earlier she has remarked
on qualities of the books and articles sent to her by Mrs. Howe with self-deprecating
appreciation, as when she asks for explanations of meanings "beyond my powers
of comprehension," yet now she sees that the protective timidity of X107 covers
for unacknowledged privilege: home as a clean and lovely place that she aban-

doned, regular meals, and presumably schooling. Some students felt that Maimie showed a lack of sympathy for mental illness (not seeing how Maimie refers it to dominant definitions), but most of them focused on the primacy of the value placed on a self-revelation that works through to a common humanity rather than merely inducing pity. They note how Maimie moves from the superficial symptom of the pseudonym to more writerly complaints about originality and authenticity which contrast markedly with her earlier, clearly derivative critical judgments:

> I don't share her viewpoint. (I don't like to even think that "X107," so I've got her fixed as Ruth Ramsey, and that because she reminds me of Ruth who was an associate of mine at one time, and who wasn't unlike X107 in her utterances—so X107 is now Ruth Ramsey to me.) The viewpoint about people knowing about her past and the prison term, etc. . . . I'd have liked her to be original enough to want to live now in the open. *I am what I am*. It sticks in one's throat at first to admit it, but it gets easier. . . .
>
> I am afraid you will think I take a great deal on myself to criticise anything which has so much in it to excite pity and not criticism. . . . I warn you that I am practicing a code now that admits of no cheap sentimentality, for I find that is as bad—perhaps worse—than cold indifference. (373–74)

Maimie's supposed "failure" to produce an autobiography has clear relevance to students' frequent opinion that *The Maimie Papers* "just ends," as opposed to the artful pulling together of textual elements in more literary works. The opinion asks that the class pay attention to what gives nonfictional works the "sense of an ending." Does the fact that the letters stop so suddenly deprive the reader of that sense? What themes does the final silence bring to an end? How does this ending reflect Maimie Pinzer's final view of the human purpose of storytelling? Maimie's coming to self-confidence about her own perceptions of "errant" girls (her quotation marks, by this point) and what they need coincides with her rejection of benefactors' patronizing and judgmental interference, that of the "Rescue Band," Mrs. Yerkes, and the woman dubbed "Creeping Jesus" who tries to persuade girls to leave houses of prostitution though she herself "never speaks ten words without religious references" (345). But she also more subtly suggests, despite the ritual incantations of goodness, that certainly Mr. Welch and even Mrs. Howe do not understand about her as much as they think nor as much as do the girls whom she is committed to helping. Describing how a first girl inducts a second into her home by telling stories about the photographs, the books, Maimie herself, and other household lore, Maimie writes to Howe, "This second girl generally comes in knowing more about me and my affairs than you do—really" (342).

With self-referential insight Maimie demonstrates how the development of taste accompanies the development of intimacy and the capacity to tell stories

about "our little circle," so that the best therapy attends the girl's conviction that
she can "be one of us" (343).[5] Students speculate, initially, that, if not dead, then
Maimie might well have slipped back into a life of prostitution, perhaps at her age
and condition of life more degrading than she could admit to her correspondents.
But I like to suggest a different but related possibility, that having discovered the
importance of ongoing engagements with those whom she sought to help
through developing a sense of their own agency and worth—not as a benefactress
but, rather, as a kindred spirit who understood because she had been there—she
sensed something of the barriers keeping even Mrs. Howe from understanding
her as she tried to understand others. In the penultimate letter of 1918 she
describes nursing others through the influenza epidemic, along with the loss of
her sister-in-law and her own unborn baby. She works at raising her deceased
sister-in-law's children and has not "the remotest idea as to plans for the future"
(414). Over four years later the last letter refers to uneven correspondence
(including her having failed to write for over a year after receipt of a letter), and
she reports living in a resident hotel and teaching English to a Filipino student.
Significantly, the end of the letter begins, "You haven't any idea of what I am
thinking of these days" (416). The rhetorical need to ask for advice has receded
to an empty convention, here only a promise to do so at some time in the future
because "just now I can't go into it." Instead, a final paragraph circumscribes both
an intellectual aspiration very much intact and a skepticism about formal education appropriate to such formidable self-education: "I want to go to school—i.e., I
want to take up the study of something. I am fearful lest my equipment is inadequate. I haven't any idea of what I should aim for, and above it all, I am so afraid
that I overestimate the worthwhileness of it. I haven't discussed this with Ira,
mainly because in his estimation I know now more than anyone alive! However,
I know what I have yet to know" (416). The line "I am so afraid that I overestimate the worthwhileness of it" followed by "I know what I have yet to know" suggests a revisionary view of her own educative agency and a revision, too, in how
to read this sense of an ending.

Whether or not Maimie could have written and chose not to or simply suc-
cumbed to her life's exigencies, her progress justifies a story that becomes entirely
oral, with the social interactions it thrives on replacing the formal correspondence to her benefactors. In response to a question about what kind of genre the
letters as a whole represent, students distinguish the work not only from autobiography, realism, and naturalism but also from an oral history, which is often
more like a written tradition in its recording of a life story, told in a narrative past
tense and overviewing the whole of a life lived up to the point at which narration
begins. Part essay, part life story, part social philosophy, now a nongenre and now
an outlaw genre, some agree that what at first seemed a disappointing nonending
in fact approaches a kind of meta-realism. Life changes have a recursive effect on
prior telling, and the writer evinces the ultimate control of leaving the writing.
Maimie's relation to the real bears only tangential relation to what literary critics
have called "realism" in the writing of fiction; no -ism applies well here because
she conceives no difference between her relationship with those to whom she

writes and the writing itself: her poses, confessions, pleas, and, finally, her self-reflective explanation of her own differences and allegiances. Yet in its unraveling of the connections between economic need and the writing itself lies a critique of the social relations on which the correspondence relies. And all agree, too, that Maimie has rearticulated the terms of her own legitimacy and, in so doing, has called into question the basis of the correspondence's intimacy and purpose.

Now students refer back to *The Octopus* in order to take up more global issues about how writing relates to social injustice and social change. In creating the character of Presley, a participant-observer desirous of "capturing" the struggle of ranchers against the railroad and banks in California's San Joaquin Valley, Norris's fiction also presents complex autobiographical self-reference. The literary forms to which Presley most often refers, romance and epic—the heroic genres—not coincidentally inform Norris's own description. The obvious difference in the fictional and nonfictional status of novel and letters notwithstanding, both writers reveal understandings about literature and genre have self-referential relevance to how they think about the literary qualities of their own work in relation to the lives of what Norris conceives as "the masses" and what Pinzer regards as "unfortunates" like herself. Norris's writer-observer Presley aspires to a great epic poem about the ranchers' struggle with the railroad, and Norris comes to California to research that same struggle and write about it in extremely lyrical prose. Both maintain their distance from social turmoil, but Presley becomes ridiculous the moment he tries to resolve felt tensions between writing and acting. It would be hard not to see some correspondence between Presley's coming to terms with a necessary impotence and Norris's turning Presley toward the shepherd Vanamee's mystically optimistic romanticism. The writer's conflicted will to expression and to action climaxes in a scene in which Presley frightens himself into hysteria by throwing a silly, impotent bomb, only to feel prostrate with relief when the bomb fails to kill S. Behrman, the railroad magnate. Later he "discovers," in direct confrontation with the banker Shelgrim, that he has misconceived problems and misdirected his energies; that is, he feels himself pitifully outargued by the authoritative overview of corporate power. It occurs neither to Presley nor, presumably, to Norris that an actual participant in the struggle might also tell its story; protagonist and author both imagine a heroic tale that must be produced by the outsider-observer.

Because the class's consideration of *The Octopus* has understood both narrative discussion of genre and the character of Presley as self-referential, it now mitigates against the critical fashion to take a fiction as *only* a fiction, suspending disbelief in any writer's agency or responsibility. Even without the pressure from his publisher to make the moral dilemma of the contest between ranchers and railroad more "equal-handed," the choice of a figural consciousness so much more detached from the working-class characters than from the potentially "heroic" or "tragic" ranchers mediates any portrait of their suffering, a suffering depicted primarily in sentimental vignettes. Where does the story of Mrs. Hooven's gradual starvation and her daughter Minna's inevitable prostitution—

partly sentimental realism and partly naturalistic melodrama—fit into the self-referential discussions of the epic, the heroic, and the romantic? Although Norris does not heroize his own relation to his characters' supposedly "real" experience, yet—as so often in American fiction—when he gets closest to addressing what writing may or may not have to do with social action, he thrusts his alter ego into fits of self-abnegation and the intellectual's ultimately passive cynicism about social change, retreating, in the end, to the latent romance that has hovered behind much of the prose. Yet neither the plight of workers nor the idyll of Vanamee and the two Angeles (lacking the symbolic authority of fully conceived romance) has strong structural ties to the battle between commercial and ranching interests. Though narration has at regular intervals distanced itself from the effete, browbeating, even effeminate side of Presley, Norris ends with narrative encomiums to a kind of generative fatalism that couples an almost perfect cynicism with a romantic paean to necessary cycles. The "WHEAT," capitalized like an earlier inchoate "FORCE," becomes the only agency in a book that comes down on the side of an inevitable distance between social action and writing, with the writer's attempts to portray social turmoil always already doomed. Despite the triumph of corporate capital, the ruin of the ranchers, and the total destruction of all the book's working poor, the "WHEAT" moves onto ships "to feed thousands of starving scarecrows on the barren plains of India," and, wondrously, "the individual suffers but the race goes on" (whose suffering and whose race?): "The larger view always and through all shams, all wickednesses, discovers the truth that will, in the end, prevail, and all things surely, inevitably, resistlessly work together for good" (458).

A class's comparative invocation of an earlier reading of *The Octopus* works to suggest that Norris's writing, incorporating much of a romantic realist's representation into a naturalist's design, should demonstrate that Norris has no more "control" over his ideological framework than does Maimie Pinzer over that of her letters. Rather, each in some way exemplifies the conflicts represented, conflicts that may or may not be articulated in the texts as such. Although the fictive world and the naturalist's premise may seem to endow Norris with more self-consciously artful "distance" from his subject, such distance becomes itself part of conflicted fictional representation. In Norris's case, narration has increasingly conflicted relation to Presley as figural consciousness, both mocking his effete detachment yet simulating his insights and social judgments. In Pinzer's case the immediacy of the letters' address, their presentation as self-validation and justification, initially make Maimie's motivations vulnerable to charges that self-serving overcomes the formal or "aesthetic" values associated with art.[6] Yet an overall logic orders a development that increasingly displaces the values of genres received as literary with those of an oral storytelling inseparable from both social solidarity and social change.

Both Pinzer and Norris face the problems of taking real-life experience as subject matter for writing. That Norris retreats to a romantic idealization of stable order without moral demands for social action should interest us no more than that Pinzer wrote beyond her audience's conception of the reasons for writing and, therefore, disappeared into a world more characterized by oral stories told for therapeutic or salvational ends (the felt validation for most orature, after all) than by stories meant to publish and sell as literature.[7] In the experiential present tense of a perennially fraught immediacy, the letters unfold a growth toward a storytelling self-sufficiency unnoticed by either Mrs. Howe or Mr. Welsh, though moved forward by wide reading in any number of genres. In review, students remember that they initially complained that Maimie's letters repetitively document her daily circumstances, seemingly important to her but for them bearing a tedious verisimilitude. When asked questions about an implied audience, they easily named Fanny Howe and Mr. Welch as Maimie's straightforward addressees, talking about Maimie's narration as though this audience mandated a unitary persona. Now they find evidence of multiple and developing personae, double consciousness, irony, and complex negotiations of her correspondents' roles at every turn. In contrast, the students remember immediately understanding as literary Norris's overt encomiums to Presley's—and presumably his own—attempts to understand his own role as "a poet of the people." Having engaged the text as *literature*, they no longer experience it primarily as an activity of social distancing but, instead, as an interpretive activity.

The theoretical issues emerging in teaching *The Maimie Papers* help distinguish the work from works that necessarily describe the suffering of the poor from above, as characters whose suffering represents some aesthetic dilemma for the writer, even though their subjectivity has no representation in writing. In addition to arguing for the explicit relation of *The Maimie Papers* to aesthetic traditions and problems (as opposed to its conventional status as a social or historical "document"), I want to recommend a paradigm for encouraging all students to take their own readerly assumptions as part of intellectual difficulty and then to move forward to consider how writerly positioning might also affect how to read. Especially when interpreting works embedded in experience not one's own, in an environment in which issues of class may differ, conflict, or overlap with issues of gender, race, ethnicity, sexuality, and other social categories, it seems especially important for teachers of working-class materials to work with and through, rather than simply acknowledge, the importance of relational social positions. The distance between *The Octopus* and *The Maimie Papers* is not only that between what critics have considered literature or not but also between very differently situated conflicts regarding writing and social action.

Pedagogically, the sequence of tasks and discussion has moved readerly concerns closer to writerly ones, with "What does it mean?" at least temporarily displaced by "How does the writing represent the life?" Even without Mikhail Bakhtin or concepts of heteroglossia or the dialogical, such discussion encourages students to reflect on how taking Maimie Pinzer seriously as a "writer" of "literature" means changing our conceptions of both.[8] For writers, one's own experience does not necessarily disallow imaginative creation of very differently placed social experience; nevertheless, writing always in some way embodies felt social tensions of which writers are more or less aware, and perhaps, especially with those distances they understand as simply natural, a part of the way the world is.

For readers, critical understanding that writing embodies social tensions very differently for those writing from different social positions need not imply an essentialism that sees some straightforward relation between a writer's social class and the interests served by that writing.[9] Rather than an autobiography conceived retrospectively and ordered according to an overview of development that fits some received paradigm of knowledge and value, Maimie Pinzer's letters develop in form, structure, style, and theme even while in some ways still participating in what they resist.[10] The analytical tasks performed by groups of students ideally help them see the degree to which they associate the literary with the privilege of control over one's own life and, by extension, with control over one's own life-as-text.

Read relationally, *The Maimie Papers* and *The Octopus* suggest alternative and differently complex cases of writers representing social changes contemporary to their own lives—cases suggesting that writing about experience one vicariously witnesses or imagines has as conflicted relation to social experience as has writing about experience as it happens—in the conflicted realm of a present only just become a narrated past. And if, as Roland Barthes suggested in *S/Z*, literature has as its goal the conversion of the reader into the writer, then the ultimate accolade to reading is that it encourages us to become writers, to undertake new projects. Thus, I am pleased when a student moves from thinking about her own positioning to thinking about the writer's positioning to suggesting excitedly that she would not be able to judge the explicitly literary value of Maimie's letters until she had read them all with an eye to just that, editing with different criteria than those steering Rosen and Davidson. (And is there any greater testimony to editorial work than inspiring one to imagine a new edition based on one's own interpretive logic?) Other students criticize the representation of the letters on the book's back cover, which identifies its relevance to women's studies, history, and Jewish studies but not to literary studies. They find the mirror figure cited in the *New York Times*'s blurb inadequate to Maimie's development ("Fanny Howe became a mirror in which Maimie could know, speak and feel her thoughts, unacceptable though many of them were to polite society and, often, to Maimie herself") and they reject as condescending the domestic verb *spicing*, the trivializing "tale of woe," and the devaluative adjectives and genres in the *Atlantic Monthly*'s plug: "Maimie wrote vividly and well, spicing her tale of woe with sharp little vignettes, conversations, and quirky reflections."

Considering readerly/writerly relations not only necessitates self-reflective analyses of social positioning, but it also discourages the tendency to take as givens the generic parameters of literary tradition (so that, e.g., only novels illuminate other novels). Students have familiarity with criticism that takes as formally irrelevant any consideration of an author's lived relation to the social worlds she or he creates, and they take classes in literature which proceed as though the meanings of texts reside somehow "in" the texts themselves. Any activities or tasks that involve locating the desire to read and to write also involve negotiating conscious and unconscious personae, complex relations among desire, knowledge, fantasy, and the real that make all representations to some degree conflicted. Yet coming to an understanding that nongenres, mixed genres, and outlaw genres may effectively and artfully resist the differentials of power that characterize dominant genres means coming to an understanding that Norris (or James or Faulkner or any other writer of privilege) does not necessarily have more aesthetic control over his work than do writers such as Maimie Pinzer who stand outside dominant genres and traditions. The art of writing against the grain of received notions of the literary—while still admiring Michel Eyquem de Montaigne, Charles Dickens, and Wilde, among others—may merge with the art of forging a writing at all, a writing that needs to both learn from and yet resist dominant constructions of knowledge and power in order to assert its own value.

The point, after all, is not simply that Maimie Pinzer understands more about chronic hardship than either Norris or ourselves as readers—though a respect for the experiential wisdom of her social philosophy should follow from discussion. Rather, when students complain that she lacks conscious control or design of the kind they associate with autobiography or literature, they measure her against some misconstrued idea of literary art as fundamentally intentional, monological, controlled, and, perhaps most important, formally related to the literary genres familiar to them. Critical and comparative reading should illustrate that both those with little power or privilege and those with much bring their social baggage with them to understanding readerly/writerly relations. Because the weight of pedagogy has for so long been behind the formal training in genres and traditions attached to the great canonical books—and therefore behind any number of implicit connections between social and aesthetic value—students may express understandable dismay when confronted with a kind of readerly disability that has as much to do with their own lived experience as it has to do with textual experience. So that, when they initially see a singular, flat, descriptive prose, they do so because of a practiced inattention to any position that must negotiate multiple, sometimes conflicted audiences with the most direct personal consequences. As a consequence for the act of writing itself, the more intimate audience listening as "one of us" replaces any of the multiple audiences negotiated by Maimie as she wrote. And when a resisting commitment to social action and interaction overtakes the status of writing itself, the privileged classroom faces its own ultimate critique.

NOTES

1. I adapt here the readerly/writerly distinction made by Roland Barthes in S/Z to distinguish practices that consume the text (a readerly naming of signifieds) from practices that produce the text (a writerly extension of the play of signifiers); here, I intend *readerly* to suggest "reading while thinking about our own position as readers" and *writerly* to signify "reading while thinking about the writer's position." I do not, unlike Barthes, extend this distinction to texts.

Part of the pedagogical problem becomes engaging students in the theoretical questions that inform criticism in classes with literary texts as primary sources. Though not always in agreement with students' evaluations, many resent taking literature classes they view as "theory heavy" or "top-loaded with theory," even though they may willingly engage in theoretical arguments in the context of discussing literary texts. Here I try to represent how I negotiate theoretical issues in classes devoted primarily to working with texts read as literature.

2. Although my classes have predominantly middle-class students, working-class students and students with self-identifications that otherwise marginalize them may also participate in the responses I describe here as belonging simply to "students." Whether internalizations of dominant values and censored self-presentations produce conformity or whether the subservient tonalities of especially the early letters discourage sympathetic readings, resistance to thinking of Maimie's letters as artful easily dominates initial responses to reading.

3. In describing classroom tasks and discussion, I follow the lead of my students in calling Maimie Pinzer "Maimie" throughout, even though it would no more occur to them to call Norris "Frank" than to call Shakespeare "William." Calling attention to this asymmetry of naming often leads to discussion about both the power relations affecting who calls whom by their first names and the conflictual sense in which "Maimie" both responds to the implied intimacy of the letters and at the same time might subconsciously diminish her status as a writer.

4. Usefully, some students here relate how their own sense of Mrs. Howe's status as benefactress and Maimie's as the needy victim shaped their initial presumption that if Maimie grows, it must be because of contact with the better educated, more genteel woman. They may even consider the implications and consequences of formal versus informal education, admitting to a presumption that Maimie's efforts to educate herself must necessarily fall short of a "real" education.

5. If ever there were a temptation to introduce external argument, this kind of discussion seems to ask for reference to key passages in Pierre Bourdieu's *Distinction: A Social Critique of the Judgement of Taste*; despite Bourdieu's own predilections of class, he lays out what most cultural theory has come to accept, that is, how what most conceive of as chosen "taste" comes to us through cultural processes.

6. In previous classes discussion has noted the asymmetry of which writers' works have stood as self-explanatory and which have had their motivations and characters always under a skeptical scrutiny.

7. My interpretive emphasis here differs from Ruth Rosen's hypothesis that Maimie may have stopped writing simply because, as she postulates in her introduction to *The Maimie Papers*, "with her husband available to provide the support, intimacy, and friendship which she had shared with Mrs. Howe, Maimie found less urgency to write as frequently" (xix–xx).

8. For an example of dialogical analysis of writerly desire, I refer interested students to the explications in Peter Hitchcock's *Dialogics of the Oppressed*.

9. This argument usefully coincides with Walter Benn Michaels's insight that the logic of naturalism in general "served the interests not of any individual or any group of individuals but of the money economy itself" (178), such that the personification of the economy and the dehumanization of characters propels a kind of category mistake. Charitably, Michaels sees this figurative mistake as providing "a singularly compelling image of the naturalist distinction between material and identity. Failing to be a person, it images by the way it isn't a person the condition in naturalism of the possibility of persons" (180).

10. Perhaps those explicating colonial and postcolonial/postindependence literary resistance have argued most strongly for the idea that resistance is always in some way complicit with what it resists. Jenny Sharpe's "Figures of Colonial Resistance" finds an emphasis on the partial, complicit nature of literary resistance common to such theorists as Gayatri Spivak, Homi Bhabha, Abdul Jan Mohamad, and Benita Parry. Whether con-

ceived as an "out-law genre" (see Kora Caplan's "Resisting Autobiography: Out-Law Genres and Transnational Feminist Subjects") or as a form of resistance that responds in opposition to the genres that Maimie recognized as such (see the last chapter, in particular, of my *The Tragedy and Comedy of Resistance: Reading Modernity through Black Women's Fiction*), The Maimie Papers well illustrates the negotiated terrain of writers with less power than their multiple audiences writing directly for those who have power over their lives and indirectly for later audiences who may share all or only some of the habits of reading from above.

REFERENCES

Bakhtin, Mikhail. *The Dialogical Imagination: Four Essays by M. M. Bakhtin.* Translated by Caryl Emerson and Michael Holquist. Austin: University of Texas Press, 1981.

Barthes, Roland. *S/Z.* Translated by Richard Miller, with a preface by Richard Howard. New York: Hill and Wang, 1974.

Bhabha, Homi K. "Interrogating Identity: The Postcolonial Prerogative." In *Anatomy of Racism,* edited by David Theo Goldberg, 183–209. Minneapolis: University of Minnesota Press, 1990.

Bourdeiu, Pierre. *Distinction: A Social Critique of the Judgement of Taste.* Translated by Richard Nice. Cambridge: Harvard University Press, 1984.

Butler, Judith. *Bodies That Matter: On the Discursive Limits of "Sex."* New York and London: Routledge, 1993.

Choy, Christine, director. *Who Killed Vincent Chin?* Videorecording, 83 min. Film New Now Foundation and WTVS, Detroit. New York: Filmakers Library, 1988.

Davis, Rebecca Harding. *Life in the Iron Mills.* 1861. Reprint. New York: The Feminist Press, 1972.

Hitchcock, Peter. *Dialogics of the Oppressed.* Minneapolis and London: University of Minnesota Press, 1993.

Kaplan, Cora. "Resisting Autobiography: Out-Law Genres and Transnational Feminist Subjects." In *De/Colonizing the Subject: The Politics of Gender in Women's Autobiography,* edited by Sidonie Smith and Julia Watson, 115–38. Minneapolis: University of Minnesota Press, 1992.

Michaels, Walter Benn. *The Gold Standard and the Logic of Naturalism.* Berkeley, Los Angeles, and London: University of California Press, 1987.

Norris, Frank. *The Octopus.* 1900. Reprint, New York and Scarborough: New American Library, 1964.

Pinzer, Maimie [pseud.] *The Maimie Papers: Letters from an Ex-Prostitute,* edited by Ruth Rosen and Sue Davidson. New York: The Feminist Press and Indiana University Press in cooperation with the Schlesinger Library of Radcliffe College, 1977.

Sharpe, Jenny. "Figures of Colonial Resistance." *Modern Fiction Studies* 35, no. 1 (1989): 137–55.

Slemon, Stephen. "Unsettling the Empire: Resistance Theory for the Second World." *World Literature Written in English* 2 (1990): 30–41.

Taylor, Carole Anne. *The Tragedy and Comedy of Resistance: Reading Modernity through Black Women's Fiction.* Philadelphia: University of Pennsylvania Press, 2000.

Between Theories and Anti-Theories

Moving Toward Marginal Women's Subjectivities

Roxanne Rimstead

Paulo Freire has urged that shifts in theory be grounded in human narratives. Since these narratives are a location in which the oppressed may imagine liberation in the context of their own experiences, Freire notes, they yield knowledge about the particularities of people's suffering and the multiple possibilities for their emancipation (xi–xii). Especially in the context of a postmodern world in which subjectivities have become unmoored from previous narratives of social justice, Freire encourages academics to listen to and ground our own educational praxis in the language of everyday experiences (Freire and Giroux, ix–xi). Yet, within the context of current literary discourse, for feminist critics to turn their attention to the narratives of marginal women is as problematic as it is challenging. Tony Bennett has noted in *Outside Literature* that there is a struggle, a "wresting" of discourse materials needed in order even to begin to speak from or about a place outside "Literature": "There is no ready-made theoretical position outside aesthetic discourse which can simply be taken up and occupied. Such a space requires a degree of fashioning; it must be organized and above all won" (10). Whereas Bennett would suggest we win that place by scientifically analyzing and exposing a hierarchy of discourses within the academy, Freire's concept of cultural struggle urges academics to look beyond the limits of academic perception and actively engage with oppressed groups to help them achieve subjecthood and to learn from them. But, given the demands of established literary discourse, of which mainstream feminist criticism is now a part, populist feminist critics cannot move directly beyond theoretical exclusions toward marginal subjects; we must learn to move consciously between those theoretical positions we inherit and sometimes oppose and those I call, for the purposes of this discussion, anti-Theory.

ANTI-WHAT?

By *anti-Theories* I do not mean antitheoretical discourse that mistrusts all theoretical formulations or anti-intellectual discourse or even the resistance to poststructuralist theory described by Paul de Man as generalized resistance to theory. Anti-Theories, as I see them, question the exclusions of Theory when it assumes its own primacy above other theories or other ways of knowing culture and marginality—for example, through scientific, homogenizing, or totalizing abstractions. By anti-Theories of marginal women's subjectivities, I mean those discussions about reading and interpreting marginal voices, often quite theoretical themselves, which steadily work toward political agency in the form of pop-

ulist goals or coalition politics. They constitute an oppositional force within academic feminist criticism by trying to bring feminist literary criticism back to a
more direct interest in community and everyday life—or, in political terms, back
to praxis. While some anti-Theories reach beyond theory into the area of experiences and particularities of concrete subjects, others scrutinize Theory to expose
its own subjective blindspots, which sometimes reduce the complexity of marginal subjects, or eclipse them altogether. Finally, these critical gestures toward
greater community alliance are not simply acts of faith and often include, as part
of their own political self-reflexivity, questions about the nature of political coalition and the claim to know and access marginal subjectivities as an alternative
form of knowledge.[1]

In the early days of "authentic realism" in American feminist criticism (1970s),
the problematic of moving back and forth between androcentric Theory and
women's everyday experience was resolved by a veering away from theory and
toward a direct assertion of the preeminent truth-value of experience and subjectivity. As Sara Mills has observed in *Feminist Readings/Feminists Reading*, at that
stage in experientially based criticism, the claims on the text were unabashedly
prescriptive, privileging authenticity as a measure of the social effect of the text
to challenge the status quo by correcting misrepresentations. Authentic realism
implied an antitheoretical stance because, as it sought to make literary texts
accessible to more women, it also encouraged a more plain-speaking, less jargon-
ridden form of critical inquiry and it challenged the received values enshrined in
that discourse. In "unacademic" language grassroots discussion groups probed the
transformational power of autobiographical and confessional texts in respect to
the lives and experiences of ordinary women readers, an act that by its very existence raised important questions about knowledge claims in critical discourse and
the social effect of literature (Mills). But current poststructuralist debates on
claiming of knowledge and experience across the disciplines have developed
more complex attitudes about constructing knowledge—attitudes that mistrust
the representationist assumptions about a concrete reality existing out there,
waiting for a purer, truer form of representation.[2]

Chris Weedon has critiqued the earlier strains of antitheoretical and experiential criticism in *Feminist Practice and Poststructuralist Theory* through a deconstruction of the fiction-reality dichotomy and a more complex understanding of
the relation between texts and everyday reality. But, while more complex representationist theories have emerged, it has sometimes been at the expense of
neglecting realist texts altogether and privileging only those texts that consciously experiment with postmodernist forms and playfully deferred subjects.
Rita Felski, among others, has expressed a concern with this neglect and has
argued for reinstating the value of those realist texts in the shadow of a postmodernist feminist canon. In *Beyond Feminist Aesthetics: Feminist Literature and Social
Change* she argues at length for the political need and theoretical efficacy to rein-
state the value of realist literature as a vital part of an oppositional feminist discourse. Felski has observed that certain types of feminist literary theory, especially
those influenced by poststructuralism, have carried the implicit assumption that a

concern for subjectivity based in lived reality is anachronistic and naive. She concludes that there is, consequently, a need to defend the theoretical validity of a culturally based feminist criticism:

> [I]t becomes possible to see the debate between "experiential" and "post-structuralist" feminism does not lend itself to simple resolution by adjudicating their respective validity as theories, but springs from conflicting ideological interests: on the one hand a populist position which seeks to link texts to everyday life practices in the hope of affecting direct social change, on the other the emergence of an academic feminism with often quite different affiliations and professional commitment to more rigorous and intellectually sophisticated, and hence necessarily more esoteric, forms of analysis. (11)

Bella Brodzki and Celeste Schenck have also noted that the complex theorizing practiced by feminist deconstructionists may have served to legitimate feminist discourse professionally but that it may be time to "uncouple" feminism and deconstruction in order to look at other forms of feminist theorizing and the politics of theory itself. As another critic, R. Radhakrishnan, has so succinctly put it, once again linking theoretical schools to subject positions grounded in power relations, "Whereas the dominant position requires acts of self-deconstruction, the subordinant position entails collective self-construction" (277). Yet those of us who prefer the ideological positioning of collective self-construction and populist feminism—and I use the term *populist*[3] here, as Felski does, in an affirmative sense—are still in need of more wide-ranging theories and reading practices to help us make these links between art and everyday life.

SUBJECTIVITIES

The plural form of *subjectivity—subjectivities*—is now fashionable within the context of postcolonial and poststructuralist debates because it invokes, paradoxically, both a sense of inclusiveness of other identities and a sense of playfully deferred identities. One notable exception to this generally blurred invocation of the term is Regenia Gagnier's astute theoretical introduction to her recent study *Subjectivities: A History of Self-Representation in Britain (1832–1920)*, which begins by stating that subjectivity, according to cultural studies, is broader than that previously known within the realm of literary studies. Not only did literary studies tend to limit the choice of texts to those reflecting bourgeois subjectivities, Gagnier observes, but the questions asked of those subjectivities were not broad enough or probing enough to reveal the full cultural role of subjectivity. She reviews a wide range of definitions now circulating actively in academic discourse: first, "the subject is a subject to itself, an 'I'"; second, and simultaneously, it is a subject to others appearing as the "Other," which often leads it to construct itself, especially in the case of groups, communities, classes, and nations, in opposition to others; third, the subject is one of knowledge, especially in terms of "the discourse of social institutions which circumscribe its terms of being"; fourth, the subject is a body separate from others (except in the case of a pregnant woman) and dependent upon its concrete environment; fifth, the subject is often identified, despite challenges by deconstructionists, as the site of subjective knowledge as opposed to objective knowledge, in other words with the partial and particular view of the world rather than the Cartesian and hypothetical universal view; and, finally, the subject is also a textual convention, or, as Gagnier describes it: "The 'I' is the self-present subject of the sentence as well as the subject 'subjected' to the symbolic order of the language in which one is writing" (8–9).

Gagnier's is not an exhaustive list, but it is complete enough to hint at the complex theorizing of subjectivity in the context of current academic discourse and to show how precisely defined the use of the term should be to avoid blurring and slippage among these applications. For example, marginal women's subjectivities are represented in current academic discourse, more often than not, in terms of Gagnier's second definition—emphasizing how working-class and poor women are defined as Other in terms of both class and gender. Yet, increasingly, some of the more radical critics aligned with these women are willing to ask, like the proponents of a Marxist history-from-below tradition, how working-class and poor women experience themselves as *I*, as Other, and also through any of the other applications (e.g., according to Gagnier's fourth definition, we might also ask how the working-class or poor subject might experience her body differently because it is classed as well as gendered). As Patrick Brantlinger notes, however, rendering the subject more theoretically complex is not in and of itself an oppositional act, and, therefore, the cultural critic who claims to be critiquing dominant culture, must posit more than increasingly complex ways of representing the subject or exposing hegemonic misrepresentation; she must also posit through her critique alternative social orders (145).

Interestingly enough, populist feminist critics seldom spend publication time rigorously defining their precise theoretical application of the term *subjectivities*; they usually focus, instead, on the importance of listening more closely to the heterogeneous and complex composition of classed and gendered subjectivities as they are represented by the voices of marginal subjects themselves and the problematics of listening to and speaking for others. For example, populist critics such as Barbara Christian, bell hooks, and Janet Zandy, whose anti-Theories I will discuss shortly, urge the study of utterances by marginal women as the first and primary step in accessing their subjectivities and look to the voices and the concrete subjects in their communities as more than objects of study but, foremost, as subjects capable of imparting knowledge about their own meanings and imaginings. That is not to assume that we can access these subjectivities purely and simply through good faith and solidarity but rather that we listen closely to the idiom, the texture, and the testimonial function of the stories in which subjectivities are expressed.

Understanding marginalized subjectivities in terms of class, race, and gender should involve a radical critique of our own categories of analysis, as well as the context of our inquiry, and how and why we invoke marginalized subjects from our relatively privileged positions as academics. For example, it is important to remember that current inquiries about class and gender come after an embattled era, when Marxists and feminists—with socialist feminists caught in between—vied for the primacy of their respective categories of analysis: class and gender. The following excerpt from "The Very Last Feminist Poem," by the little-known Canadian writer and propagandist for Marxism, Sharon Stevenson, dramatizes a socialist feminist's struggle with conflicting subjectivities: on the one hand, a feminist subjectivity she fears is less politically potent than a man's and bourgeois in its self-absorbed nature and, on the other hand, a Marxist subjectivity that will not make room for a woman's private concerns and yet cannot resist the concreteness and emotional texture of those experiences either:

> if I were, for instance, Chris Marlowe
> (dead soon after)
> I might be thinking a great deal of the future
> of possibility
> of how to affect change
> if only I were a man.
> instead my mind runs in argument
> over & over again
> with the husband
> the lovers
> the absence of child
> held small in the womb
> seeming lack of purpose
> chaos in day-to-day life
>
> & subjectivity
> rushes soft & clinging
> along the thighs
> before nestling in the brain
> as the strongest weapon
> of the bourgeoisie.
>
>   (11. 9–20)

The speaker's sensuous diction reveals ambivalence over her womanly subjectivity, which she rejects as alien and invasive on the surface but "clinging" and "nestling" in a softly sensual way. As a Marxist, she despairs of her lack of focus on the public sphere and her distraction from a historical mission—a distraction that leaves her wanting beside Marlowe, a man remembered by history as both artist and political agent. Yet her guiltily confessional moment does invoke a different scene of historical struggle: the early stage of socialist feminism, when highly politicized women experienced their subjectivities (and their political souls for that matter) as contested territory.[4]

This historic tug-of-war with the fundamentally conflicting notions of public and private subjectivity in Marxism and feminism warrants more careful study because the assertion of the primacy of one category over the other was more than theoretical "nitpicking," as Josephine Donovan noted in *Feminist Theory: The Intellectual Traditions of American Feminism.* The conflict implied questions of loyalties to various communities and different "revolutionary strateg[ies]" (87). In the early days of socialist feminism in U.S. academia, revolutionary strategy depended not only on where one's primary loyalties lay in terms of theory, Donovan notes, but also on how theory extended into strategy—especially, how one perceived the formation of revolutionary consciousness in oneself and others as subjects of history, for example, whether working-class women would be brought to class consciousness through the efforts of an educated elite or through their own insights into oppression.

THEORIES OF THE CLASSED AND GENDERED SUBJECT

It is equally necessary for feminist theory to acknowledge that gender is only one of the many determining influences upon subjectivity, ranging from macrostructures such as class, nationality, and race down to microstructures such as the accidents of personal history, which do not simply exist alongside gender distinctions, but actively influence and are influenced by them. To define gender as the primary explanation of all social relations, to speak of the male and female subject in abstract and ahistorical terms, is in fact ultimately counterproductive for feminism, in that such an account can offer no explanation of how existing forms of gender inequality can be changed.

—Rita Felski, *Beyond Feminist Aesthetics*

Most schools of feminist theory are now demanding that the theoretical basis of feminist coalition has to be more historically and socially informed than an ideal-ized category of gender. And the inclusion of marginal subjectivities is central to this project of informed coalition among women. But the great majority of acade-mic feminists are still theorizing from a position of privileged status (one of sev-eral types: economic, racial, ethnic, educational, social, professional, and cultural), which tends to idealize the relation of a pluralist feminist discourse to lived marginality. An idealist feminist discourse claims to transcend elitism and unfold truths about female subjectivity that apply to all women, no matter how different their stories may be. For example, Elaine Showalter's pioneering 1982 essay, "Feminist Criticism in the Wilderness," posited a theory of culture whereby all women were represented as culturally marginalized and thus part of a binding reality. Furthermore, Showalter claimed, "It is in the emphasis on the binding force of women's culture that this approach differs from Marxist theories of cul-tural hegemony" (27). Showalter may be seen as having posited, first, an idealized concept of collective female culture as a rallying cry to theory and, second, a the-ory that by its very nature would not make a significant place for the knowledge that marginalized women have of difference and hegemony in their everyday lives. As evidenced by Donna Perry's more recent overview of the discipline in

"Procne's Song: The Task of Feminist Literary Criticism," mainstream, academic feminist criticism still posits the concept of a community of female readers and writers that ultimately transcends class and race. Through the rather optimistic notion that the feminist critic is one consciously "writing to and for the converted," Perry claims that dissenting voices and differences among feminists are able to emerge and challenge what those shared concerns are (302–3). As anyone knows from looking at the class and racial makeup of student and faculty populations and attendance at academic conferences, however, women do not all speak with one transcendent and homogeneous voice: we are not all being heard through "the voice" of academic feminism.

High theorists as well as populists are increasingly arguing that the assumptions behind gender-specific categories of analysis may detract from theoretical rigor by failing to recognize women's different social locations and subject positions, both group and individual. For example, Jeanne Costello's "Taking the 'Woman' out of Women's Autobiography: The Perils and Potentials of Theorizing Female Subjectivities" calls into question not only the homogenizing of the female subject through disregard for social forces such as class, gender, and sexual orientation but also the whole strategy of still creating gender-specific categories of texts at this point in feminist criticism. Costello criticizes recent theories of women's life writing, in particular those based on the application of psychological gender theories such as Nancy Chodorow's and Carol Gilligan's, showing how essentialism often creeps into feminist practices of reading and questioning women's texts. Judith Butler's *Gender Trouble* also suggests dismantling the gender paradigm as a gesture toward greater theoretical rigor. As an antidote to the homogenizing aspect of heterosexual feminist identity politics in high theory, Butler prescribes even higher theory: "a critical genealogy of [feminism's] own legitimating practices" (5). But her own genealogy is historically lopsided on the side of academic feminism, leaving out the dissenting voices, the anti-Theorists among feminism's populist critics and activists who have traditionally exceeded Theory in their capacity to embrace heterogeneity by going outside the academy among those very women whom Theory has excluded. Consider, for example, Sheila Baxter, activist and welfare mother, who compiled a collection of interviews with poor women in 1988 in Vancouver, *No Way to Live: Poor Women Speak Out*, and included women of diverse racial and ethnic groups, lesbian women, elderly women, single women, married women, handicapped women, and so on.[5]

By invoking unproblematized claims of identity and macropolitical goals, populist critics may be as falsely idealistic about a common community of women as practitioners of high theory. Populists, however, do not need to rely exclusively on increasingly complex theory to invoke the heterogeneity of subjects in their community because the very practice of their cultural critique is linked to recovering and exploring the particular and heterogeneous voices of concrete subjects. With our eyes on the complexity of everyday life, we are more likely to see that alliances between a given individual and various communities and subcultures, with their accompanying constructions of identity, are tentative because they shift with material circumstances, age, sexual orientation, race, ethnicity, and so on.[6]

In the last two decades, in particular, feminists have advanced beyond the dispute over the primary identity designation (class or gender?) and refined the discussion by asking how class, race, and gender work as interacting contexts that construct the subject. This challenge has arisen partly from anti-Theories such as Janet Zandy's, when she asserts empirically the importance of women's gendered difference within the working class: "The boundaries and texture of working-class women's lives are not the same as men's. Not separate, but not the same" (7). And the relation between class and gender has also been problematized by theorizing class differently. For example, Christine Delphy in *Close to Home: A Materialist Analysis of Women's Oppression* has challenged the Marxist conception of class identity with an alternative theoretical formulation; instead of class identity based solely in market modes of production (the public sphere), she posits the construction of working-class identity within the domestic mode of production (the private sphere). Of particular interest in Delphy's challenge is the method of bringing her own empirical observations of rural women in everyday life to bear on intellectual Marxism—yet not in a scientific or even a methodologically systematic way but, rather, in a descriptive way that shows the complexity of lives that exceed Theory (ix, 43–46).

Materialist feminists, especially in British feminist theory, have also called for greater rigor in theorizing the classed and gendered subject through consideration of a more psychologically complex subject. For example, Carolyn Steedman has described how necessary it is to allow an unconscious life to working-class childhoods in order to understand the individual formations of class consciousness and the different textures of classed and gendered experiences. She attributes the devaluation of the unconscious in class theory to gender bias. What Steedman terms the "refusal of a complicated psychology to those living in material distress" has come about, she suggests, not only because of the privileging of experiences of working-class men as a source of knowledge about class identity but also because of the generally debased position of mental life in Marxist philosophy and the fact that the theory of emotional and psychological selfhood was executed by people in a central class relationship to the dominant culture (285).

Materialist feminists have been discussing subjectivities recently in two significantly different ways: while some generate what I call anti-Theories to explain the utterances of working-class and poor women as subjects of oppositional culture, others have approached class and gender through "high theory," as inscriptions that need to be decoded by engaged critics applying oppositional reading practices to texts. In other words, while some feminists write anti-Theories to locate the potential for agency and cultural opposition in marginal women's voices, themselves as subjects of knowledge, others are working on new theories to refine how we read class and gender in these voices and more traditional canonical texts as objects of knowledge, thus locating the potential for agency with intellectuals in the act of critical analysis itself. The purpose of the discussion here is not to valorize one method over the other but, instead, to show how anti-Theories often function to balance theories and bring them back to political praxis and a more concretely inclusive sense of community and culture.

In "Pandora's Box: Subjectivity, Class and Sexuality in Socialist-Feminist Criticism" Cora Kaplan suggests that we reframe the theoretical debate about one social construct—either class or gender—containing or taking precedence over the other by studying texts in terms of how the speaking subject is constructed by class and gender, given that they interact reciprocally and in a complex way upon the speaking subject (346, 364). Class and gender work upon the subject as reciprocal processes, she argues, rather than fixed contents or static territories that definitively can be located in and around the subject. Kaplan suggests that fiction, in general, can reveal subjectivities if we study it as "the ordering of the imagination," as the site of expressions of "hidden" or taken-for-granted ideological beliefs about the self and other classes of women, especially in respect to a history of conventional formulations of femininity: "Literary texts give these simultaneous inscriptions narrative form, pointing towards and opening up the fragmentary nature of social and psychic identity, drawing out the ways in which social meaning is psychically represented. It is this symbolic shaping of class that we should examine in fiction" (359). In addition to identifying the "construction of dominant definitions of the inner lives of working-class women," Kaplan suggests, therefore, that we learn "how dominant definitions of both class and gender are lived by these women" (361). She implies that taking class and gender into account in "a more complex way" would mean, in addition to the appropriation of semiotic and psychoanalytical methodologies by materialist feminists, turning to "non-literary sources, to the discourses in which [working-class women] themselves [speak]" (361). But she adds that the integration of these voices fall beyond the theoretical scope of her own essay, perhaps because at this point her theory necessarily heads into the uncharted area of anti-Theory.

Catherine Belsey, on the other hand, in her essay "Constructing the Subject: Deconstructing the Text," does not discuss the possibility of counterhegemonic knowledge coming from the utterances of ordinary women. Belsey implies that the power to challenge ideology lies in the hands of a reader-critic who can discover contradictory subjectivities by deconstructing the canonized text: "Having created a canon of acceptable texts, criticism then provides them with acceptable interpretations, thus effectively censoring any elements in them which come into collision with the dominant ideology. To deconstruct the text, on the other hand, is to open it, to release the possible positions of its intelligibility, including those that reveal the partiality (in both senses) of the ideology inscribed in the text" (58, 51). Belsey's use of the term *subjectivity* may be partly explained by the concept of ideology to which she subscribes, that of the Althusserian school, which defines *ideology* as a determinate and dominant force of misrepresentation acting upon all subjects to create false and partial consciousness. Given this context, Belsey refers to subjectivity as though it were an ideologically determined location that is knowable or partially knowable through discourse analysis, historical analysis, psychoanalysis, and deconstruction—in short, through scientific or objective means. This implies that a woman's own narratives about herself and her lived realities are not potent enough to challenge the misrepresentations (and thus hegemony) that ideology imposes—unless, perhaps, the subject herself is capable of applying a method of deconstruction to open her own utterance and see how ideology is operating within it.

By comparing Kaplan's and Belsey's theorization of the subject, we can see that Kaplan's discussion of subjectivity implies more faith in individual agency and in personal formulations of lived experience as an additional source of knowledge in challenging oppressive ideologies. Kaplan's use of the term valorizes subjectivity as a way of knowing, as politically grounded perspectives and sensibilities through which we can know and feel, rather than merely deconstruct and map, the female subject. Thus, as noted earlier, Kaplan invites emergent voices into the process of oppositional analysis as epistemologically valid subjects, though she stops short of theorizing how this might be done. The nuances between the two theorists' concepts of subjectivity illustrate how materialist feminists must struggle with residual and somewhat divergent Marxist theories about ideology and subjectivity while striking out with new feminist theory to explore subjects that have previously been off the map.[7]

I would agree that it is useful to be vigilant about the dangers of mystifying subjectivity and prioritizing it above other forms of knowledge, practices that Weedon links with assumptions in humanist discourse of the free, self-determining individual and those of certain radical and essentialist theories of gender (78–79) and which Belsey also links with assumptions of autonomous agency ("Literature" 51–52). But the fact remains that theories that are not informed by these subjectivities, even when acknowledging the voices of working-class women as worthy *objects* of study, have tended to be too abstract or too idealist to bring us much closer to any "inside" knowledge of what Zandy referred to as "the boundaries and textures of working-class women's lives" (7). It seems that the mundane and messy sphere of material struggle, class identification, complicity, and the complexity of life in the concrete world have not been able to emerge through highly abstract language and theory of literary discourse; whereas these subjectivities are palpable in testimonies about the lived experiences of class and poverty.

UNDERSTANDING SUBJECTIVITIES

Among the theories and anti-Theories of materialist feminism there emerge nuanced but significant differences between projects to map marginal women's subjectivities and those that claim to access them as knowledge and cultural exchange. These projects are not necessarily separate—and sometimes one critic will attempt both in the course of a particular work—but it is interesting how the choice to "map" subjectivities often signals that the critic is about to write from a more distanced, bird's-eye view, so to speak, rather than from the more closely identified position of coalition with the marginalized community itself. Although both of these projects are invaluable to feminist criticism and cultural studies, anti-Theories are the more devalued of the two. Critics who place greater value on the power of marginal voices to inform reading and writing practices are often seen by the literary establishment, at worst, as anti-intellectual and, at best, as less academically rigorous than those who confine their methods to archival research or abstract theorizing about these voices as objects of study.

I have already mentioned that Zandy's introduction to *Calling Home: Working-Class Women's Writing—An Anthology* constitutes what I would call an anti-Theory based on accessing working-class women's voices and reading them "from the inside out" (9). Zandy has suggested that working-class women in late capitalism in the United States experience a special kind of cultural exclusion, one which is so pervasive that it denies us a cultural home. This severe experience of muting requires, more than the academic mapping of difference, the cultural accessing of stories, memory, and subjectivities specific to this community of women. Cultural accessing comes with assumptions that the phenomenological potential of reading will allow it to play a role in social therapy and in identity construction. For example, Zandy calls for an intertextual rather than theory-oriented cultural criticism, one which would allow us to bypass complexly exclusionary Theory and claim access to a cultural home through a process of recognition and retrieval, a collaborative process between reader and writer.

Zandy is pragmatic and respectful in her discussion of working-class women's utterances, expressing a great faith in the internal coherence of these voices and their potential to inform the oppositional reader: "To try to fit this literature into the neat academic categories of genre or period is like squeezing a wilderness into a cultivated park. Despite its diversity and unconventional literary forms, working-class literature is not a mass of dangling parts but a collective body of work. To see these connections, one has to look from the inside out, that is, through the impulses and intentions of the literature itself" (9). While affirming the coherence of working-class texts as a body, Zandy also affirms the uncontainable nature of these utterances in the image of the wilderness. This motif recalls Showalter's paradigm of cultural muting described in "Feminist Criticism in the Wilderness" but stresses heterogeneity, class differences, and lack of cultural access as realities within a nonidealized cultural wilderness. Furthermore, Zandy implies that accessing the inside of working-class women's experience of cultural wilderness is possible by assembling voices that come from the inside of these experiences not in terms of essence but, rather, in terms of point of view: "I looked for pieces from the inside of working-class experience either by virtue of the author having been born into the working class or through close political and cultural identification with working-class life" (8). Thus, the inside of this community is determined by a sense of coalition-based empathy, political analysis, or an insider's knowledge of experience, rather than essence.

In her brief discussion of intentionality, Zandy gives the impression that she has been selective in drawing together narratives that express subjectivities based on collectivity and struggle. This selectivity makes the project of reading "from the inside out" one partly dependent on the inside of a consciously idealist (vs. idealized) category of narratives which has been fashioned by the critic for, by, or about a particular group of working-class women or women who empathize with this position—all of whom have achieved an awareness of the importance of struggle (10). What I am saying here is that the claim to read from the inside, in this case, is more a politically demarcated space than a theoretical one; it comes to mean reading from the inside of a community of women writers and readers who are brought together through political coalition. To use Zandy's own distinction, then, she implies that we strive not only to read from inside a space (a cultural home) of class knowledge but also, more specifically, inside a space of willed class solidarity: "Class knowledge comes from experience and story, history and memory, and from the urgency of witnessing. Class solidarity is born from perception of common struggles and common enemies" (8), By distinguishing between the search for class knowledge, which tolerates heterogeneity, and that of class solidarity, which wills commonality, Zandy avoids having to idealize the stories of working-class women, as earlier categories of proletarian literature did.

Although avoiding the word *populist*, probably because of its negative political implications under Reaganomics, Zandy's populist goals are overt; they outweigh any merely ethnographic concerns for broader representation and are the clearest aspect of her anti-Theory. When she gives priority to a reading practice and a form of critical discourse that "would not alienate working-class people from their own texts and would not privilege the critic at the expense of the writer," her commitment to make her own theory more accessible, relevant, and serviceable to a community of readers and writers among working-class women represents a stronger bond with the concerns and sensibilities of this community than with the abstract notions of class and gender (10). This bond is perhaps one reason why her concept of reading from the inside out remains inadequately theorized for academic consumption (especially on the point of intentionality)— inadequate, that is, given the bourgeois tradition of literary discourse to speak an academic insiders' language.

The exclusionary aspect of theoretical language and theoretical practice has been eloquently challenged by Barbara Christian in "The Race for Theory." For example, Christian maintains that African Americans have always had to theorize as a strategy for survival. Although their theories have not been academically sanctioned, they have always been a race whose members theorized their own oppression to make sense of their world. In the present academic climate, however, Christian argues that African American critics and other radical critics often feel pressured by the institutional exigency of creating and prescribing one Theory that will contain or homogenize the voices under study: "Some of us are continually harassed to invent wholesale theories, regardless of the complexity of the literature we study. . . . I consider it presumptuous of me to invent a theory of how we ought to read. Instead, I think we need to read the works of our writers in our various ways and remain open to the intricacies of the intersection of language, class, race, and gender in the literature" (570). Christian's solution to the race for theory, which she sees taking place at the expense of recognizing difference, is twofold: first, to valorize theoretical formulations other than those of "high" criticism by learning to listen to the theory couched in the ordinary or the poetic language of the people themselves; and, second, to ground theory constantly in the practice of reading the literature of people who are not usually heard, because, Christain notes, "theorizing is of necessity based on our multiplicity of experiences" (577). The bottom line she sees for engaged critics from oppressed groups is to always ethically interrogate our own praxis by asking "For whom are we doing what we are doing when we do literary criticism?" Grounding our inquiry in feelings of coalition and our own subjective experiences of class and gender—as well as our concepts of these forces—will bind us more faithfully to the community about whom we write and help us to resist acculturation in an academic community that often pressures us to deal in the currency of theories and authorities that are alien to our subjective experiences.

Though the current fashion is to engage in critical discourse about marginal subjectivities, we may still devalue those same subjectivities through institutional discourse and reading practices. In *Yearning: Race, Gender, and Cultural Politics* bell hooks has noted: "Too often, it seems, the point is to promote the appearance of difference within intellectual discourse, a 'celebration' that fails to ask who is sponsoring the party and who is extending the invitations. For who is controlling this new discourse? Who is getting hired to teach it, and where? Who's getting paid to write about it?" (54). hooks suggests that white academics refuse to perceive the existence of a special psychosocial cultural space based on black sensibilities and experiences: "The tendency to overvalue work by white scholars, coupled with the suggestion that such work constitutes the only relevant discourse, evades the issue of potential inaccessible locations—spaces white theorists cannot occupy. Without reinscribing an essentialist standpoint, it is crucial that we neither ignore nor deny that such locations exist" (55).[8] Yet, according to hooks, stepping forward and signifying difference subjectively in the academy provokes negative feedback, as long as it occurs within a feminist movement in which well-intentioned, but nonetheless privileged, white women impose a transcendent and idealized "notion of friendship and sisterly bonding . . . based on principles of seamless harmony" and an unacknowledged code for "nice, nice behavior" (89).

Without making subjectivity the exclusive or even the preeminent source of knowledge about life and culture on the margins, populist critics such as Zandy, Christian, and hooks are beginning to present us with a clearer image of how the academic world pushes marginal voices to the outside via theories and institutional practices that actively, though often unintentionally, assert a hierarchy of subjectivities. Anti-Theories show feminists how the wilderness of female culture has already been colonized by classist and racist values and that the way back to a history of that colonization should include, as well as a collection of muted voices inscribed in narratives, the critic's own subjective knowledge and even her or his own oppositional idiom. For example, Christian has described how accessing knowledge through texts is a way of feeling connected with her own community of women and men and a means of cultural survival: "What I write and how I write is done in order to save my life. And I mean that literally. For me, literature is a way of knowing that I am not hallucinating, that whatever I feel/know is. It is an affirmation that sensuality is intelligence, that sensual language is language that makes sense" (578). And bell hooks recalls that her attempts to use language from the vernacular invariably met with editors' corrections, which she herself accepted until she realized how "disempowering it was for people from underprivileged backgrounds to consciously censor our speech so as to 'fit better' in settings where we are perceived as not belonging" (90). Similarly, writing about the politics of representation in Canadian native women's writing, Barbara Godard has noted that the literary institution has asserted "its authority monologically by refusing to engage in dialogue with these alternate discourses" (186). Godard explains that so few subject positions are left open to native writers, given the literary institution's enforcement of a limited author position, that their subjectivities and idiom are sometimes rejected by publishers—in Lenore Keeshig-Tobias's words, for sounding "too Indian" or "not Indian enough" (qtd. in Godard 186). As an English literature professor of East Asian origin in Canada, Arun Mukherjee has reported that students may also participate in discouraging a discourse of cultural difference by reasserting a dominant apolitical and ahistorical humanist discourse. Mukherjee explains how students may resist oppositional readings of texts and embrace, instead, a "prophylactic view of literature," described by Richard Ohmann as filtering subversive content from even the most provocative texts (qtd. in Mukherjee 27–28). Important steps in oppositional criticism are, therefore, not only the recovery of marginal subjectivities but also the exposure of a hierarchy of subjectivities within theoretical discourse and the exposure of academic discourse as an insider discourse subjectively formed in the interests of that reigning group. For, as Terry Eagleton noted in *Literary Theory: An Introduction*, you may speak a "regional dialect" of critical discourse, "but you must not sound as though you are speaking another language altogether" for "to do so is to recognize in the sharpest way that critical discourse is power": "To be on the inside of the discourse itself is to be blind to this power, for what is more natural and non-dominative than to speak one's own tongue?" (210). There is a terrible irony here. Pronouncing difference within a tightly policed formal discourse risks pushing populist critics further toward the margins, yet in order to move closer to marginal women's subjectivities we must speak different critical languages through which we can construct a more radical subjecthood. And so we move between theory and anti-Theory, not so much playfully as critically—not celebrating detachment but, rather, looking for a home.

NOTES

I am grateful to Chin Bannerjee for his comments on an early draft of this essay. He helped me see that I was indeed reaching for a theory of anti-Theory.

1. For examples of such self-questioning, see Linda Alcoff's "The Problem of Speaking for Others"; and John McGuigan's *Cultural Populism*. Full documentation for these and other sources mentioned in these notes can be found in the references.

2. See, e.g., Joan Wallach Scott's "Experience"; and Mary E. Hawkesworth's "Knowers, Knowing, Known: Feminist Theory and Claims of Truth."

3. See McGuigan's discussion of the complex etymology of the term *populist* in *Cultural Populism*.

4. For a good overview of the theoretical dilemmas of socialist feminists, see Louise C. Johnson's summary "Socialist Feminisms."

5. For further critiques of gender as a category of analysis, see Joan Wallach Scott, "Gender: A Useful Category for Historical Analysis"; Felski, "Subjectivity and Feminism," in *Beyond Feminist Aesthetics*; and Sandra Harding, "The Instability of the Analytical Categories of Feminist Theory."

6. For more detailed theoretical discussion about coalition politics and reading practices, see Caren Kaplan, "Resisting Autobiography: Outlaw Genres and Transnational Feminist Subjects"; and Radhakrishnan, "Negotiating Subject Positions in an Uneven World."

7. On accessing women's subjectivities through fiction, see also Weedon, *Feminist Practice*, 74–113; Felski, *Beyond Feminist Aesthetics*, 51–85; and Paula Rabinowitz, "The Great Mother: Female Working-Class Subjectivity."

8. See also Steedman, *Landscape for a Good Woman*; and Arun Mukherjee, *Towards an Aesthetics of Opposition*, on the topic of informed and subjective reading by insiders in marginalized groups.

REFERENCES

Alcoff, Linda. "The Problem of Speaking for Others." *Cultural Critique* 16 (winter 1991): 5–32.

Baxter, Sheila. *No Way to Live: Poor Women Speak Out*. Vancouver: New Star Books, 1988.

Belsey, Catherine. "Constructing the Subject: Deconstructing the Text." In *Feminist Criticism and Social Change*, edited by Judith Newton and Deborah Rosenfelt, 45–64. New York: Methuen, 1985.

———. "Literature, History, Politics." In *Literature and History*, 1983. Reprinted in *Modern Criticism and Theory: A Reader*, edited by David Lodge, 400–10. London: Longman, 1988.

Bennett, Tony. *Outside Literature*. London and New York: Routledge, 1990.

Brantlinger, Patrick. *Crusoe's Footprints: Cultural Studies in Britain and America*. New York: Routledge, 1990.

Brodzki, Bella, and Celeste Schenck. "Criticus Interruptus: Uncoupling Feminism and Deconstruction." In *Feminism and Institutions: Dialogues on Feminist Theory*, edited by Linda Kaufman, 194–208. Cambridge, Mass.: Basil Blackwell, 1989.

Butler, Judith. *Gender Trouble*. New York: Routledge, 1990.

Christian, Barbara. "The Race for Theory." In *Women, Class, and the Feminist Imagination*, edited by Karen V. Hansen and Illene J. Philipson, 568–79. Philadelphia: Temple University Press, 1990.

Costello, Jeanne. "Taking the 'Woman' out of Women's Autobiography: The Perils and Potentials of Theorizing Female Subjectivities." *Diacritics: Feminist Miscellanies* 21, nos. 2 and 3 (summer–fall 1991): 123–34.

Delphy, Christine. *Close to Home: A Materialist Analysis of Women's Oppression*, edited and translated by Diana Leonard. Amherst: University Press of Massachusetts, 1984.

de Man, Paul. "The Resistance to Theory." *Yale French Studies* 63 (1982). Reprinted in *Modern Criticism and Theory: A Reader*, edited by David Lodge, 355–71. London: Longman, 1988.

Donovan, Josephine. *Feminist Theory: The Intellectual Traditions of American Feminism*. New York: Ungar, 1987.

Eagleton, Terry. *Literary Theory: An Introduction*. Oxford: Basil Blackwell, 1983.

Felski, Rita. *Beyond Feminist Aesthetics: Feminist Literature and Social Change*. Cambridge: Harvard University Press, 1989.

Freire, Paulo. Foreword to *Paulo Freire: A Critical Encounter*, edited by Peter McLaren and Peter Leonard, ix–xii. London: Routledge, 1993.

————, and Henry A. Giroux. "Pedagogy, Popular Culture, and Public Life: An Introduction." In *Popular Culture: Schooling and Everyday Life*, edited by Henry A. Giroux and Roger Simon, vii–xii. New York: Bergin and Garvey, 1989.

Gagnier, Regenia. *Subjectivities: A History of Self-Representation in Britain (1832–1920)*. New York: Oxford University Press, 1989.

Godard, Barbara. "The Politics of Representation: Some Native Canadian Women Writers." In *Native Writers and Canadian Writing*, edited by W. H. New, 183–228. *Canadian Literature*, special issue. Vancouver: University Press of British Columbia, 1990.

Harding, Sandra. "The Instability of the Analytical Categories of Feminist Theory." In *Feminist Theory in Practice and Process*, edited by Micheline R. Malson, Jean F. O'Barr, Sara Westphal-Wihl, and Mary Wyer, 15–34. Chicago: Chicago University Press, 1986.

Hawkesworth, Mary E. "Knowers, Knowing, Known: Feminist Theory and Claims of Truth." In *Feminist Theory in Practice and Process*, edited by Micheline R. Malson, Jean F. O'Barr, Sara Westphal-Wihl, and Mary Wyer, 327–51. Chicago: Chicago University Press, 1986.

hooks, bell. *Yearning: Race, Gender, and Cultural Politics*. Toronto: Between the Lines, 1990.

Johnson, Louise C. "Socialist Feminisms." In *Feminist Knowledge: Critique and Construct*, edited by Sneja Gunew, 304–31. New York: Routledge, 1990.

Kaplan, Caren. "Resisting Autobiography: Outlaw Genres and Transnational Feminist Subjects." In *De/Colonizing the Subject: The Politics of Gender in Women's Autobiography*, edited by Sidonie Smith and Julia Watson, 115–38. Minneapolis: University of Minnesota Press, 1992.

Kaplan, Cora. "Pandora's Box: Subjectivity, Class and Sexuality in Socialist-Feminist Criticism." In *British Feminist Thought: A Reader*, edited by Terry Lovell, 345–66. London: Basil Blackwell, 1990.

Mills, Sara. "Authentic Realism." In *Feminist Readings/Feminists Reading*, edited by Sara Mills, Lynne Pearce, Sue Spaull, and Elaine Millard, 51–82. Charlottesville: University Press of Virginia, 1989.

Mukherjee, Arun. *Towards an Aesthetics of Opposition: Essays on Literature, Criticism and Cultural Imperialism*. Ontario: Williams-Wallace, 1988.

Perry, Donna. "Procne's Song: The Task of Feminist Literary Criticism." In *Gender/Body/Knowledge: Feminist Reconstructions of Being and Knowing*, edited by Alison Jaggar and Susan Bordo, 293–308. New Brunswick, N.J.: Rutgers University Press, 1989.

Rabinowitz, Paula. "The Great Mother: Female Working-Class Subjectivity." In *Labour and Desire: Women's Revolutionary Fiction in Depression America*, 97–136. Chapel Hill: North Carolina University Press, 1991.

Radhakrishnan, R. "Negotiating Subject Positions in an Uneven World." In *Feminism and Institutions: Dialogues on Feminist Theory*, edited by Linda Kaufman, 276–91. Cambridge, Mass.: Basil Blackwell, 1989.

Scott, Joan Wallach. "Experience." In *Feminists Theorize the Political*, edited by Judith Butler and Joan W. Scott, 22–40. New York: Routledge, 1992.

———. "Gender: A Useful Category for Historical Analysis." In *Gender and the Politics of History*. New York: Columbia University Press, 1988.

Showalter, Elaine. "Feminist Criticism in the Wilderness." In *Writing and Sexual Difference*, edited by Elizabeth Abel, 9–35. Chicago: Chicago University Press, 1982.

Steedman, Carolyn. *Landscape for a Good Woman*. London: Virago, 1986.

Stevenson, Sharon. "The Very Last Feminist Poem." In *Gold Earrings: Selected Poetry*. Vancouver: Pulp Press, 1984.

Weedon, Chris. *Feminist Practice and Poststructuralist Theory*. Oxford: Basil Blackwell, 1987.

Zandy, Janet, ed. *Calling Home: Working-Class Women's Writing—An Anthology*. New Brunswick, N.J.: Rutgers University Press, 1990.

'People Who Might Have Been You'

Agency and the Damaged Self in Tillie Olsen's *Yonnondio*

Lisa Orr

Reading Tillie Olsen's *Yonnondio* makes me tired and unhappy. In my mind, I am back in the neighborhood where I grew up. Surrounded by corner bars and turn-of-the-century factories, we lived our lives by the rhythms of the unemployment rate. When times were good, we tried to pay off our bills: five dollars a month to the dentist, more money down on the credit cards. When times were bad, we juggled who got paid that month by how nasty their demands for payment sounded: who would turn off service first, the phone company or the gas and electric? With each layoff we sank deeper into debt. With each plant closing my parents found fewer jobs that paid more than minimum wage. There was no money to move, and there certainly wasn't enough to stay. For us, living constantly in the red, escape seemed impossible.

I got out on other people's money—economic opportunity grants and scholar-ships. Reading *Yonnondio* renewed the guilt I feel about the others left behind, because *Yonnondio* is stunningly accurate in the oppressive, hopeless feelings it reproduces. The sense of "horror . . . on everything," which critic Annie Gottlieb unfortunately characterizes as melodramatic, is actually one of the most authenti-cally reproduced aspects of working-class life in the book.[1]

I have spent years hiding that part of my life. Finding a book that proved that literature could include the lives of working-class people was wonderful. But the fact remains that reading this book does not feel empowering to me. If anything, it makes me want to start taking the rungs two at a time on my way to the bour-geoisie. I don't want to identify with the working class in this book—it is just too painful.

The reader experiences what the characters feel: hopes collapse with the knowledge that life will continually beat one down. I have watched this sense that nothing can change prevent fellow workers from voting, participating in a union, turning in companies that violate safety codes—in short, from attempting anything that might improve their living conditions. The possibility of a person's having any effect on the system appears nil.

Disturbed by this hopelessness reflected in *Yonnondio* and in my own experi-ence, I turned to Ernesto Laclau's *New Reflections on the Revolution of Our Time* to examine the question of agency. Writing in the late 1980s, in the midst of the transformations of various "socialist" countries into free-market economies, Laclau observes that classical Marxism cannot account for the survival of capitalist states. This leads him to reexamine Marx's argument that the proletariat will inevitably overthrow capitalism.[2]

What Marx could not foresee was the extent to which capitalism could create an efficient, nondisruptive worker who would readily produce and consume products. Capitalism's longevity has led neo-Marxists such as Louis Althusser to posit that ideology creates the subjects necessary to perpetuate capitalism.[3] But if workers are entirely determined by outside forces, they will, according to Laclau, be incapable of overthrowing capitalism.[4]

Rather than accept this conclusion, Laclau notes that the belief that the worker is constructed by the system does not account for all the historical effects of capitalism. As he points out, capitalism has disrupted the lives of workers, but it has also generated unions and strikes, as well as worker-organized destruction of machinery.[5] The system has defined groups of people who are linked by economic circumstances. Eventually this group will disband; the individual members dispersing to join other groups defined by different circumstances, such as race or gender. In this way, Laclau believes, the voices of opposition become stronger, as they can rally against numerous points.[6]

Thus, for Laclau, the distinction between subjects who are completely inscribed by social forces and free agents who create their own society is an artificial one. The reality is constantly sliding between these two extremes. It is in this sense that Laclau sees a possibility of agency.

Olsen too sees capitalism as damaging people, who nonetheless retain some sense of human agency. Olsen, however, does not pass over the "ravages of circumstance" inflicted on workers by capitalism as easily as Laclau does.[7] Her novel shows us the human cost of the system Laclau so optimistically views as generating its own downfall. For example, *Yonnondio* demonstrates how economic status has a direct effect on behavior. When times are good—such as when the Holbrooks begin their life on the farm—Jim and Anna are happier together and kinder to their children. When money is tight, Jim cuffs them all around, and Anna strikes the children. She realizes, "'Twasn't them I was beatin up on. Somethin just seems to get into me when I have something to hit."[8] The text takes a forgiving attitude toward Jim and Anna. The constant money worries, Jim's crippling, dangerous work, and Anna's struggle to care for her children without even the basics create tension and anger that cannot always be contained.

Significantly, we don't learn what Jim and Anna look like until they leave the mining town. Jim, on the way to the farm, wears "a look of being intoxicated, his heavy brown hair blowing back, his blue eyes glittering" (25). Later, at the barn dance, we see Anna with her "black eyes laughing, her black hair smooth and shiny to purple" (31). This is the most personal description the two receive in the novel. By the time they are described again, in Omaha, their personal traits are subsumed by the suffering or sullen appearance of most of their class. Anna's "great dark eyes" are lost "down a terrace of sunken flesh," and all that remains familiar of Jim is the strange blue of his eyes (48). In this sense capitalism does appear to be turning human beings into anonymous, identity-less workers.

The belief that the system cannot be changed is, as Laclau points out, paralyzing. Even the reader is conditioned to feel hopeless in this novel: we learn from experience to dread the bad times sure to follow any respite. Thus, when Olsen writes "in everyone's heart coiled the fear of a blowup," describing the family's final days at the mining town, she does more than create suspense (17). Suspense is only possible when there is a possibility that an incident may be averted. But Olsen's reference to a facile company statement on the "unavoidable catastrophe" indicates that this is an oft-repeated tragedy (20). The incompetence of the bosses, the gas-filled caves, the untimbered roofs make an "accident" not only difficult to avoid, but inevitable.

Outside forces collude to keep the Holbrooks down. Once at the farm, their neighbor Benson warns them, "You can't make a go of it . . . bad or good year, the bank swallows everything up and keeps you owin 'em" (31). Anna's "cumulating vision of hostile, overwhelming forces" is based on fact: the banks, the bosses, and the landlords all have a stake in extracting profit from the Holbrooks (93). No wonder Mazie cannot enjoy her family's fireworks. "O it's us again," she rejoices for a moment, but then realizes, "Now something bad's going to have to happen. Again" (107).

Jim's misguided optimism at getting work at the packinghouse—"Didn't I tell you we'd manage? Good times comin, honey, good times"—is no antidote (104). His failure to analyze the forces that shape his life leads him to believe that a few more pennies a day will make a difference. The reader, like Jim's friend Kryckszi, knows better.

These ominous passages must not be read simply as foreshadowing. Olsen clearly is not interested in aesthetic effects alone, as her comments during the blowup scene at the mine illustrate: "And could you not make a cameo of this and pin it onto your aesthetic hearts? . . . Surely it is classical enough for you— the Greek marble of the women, the simple, flowing lines of sorrow" (20). Olsen's foreshadowing carries a political message: "hostile forces" attempt to convince working people that they are helpless, that nothing will ever get better, that resistance is useless.

With this knowledge, we can understand why Mazie is afraid to hope any longer. At one point she allows herself to pretend she is back on the farm, but then harshly chastises herself: the grief, the mourning is too hard to bear (100). This is how a working-class child is forced to cripple her own imagination. With even imaginative escape a cause of pain, the future for Mazie appears unalterably bleak.

According to many critics, what *Yonnondio* offers as a source of hope is the transcendence of the individual, such as the survival of "Anna's remarkable character."[9] The final scene, in which baby Bess discovers her ability to affect the world around her, has also been read as an illustration of that fundamental optimism (132). But to read this novel as only a story of the "rebirth of the spirit," as a *Village Voice* critic rhapsodizes on my edition's back cover, is to gloss over what it has to tell us about the destruction that capitalism causes, the destruction that Laclau so easily passes over. These critics are ignoring what actually occurs in the novel: while Olsen imagines children born with a self intact, their circumstances crush it out of them. No workers survive undamaged. At best they manage to retain something of their identity. This is why Olsen's novel focuses on retaining a sense of self, while at the same time she has been quoted as saying, "It is irrelevant to even talk of a core of Self when circumstances do not sustain its expression or development, when life has tampered with it and harmed it."[10] Worrying about having a self, she suggests, is a luxury. But it is also a form of resistance.

Anna knows the value of keeping one's inner self alive, and tries to pass this knowledge on to her children. On the one day when Anna is free of her daily routine—the day she and the children pick dandelion greens—Anna repieces the parts of herself that have been scattered by the various demands on her.

At first it seems that Anna's escape comes at the expense of her children. She wears a "remote, shining look . . . on her face, as if she had forgotten them, as if she . . . was not their mother any more" (100). Later, "Mazie felt the strange happiness in her mother's body, happiness that had nothing to do with them, with her; happiness and farness and selfness" (101). Her mother's distance is profoundly disturbing to Mazie, who longs to snap her fingers under her mother's nose.

But having momentarily recovered a selfhood, Anna can offer her children the kind of mothering that gets lost in caring for everyday needs. Her fingers stroke Mazie "into happiness and intactness and selfness" (102). In this mood Anna can heal the "hurt and fear and want and shame" that she ordinarily cannot redress (102).

The interlude does not last long. A whiff of the packinghouse brings back "the mother alertness, attunement, in her bounded body" (102). But even after her return to boundedness, she uses a phrase the children have never heard her say before: "Holy Meroly" (102). Something of the Anna who is more than clotheswasher, cook, or cleaning lady survives.

In interviews, Olsen insists that "her involvement in a 'full extended family life' did not fracture her selfhood."[11] Anna cannot be conflated with Olsen, but Olsen's insistence suggests we should read this scene carefully. The fact that the packinghouse smell brings Anna back to motherhood is significant. It is not motherhood that limits women, it is motherhood in these economic circumstances. While Anna has been ill, "a separation, a distance—something broken and new and tremulous—ha[s] been born in her" (93). It is free to develop because the house is neglected, a neighbor tends the baby, someone else prepares the meals—for a while she is free of her deadening routine.

In Laclau's terms, the Anna who sits under a tree stroking Mazie's hair is not the same Anna who hits her children. Olsen optimistically sees the Anna who sings to her children as Anna's "real self" who can bring out the "selves" within her children; to Laclau this very fragmentation precludes any essential self, which, to use his terms, is both "blocked" and "affirmed" by the forces arrayed against it.[12] But Laclau would agree that Anna is not reducible to the sum of capitalism's effects on a working-class wife. The Anna who stubbornly insists "Better . . . to be a cripple and alive than dead, not able to feel anything" is a source of resistance in the novel (37).

Mazie, too, resists the "inevitable . . . reduction of iron-willed humans to scrap."[13] Repeatedly she seeks confirmation from those around her that she is a human being. In the first chapter she seeks out her father in order "to force him into some recognition of her existence, her desire, her emotions" (8). When the family moves to Omaha, Mazie feels most threatened by the anonymous faces passing her on the street, "faces that knew her not, that saw her not" (69).

Yonnondio demonstrates repeatedly how ugliness can crush the spirit. For Mazie the shock of the city is so great that she wanders in a dream until a drunken passerby knocks her down. Later, she suddenly notices the morbid, depressing stories Ben has been telling Jimmie, and realizes they are destructive. As the narrator explains, "The conjurer is working spells on Anna's children. Subtly into waking and dreaming, into imagination and everyday doings and play, shaping, altering them" (108). The poems Ben recites are part of the spell, hardening them, numbing their senses. Mazie seeks out happier children's stories from her parents, but her father can no longer tell them: "The day at Cudahy's has thieved Pop's text" (101). Anna might remember some, but by the time she finishes her household chores, "it is too late for texts" (110).

Thus Anna, dreaming of a future on the farm and beautiful things to keep, is not succumbing to bourgeois brainwashing. She is not a materialist dreaming of acquiring objects for the sake of status. She simply knows the price of raising children in such surroundings. An ugly world is as deadening to the senses as meaningless, monotonous work. Locating beauty is not an empty aesthetic exercise but a tool for survival.

In the struggle to maintain selfhood, Mazie has an advantage that Anna and perhaps Ben share. She has a gift for finding beauty in surprising places, and she uses this gift to resist the numbing effects of her circumstances.

Beauty is what helps Mazie survive. In the mining town she finds release from pain in the "purty tongues" on the burning culm (10). When horrible memories of her abduction by McEvoy haunt her, she pushes them away by finding beauty wherever she can: "Butterflies live behind your eyes, Will. . . . Go ahead and try it—push your finger in your eye and you'll see 'em, butterfly wings" (43). The entire family can enjoy obvious beauty when it presents itself, as when they sing together at Else and Alex's house, or when they are watching the fireworks. It provides a saner release than damaging each other, or feeding nail-filled meat to dogs, as the men in the neighborhood do. But Mazie's gift for discovering hidden beauty is a rare one, and even more surprising considering her surroundings. For this reason Old Man Caldwell is amazed when Mazie speculates on whether stars are "lamps in houses up there, or flowers growin in the night" (32). "Children have marvelous minds. I hate to see what life does to 'em," he tells Anna (34).

Not all of Mazie's attempts succeed. The corn silk she treasures turns brown; her homemade perfume smells, but not pleasantly. That she continues to try is thanks to Anna, who uses precious energy scrubbing out an ink bottle to catch sunlight in the window.

Ultimately, this sense of self and sensitivity to beauty will be politically useful. In Olsen's original plan for the book, "Mazie was to grow up to become an artist, a writer who could tell the experiences of her people, her mother especially living in her memory. In Mazie's achievement, political consciousness and personal creativity were to coalesce."[14]

The world the Holbrooks live in is not sympathetic to creativity—next to everyday needs, it appears trivial. When Anna dreamily suggests that the mist on the river looks like "soft laundry blowin on a line," Jim responds, "You fixin to get sick on me again?" (93). Minutes later, Anna squelches Ben in a similar way. Ben admires the way she folds the clean laundry, and asks, "Are you making it a sunflower? Can I try trees and branches?" Anna responds fiercely, "You touch that wash with your dirty hands, and you'll never touch another thing" (94). Maintaining creativity in spite of such rebuffs is an everyday challenge for Anna's children.

A later passage, in which Anna begins speaking, is even more revealing:

> "Jim, a man came by today and for a quarter a week if we start now, a kid gets three hundred dollars when he's sixteen. For a sure edjication."
>
> Jim jabbed at Ben's arm, shadow-punched at his face. "Don't you know how to duck yet?"
>
> Holding his father's hand to stay it: "Guess what, Poppa? We blewed soap bubbles today with green onions." (94)

Anna wants to educate her children out of the working class, but Jim is more concerned with teaching them the skills they will need to survive within it. Ben's answer is something altogether different. His answer indicates he shares Mazie's gift for finding beauty in the humblest things. With such a gift, he can survive without giving up his working-class roots. Of the three, only Ben's view has the potential to create change.

Deborah Rosenfelt has written that Olsen "has not wanted to be misread as encouraging a withdrawal from political activism for the sake of 'art' or self-fulfillment."[15] Rather, her stated purpose has been paraphrased as the responsibility to "'voice the unvoiced,' to speak for all those millions like us whose lives are such that they can never come to writing. . . . In our brutal and inhuman society we injure each other, she reminds us, and any person who achieves recognition does so at the expense of others; this fact we must always remember, not with guilt but with a sense of responsibility to articulate the realities we come from."[16]

Mazie is suited to be the voice of her people by the fact that she feels a connectedness between herself and others, even when she would rather not. Her meeting with the deformed Erina at first seems like a repeat of the McEvoy incident, but Mazie is older now and part of her understands that private suffering is not necessarily a sign of private fault. Still, this connectedness is frightening; at first it seems merely like a doubling of one's own pain. Mazie shudders over a dream she had of being Erina: "Last night I was your body. Go away" (119). Erina would understand Mazie's dream of drinking from the Big Dipper; Erina finds happiness watching a bird play in a saucer of water. Olsen is aware, and probably Mazie is, too, that Erina is what Mazie would have been had she been even less fortunate. Erina reflects Olsen's knowledge that "there is so much more to people than their lives permit them to be. It almost kills you how much is lost and wasted in people who might have been you."[17]

Mazie's sense of connectedness prevents *Yonnondio* from being a story of individual success. All of Olsen's characters are individuals, but they are not isolated. Jim's lament that he has no way to buy the foods the doctor says Anna needs is echoed by a "million swollen throats" (78). When Anna goes to the clinic, she is surrounded by "distorted faces of pain," all with their private griefs, which, however, they experience as a result of their shared economic circumstances (82). As Laclau would argue, that part of the self which is shaped by capitalism forms a common link among these people.

If Mazie does appear to have a special gift, it is one preserved by what Olsen in *Silences* calls "chancy luck" as much as by her own effort.[18] *Yonnondio* does not imply that Mazie deserves special credit. Some critics find this disturbing. "If 'circumstances' are to be blamed for one's failure or 'silences,'" writes Abigail Martin, "then is one free to take credit for any successes achieved?"[19] The answer, I feel, must be no. Anyone who has escaped from that life knows that equally deserving people are left behind. Circumstances account as much for successes as failures.

If Mazie became a writer only to pat herself on the back for her success, she would be implying that all those she left behind had somehow not worked hard enough to escape. The Holbrooks work hard and still have nothing to show for it because outside forces work against them.

Mazie, if a self-absorbed artist, would not be a voice for her silenced class. The fact that Mazie has been damaged, that even the "terrible lands of dream" offer no escape to her, makes her the better activist (112). When Caldwell tells Mazie "Whatever happens, remember, everything, the nourishment, the roots you need, are where you are now," he is pushing her to remain loyal to her class (38). But he is also reminding her of the source of her political usefulness. The conditions that make her life too horrible to escape even in dreams are the very conditions that make her a potential agent for revolutionary change.

Mazie can interact with and change the structure because the structure has partially created in her a person capable of undermining it. As Laclau explains, human beings create their own identities in the decisions they make, decisions that are made possible by the gaps in the structure. Thus "the constitution of a social identity is an act of power and . . . identity as such is power."[20]

As we have seen, this leaves us with a subject who is divided and unpredictable. But Laclau sees this fragmented subject as a source of optimism. In his words, "One of the consequences of fragmentation is that the issues, which are the rallying point for the various social struggles, acquire greater autonomy and face the political system with growing demands. They thus become more difficult to manipulate and disregard."[21]

Tillie Olsen's work demonstrates the importance of this divided self, even though she is also obviously advocating a communist revolution. Rosenfelt has written that Olsen "found herself unable to document the political vision of social revolution as authentically and nonrhetorically as she was able to portray the ravages of circumstance on families and individuals and the redeeming moments between them."[22] But the two subjects are not necessarily exclusive. In portraying individuals in moments when they are something more than products of the system, something more than victims, Olsen can also be writing subversive prose. In doing so, she prefigures Laclau by almost sixty years.

Laclau's optimism about the fragmented self is then justified. As he predicted, the system has produced an individual who has the potential to overthrow it. Rereading *Yonnondio* with Laclau in mind helps me see room for hope in it. *Yonnondio* does not merely reproduce that despair which can be so crippling and antirevolutionary. Ultimately, Laclau helped me understand what originally seemed like a contradiction in Olsen. Olsen can say in the same interview, "I am a destroyed person" and "I am a survivor," because they are both true at once."[23]

NOTES

1. Annie Gottlieb, "A Writer's Sounds and Silences," review of *Yonnondio*, by Tillie Olsen, *New York Times Book Review*, 31 March 1974, 5.

2. Ernesto Laclau, *New Reflections on the Revolution of Our Time* (New York: Verso, 1990).

3. Louis Althusser, "Ideology and Ideological State Apparatuses," in *Lenin and Philosophy* (New York: Monthly Review Press, 1971).

4. Laclau, *New Reflections*, 51.

5. Ibid., 39.

6. Ibid., 32.

7. Deborah Rosenfelt, "From the Thirties: Tillie Olsen and the Radical Tradition," in *Feminist Criticism and Social Change*, ed. Judith Newton and Deborah Rosenfelt (New York: Methuen, 1985), 236.

8. Tillie Olsen, *Yonnondio: From the Thirties* (1974; New York: Delta-Bantam Doubleday Dell, 1989), 7. Subsequent citations are from this edition and given directly in the text.

9. Michael Staub, "The Struggle for 'Selfness' Through Speech in Olsen's *Yonnondio: From the Thirties*," *Studies in American Fiction* 16 (1988): 131–39, 137.

10. Erika Duncan, "Coming of Age in the Thirties: A Portrait of Tillie Olsen," *Book Forum* 6 (1982): 207–21.

11. Selma Burkom and Margaret Williams, "De-Riddling Tillie Olsen's Writings," *San Jose Studies* 2 (1976): 67–83.

12. Laclau, *New Reflections* 21.

13. Rose Kamel, "Literary Foremothers and Writers' Silences": Tillie Olsen's Autobiographical Fiction," *MELUS* 12 (1985): 55–73.

14. Rosenfelt, "From the Thirties," 233.

15. Ibid., 225.

16. Sandy Boucher, "Tillie Olsen Is a Survivor," *California Living Magazine*, 10 February 1974, 23.

17. Kenneth Turan, "Breaking Silence," *New West*, 28 August 1978, 59.

18. Tillie Olsen, *Silences* (1978; New York: Delta-Bantam Doubleday Dell, 1989), 39.

19. Abigail Martin, *Tillie Olsen*, Boise State University Western Writers Series 65, ed. Wayne Chatterton and James H. Maguire (Boise, Idaho: Boise State University Press, 1984), 17.

20. Laclau, *New Reflections*, 31.

21. Ibid., 82.

22. Rosenfelt, "From the Thirties," 236.

23. Boucher, "Tillie Olsen," 24.

Industrial Music

Contemporary American Working-Class Poetry and Modernism

Julia Stein

Tom Wayman, a Canadian poet living in Vancouver, has labored to create a movement of North American work writers for the last twenty years. After he earned his master of fine arts degree from the University of California–Irvine, he published *Beaton Abbot's Got the Contract* (1974), his first anthology of work poetry. Two more anthologies of work poetry followed—*A Government Job at Last* (1975) and *Going for Coffee* (1981)—plus a 1983 book of essays, *Inside Job: Essays on the New Work Writing*. His own poetry, published in over nine books, includes many poems about his job assembling trucks in a factory. Wayman's essays, poetry, and anthologies began a new dialogue throughout North America on work writing. Many small presses and literary magazines, in both Canada and the United States, have published working-class literature from 1970 through 1994.

In 1990 university presses published two anthologies of proletarian literature: Janet Zandy's *Calling Home*, the first American anthology of working-class women's writing, published by Rutgers University Press; and Peter Oresick and Nicholas Coles's *Working Classics: Poems on Industrial Life*, published by University of Illinois Press. Zandy includes over sixty authors—poets, fiction writers, and nonfiction writers; the poets range from Tillie Olsen, who began writing in the 1930s, to Chris Llewellyn, who first published in the 1980s. Oresick and Coles, in their introduction, say they included "169 poems by 74 poets," all written after 1945 (xxii). Zandy includes writing on many subjects derived from the feminist movement—home, sex, marriage, birth—but makes no mention of Wayman's anthologies. Oresick's and Coles's anthology is about industrial work. They only quote from one living poet, Tom Wayman, calling his poetry anthologies "pioneering collections" (xxiv), and their editorial criteria are shaped by Wayman's ideas in *Inside Job*.

In *Inside Job* Wayman puts forth a literary history in which romantic poetry has a negative influence on contemporary literature. He offers three criteria for work poetry: it should use "internal realism"; it should play down such traditional subjects as love, nature, and death and, instead, describe work; and it should avoid nonrealistic modernism and experimental poetry. In the rest of this essay I would like to discuss Wayman's three criteria. I would like to look at a few outstanding working-class writers to see how well their work reflects Wayman's theories. Because a large body of contemporary working-class poetry has been produced in the last twenty-four years, it seems an appropriate time for an assessment both of Wayman's theory and of this poetry.

I would like to begin with Wayman's comments on literary history. He argues

that European romantic poetry—with love, death, and nature as its main subjects—has been an important, but negative, influence on North American
poetry. He thinks that romantic poetry causes many readers to lose interest in
poetry while they attend school: "To most people, thanks in large part to high
school English curriculums, the words 'poetic' and 'romantic' are synonymous.
And romantic poetry as introduced to us in school is an archetype of escape from
reality in art" (26). He thinks most poets continue to write about irrelevancies. In
industrial society, he says, love, nature, and death are not central to our lives. He
argues that work is the governing factor in our lives and, thus, work writing
should be central to literature. He says that work poetry "leads in breaking the
remaining shackles of romanticism in art—obscurity, escape—in order to help us
learn more about the everyday world we inhabit" (26).

Wayman's characterization of romanticism and its relationship to the working
class is not accurate. There was a working-class audience that once eagerly read
romantic poets. E. P. Thompson, in his book *The Making of the English Working
Class*, has shown how a British workers' audience was created by 1830. Hawkers
"went round the working-class districts, hawking chapbooks, almanacs, dying
speeches, and . . . Radical periodicals" (788). The working-class autodidacts created group reading circles in taverns and coffeehouses as well as reading rooms.
From 1810 to 1830 the radical presses aimed at this working-class audience led an
assault on government libel laws and stamp taxes. This radical assault forced the
government to finally give the working class free speech by 1830. Thompson says,
"This was the culture—with its eager disputations around the booksellers' stalls,
in the taverns, work-shops, and coffeehouses—which Shelley saluted in his 'Song
to the Men of England' and within which the genius of Dickens matured" (790).
Thompson argues that this working class was part of the national British literary
audience by 1819. Working people read middle-class radicals: Percy Bysshe
Shelley, Lord Byron, and, later, Elizabeth Barrett Browning. Browning's "Song of
the Children" was an immensely popular poem protesting against the brutal
abuse of children working in mines and factories. They read worker-writers such
as Ebenezer Eliot, the corn-tax rhymer, and Thomas Hood.

Anglo-Americans brought this radical popular culture with them to the
Americas by the 1830s. Barbara Wertheimer, in *We Were There: The Story of
Working Women in America*, discusses the New England mill women at Lowell,
Massachusetts, who during the 1830s and 1840s "read the protest journals of the
day and followed accounts of strikes on the docks and in the cities" (65). After
work they attended lectures, sewing circles, and literary "improvement circles."
Wertheimer said that "out of one of these circles grew the *Lowell Offering*, the first
journal ever written by and for mill women," which printed their poetry (65).
Mill women began a new work literature in which workers wrote about their jobs.

Besides occupational groups such as mill workers and, later, miners, immigrants created work literature. Beginning in the 1840s, German immigrants
arrived in the United States, bringing with them "the German dream of a
working-class Socialist culture separate from and opposed to the evolving mass
culture" (Buhle 9). Carol Poore, in her article "German-American Socialist

Culture" writes, "Not only did they produce a large body of original literature (poetry, drama, fiction) but they also established a flourishing network of newspapers, theaters, and other organizations aimed at large numbers of German-speaking workers" (14). This poetry, influenced by such romantic poets as Heinrich Heine, "expressed the sufferings of the proletarians and their utopian mission in a hortatory, often moralistic way" (15). German American workers' culture and its institutions were widely copied by later-arriving immigrants such as the Finns, Ukrainians, South Slavs, and Eastern European Jews.

By the first decade of the twentieth century the working-class reading audience was massive. In his book *The Radical Novel in the United States, 1900–1954*, Walter B. Rideout writes about the radical press in 1912: "in that year alone 323 papers and periodicals with various shades of red were devoted to Socialism. The important periodicals by virtue of the size of their distribution were the monthly *Wilshire's Magazine* (400,000) and the two weeklies, *The Rip-Saw* (200,000) and *The Appeal to Reason* . . . over 500,000" (99). One of these periodicals was a literary magazine. In 1901 young New York intellectuals put out the *Comrade*, the first socialist literary magazine in the United States. Literature critics writing in the *Comrade* were highly critical of genres favored by socialist fiction writers—the moral-sentimental tale, the utopian novel, and the romance—and they called for realism (Rideout 24). Thus, the socialist critique of romanticism began seven decades ago.

After 1900 English-language poets emerged out of the Industrial Workers of the World (IWW, or Wobblies). The IWW encouraged working people to write songs and poems, printing these pieces in Wobbly newspapers. Cary Nelson, in *Repression and Recovery: Modern American Poetry and the Politics of Cultural Memory 1910–1945*, mentions three Wobbly poets—Covington Hall (1871–1951), Arturo Giovannitti (1884–1959), and Ralph Chaplin (1887–1961)—who "built strong popular reputations, and have remained important to those interested in labor history and culture" (62).

Like the Wobblies, Wayman wants to encourage working people to create their own culture. He applauds the Wobblies' efforts to organize U.S. workers from 1900 until the early 1920s. Though Marxists, the IWW's members differed sharply from those of the Socialist Party. The Wobblies promoted direct action through strikes, free speech fights, boycotts, and demonstrations. They distrusted the socialist's emphasis on political elections, distrusted any person who "represented" the workers in politics or permanent trade unions. The IWW had its own definition of working class. This definition included industrial workers—longshoremen and garment workers—as well as loggers in logging camps, migrant workers on the farms, miners, fishermen, and homeless in the hobo camps. Their inclusion of migrant labor, the unemployed, and the hoboes made them different from East Coast Marxist groups, which only wanted to organize the industrial proletariat. Traditional Marxists ignored what Marx called the *lumpenproletariat*, the homeless or unemployed, because Marx thought the lumpenproletariat was irrelevant to the class struggle.

When I speak of contemporary working-class poets, I will use the Wobbly definition, including both those who write about eastern or midwestern factory work, as well as those who write about migrant work and class struggle in other parts of the country. I will refer to such contemporary poets of the working class as Philip Levine and Jim Daniels, who write about auto work in Detroit, the industrial heartland; Jimmy Santiago Baca from New Mexico, who describes how Chicano small farmers lost their land to the government; Tom McGrath from North Dakota and Wilma McDaniel from Oklahoma, both of whom deal with the conflicts between migrant farm laborers and large farmers.

Wayman developed his critical ideas while collecting poems for his anthologies. In *Inside Job* he says he was dissatisfied with his first collection, *Beaton Abbot's Got the Contract*, because he feels that the poems written by outsiders, people observing other people work, were not as good as those written by insiders, people doing the jobs. (Unfortunately, he neglects to include examples of these flawed poems in *Inside Job*.) While thinking over these problems, he says that he presented some poems by insiders to a working-class audience:

> The enthusiastic reception the new work poems have received from those working at the jobs depicted—irrespective of the poet's background, or how long the poet has been employed, or whether the poet still works there—is testimony to the truth and power of these poems, I feel. (21)

Wayman thinks that poetry by insiders is "more honest, deeper, richer . . . with an immense strengthening of the art both in complexity and aesthetics" than poetry by outsiders (48). When Wayman argues for insiders creating poetry, he carries on the Wobbly tradition of distrusting "professionals" and "representatives" who claim to represent workers, insisting that the workers "must act" (49).

Wayman argues that contemporary work poets write a "lyric as documentary," which uses anecdotal accounts of work events. He refers to John Lent, another Canadian poet and critic, who says that work poets document many different worlds of work. Wayman says Lent recognized that this lyrical documentary is "an extension of William Carlos Williams' poetics" (23). He says that, as working-class people read contemporary poetry, they discover that:

> Modern poems can be short, concise, unrhymed, anecdotal—exactly like the conversations in which the industrial culture itself is transmitted: People whose daily work leaves them without time, energy, or self-confidence for longer forms find contemporary poetry a handy vehicle to express what they feel is important to their lives. (71)

Work poets, he thinks, are influenced by Williams's poetry, especially his short, unrhymed lyrics based on the "raw facts of ordinary life" (23).

When Wayman insists that work writing is primary, and then anthologizes work writers, he acts within a historical tradition of Marxism. Earlier I mentioned how the IWW encouraged work literature. Granville Hicks and Michael Gold, two socialist realist critics in the 1920s and 1930s who were close to the Communist Party, also used Marxist theory to argue that production was central to human existence and that work writing was central to literature. Wayman and the social realist critics are interested in writing about blue-collar work; both want this writing to have technical precision and to use a work vocabulary.

Though Wayman shares many ideas with 1930s critics, he calls contemporary work poetry "internal realism," claiming it is quite different from 1930s socialist realism, which he calls "external realism." He defines external realism as literature dominated by a vision of the great day when socialism would arrive; he adds that most external realist writing was created by outsiders observing other people work. He gives examples of external realism as Russian socialist realism and Diego Rivera's 1930s murals of the auto industry at the Detroit Institute of Art. Wayman even faults 1930s work writing by "participants inside the industrial process" (47). This future-oriented work poetry, Wayman feels, does not accurately describe daily work because "the poet uses an external ideological framework to try to bend or alter what is happening to fit a preconceived pattern" (47).

Wayman fails to see how 1930s poetry is connected both to modernism and to previous radical traditions. Nelson, who has carefully reread proletarian poetry of the 1920s and 1930s, comments that proletarian poets were writing modernist lyrics from 1914 on:

> Indeed one of the more striking things about the gradual emergence of modernist forms in American protest poetry—from Arturo Giovanetti's prose poems of 1914 to Anna Louise Strong's free verse of 1919 to Lola Ridge's and Charles Reznikoff's imagist poems about immigrants in America, on through the poets of *We Gather Strength* (1933) is the lack of sense of radical break with the past. (25)

Proletarian poets did have a strong sense of the past. Nelson comments that Marcus Graham's *Anthology of Revolutionary Poetry* (1929) included "The Forerunners," such as William Blake, Shelley, Walt Whitman, William Morris, and poets who published in *The Comrade* as well as the "the moderns." Both the forerunners—Blake, Shelley, and the IWW poets—and the 1930s work writers had utopian dreams. The 1930s poets were the latest in a long history of writers who had utopian visions, stretching back to Shelley, Heine, and other romantics.

Nelson thinks that 1930s proletarian poetry was *not* dominated by the Communist Party's theories of socialist realism:

> Yet, unlike proletarian fiction, poetry was rarely pressed to abandon all marks of stylistic and political idiosyncrasy. Indeed, even writers who generally had little patience with what they considered to be the bourgeois cult of individualism left considerable space for poetry to register individual experience, conflicts about political commitment, and linguistic effects that suggested the peculiarity of an individual landscape. (150)

Nelson argues that the Communist Party asks merely "clear sympathy for the working class," and Communist-dominated journals "often settled quite happily for revealing portrayals of working-class life" (163). He discusses various 1930s labor poets: Mike Gold's found poems were taken from workers' letters to the *Daily Worker*; Joseph Kalar was a mystic poet who worked in paper mills; Sol Funaroff, influenced by Eliot, combined "abstract manifesto and personal lyricism"; Edwin Rolfe's complex lyrics are clearly influenced by Ezra Pound, T. S. Eliot, and Williams (150–51). Kenneth Patchen was most influenced by W. H. Auden, Hart Crane, and Whitman.

Furthermore, the Communist-influenced proletarian arts movement did have some real accomplishments. The *New Masses* and the magazine put out by the John Reed Clubs published many new (and old) working-class writers: Michael Gold, James Farrell, Richard Wright, Langston Hughes, Erskine Caldwell, Tillie Olsen, and others. These magazines, the critics who wrote for them, and the John Reed clubs created a support system crucial for working-class writers, encouraging them to write about lives that had been dismissed as trash, as garbage unfit for literature. Nelson argues that the myth of Communist Party domination was started by Philip Rahv's "polemical 1939 *Southern Review* essay, 'Proletarian Literature: A Political Autopsy.'" In discussing Rahv's essay, Nelson argues that "the poetry is too diverse to fit any simple model of party influence" (163–64). The myths Rahv created about 1930s poetry have remained with us until the 1990s.

Wayman argues that contemporary work writers use internal realism, which is characterized by "the abandonment of heaven" (40). He thinks that internal realism accurately reflects the experiences of the postwar working class, which has abandoned any faith that "participation in the work force will lead to any particular future, let alone a glorious socialist one" (40). Instead, internal realism concentrates on the here and now, the minutiae of daily life. New working-class writers who give nitty-gritty descriptions of work life as they experience it on their jobs are, he thinks, a reflection of working-class consciousness in this period.

Philip Levine's poetry illustrates internal realism. The white and black male factory workers in Levine's poems lack hope for a socialist heaven on earth. The poems describe working in a bleak factory. In 1948 his brother curses his job, angrily saying, "You can have it" in a poem with that title published in Levine's *7 Years from Somewhere* (1979). In "Sweet Will," from Levine's *Sweet Will* (1985) and reprinted in Oresick and Coles (146–47), the narrator's coworker gets drunk on the job every Friday night, falls to the oily shop floor, and sleeps in his own blood. The young man in "The Everlasting Sunday," from Levine's *Not This Pig* (1968), set during the late 1940s, loses his youth in the numb loneliness of his awful job:

> Bowed my head
> into the cold grey
> soup of the wash trough,
> talked with men
> who couldn't talk.

> (reprinted in Oresick and Coles 138)

Twenty years later, the narrator in "Coming Home, Detroit, 1968," finds the city burning up, the people with

> charred faces, the eyes
> boarded up, the rubble of innards, the cry
> of wet smoke hanging in your throat
>
> (Levine, *Selected Poems* 75)

A sense of hopelessness pervades Levine's factory poems.

Like the people in Levine's poems, Jim Daniels's Detroit white factory workers have no belief in a socialist future. In "Recycled Lunchbucket" Daniels writes:

> I wiped it clean, sprayed black paint
> over the farm animals, the barn.
> Then it looked like the others in the factory:
> small black houses, our little coffins.
>
> (Daniels, *Places Everyone* 69)

Daniels's internal realism is very much like the minimalism, or "new realism," of such writers as Raymond Carver and Bobby Anne Mason, two working-class fiction writers. The auto workers in Daniels's poem don't try to escape their "little coffins," just as the characters in Carver's and Mason's stories usually accept their small coffins. The inhabitants of internal realist poems or minimalist fiction make minimal demands on reality, certainly no utopian demands. This realism of the late twentieth century is quite different from Honoré de Balzac's nineteenth-century bourgeois realism.

Wayman's concept of internal realism aptly characterizes a mood of many labor poets, yet this concept poses problems. Bruce Robbins, in *The Servant's Hand*, refers to Kenneth Burke's critique of proletarian realism in the 1930s: "Burke is afraid, that a 'discourse weighted with symbols of proletarian life and exploitation might succeed only in isolating workers' agony,'" if that discourse is dissociated from utopian visions that "effectively mobilize allegiance and action" (5). Robbins states that Burke argues:

> To mobilize those whom the image of the alienated worker leaves unmoved, what is needed is to replace the usual realism of the present with a rhetoric . . . projecting images of the desirable (future) while it also reaches back to engage with the compromised values of the uncon-verted. (5)

Robbins argues that realism must be altered to make room for "unrealistic visions or fictions of shared fate" (6). During the 1930s writers usually combined utopian visions and images of workers' agony, while by the 1980s the alternative visions had nearly vanished. Robbins's argument is probably even more crucial to the 1990s than to the 1930s. Furthur, Robbins analyzes in *The Servant's Hand* the servants in literature, a job dominated by women, as he looks at work literature taking place in the boudoir and kitchen rather than factory floor.

While Kenneth Burke and Bruce Robbins developed one critique of proletarian realism, feminist critics in the 1980s began a second critique. Wayman (as well as 1930s socialist realists) encouraged labor poets to write primarily about the job rather than about love or reproduction. Two feminist critics, Alice Kessler-Harris and Paul Lauter, mention that "less than a quarter of all women . . . worked outside the home during most of the 1930s" (x). These critics say that in the 1930s "women writers of the Left chose to flout male convention and to write about themes that fell outside the frameworks of their male peers. . . . [In] her novella, The Girl, Meridel Le Sueur focuses on the regenerative power of pregnancy" (xiii–xiv). The two critics also quote Deborah Rosenfelt's discussion of Tillie Olsen's novel, Yonnondio: "The major transformation is based on . . . the regenerative life cycle of which mother and daughter are a part . . . and nurturing that creative capacity in the young is shown in Yonnondio to be an essential precondition to social change" (xiv). Feminist critics think women's "work" includes work within the home and the reproduction of life in the family. These critics do not see production as central to working-class writing but, rather, only as one facet of it. Contemporary female working-class poets continue to write powerfully about reproduction, while also raising new feminist issues. African American poet Audre Lorde broke new ground by writing about her breast cancer.

Another feminist critic, Janet Zandy, in her anthology Calling Home, includes literature that points to differences in the domestic labor of working-class and middle-class women. For example, Marge Piercy, in "Out of the Rubbish," from My Mother's Body (1985), describes how her mother labored to fix up their shabby house:

> If we make curtains
> of the rose-bedecked table
> cloth, the stain won't show
> and it will be cheerful.
>
> (reprinted in Zandy 123)

Piercy's poem points out that a working-class woman is a laborer who has to make her own curtains, while a middle-class woman is a consumer who buys her drapes. In the introduction to her book Zandy also contrasts working-class with middle-class women when she discusses "home":

> Working-class women have not found a home in middle-class America. Not really. Recalling the struggle against the dirt and filth of poverty, they try to make of their small and modest homes, safe, clean places. The curtains are changed; the glass doors polished with vinegar, the front stoop swept. . . . These homes . . . can blow over with the slightest shift in economic winds. (1–2)

Many female working-class writers from the 1930s to the 1990s write about how economic forces destroyed poor people's homes and families. Grace Lumpkin's 1930s novel about the Gastonia strike, *To Make My Bread* (1932), describes the evictions of the strikers' families from their company-owned homes (reprinted in Salzman 127). During the 1980s Wilma McDaniel wrote *Primer for Buford*. Many poems deal with how the dust bowl catastrophe, both economic and environmental, affected the Okie family: "Green Grape Pie" talks of how children coped with starvation; "Aunt Sula's Quilt" tells how the neighbors gave Aunt Sula a going-away gift before she left for California; "Via Dolorosa" recounts how Okie mothers suffered on the migration westward. As McDaniel aged, she realized that Okie history and customs were not being transmitted to the younger generation in California. She then wrote *Primer for Buford* for Uncle Claudie Windham's grandson Buford, who

> don't know nothing
> his daddy done
> when he was boy in Oklahoma.
>
> ("Primer for Buford" 15)

She gives an epic story of an Okie family.

Men, as well as women, write about how political or economic forces push people from their homes. Jimmy Santiago Baca, in his poem "Roots" from *Black Mesa Poems*, describes how his father lost his land—his family's home for generations—to the government; his family wound up as immigrants and exiles in their own land. In *Martin and Meditations on South Valley*, Baca describes how his narrator, Martin, builds his family a home, and also has a fine piece about Martin's wife giving birth. Both McDaniel and Baca create their own working-class visions of domestic labor. From the Wobbly hoboes to McDaniel's Okies in their jalopies to Baca's Chicanos, homelessness has been central to this poetry.

Wayman does make one very cogent point when he argues that our economic position influences our relationship to nature, love, and death. There are great differences between those, like William Wordsworth, who have the income leisurely to contemplate a landscape versus those, like Thomas McGrath, who work on the land as a farm laborer. Jim Daniels does not describe a lovely landscape in "Still Lives in Detroit #2, Parking Lot, Ford Sterling Plant" in *Places Everyone*. Instead he writes of "a barren landscape decaying under the grey sky" (reprinted in Oresick and Coles 54). In the 1930s Muriel Rukeyser published her long epic, *U.S. 1*, about hundreds of miners in West Virginia who were dying from work-induced lung disease. *Working Classics* also includes two of many poems written in the 1980s about the Triangle Shirtwaist Company fire: Mary Fell's "The Triangle Fire," from her collection *The Persistence of Memory*; and a section from Chris Llewellyn's book, *Fragments from the Fire*. From the 1930s through the 1980s labor poets have created a poetry of industrial disasters and polluted landscapes.

Wayman proposes both a subject matter—work—and a method—the lyric as documentary. At the same time, he attacks all forms of nonrealist writing. He writes that, in the early parts of the century,

> What was new in poetry were certain experiments in form—including surrealism, sound poetry, automatic writing, the unconventional re-arrangement of words on page: Some writers today still imagine that what was startling half a century ago must remain the path to the future. But in our time the new in poetry is to be found rather in content, specifically this content. (*Inside Job* 72)

Wayman ignores the politics and content of modernist poetry. Both Dada and surrealism blasted out protests against the debacle of European society and the French surrealists made scathing critiques of society, allying themselves first with the Communist Party in the 1920s and then with the Trotskyites in the 1930s. They dismissed realism as unable to provoke any real change in society; they wanted to forge a new language using nonrealistic art forms because "to propose a new language is to propose a changed life for men and an alternative and revolutionized society" (Short 303).

Wayman is blind to the sociopolitical critique of the original surrealism or of Dada, so he is also blind to how this critique has been continued by at least some of the subsequent generations of modernist poets. A small French Trotskyist sect merged with Dada artists in the 1950s to produce the International Situationists, who were the theoreticians for the May 1968 French uprising. Their ideas inspired much postmodernist art; a small group of northern California situationists started *Process World*, an avant-garde San Francisco magazine for workers in the information-processing industries (Ward). A feminist Trotskyist group, the Freedom Socialist Party, includes two contemporary Bay Area poets, Nelly Wong and Merle Woo, and the late Karen Brodine was also a member. A politicized modernism, drawing on both Marxism and the French avant-garde, has been integral to twentieth-century poetry from the 1920s up to the 1990s.

Wayman feels that most nonrealist art is escapist literature that keeps people confused about their lives in industrial society. He thinks nonrealist art promotes the interest of the bourgeois class, asserting that this class wants people confused and mystified about everyday reality. Wayman condemns four forms of nonrealistic art: magical realism, myth, symbolism, and alternate visions. After briefly discussing his criticism of each form, I would like to compare Wayman's criticism with some poetry by contemporary working-class poets.

Wayman dislikes magical realism; he calls Gabriel García Márquez's magical realism "a bizarre and arbitrary surrealism" that "eases the reader's flight into fantasy" (16). But other literary scholars view magical realism as an integral part of Chicano literature about the working class. At the 1991 Modern Language Association conference, in a session titled Relations between U.S. Hispanic and Latin American Literature, Carl Guitterez-Jones presented a paper entitled "The Magical in Morales's *Brick People*," a novel about Chicano workers in a brick factory. Baca, a Chicano poet, has many magical figures in "Meditation on South

Valley" (the title poem from *Martin and Meditation on South Valley*) including *curanderas* (spirit healers) and *brujas* (witches). *Curanderas* and *brujas* have been part of Chicano and Mexicano culture for centuries. Wayman, however, does not account for the cultural significance of this style of literature.

Wayman dismisses symbolism and myth in literature as a result of social hierarchies. He says critics like symbolism and myth in writing because the ability to understand Greek and Roman myths or to decode obscure symbolism can be accomplished only by an educated, often upper-class, minority. He regards myths as an outdated means that earlier civilizations used to comprehend their world; this knowledge, he feels, has largely disappeared from the general population. Literature relying heavily on myth and symbol, he argues, bears the subtext that ordinary, daily life is not important as literature.

Wayman praises feminist, Chicano, and black writing, yet all these literatures have accepted mythical writing and symbolism as relevant to contemporary audiences. Feminists have rewritten many Greek and Roman myths to the delight of women's audiences. Alta rewrote the Orpheus myth from the viewpoint of Eurydice, while Greek actress Melina Mercouri acted in the film *Crime of Passion*, a feminist retelling of Medea. Native American poets—including Simon Ortiz, Wendy Rose, and Leslie Marmon Silko—have written poems using Native American symbolism and mythical characters. Third World cultural nationalisms in the 1960s encouraged Chicanos, blacks, Native Americans, and Asian American writers to use their religious symbols and mythic past, forging connections between their past and the present.

This brings us back to McDaniel, who is part Native American and part Euro-American. She uses Christian symbolism to such a great extent in *Sister Vadya's Song* that she sounds often like a present-day biblical prophet. In "Kinship" she writes:

> the Bible
> has seeped into the marrow
> of our souls
> Old Testament
> and New
> We have both seen the wicked
> in great power.
>
> (38)

The characters in *Sister Vadya's Song* live in a Bible-saturated world: in "Close Neighbors" Jesus and his mother "live down the Okie Road only a/little piece" (66); in "Psalms" Odie Hicks in his California exile

> might as well been
> sitting by the rivers of
> Babylon
> the muddy Kings held him
> as tight.
>
> (62)

McDaniel fuses her deep spirituality with politics in *Primer for Buford*. In "Red Is for Martyrs" the priest strangely wears the red vestments honoring Saint Matthew, the patron saint of tax collectors. The poet, believing that the real martyrs are the young men who died in the war, wants back the taxes that paid for their deaths. McDaniel's deep religious beliefs are typical of many in the working class. Thompson, in *The Making of the English Working Class*, discusses the many religious revivals among the English rural and urban poor in the early nineteenth century. When many of these poor Christians, like McDaniel, became politicized, they expressed their politics using biblical discourse—in revival-style meetings, politicized hymns, and religious slogans (438–39). Thompson's research and McDaniel's writings show that symbolism and spirituality are important to European American working-class writers also.

Wayman dismisses literature that imagines alternative possibilities. He does admit that some critics defend visionary literature, as it "provides a vision of other human possibilities, often of an ideal world or situation" (*Inside Job* 17). But he immediately criticizes visionary literature, if it is in any way disconnected from daily work, as one more escape fantasy. He writes as if no such visionary literature dealing with production exists. But the writings of Marxist critic Christopher Caudwell inspired labor poets such as McGrath to write visionary literature that was connected with daily work.

A young British Marxist poet and critic, Caudwell wrote *Illusion and Reality*, which had a great impact on post–World War II leftist intellectuals in England and New York. Caudwell gave a Marxist rationale for the spiritual in art and for alternative visions. Caudwell argued that poetry, the rhythmical language of public emotion, is necessary for the economic well-being of tribal societies. He used the example of a harvest. Before the harvest the tribe will have a public festival in which it uses poetry to call up a fantasy of the harvest:

> As man by the violence of the dance, the screams of the music, and the hypnotic rhythm of the verse is alienated from present reality, which does not contain the unsown harvest, so he is projected into the phantastic world in which these things phantastically exist. That world becomes more real, and even when the music dies away the ungrown harvest has a greater reality for him, spurring him on to the labours necessary for its accomplishment. (27)

Here poetry gives the alternative visions that help channel human instincts into economic activities.

Thompson recalls how British and American leftist literary critics and intellectuals hotly debated Caudwell's theories during the late 1940s. In a long essay on McGrath collected in Frederick Stern's *The Revolutionary Poet in the United States*, Thompson writes that Gertrude R. Levy's book *The Gate of Horn*, which examines totemism and cave art in Lascaux, vindicated Caudwell's view of tribal art. Cave art and tribal art both had complex symbolism that embodied the tribe's totems. Thompson discusses how both Levy and Caudwell helped Marxists understand how the shaman or artist in tribal society led the religious rituals that promoted the economic well-being of the tribe. These ideas about the artist as visionary shaman clearly influenced many 1950s and 1960s poets, such as the Beats and Tom McGrath.

Both Levy and Caudwell clearly influenced McGrath. McGrath entitled one novel *The Gates of Ivory, the Gates of Horn* and introduces part 4 of his epic poem *Letter to an Imaginary Friend* with the Caudwell quotation about how the tribe uses collective emotion to call up the fantasy of the harvest. McGrath, in "A Note on Parts Three and Four of *Letter to an Imaginary Friend*" (1985), explains that he borrows heavily from Hopi myth, especially Hopi symbolism of resurrection and renewal. He repeatedly calls himself "a resurrectionist man" who acts very much like a Native American shaman. McGrath sees his whole epic poem as a kachina that will help fulfill Hopi prophecy: ending the present world, the Hopi Fourth World; and ushering in the Hopis' Fifth World, which he identifies as the postcapitalist world. Of course, he also has wonderful descriptions of work throughout his epic poem, from his joining a farm labor crew in his early teens to his working as a woodcutter during the depression. He describes how he "sweated and froze" in the migrant woodcutting crew and how he

> participated in the solidarity of forlorn men
> Firm on our margin of poverty and cold
> Communitas
> Holy City
> Laughter at forty below
> Round Song
> The chimes of comradeship that comes once maybe
> In the Winter of the Blue Snow.
>
> (*Letter*, parts 1–2, 46)

This round song of the woodcutters is McGrath's utopian vision of labor solidarity, which could constitute a new world of *communitas* in the future. McGrath was part of a small group of poets who, throughout the postwar years, still retained their utopian visions.

Thompson argues that McGrath is not an isolated literary figure but, rather, is representative of an important leftist current from the 1940s through the 1980s. Memory of this current has been erased:

> I find, rather often, a curious amnesia within American radical culture as to certain moments in its own past. . . . Not only some part of the 1930s but a large amount in the 1940s has fallen out of polite discourse.
>
> Orthodox academicism and post-Trotskyist criticism and historiography have obliterated this moment under some general theory of the universal contamination of "Stalinism." ("Homage to Thomas McGrath" reprinted in Stern 113)

Thompson tells how McGrath was part of a British and North American dissi-
dent group that used Caudwell and Levy to battle Communist orthodoxy within
the Communist Party during the 1950s. When the dissidents lost to the party
bureaucrats, McGrath and many others left the Communist Party. McGrath
remained an independent radical whose nonorthodox radicalism permeated his
poetry. Thompson thinks that McGrath's trajectory was typical of his generation.
Thompson himself, as well as many other British and North American leftist
intellectuals, shared this history from the 1940s through the 1980s. Though these
British and American writers split from the Communist Party, they still remained
political radicals, and their politics were central to their literary work. Nelson
mentions some of the radical writers continuing to publish individual poems as
well as complete books in the 1940s and 1950s: "Langston Hughes, Muriel
Rukeyser, Kenneth Fearing, Alfred Hayes, Don West, Genevieve Taggard, Norman
Rosten, Edwin Rolfe, Thomas McGrath, Aaron Kramer, Ruth Lechlitner, Walter
Lowenfels, Melvin Tolson, Olga Cabral and others" (166). Many of these poets
continued to publish through the 1990s, their work developing with each decade,
largely appearing in small press editions and alternative magazines, yet they have
been largely ignored.

The North American literary establishment has successfully marginalized
these poets as part of a larger effort to "imagine that radical political poetry as a
whole came to an end in America in 1939" (Nelson 164). Unfortunately, many
young working-class writers have never heard of these poets or their history.
Nelson argues that ignorance of radical literary history "suggests how successful
has been the process of repression and the construction of a diminished, sanitized
cultural memory" (166).

Wayman criticizes modernism and visionary poetry in this landscape of cultural amnesia described by Thompson. The New Critics and the myth critics not
only buried leftist history but also stripped the politics out of modernist texts.
Wayman seems to be responding to the landscape that he sees before him: a
derivative modernism totally divorced from any social or political content and a
new generation whose members were beginning to write working-class literature.
But Wayman overstates his case when he dismisses all postwar literature influenced by nonrealistic modernism.

All of working-class poetry from 1820 to the present needs to be retrieved and
studied. Contemporary work poets can no longer hold on to their cultural amnesia, no longer remain in ignorance of their history. Perhaps as labor poets, both
historical and contemporary, receive more critical attention, the belief that labor
poets need to use realism will be debated. Nelson uses poststructuralist theory to
deconstruct twentieth-century literary history, and in the process he retrieves
proletarian poetry from the early twentieth century for the 1990s. Poststructuralist
theory, if applied to working-class poetry, could also lead to a reexamination of
realism, representation, and labor poetry. From the Wobblies to the poststruc-
turalists the basic question is: Who represents the working class? With an
immensely diverse and complex working class, can a handful of writers "represent" or give a "realistic" portrait of the whole class?

Wayman has carried on the tradition of Wobbly dissent, and that is courageous.

I have used the Wobbly definition of the working class rather than the traditional Marxist one. The Wobbly definition included the homeless and the unemployed, as well as preindustrial workers such as farm laborers, fishermen and miners. If work literature includes preindustrial workers, then could it also include workers in a postindustrial economy now developing in the United States? The postindustrial working class has its homeless, part-time, and marginalized workers, many of whom are women. Clearly, the nature of the postindustrial working class and the beginnings of a postindustrial work literature in such magazines as *Processed World* should be studied further. Literary critics of noncanonical working-class literature need to recover and study all of the past literature, as well as look with open eyes at how this literature is changing in the present.

BIBLIOGRAPHY

Aaron, Daniel. *Writers on the Left*. New York: Harcourt, Brace and World, 1961.
Baca, Jimmy Santiago. *Black Mesa Poems*. New York: New Directions, 1986.
———. *Immigrants in Our Own Land*. Baton Rouge: Louisiana State University Press, 1979.
———. *Martin and Meditation on the South Valley*. New York: New Directions, 1987.
Bold, Alan. *The Penguin Book of Socialist Verse*. Baltimore: Penguin Books, 1970.
Brodine, Karen. *Illegal Assembly*. Brooklyn: Hanging Loose Press, 1980.
———. *Women Sitting at the Machine, Thinking*. Seattle: Red Letter Press, 1990.
Buhle, Paul, ed. *The Origins of Left Culture in the United States: 1880–1940*. *Cultural Correspondence*, nos. 6–7, and *Green Mountain Irregulars*, no. 6 (spring 1978).
Caudwell, Christopher. *Illusion and Reality*. New York: International Publishers, 1937.
Clubbe, John, ed. *Selected Poems of Thomas Hood*. Cambridge: Harvard University Press, 1970.
Coiner, Constance. "'Pessimism of the Mind, Optimism of the Will': Literature of Resistance." Ph.D. diss., University of California–Los Angeles, 1987.
Coleman, Mary Jane. *Take One Blood Red Rose*. Minneapolis: West End Press, 1980.
Daniels, Jim. *Places/Everyone*. Madison: University of Wisconsin Press, 1985.
———. *Punching Out*. Detroit: Wayne State University Press, 1990.
Fell, Mary. *The Persistence of Memory*. New York: Random House, 1984.
Giovanitti, Arturo. *Arrows in the Gale*. Riverside, Conn.: Hillacre Brookhouse, 1914.
Grahn, Judy. *The Work of a Common Woman*. New York: St. Martin's Press, 1978.
Howe, Irving. *World of Our Fathers*. New York: Harcourt Brace Jovanovich, 1976.
Harris, Marie, and Kathellen Aguero, eds. *A Gift of Tongues: Critical Challenges in Contemporary American Poetry*. Athens: University of Georgia Press, 1987.
Kessler-Harris, Alice, and Paul Lauter. Introduction to *The Unpossessed*, by Tess Slesinger. Old Westbury, N.Y.: The Feminist Press, 1984.
Kornbluh, Joyce, ed. *Rebel Voices, An I.W.W. Anthology*. Ann Arbor: University of Michigan Press, 1964.
Laska, Peter J. *D.C. images and other poems*. Beckley, W.V.: Mountain Union Books, 1975.
Levine, Philip. *1993*. New York: Atheneum, 1974.
———. *Selected Poems*. New York: Atheneum, 1984.
———. *They Feed They Lion*. New York: Atheneum, 1972.
———. *What Work Is*. New York: Alfred A. Knopf, 1991.
Levy, Gertrude R. *The Gate of Horn*. London: Faber and Faber, 1948.
Llewellyn, Chris. *Fragments from the Fire*. New York: Viking, 1986.

McDaniel, Wilma. *A Primer for Buford*. Brooklyn: Hanging Loose Press, 1990.

———. *Sister Vadya's Song*. Brooklyn, N.Y.: Hanging Loose Press, 1982.

McGrath, Thomas. *The Gates of Ivory, The Gates of Horn*. New York: Mainstream Publishers, 1957.

———. *Letter to an Imaginary Friend: Parts 1 and 2*. Chicago: Swallow Press, 1962.

———. *Letter to an Imaginary Friend: Parts 3 and 4*. Port Townsend, Wash.: Copper Canyon Press, 1985.

———. *Selected Poems, 1938–1988*. Port Townsend, Wash.: Copper Canyon Press, 1988.

Nelson, Cary. *Repression and Recovery in Modern American Poetry and the Politics of Cultural Memory, 1910–1945*. Madison: University of Wisconsin Press, 1989.

Oresick, Peter, and Nicholas Coles, eds. *Working Classics: Poems on Industrial Life*. Chicago: University of Illinois Press, 1990.

Patchen, Kenneth. *Before the Brave*. New York: Random House, 1936.

Poore, Carol. "German-American Socialist Culture." In Buhle, ed., *Origins of Left Culture*.

Rideout, Walter B. *The Radical Novel in the United States, 1900–1954*. Cambridge: Harvard University Press, 1965.

Robbins, Bruce. *The Servant's Hand*. New York: Columbia University Press, 1986.

Rukeyser, Muriel. *The Collected Poems of Muriel Rukeyser*. (New York: McGraw-Hill, 1982).

Salzman, Jack, ed. *Years of Protest, A Collection of American Writers of the 1930s*. Indianapolis: Bobbs-Merrill Educational Publishing, 1967.

Shelley, Percy B. "Song to the Men of England." *The Complete Works of Percy B. Shelley*, 31:288–89. New York: Gordian Press.

Short, Robert. "Dada and Surrealism." In *Modernism*, 292–308. New York: Penguin Books, 1976.

Stern, Frederick, ed. *The Revolutionary Poet in the United States: The Poetry of Thomas McGrath*. Columbia: University of Missouri Press, 1988.

Tarlen, Carol. "Today." Poem, copy in author's collection, n.d.

Thompson, E. P. "Homage to Thomas McGrath." In *The Revolutionary Poet in the United States*, edited by Frederick Stern. Columbia: University of Missouri Press, 1988.

———. *The Making of the English Working Class*. London: Victor Golancz, 1980.

Voss, Fred. *Goodstone*. Long Beach, Calif.: Events Horizon Press, 1991.

———. *Survivor*. Long Beach, Calif.: Guillotine Press, 1989.

Ward, Tom. "The Situationists Reconsidered.: In *Cultures in Contention*, 144–64. Seattle: Real Comet Press, 1985.

Wayman, Tom. *Beaton Abbott's Got the Contract: An Anthology of Working Poems*. Edmonton, Alta.: Newest Press, 1974.

———. *Going for Coffee:An Anthology of Contemporary North American Working Poems*. Madiera Park, B.C.: Harbour Publishing, 1981.

———. *A Government Job at Last: An Anthology of Working Poems, Mainly Canadian*. Vancouver, B.C.: MacLeod, 1975.

———. *Inside Job: Essays on the New Work Writing*. Madiera Park, B.C.: Harbour Publishing, 1983.

———. *Introducing Tom Wayman: Selected Poems, 1973–1980*. Princeton N.J.: Ontario Review Press, 1980.

Wertheimer, Barbara. *We Were There: The Story of Working Women in America*. New York: Pantheon Books, 1977.

Wright, James. *The Branch Will Not Break*. Middletown, Conn.: Wesleyan University Press, 1959.

Zandy, Janet, ed. *Calling Home: Working-Class Women's Writings*. New Brunswick, N.J.: Rutgers University Press, 1990.

U.S. Working-Class Women's Fiction

Notes Toward an Overview

Constance Coiner

A Partial History of Efforts to Promote Working-Class Women's Writing

We now have in print a discrete body of work that can be identified as writing by or about U.S. working-class women.[1] The Feminist Press, founded in 1970 by Florence Howe and Paul Lauter, has a distinguished history of publishing and reprinting working-class women's writing—including, among numerous other titles, Rebecca Harding Davis's *Life in the Iron Mills*, the first significant portrait in U.S. literature of industrial workers' lives (1861; 1972; a 1985 edition contains additional stories by Harding Davis); Agnes Smedley's *Daughter of Earth* (1929; 1973; 1987); *Women Working: An Anthology of Stories and Poems*, edited by Nancy Hoffman and Florence Howe (1979); Paule Marshall's *Brown Girl, Brownstones* (1959; 1981) and *Reena and Other Stories* (1984); Meridel Le Sueur's *Ripening: Selected Work, 1927–1980*, edited by Elaine Hedges (1982; 1990); Josephine Herbst's *Rope of Gold* (1939; 1984); and *Writing Red: An Anthology of American Women Writers, 1930–1940*, edited by Charlotte Nekola and Paula Rabinowitz (1987).

West End Press, largely through the efforts of John Crawford, since 1976 has published and reprinted literature by working-class women writers, including Meridel Le Sueur, Paula Gunn Allen, Wendy Rose, Cherríe Moraga, and Nellie Wong. Arno Press has reprinted some working-class women's writing, including two of Herbst's novels, *Money for Love* (1929; 1977) and *Nothing Is Sacred* (1928; 1977). The ILR Press (the press of the School of Industrial and Labor Relations at Cornell University) has begun a Literature of American Labor Series that includes Theresa Serber Malkiel's *The Diary of a Shirtwaist Striker* (1910; 1990). A note in texts published in the ILR series explains its purpose: to "bring back into print some of the best literature that has emerged from the labor movement" in the United States and Canada. "We are defining literature broadly," the note continues, to include "novels, biographies, autobiographies, and journalism."

The Politics of Literature: Dissenting Essays on the Teaching of English, edited by Louis Kampf and Lauter (1972), raises issues still relevant for scholars of working-class writing, who are "up against the great tradition," to borrow the title of one of the collection's essays. And, since its inception in 1975, the journal *Radical Teacher* has consistently supported working-class studies, as has the Radical Caucus of the Modern Language Association (MLA). Since 1968 the caucus has organized MLA sessions addressing working-class concerns, including working-class women's writing.

Tillie Olsen's *Tell Me a Riddle* (1961) and *Yonnondio: From the Thirties* (1974) are prominent among working-class texts. Olsen has also worked to restore forgotten, out-of-print women's writing, especially working-class women's writing. Shelley Fisher Fishkin gives us Florence Howe's account of Olsen's role in The Feminist Press:

> In 1970, when Tillie Olsen "gave *Life in the Iron Mills* to The Feminist Press and said she had written a biographical and literary afterword that we could have as well, that changed the whole course of publishing for the Feminist Press." Up to that point The Feminist Press had planned to bring out "short biographical pamphlets about writers and women of distinction in all kinds of work, and . . . feminist children's books," observes Howe, "but we had not thought of doing works from the past until [Tillie] handed [us] *Life in the Iron Mills*, and followed that up the following year with *Daughter of Earth*." A key chapter of publishing history was in the making. At first "The Feminist Press had the reprint field to itself." Then other publishers jumped in—Virago and the Women's Press in the mid '70s, and Beacon, Rutgers, Pandora, Illinois, ILR Press, Oxford, and scores of others in the '80s. (5)

Moreover, Olsen has tirelessly encouraged and promoted working-class women writers—with Linda McCarriston, an Irish American poet (*Eva-Mary*, 1991), and Fae Myenne Ng, a Chinese American fiction writer (*Bone*, 1993), providing only two recent examples.

The pioneering work of The Feminist Press, *Radical Teacher*, the Radical Caucus of the MLA, and others has been furthered by publications such as Janet Zandy's anthology *Calling Home: Working-Class Women's Writings* (1990); Peter Oresick and Nicholas Coles's edited collection *Working Classics: Poems of Industrial Life* (1990); Paula Rabinowitz's *Labor and Desire: Women's Revolutionary Fiction in Depression America* (1991); Laura Hapke's *Tales of a Working Girl: Wage-Earning Women in American Literature, 1890–1925* (1992); Jon Christian Suggs's edited volume, *American Proletarian Culture: The Twenties and Thirties* (1993); Coles's "Democratizing Literature: Issues in Teaching Working-Class Literature" (*College English* [November 1986]); and Pam Annas's "Pass the Cake: The Politics of Gender, Class, and Text in the Academic Workplace" (*Working-Class Women in the Academy: Laborers in the Knowledge Factory*, edited by Michelle Tokarczyk and Elizabeth A. Fay [1993]). Moreover, biographies of Josephine Herbst (by Elinor Langer, 1984), Agnes Smedley (by Janice R. and Stephen R. MacKinnon, 1988), and Mary Heaton Vorse (by Dee Garrison, 1989) have appeared.

Such publications and efforts signal that working-class writing may be emerging as a visible, if not yet "legitimate," category of literary studies. (I agree, however, with Lillian Robinson's assertion—especially when it is applied to English departments—that "the most massive and brutal attempts to deny the existence of an analytic category occur with respect to class" [66]). Theorizing working-class writing is linked to and extends the efforts of those expanding the literary canon and examining the aesthetic and political bases on which it is constructed.

Theorizing working-class writing is also linked to the work of scholars revisioning the 1930s literary Left.[2]

TOWARD A DEFINITION OF WORKING-CLASS WRITING

Since the 1960s, U.S. working-class writing has been variously defined. In an important essay in *Culture and Crisis in Britain in the '30s* (1979) Carole Snee uses the term "working-class writing" to denote works written by a member of the working class, whether or not the writer has class consciousness. In charting working-class writing in a pioneering essay first appearing in *Radical Teacher* (1979), Lauter deliberately employs "relatively loose definitions" and "broad categories." He discusses texts "by *and* about working people, written and oral forms, 'high,' 'popular,' and 'mass' culture." He designates as members of the working class "those who sell their labor for wages; who create in that labor and have taken from them 'surplus value,' to use Marx's phrase; who have relatively little control over the nature or products of their work; and who are not 'professionals' or 'managers.'" Lauter refers "to people who, to improve their lot, must either move in *solidarity* with their class or leave it (for example, to become managers)," and he includes not only factory workers but also slaves, farm laborers, and those who work in the home (110).[3] Of course, working-class writing often coincides with other literary categories (e.g., writing by women, radicals, and people of color may also qualify as that of the working class).[4]

Working-class writing cannot be clearly delineated from bourgeois texts. As Terry Eagleton observes:

> The languages and devices a writer finds to hand are already saturated with certain ideological modes of perception, certain codified ways of interpreting reality; and the extent to which he can modify or remake those languages depends on more than his personal genius. It depends on whether, at that point in history, "ideology" is such that they must and can be changed. (*Marxism and Literary Criticism* 26–27)

Working-class writing of necessity exists within the dominant cultural formation. But, because ideology is contradictory rather than homogeneous, working-class writing can variously interrogate, emulate, challenge, and appropriate the forms of the dominant culture while straining beyond them.

Mary Jacobus and Rachel Blau DuPlessis, in their work on women writers, help illuminate this fundamental tension within working-class women's writing. As Jacobus argues, women writers, "at once within this culture and outside it," must simultaneously challenge cultural terms and work within them (20). Acknowledging Jacobus's work, DuPlessis notes that women writers experience a "split between alien critic and inheritor." They are "neither wholly 'subcultural' nor, certainly, wholly main-cultural, but negotiate difference and sameness, marginality and inclusion in a constant dialogue" (43). (DuPlessis reminds us that W. E. B. Du Bois first postulated this "double consciousness" for African

Americans, who constantly negotiate with the dominant culture.) Such a split
occurs with working-class women writers as well.

"To approach working-class culture," Lauter argues "we must lay aside many of
our presuppositions about what literature is and *is not*": "We must begin by asking
in what forms, on what themes, in what circumstances, and to what ends working
people spoke and sang to one another. How did they gather, examine, transmit,
and renew their experiences? First, we need a broader definition of what we can
call 'literature'" (111). In her introduction to her study of working-class British
literature, *The Industrial Muse* (1974), Martha Vicinus similarly calls for a broader
definition of literature: "What we call literature, and what we teach, is what the
middle class—and not the working class—produced. Our definitions of literature
and our canons of taste are class bound; we currently exclude street literature,
songs, hymns, dialect and oral storytelling, but they were the most popular forms
used by the working class" (1).

Lillian Robinson's *Sex, Class, and Culture* (1978; reissued in 1986) also unmasks
the class-bound nature of what universities consider "literature" and calls for "a
radical redefinition" of the term (224). "Working/Women/Writing," one of the
dozen essays (all written by Robinson), examines the personal histories—collected in the scrapbook *I Am a Woman Worker*[5]—of rank-and-file female factory
workers who studied at the Associated Schools for Workers in the 1920 and
1930s. (Perhaps the best known among these schools was the Bryn Mawr summer
institute, the subject of a memorable documentary, *The Women of Summer* [1985],
and of recent work by Karyn L. Hollis [see references].) About *I Am a Woman
Worker*, Robinson concludes:

> I wish to suggest that, whatever we have been taught, clichés or senti-
> mentality need not be signals of meretricious prose, and that ultimately
> it is honest writing for which criticism should be looking. It is essential
> to recognize literature that can enhance our understanding of the condi-
> tions that define women's lives, and, in order to gain insight into what
> women experience, I do not feel that we have to "relax our standards."
> Instead, writing like this can force a reevaluation and a reordering of
> those standards and turn them on their heads. And this sort of process,
> this sort of reading, tells us something we urgently need to know about
> both women and literature. (252–53)

Robinson reminds us that working-class women's writing "gives form to the experiences of the *majority* of women" (225; my emphasis). She offers an alternative
standard for literature, shocking for its simplicity and for its revolutionary implications: it "should help us learn about the way things are, in as much depth and
fullness as possible and by any means necessary" (230).

Lauter notes the importance of comparing African American and Euro-
American working-class cultural materials. "Almost all writing produced by
African-Americans is, by any definition, working-class literature," Lauter rightly
asserts, observing that "most of the authors have working-class origins, and their

subjects and audiences are generally working-class people like themselves" (119). Although African American and Euro-American working-class cultural forms derive from different traditions, if we examine how these forms were produced and how they functioned within working-class communities, some important similarities emerge. In *Black Culture and Black Consciousness: Afro-American Folk Thought from Slavery to Freedom* (1977), for example—which Lauter considers "required reading" for those interested in working-class cultural forms—Lawrence Levine has collected firsthand descriptions of the creation of spirituals, mainly in postbellum African American churches. Levine found that originality and innovative form, both prized by the bourgeois aesthetic, were not primary considerations in creating spirituals. New songs, which varied tunes and lyrics familiar to people's communities, were deliberately constructed from old ones. Moreover, like oral storytelling, the spirituals were often created communally, with an individual's creation often considered less significant than that of a group.

Indeed, as Lauter observes, "Much working-class art is created and experienced in group situations—not in the privacy of a study, but in the church . . . the work site, the meeting hall, the quilting bee, or the picket line. It is thus rooted in the experiences of a particular group of people facing particular problems at a particular time. It is not conceived as timeless and transcendent" (113–14). Similarly, the contributors to *I Am a Woman Worker* violated "a fundamental precept of bourgeois aesthetics that good art . . . celebrates what is unique and even eccentric in human experience or human personality. Individual achievement and subjective isolation are the norm, whether the achievement and the isolation be that of the artist or the character" (Robinson 226). The contributors to *I Am a Woman Worker*, in contrast, "wrote about their lives in order to develop their potential as part of their class and its struggle—a commitment that they did not separate from self-actualization." Although Robinson does not dismiss the importance of oppressed people's writing as a means of establishing identity, she is "even more impressed by the notion that doing so may be understood as a process that integrates one into one's community and helps to create and unite the community itself, instead of underscoring the purportedly inherent conflict between the individual and the group" (232).

Toward Theorizing Working-Class Writing

Fiction by working-class women writers that comes immediately to mind includes Harriette Arnow's *The Dollmaker* (1954; 1972); Meredith Tax's *Rivington Street* (1982); Bobbie Ann Mason's *Shiloh and Other Stories* (1982) and *In Country* (1985); Carolyn Chute's *The Beans of Egypt, Maine* (1985), *Letourneau's Used Auto Parts* (1989), and *Merry Men* (1993); Denise Giardina's *Storming Heaven* (1987) and its sequel, *The Unquiet Earth* (1992); Barbara Kingsolver's *The Bean Trees* (1988) and *Animal Dreams* (1990); and Dorothy Allison's *Trash* (1988) and *Bastard out of Carolina* (1992). And yet there are still relatively few scholars addressing working-class writing. While there are differences among scholars' approaches to theorizing working-class writing, they share the recognition that canonical views of the nature and status of "literature" have seriously impeded attempts to understand and value working-class discourse. These scholars have variously argued that we must look through something other than "aesthetic" lenses when evaluating working-class writing.

I suggest that all these scholars are looking through various pragmatic lenses: that is, they are looking at connections between discourse and society, asking, among many other questions, how society shapes discourse and how discourse shapes society. Those employing pragmatic lenses are less preoccupied with the undecidability of meaning than with language uses. They think of language, as Eagleton has put it, "as something we *do*" (*Literary* 147).

If extended to working-class writing, an argument Annette Kolodny made in 1980 about women writers partly explains working-class writing's current marginal status in the literary canon. Discussing writers such as Charlotte Perkins Gilman, whose work dropped out of sight until The Feminist Press reissued *The Yellow Wallpaper* in 1973, Kolodny argued that the reason for Gilman's disappearance

> may not be due to any intrinsic lack of merit in the work but, instead, to an incapacity of predominantly male readers—those readers who have traditionally been invested with the authority to record literary history—to interpret competently and appreciate fully women's texts. Such readers may have been as unacquainted with the texts' real-world contexts as with their informing literary contexts. The result was that these readers did not read the texts well; and, blaming the difficulty on *what* was read rather than on *how* it was read, they accorded the text—and not themselves—diminished status. (590)

Change *male readers* to *readers from the professional-managerial class*—the class in which most literary agents, editors, reviewers, taste-making intellectuals, critics, and professors reside—and we begin to see that canon-making aesthetic values arise partly out of class conflict.

Working-class writing offers its readers something rarely found in modern and postmodern art. While modern/postmodern art strives to renew our perception of the world, it seldom accounts for the causes of our perception's "initial numbness" (Jameson 374). In contrast, working-class texts foreground some of the causes—the trappings of an economic system that transforms humans into commodities. Working-class writing unmasks the fact of work and production, which is, as Jameson notes, "the very key to genuine historical thinking" and "a secret as carefully concealed as anything else in our culture" (407).

To view working-class discourse through other than canonical aesthetic lenses is, however, not enough. We must also explore other-than-canonical ways of reading that discourse. Theorizing working-class writing begins in recognizing that the term *literature* has long implied "aesthetic" (or what I will call "romantic") ways of reading and thinking about discourse and, second, in recognizing that some working-class writers disrupt those ways of reading and thinking. To avoid the trap of trying to evaluate writings by the very standards those writings challenge, I propose, as have others, that we examine those works and ways of reading them not from an aesthetic or romantic perspective but, rather, from a *pragmatic* one.

Long-standing principles of romantic reading theory aim to guarantee that individual readers become passive receivers or appreciators of canonical discourses and the cultural values they embody. Pragmatic reading strategies, on the other hand, require close scrutiny of language structures such as figuration—but structures viewed not as aesthetic components but, rather, as tools with which writers and readers make texts do various sorts of social or cultural work. By *cultural work* I mean the work any text does, implicitly or explicitly, to support or subvert the dominant culture. (Both supporting and subverting elements are often present in any single given text, even in one clearly intent on subversion.) The working-class discourse with which some of us are concerned disrupts romantic passivity by demanding that readers become active interrogators of texts and cultural values, at times questioners and critics of meanings, at times participants in constructing meaning.

Stylistic experiments to draw readers into collaboration are, of course, as old as the activities of reading and writing; such experiments probably date from the writer who first consciously used ellipsis for the purpose of forcing a reader to fill in the gap. Many of those experiments have arisen from a recognition, at least as old as Plato's *Phaedrus* (with its own experiments with disrupting passive reading), that reading tends to be a privatized, individual—rather than communal—activity. J. Paul Hunter comments on one genre, the novel, in relation to reading's solitariness. Hunter is concerned with ways in which the reading process and the central subject of the modern novel "seem to have a common meeting ground in their attention to isolation. . . . the act of reading a novel is, like the act of contemplating one's own consciousness, an anti-social (or at least asocial) act—very different from the sociality involved in hearing a story or attending the performance of a play" (42). It is certainly the case that many writers, for a variety of political and aesthetic reasons, have exploited the individualistic tendencies of the act of reading, while other writers—again, for a variety of political and aesthetic reasons—have attempted to disrupt this isolation. Most of the scholars theorizing working-class writing, however, are concerned with formal experiments that attempt to subvert traditional notions of bourgeois individualism and promote collective social change.

M. M. Bakhtin and V. N. Volosinov's theories of discourse provide some useful tools for pragmatic reading strategies. Bakhtin's concept of "heteroglossia"—a "multiplicity of social voices and a wide variety of their links and interrelationships" (*Dialogic* 263)—provides one tool for examining working-class discourse, much of which is heteroglossic. Of course, working-class writers are not the only writers to experiment with heteroglossia. Many others have experimented with versions of the multivocality Bakhtin identifies as characteristic of the novel's form. Those attempting to theorize working-class writing, however, are concerned with the ways in which the formal explorations of some working-class writers derive from their desire to oppose the ideology of individualism and other "naturalized" cultural values.

A second tool we can draw from Bakhtin and Volosinov is their concept of the "dialogic" nature of all discourse. Volosinov finds that all "verbal performance in print" engages in "ideological colloquy of large scale: it responds to something, objects to something, affirms something, anticipates possible responses and objections, seeks support, and so on" (95). Heteroglossia and the dialogic provide critical lenses for viewing the resistance embodied in working-class texts.

Bakhtin and Volosinov's version of pragmatics provides several additional tools. Volosinov suggests "little behavioral *genres*" as subdivisions of heteroglossia and discourse's dialogic structure. Examples of "little behavioral genres" include "the full-fledged question, exclamation, command, request" (96).[6] Some of these rhetorical genres have been contemplated extensively within British and American speech-act theory, and in my own work I have drawn on a few insights of speech-act analysis to examine structures of commands, urgings, and pleas as those structures contribute to the dialogic character of Tillie Olsen's and Meridel Le Sueur's writing (see, e.g., " 'No One's Private Ground': A Bakhtinian Reading of Tillie Olsen's *Tell Me a Riddle*,"[7] *Feminist Studies* 18 [summer 1992]: 257–81, which is part of *Better Red: The Writing and Resistance of Tillie Olsen and Meridel Le Sueur* (1995).

Peter Hitchcock, who proceeds from what I am terming a pragmatic approach, believes that "the multiple voicing of working-class fiction represents not only its most salient aesthetic quality, but also its specific internal polemic" (2). About one of his additions to Bakhtinian theory Hitchcock says, "To adequately explain the class purview of working-class fiction Bakhtin's theory of voicing must be tempered by a theory of silence; for to understand the dialogism of the oppressed one must articulate the dialogism of the suppressed, those ideological and institutional relations that have often left working-class and women's utterances unuttered" (44). In my own work I have found Bakhtinian language theory and the issue of silences to be vital to the study of working-class women's discourse.

In calling attention to a pragmatic perspective, I want to emphasize again that those attempting to theorize working-class writing are not interested in the romantic training of readers to "appreciate" the rhetorical tools of working-class writing as aesthetic devices peculiar to an "elevated" literary realm. Rather, we want readers to decipher the cultural work done by working-class texts and the ways in which readers are invited to participate in that cultural work.

Because the methods of historical analysis and those of literary analysis, long viewed as separable disciplines, have not equipped us to read working-class writing, most scholars of working-class writing are also allied with those encouraging people to cross traditional categorical boundaries, including those dividing genres and academic disciplines. Such divisions have long been under scrutiny in feminist theory, but challenging them seems particularly crucial for theorizing working-class writing. In "History as Usual? Feminism and the 'New Historicism,'" Judith Newton suggests for academics an enlarged collectivity: "I can see it now—a materialist feminist literary/historical critic working with a 'New Women Historian' and, in a brave move beyond the dyadic bond, with a cultural materialist too, and perhaps with others as well" (120). Historian Joan Scott has also transgressed traditional boundaries between history and literary theory. Rather than viewing literature as residing in an elevated, transcendent, "universal" realm untainted by history, Scott argues that history and literature are both "forms of knowledge, whether we take them as disciplines or as bodies of cultural information" (8). And in "Literature as Women's History" Nancy Armstrong attacks disciplinary boundaries, outlining "an antidisciplinary notion of culture" that would not sharply delineate between "literary" and "nonliterary" discourse. In arguing that working-class writing often challenges such boundaries, my aim—like that of Newton, Armstrong, and others—is to problematize such boundaries in order "to overcome," as Armstrong has so straightforwardly put it, "the divisions of knowledge that prevent us from understanding who we are and what we do" (367–68).

If, however, we are to challenge traditional boundaries, we must, as I have suggested, carefully examine and rework long-standing cultural assumptions about what it means "to read." Armstrong expresses this concern in a reference to figurational reading of some nonliterary texts by women. She notes that these texts must be "read with all the attention to technical detail that a literary text alone has formerly deserved" (356). Armstrong advocates what I would call a pragmatic approach to reading. As she recognizes, reading methods that reserve complex analysis, such as figurational scrutiny, for literary texts obscure many of the rhetorical and cultural complexities marking much nonliterary discourse.

In "Reading Ourselves: Toward a Feminist Theory of Reading" Patrocinio P. Schweickart has noted a similar problem in what she terms the "utopian" impulses in reading theory, by which she means the attention on the (variously problematized) relationship between text and reader to the exclusion of considering the text's and reader's historical situations. Such bracketing has produced many reading theories that overlook "issues of race, class, and sex, and give no hint of the conflicts, sufferings and passions that attend these realities" (35). Reading theory's movement away from utopian disregard for gender issues, for example, would include consideration of how gender is inscribed in texts and the roles played by the reader's gender in the reading process. Recognizing that "literature acts on the world by acting on its readers," Schweickart calls for reading theory and pedagogy that generate active readers who will scrutinize a text for "the nature of the choices proffered by the text and, equally important, what the text precludes" (39, 50). Schweickart argues that dialogue between feminist theory and reader-response theory provides the best possibilities for replacing utopian theory.

David Bartine's work is also useful to those attempting to theorize working-class writing. Bartine has traced the 250-year history of what he calls "romantic reading theory" in U.S. education and culture and the long-eclipsed "pragmatic" alternatives to romantic theory. Bartine argues that attempts to dismantle cultural myths and canons provide an "incomplete solution to the problem without reconstructing, according to a radically different plan, the reading activity and the reader" (55). Bartine, like Armstrong, argues for employing pragmatic reading methods such as complex figurational analysis in a multiplicity of literary and nonliterary texts, and he believes that the rudiments of such analysis can be introduced to students at an early age and systematically developed throughout their education. Armstrong, Schweickart, and Bartine recognize the need to reteach readers to see what they have been systematically taught to overlook.

Because theorizing working-class women's writing at points coincides with the materialist-feminist approach to culture outlined in Judith Newton and Deborah Rosenfelt's introduction to *Feminist Criticism and Social Change* (1985), I want to call attention to this introduction as a useful starting point for approaching working-class women's writing. Working-class studies, committed as much to historic and economic concerns as to gender relations, often lies within the province of materialist feminism, opposing the flight from history evident in much literary theory, including much feminist criticism. Eagleton rightly identifies "the *extremism*" of much literary theory as "its obstinate, perverse, endlessly resourceful refusal to countenance social and historical realities," even though "'extremism' is a term more commonly used" to dismiss those who "call attention to literature's role in actual life" (*Literary* 196). Scholars approaching working-class writing have often done so dialectically, embracing contradictions and locating "in the same situation," as Newton and Rosenfelt have put it, both "the forces of oppression and the seeds of resistance" (xxii).

The Obfuscation of Class as a Category of Literary Analysis

New constituencies have emerged in the advanced industrial world during the past two decades—feminists, national minorities, peace and anti-intervention activists, environmentalists, gays and lesbians, AIDS activists, tenants and other neighborhood groups—that have kept radical tendencies alive after the eclipse of the New Left. Whereas Old Leftists considered the working class to be the decisive revolutionary protagonist, many leftists now believe we must confront multiple and overlapping forms of domination (class, patriarchal, racial, bureaucratic, consumer, and media related) without reducing that reality to any one of its elements. The new social movements must build ties to working-class and labor struggles, but the class dimension of domination must be taken into account without minimizing other such dimensions.

Yet, although many Old Left intellectuals mistakenly subordinated all social issues to those of class, at this historical juncture—as is suggested by the relatively few scholars focusing on working-class writing—class is not a fashionable category of analysis among literary critics, including feminists. Canon reformation has legitimized the study of literary texts by women and people of color, but multicultural educational reform will defeat its egalitarian purpose if gender and racial identities are allowed to suppress class identities.

Despite its place in the now familiar list—race, gender, class, ethnicity, sexuality, and disability—class is often the least addressed of these issues. There may be several explanations for this more specific than the nature of U.S. academic liberalism. One may be that few people of working-class origin make it into the ranks of the professoriat; so few people with an "insider's" sensitivity to this issue are undertaking scholarship and shaping curricula.[8] Another explanation may be that many faculty and students have imbibed, at least to a certain degree, the myth of classlessness in the United States, a myth that has been used historically in the United States for social control. Dispelling that myth is complicated by the fact that class origin—like sexual orientation but unlike race, gender, and some forms of ethnicity—is not always apparent, remaining hidden unless it is disclosed. In my experience at the University of California–Los Angeles and at the State University of New York–Binghamton (a medium-sized public institution that draws a majority of its students from the New York City/Long Island area), many university students of color have proudly identified themselves with their particular cultural groups, while few students of working-class origin have announced—or, in some cases, even recognized—themselves as such.

This lack of class identification among working-class students provides a third explanation for the diminished status of class as a category of analysis among literary scholars. While many students rightly exert pressure on literature departments to consider gender, race, and sexual orientation as interpretive categories and to include texts by women, people of color, and gays and lesbians in college courses, few protest exclusions based on class. Indeed, few students seem even to see class markers, typically identifying Rita Mae Brown's *Rubyfruit Jungle* (1973), for example, as a lesbian but not also a working-class novel; Sandra Cisneros's *Woman Hollering Creek* (1991) as both Chicana and women's literature but not, additionally, a working-class text; Ann Petry's *The Street* (1946) as both African American and women's writing but not a working-class novel as well.

The obfuscation of class as a category of analysis has consequences within the academy, forestalling alliances across identities of race, culture, gender, and sexuality among scholars and among our students. I am reminded of classroom experiences in which students who are active in campus groups (e.g., the Asian American Student Union, the African American Student Alliance, the Gay and Lesbian Task Force) react with surprise and confusion at their identification with the "wrong" text—the Chinese American who wonders why Eva in Olsen's "Tell Me a Riddle" "is my grandmother"; the *puertorriqueña* who says she never expected to find her "mother's story" in Olsen's *Yonnondio*; the African American who sounds an alarm when Anzia Yezierska's "Children of Loneliness" (1923) resonates more for her than Zora Neale Hurston's *Their Eyes Were Watching God* (1937).

Progressive literary scholars must expose the common working-class basis of much of the writing now identified solely on the bases of race, ethnicity, gender, and sexuality and must also create a space in cultural studies for work by Euro-American radical and working-class writers that has been ignored even in recent efforts to broaden the parameters of the U.S. literary canon. Again, I am reminded of a classroom experience: a working-class Euro-American, virulently opposed to multicultural education, recognized her miner-grandfather's struggle in Giardina's *Storming Heaven* and announced that, "if including texts like *Storming Heaven* in the curriculum is part of what multiculturalism is all about," she must begin to examine her prejudices. Anthologies such as Cherríe Moraga and Gloria Anzaldúa's *This Bridge Called My Back: Writings by Radical Women of Color* (1983) and Anzaldúa's *Making Face, Making Soul/Haciendo Caras* (1990) help students see the ways race, ethnicity, and sexual orientation *intersect with class* to produce distinctive narratives of working-class women's lives. Moreover, we can point out to our students that Zandy's *Calling Home: Working-Class Women's Writings* could be as accurately termed "multicultural" as a "working-class" anthology; its contributors include many women of color as well as Euro-American working-class women, lesbians as well as heterosexuals. And, with writings by immigrants such as the Jewish writer Anzia Yezierska, students can learn that ethnic and immigrant writing is often working-class writing as well.

Far too often students who have rejected what Richard Ohmann terms "the fatuous universalism of the right" do so by taking up a politics of identity that, as Ohmann observes, "makes any sort of embracing social movement against capitalist patriarchy hard indeed to imagine." We see on college campuses, Ohmann continues, "a politics of separate issues" with little perception "that these issues are knit together in a whole system of domination" that might be collectively opposed (33). Yet analyzing working-class writing helps in developing such perception and in students' beginning to understand that "the core curriculum is neither Shakespeare nor Alice Walker. It is accounting, computer programming, training for service jobs [for some] or for Wall Street high flying [for others], acceptance of such divisions of labor as natural and unchangeable, the quiet reproduction of inequality, and political hopelessness" (34). One way to subvert this "core curriculum" is to discuss with our students the intersections—and potential alliances—embedded in much multicultural working-class writing. As working-class writing begins to emerge as a legitimate category of literary analysis, I begin to imagine a course in multicultural working-class writing in which students do not get the sense that they have identified with the "wrong" text—a course in which identity politics is scrapped in favor of a political consciousness capable of decoding the middle-class myth and organizing to give ordinary people better life chances.

Much of my own scholarship, thus far, lies at the nexus of two related fronts in the culture wars neglected even by many progressive academics: the efforts I have been discussing to legitimate working-class writing and the struggle to preserve and revision the history of the American Left. One result of anticommunist, pro-capitalist ideology in literary studies has been, as Alan Wald points out,

> the disempowerment of the population of ordinary people who are denied a genuine history of their own cultural activities through access to authors who wrote about strikes, rebellions, mass movements, the work experience, famous political trials, the tribulations of political commitment, as well as about love, sex, the family, nature, and war from

a class-conscious, internationalist, socialist-feminist, and antiracist point of view. Instead, the population [of ordinary people] is often exclusively presented with literary role models that inculcate notions of culture that distort visions of possibilities for social transformation. ("Culture," 284–85)

Wald's remarks about the disempowerment of ordinary people remind me, again, of my disempowered "ordinary" students, who can neither hope for nor envision forms of coalition-building in an increasingly multicultural United States, partly because they lack knowledge of labor history and progressive movements for social change prior to the Civil Rights movement and feminism's second wave. My students are astonished—even incredulous—when I tell them, for example, that in 1912 in Lawrence, Massachusetts, textile workers representing about forty-five language groups united in a successful strike against long hours, pay cuts, and speed-up. And professors who in their scholarship and pedagogy are moving away from narrow conceptions of English and American literature to broader notions of "cultural studies" rarely think, despite their interdisciplinary inclinations, about the place of labor and working-class studies under that rubric. Roger Kimball's tenured (and untenured) radicals in literature and cultural studies departments have much to learn from U.S. historians such as those who composed the American Social History Project, founded by Herbert G. Gutman, and produced the groundbreaking two-volume *Who Built America? Working People and the Nation's Economy, Politics, Culture, and Society* (1989; 1992).

"Men make their own history," says Marx, "but not of their own free will; not under circumstances they themselves have chosen but under the given and inherited circumstances with which they are directly confronted." And so it is with women. Working-class women's writing often exemplifies the "audacity within confinement"—to repeat a phrase from Thomas Mann that Tillie Olsen is fond of quoting—implicitly advocated by this well-known passage from Marx. Politically and culturally, working-class women's writing represents what Williams describes as a *"pre-emergence,* active and pressing but not yet fully articulated, rather than the evident emergence which could be more confidently named" (*Marxism* 126). In necessarily "partial, scrappy, subsidiary, and preparatory" form (Trotsky 163), the most subversive of working-class women's writing strains toward the postindividual, collective, associative cultural forms of a different social order.

Toward a Bibliography of Working-Class Women's Writing in the United States

Bibliographies that include working-class women's writing can be found in the following sources:[9] Walter Rideout, *The Radical Novel in the United States, 1900–1954* (1956; reprint 1992); Jayne Loader, "Women in the Left, 1906–1941: A Bibliography of Primary Sources," *University of Michigan Papers in Women's Studies* 2 (1975): 9–82 (catalogued in libraries under the series title); Paul Lauter,

"Working-Class Women's Literature—An Introduction to Study," *Radical Teacher* 15 (1979) (reprinted in Joan E. Hartman and Ellen Messer-Davidow, eds., *Women in Print I* [1982], and in Robyn R. Warhol and Diane Price Herndl, eds., *Feminisms: An Anthology of Literary Theory and Criticism* [1991]); Cherríe Moraga and Gloria Anzaldúa, eds., *This Bridge Called My Back: Writings by Radical Women of Color*, 2d ed. (1983); Mari Jo Buhle, *Women and the American Left: A Guide to Sources* (1983); Janet Zandy, ed., *Calling Home: Working-Class Women's Writing* (1990); Paula Rabinowitz, *Labor and Desire: Women's Revolutionary Fiction in Depression America* (1991); Laura Hapke, *Tales of a Working Girl: Wage-Earning Women in American Literature, 1890–1925* (1992); Jon Christian Suggs, *American Proletarian Culture: The Twenties and Thirties*, vol. 11 of the Documentary Series of the *Dictionary of Literary Biography* (1993).

NOTES

1. For a useful discussion of the distinctions between the working class and the bourgeoisie, see the conclusion to Williams, *Culture*. Because my scholarship and teaching thus far have focused chiefly on fiction, I should acknowledge from the outset that these "notes toward an overview" will emphasize that genre.

2. Christina L. Baker, James D. Bloom, Barbara Foley, Laura Hapke, Walter Kalaidjian, Barbara Melosh, Cary Nelson, David R. Peck, Paula Rabinowitz, Deborah Rosenfelt, Suzanne Sowinska, Jon Christian Suggs, Harvey Teres, Alan Wald, and Douglas Wixson are among the literary scholars reexamining the 1930s. I also want to alert readers to *Revisioning Thirties' Culture: New Directions in Scholarship*, edited by Sherry Lee Linkon and Bill V. Mullen (1995). But it is important to underscore what Alan Wald has pointed out to scholars of the literary Left: too often radical literature has been viewed within the narrow confines of the 1930s as if that decade were an aberration in U.S. history rather than part of a sustained resistance to capitalism. As Wald argued persuasively in a presentation at the 1993 American Studies Association Convention, the Left cultural practices of the 1930s through 1960s are all linked to the same tradition. Thus, Wald is editing a series, The Radical Novel in the United States Reconsidered, of leftist novels originally published between the 1920s and the early 1960s; the novels will be paperback reprints with new introductions.

3. I have cited a reprint of Lauter's "Working-Class Women's Literature" (see references); it is a slightly edited version of the original essay with no substantial changes. The essay was also reprinted in *Feminisms: An Anthology of Literary Theory and Criticism*, ed. by Robyn R. Warhol and Diane Price Herndl (1991): 837–50. See two other relevant essays by Lauter, "American Proletarianism," in *The Columbia History of the American Novel*, ed. Emory Elliott et al. (1991): 331–56; and "Race and Gender in the Shaping of the American Literary Canon: A Case Study from the Twenties," *Feminist Studies* 9 (fall 1983): 435–63; "Race and Gender" has been reprinted in Newton and Rosenfelt, *Feminist Criticism*.

4. The categories of "radical" writing and "working-class" writing often intersect. In *Labor and Desire* Rabinowitz uses the term *revolutionary* for the more than forty depression-era novels written by women that she surveys. In "From the Thirties: Tillie Olsen and the Radical Tradition," in Newton and Rosenfelt, *Feminist Criticism*, Deborah S. Rosenfelt uses "socialist feminist" to describe the literary tradition to which Tillie Olsen belongs. I will discuss the overlapping of women's writing, working-class women's writing, and writing by women of color at other points in this essay.

5. This scrapbook, like the other collections from the Associated Schools for Workers, was a mimeographed volume. *I Am a Woman Worker* has been reissued by Arno Press (1974) in its Women in America series; the reprint is a reduced photocopy of the original.

6. See also Bakhtin, *Speech*, 60–102.

7. Expanded versions of this essay appear in Hedges and Fishkin, *Listening to Silences*; in *The Critical Response to Tillie Olsen*, ed. Kay Hoyle Nelson and Nancy Huse (1994); and in *Tillie Olsen's Tell Me a Riddle: A Casebook*, ed. Deborah Rosenfelt (1995).

8. I can offer limited evidence of some improvement on this score. Three collections of essays about intellectuals of working-class origin (many of them academics, many of them professors of English) have recently been published. See Zandy, *Liberating Memory*; Tokarczyk and Fay, *Working-Class Women*; and Dews and Law, *This Fine Place*.

9. My subject in this essay is women's writing in the United States. But for those interested in British working-class writing, see the bibliographies included in Vicinus, *Industrial Muse*, and in Hitchcock, *Working-Class Fiction*.

REFERENCES

Armstrong, Nancy. "Introduction: Literature as Women's History." *Genre* 19 (winter 1986): 347–69.

Bakhtin, M. M. *The Dialogic Imagination*, edited by Michael Holquist. Translated by Caryl Emerson and Michael Holquist. Austin: University of Texas Press, 1986.

———. *Speech Genres and Other Late Essays*, edited by Caryl Emerson and Michael Holquist. Translated by Vern W. McGee. Austin: University of Texas Press, 1986.

Bartine, David. *Reading, Criticism, and Culture: Theory and Teaching in the United States and England, 1829–1950.* Columbia: University of South Carolina Press, 1992.

Dews, C. L. Barney, and Carolyn Leste Law, eds. *This Fine Place So Far from Home: Voices of Academics from the Working Class.* Philadelphia: Temple University Press, 1995.

DuPlessis, Rachel Blau. *Writing Beyond the Ending: Narrative Strategies of Twentieth-Century Women Writers.* Bloomington: Indiana University Press, 1985.

Eagleton, Terry. *Literary Theory.* Minneapolis: University of Minnesota Press, 1983.

———. *Marxism and Literary Criticism.* Berkeley: University of California Press, 1976.

Fishkin, Shelley Fisher. "Reading, Writing and Arithmetic: The Lessons *Silences* Has Taught Us." In *Listening to Silences: New Feminist Essays*, edited by Elaine Hedges and Shelley Fisher Fishkin, 1–38. New York: Oxford University Press, 1994.

Hedges, Elaine, and Shelley Fisher Fishkin, eds. *Listening to Silences: New Feminist Essays.* New York: Oxford University Press, 1994.

Hitchcock, Peter. *Working-Class Fiction in Theory and Practice: A Reading of Alan Sillitoe.* Ann Arbor: UMI Research Press, 1989.

Hollis, Karyn L. "Liberating Voices: Autobiographical Writing at the Bryn Mawr Summer School for Women Workers, 1921–1938." *College Composition and Communication* 45, no. 1 (1994): 31–60. [Reprinted in this volume.]

———. *Resisting Voices: Writing at the Bryn Mawr Summer School for Women Workers, 1921–1938.* Carbondale: Southern Illinois University Press (forthcoming).

Hunter, J. Paul. *Before Novels: The Cultural Contexts of Eighteenth-Century English Fiction.* New York: W. W. Norton, 1990.

Jacobus, Mary. "The Difference of View." In *Women Writing and Writing About Women*, edited by Mary Jacobus. London: Croom Helm, 1979.

Jameson, Frederic. *Marxism and Form.* Princeton: Princeton University Press, 1971.

Kolodny, Annette. "Reply to Commentaries: Women Writers, Literary Historians, and Martian Readers." *New Literary History* 11 (spring 1980): 587–92.

Lauter, Paul. "Working-Class Women's Literature: An Introduction to Study." In *Women in Print I*, edited by Joan E. Hartman and Ellen Messer-Davidow, 109–25. New York: Modern Language Association of America, 1982. Originally published in *Radical Teacher* 15 (December 1979): 16–26.

Nekola, Charlotte, and Paula Rabinowitz, eds. *Writing Red: An Anthology of American Women Writers, 1930–1940*. New York: The Feminist Press, 1987.

Newton, Judith. "History as Usual? Feminism and the 'New Historicism.'" *Cultural Critique* 9 (spring 1988): 87–121.

Newton, Judith, and Deborah Rosenfelt. *Feminist Criticism and Social Change: Sex, Class, and Race in Literature and Culture*. New York: Methuen, 1985.

Ohmann, Richard. "Political Correctness and the Obfuscation of Politics." *Radical Teacher* 42 (1992): 32–34. A longer version of this essay appeared as "On 'PC' and Related Matters." *The Minnesota Review* 39 (fall/winter 1992/1993): 55–62. Reprinted in *PC Wars*, edited by Jeffrey Williams. New York: Routledge, 1995.

Rabinowitz, Paula. *Labor and Desire: Women's Revolutionary Fiction in Depression America*. Chapel Hill: University of North Carolina Press, 1991.

Rideout, Walter. *The Radical Novel in the United States, 1900–1954*. 1956. Reprint, New York: Columbia University Press, 1992.

Robinson, Lillian S. *Sex, Class, and Culture*. 1978. Reprint, New York: Routledge, 1986.

Schweickart, Patrocinio P. "Reading Ourselves: Toward a Feminist Theory of Reading." In *Gender and Reading: Essays on Readers, Texts, and Contexts*, edited by Elizabeth A. Flynn and Patricinio P. Schweickart. Baltimore: Johns Hopkins University Press, 1986.

Scott, Joan W. *Gender and the Politics of History*. New York: Columbia University Press, 1988.

Snee, Carole. "Working-Class Literature or Proletarian Writing?" In *Culture and Crisis in Britain in the '30s*, edited by Jon Clark et al. London: Lawrence and Wishart, 1979.

Tokarczyk, Michelle M., and Elizabeth A. Fay, eds. *Working-Class Women in the Academy: Laborers in the Knowledge Factory*. Amherst: University of Massachusetts Press, 1993.

Trotsky, Leon. *Literature and Revolution*. 1924. Reprint, Ann Arbor: University of Michigan Press, 1960.

Vicinus, Martha. *The Industrial Muse: A Study of Nineteenth-Century British Working-Class Literature*. New York: Barnes & Noble, 1974.

Volosinov, V. N. *Marxism and the Philosophy of Language*. Translated by Ladislav Matejka and I. R. Titunik. Cambridge: Harvard University Press, 1986.

Wald, Alan. "Culture and Commitment: U.S. Communist Writers Reconsidered." In *New Studies in the Politics and Culture of U.S. Communism*, edited by Michael E. Brown et al. New York: Monthly Review Press, 1993. Reprinted in *Writings from the Left: New Essays on Radical Culture and Politics*, edited by Alan Wald (London: Verso, 1994).

Williams, Raymond. *Culture and Society: 1780–1950*. 1958. Reprint, New York: Columbia University Press, 1983.

———. *Marxism and Literature*. Oxford: Oxford University Press, 1977.

Zandy, Janet, ed. *Calling Home: Working-Class Women's Writings*. New Brunswick, N.J.: Rutgers University Press, 1990.

———, ed. *Liberating Memory: Our Work and Our Working-Class Consciousness*. New Brunswick, N.J.: Rutgers University Press, 1995.

New Initiatives, Syllabi, and Resources

Traveling Working Class

Janet Zandy

INTRODUCTION

Wilma Elizabeth McDaniel, a prolific but not widely known working-class poet, was born in 1918, the fourth of eight children of Oklahoma sharecroppers. She and her family left the 100-degree heat and dust bowl barrenness of Oklahoma in the 1930s and migrated with thousands of others to the promised green of California. Ms. McDaniel, who now lives in Tulare, California, does not like to talk about the details of her life, the unremitting poverty and low-wage labor. Instead, she wants her poetry to tell that story. McDaniel and other working-class writers demonstrate how one single life story is inseparable from those of one's neighbors, one's region, and whole communities of working people. This story-poem about Orville Kincaid should be familiar to those who have crossed certain borders and feel ambiguous about leaving other worlds behind:

> The Academic Career of Orville Kincaid
>
> Back in the old neighborhood
> some will remember him if
> you prod them. The boy who didn't
> wear socks until he was past thirteen.
> All will remember his love of books,
> reading while he stood in line for his
> family's welfare butter and flour.
>
> But they lose him for his scholarship
> years at Oxford University, trying to
> erase who he was. Eating watercress
> sandwiches
> when he really wanted grits and gravy.
> And none of them had read of a man
> who walked out of a ten-story window
> wearing a velvet robe
> with a copy of Yeats in the pocket.

I begin with Orville Kincaid's "academic career" because in its clear and direct working-class idiom, the poem points to two important themes inherent to working-class studies: (1) the movement of some working-class people out of familiar places, out of communities, and into academic enclosures of great promise and great peril and (2) alternatives to suicide. I speak not just about the tragic suicide of individuals, but of a loss and killing of collective memory and experience.

In "Traveling Working Class" I ask you to imagine a journey that is both real and metaphoric. We are the descendants of many travelers—those who gambled on new opportunities, those who were violently torn from their homes, and those who were displaced by economic change. The literature and culture we call contemporary and American brims with tropes of migrations, border crossings, movements, disruptions, dislocations, and unsettled settlings. I use the word travel to acknowledge a degree of choice that earlier generations may not have had. But it is hardly a vacation, and it is not an easy journey. We need space to tag the necessary baggage, to draw a map of the territory, and to imagine alternative places.

LOCATIONS AND BEGINNINGS I

I'll begin with my present location. For the last twenty-five years I have lived in Rochester, New York. I didn't plan to live there—planning a future was not part of my working-class experience, getting by, working toward a better circumstance, was. How I got there seems less important to tell than what Rochester represents in terms of our larger concerns about working-class culture. Like many other medium-size U.S. cities, Rochester is a double city. It has an inner city, an outer city, and then a ring of suburbs of substantial wealth. It is the corporate headquarters for Kodak and Bausch and Lomb, and it is also a place where one-third of all city children live in poverty. Class differences are sharp in Rochester but rarely acknowledged. Rather, the media present the perspective and well-being of the business class as normative; that is, what is good for the corporation is good for the average citizen. Last year [1994], the CEO of Eastman Kodak Company was awarded a yearly salary of $6 million. I say *awarded* because I cannot imagine work that would earn that amount of money. The salary and bonuses he received were an acknowledgment from stockholders and Wall Street that he did a good job of restructuring, reengineering, and refitting the Kodak workforce. In other words, he laid off a lot of workers—seven hundred in the immediate Rochester area and ten thousand worldwide over a span of some years.

I want to pause by describing how Kodak—which has a history of paternalism and is generally less ruthless than many other corporations—went about pink-slipping, notifying workers of their job status. Workers—in this case, mostly white-collar and college-educated "employees," because the production workers had already been hit by the first wave of cuts—were called into their supervisor's office and given an envelope with a piece of paper and a booklet. Written on the paper was one of three messages: you retain your job; you may transfer to another job; or your job has been eliminated. The booklet was more interesting. Entitled "Coping with Change: How to Manage the Stress of Change," its cover depicts four stressed-out, multicultural workers clinging to a little battered boat named USS *Uncertainty* and bracing to be engulfed by the wave of CHANGE. (CHANGE is spelled out in white foam on the wave.) Imagine just losing your job and being handed this comic book on how to cope with change. It doesn't take a course in

Derrida to deconstruct the visual message: change just happens, like a big wave from out of the blue, and no one is responsible for the wave, so you better learn how to hold on to your own skimpy place in this nearly sinking boat if you want to survive. This cartoon recipe for weathering change could be dismissed as just a bad joke or caricature if it weren't clear that someone somewhere in corporate culture thought that this was a good idea and useful to people faced with the devastation of losing a job they thought was secure. The message is *you* had better change. And if you lose your place in this increasingly crowded and narrow boat, you had better learn to swim (adapt to change) or expect to be dumped into the drink and sink.

This emphasis on individual coping skills and de-emphasis on corporate responsibility are as American as apple pie and junk piles. It is also a consciousness trap. People are coaxed to individualize, personalize, and internalize economic loss. What the camera lens fails to capture in this cute picture of tidal waves of change and sinking ships are the estates on the shore, safe and secure, whose inhabitants are few but whose wealth is astronomical and growing.

At the very least, working-class studies can "de-individualize" this change and make visible the wealth on the shore—to enable people to understand what is happening to them from a larger, global, workers' perspective. Working-class studies can also claim some space where a mutuality of learning can occur, where tenured academicians can learn something from displaced workers.

Now I want to say something about the place where I teach, the Rochester Institute of Technology. In my institution, most students have little enthusiasm for the liberal arts; many feel that any course not directly related to acquiring job skills is worthless. Their feelings are understandable. Hammered by expensive tuition, juggling school and part-time jobs, and anticipating student loan payments for most of their adult lives, these students have little space for economically disengaged learning. One senior engineering student (who works thirty hours a week and comes from a working-class family) told me that his job as an engineer is to eliminate jobs. What happened, I wonder, to the notion of engineers as builders?

But even this student can be reached and can be convinced that all is not well in the corporate culture. All you have to do is ask if he knows anyone who has recently lost a job.

Here's a different perspective, from a senior business major:

Why do we put money capital ahead of the most important of all assets—human capital? I spent three years at Kodak and saw many flaws of corporate culture. However, [the] most shocking experience came this past summer at the end of my contract. I was [literally] put to work in the dark, [in] photographic paper storage. Some of the guys I worked with spent thirty years there, and I still don't know how. People were like ghosts, the only way to see someone was a small blinking red light, or a red flash light, which they were allowed to use only in certain areas. After three months of this I was getting depressed, I needed some light, sometimes I couldn't even figure out what time it was. Imagine thirty years of hard work in total darkness and then you get a cheap gold watch and "sorry about your health" note, or worse yet, a phony cartoon telling you how to cope with changes.

Isn't it about time these "worker ghosts" were seen? Isn't it about time for working-class studies?

LOCATIONS AND BEGINNINGS II

Now I want to travel back to another place and another beginning. I am a child in the 1950s, living in the shadow of Manhattan in urban, working-class New Jersey. On Sundays, when my father wasn't working the weekend shift, my family would frequently visit the graves of relatives. Those Sunday cemetery car trips are vivid in my memory, particularly the visits to my grandmother's grave in the Jewish cemetery. I see myself as a child of six or seven. I see the gray marble, the ivy, the junipers, the squiggly Hebrew letters carved everywhere. We visit Anna, my grandmother, say our prayers, and look for stones to place on top of the tombstone to mark our visit. I feel the isolation of this particular grave because all the other family members were buried in the Catholic cemetery several miles away. But in my memory it is not a sad or cheerless place.

I have not revisited that grave in nearly thirty years, at least not physically. But in my mind, I stop there often. It is through the remembrance of those visits that I feel a particular grounding, not so much in the physical location, but in story and memory, in my grandmother's hidden-from-history life story. I suspect that most of us have such hidden stories. Anna's life has been haunting me for a long time. I always tell it briefly, partially: some of the meaning of the story is the knowledge that all the strands of the story cannot be gathered up and told completely. It is the story of a very young woman who was never taught to read or write, although she was the daughter of a rabbi. She traveled alone from Europe to America, married out of her religion, and was consequently declared dead by her Orthodox family. Before she was sixteen years old, she was a wife, mother, and orphan. Over and over again, I have tried to imagine her circumstance—ostracized by her family, without literacy, raising ten children to adulthood through the Great Depression and two wars, and working all the time—in the daily battle against dirt in crowded spaces, cooking on a wood stove, scrubbing clothes on a washboard, nursing children, feeding what she called "poor souls" in the neighborhood. When she died at the age of fifty-two, she looked eighty by today's standards. Work marked her body, but it didn't destroy her humanity. She had, to borrow Toni Morrison's language, "the alien's compassion for troubled people" (149).

I tell Anna's story not to elicit a weepy, nostalgic response or a sentimentalized reverence for roots. I tell Anna's story because it is my inheritance. It is an alternative grounding to the cartoon version of generational change. I have no letters, no memoirs, no memory even of her physical touch, but I have her story told and retold by family members. And I am absolutely certain that my work rests on it and that I could not speak to you without that story in my memory and consciousness. That story is a gift, but it is also a responsibility. It is a kind of cultural haunting, a steady pressure to act out of Anna's experience. I carry it with me into the world, draw on its strength. It helps clarify my thinking. I need this story to do my work in the world. That's what I mean by memory as agency.

Now I want to think about these two locations and beginnings: There is corporate city, USA, and my grandmother's story. What do these two locations mean for mapping working-class studies and traveling working class? What do they mean for us as cultural workers?

Let's consider our map. Maps are not innocent, as Denis Wood shows in his fine book *The Power of Maps*. Maps pass themselves off as something. The power of the map lies behind the map, in the hands of the mapper. Remember those maps of the world based on power rather than geography? The United States is depicted as huge, dominating the Western Hemisphere and the globe; Africa is tiny; Central America is nearly erased.

Now I want you to consider what a map of the terrain of academic knowledge might look like. What is surveyed and mapped as "knowledge" depends a great deal on the power of the mapmaker. For a long time, the university knowledge map represented almost exclusively the interests of the ruling white elite, a minuscule minority. Some of that geography has changed, but the terrain is still contested, and despite the efforts of progressive, democratic forces in the academy to redraw that map, the representation is still highly distorted.

I am thinking now of the mapper's hands in corporate city, USA. It seems to me that disembodied corporations are the current mapmakers, defining the territory, telling students what they need to learn to get jobs in the new technological world order so that they can become part of the global "knowledge elite." You might think of it as schooling for transnationals. Corporate boards and university boards of trustees fold into the same collection of tiny, powerful elites who often unconsciously represent business interests as knowledge and as an all-pervasive reality.

It is clear that on this new corporate/education map, there is no place for my grandmother's story other than as cheap ethnic nostalgia. Nor will there be much space for labor history, workers' culture, or collective perspectives. Stories of the violence of labor struggles have enormous affective power on students, so it's no wonder they are missing from school texts.

When looking at this map, I do not travel with a sense of defeat or despair, but I do have a point of view that's been thrust on me from working at a technical institute where there is no such thing as English majors or history majors, American studies or labor studies, and no mushy liberal confusion about the direction of those in power.

It seems to me that our work is to continue the fight for the power of the map. We need to construct, reconstruct, remember, reinvent, rediscover, reconnect, and struggle for the knowledge that belongs to the majority of people, the working class.

JUNCTIONS

I want to speak more specifically about what I mean by traveling working class. Remember that scene in the movie *Thelma and Louise* when Thelma decides to get away from her husband and take a trip with her girlfriend Louise? She throws this heavy chunky suitcase on her bed and pulls out dresser drawers loaded with stuff. She pauses over her belongings—jewelry, underwear, hair dryer, socks, sweaters— what to pack? The decision is too hard. Momentarily paralyzed with indecision, she gives up and, in one great swoop, empties a whole drawer into her suitcase and greets Louise with enough matching luggage to put Elizabeth Taylor to shame.

I suspect that my tendency to overpack is not unique to me. When you live for so many years as a working-class person with a sense of imminent emergency, you develop an overcautiousness, on one hand, that is the flip side of a lack of confidence in public space, on the other. It is hard to know what you need to know and what you need to have. It took me a while to catch on that it wasn't always necessary to travel with food.

These prosaic working-class habits are not disconnected from our larger concerns about working-class knowledge and the academy. How do we pack? What class do we travel? Whose map do we use? Who stakes out the territory? Or how do we not follow in Orville Kincaid's footsteps?

Those of us who were born into working-class families encounter a juncture in our travels not faced by middle-class and upper-class people. In a myriad of subtle and not so subtle ways, we are told to adjust our language, our behavior, and perhaps our values, to get rid of all this working-class baggage and travel light if we want to "make it out." We are not expected to ask what the "it" is we are making. And who determines where we are we going? It seems to me that questions of what gets discarded, what gets transported, and who decides are at the heart of our work. For too long because of the pressures of assimilation and the denial of class difference, working-class people who have attended the academy have let others make those choices for them. We have been given the message that workers have no culture, and if they don't possess material goods, then they have nothing. For too long we have been in a double bind: erased as a presence in a class-denying society and simultaneously experiencing acute class prejudice.

There is an alternative way to travel, and I must say that, I felt this in my bones long before I knew it in my conscious mind. It was as if the working-class bodies I recognized so well knew something that my academically trained mind couldn't quite grasp. This alternative involved carrying something with me out and into the world. What? It wasn't my personal achievement or the conventional American Dream version of success (which is moribund, anyway). It certainly wasn't being cool and wearing work clothes as a fashion statement. Nor was it rejecting a decent life. I've never met any hardworking people who didn't want an easier material and physical life for their children. But they also don't want their lives ignored or forgotten or disrespected; they want the circumstances of their lives understood. And they want people who have a little power to support them and not deny them.

This process of carrying our knowledge of working-class life into the world is reciprocal. As we witness, we draw strength from our own history. Now I shall describe some considerations for equipping ourselves for building working-class studies. The first is the matter of identity.

Often when I speak to students about class, I spend some time on "decloaking," that is, making class visible in Disney-saturated America. I remind them that we all are born into a class identity, even though that identity can be mixed, hybrid, multiple, and fluid. Who writes the college tuition check is a handy class marker. And of course, our individual identities must be seen in relation to other identities—that's what *class* means. Working-class identity *is* discernible in the context of U.S. capitalism: if you're expected to dispose of it, you're probably working class. But of course, in late capitalism, disposal is not understood as the elimination of all classes and the redistribution of wealth. Rather, you're expected to take your place in a highly individualistic, competitive social Darwinism. The message: if you want to improve your material conditions—if you want the goods—then be ready to let go of that sticky, adhesive, communal sensibility. Or, to go back to our comic book—if you want to survive on that rickety boat, throw everyone else overboard!

There are alternative travel arrangements, but we have to travel with baggage that may not fit neatly into bourgeois compartments. We begin with the realization that working-class identity is not negation. *Class* defined in collective terms as shared economic circumstances and shared social and cultural practices in relation to positions of power means more than the absence or presence of things. We live in a country that is fixated on measurement or, rather, mismeasurement. Where are the tools that measure working-class cultural identity? On what grid does collective responsibility fit?

Consider how class identity travels with us from generation to generation. Our material circumstances may differ from our parents', and certainly from our grandparents', but we may still inherit certain values, attitudes, shared histories, uses of language, and even bodily postures that we reconceive, reevaluate, and restore as we move in time. This is what Stephen Jay Gould calls the "arrows" and "cycles" of cultural time—what changes and leaps forward and what circles back and is repeated. Or what Alessandro Portelli describes in oral narratives as "shuttlework," telling the tale in the present but picking up bits and pieces of the past as you go along, going back and forth in time like a shuttle (65).

It seems to me that American literature has a great deal to teach us about traveling working class. Indeed, American literature is replete with tales of travel—characters hit the open road, go down the river, and board trains. Let us briefly consider two autobiographical novels of the same time period: Anzia Yezierska's *Bread Givers* (1925) and Agnes Smedley's *Daughter of Earth* (1929). Their protagonists, Sarah and Marie, respectively, literally board trains to leave behind the chaos, dirt, and economic deprivation of their childhood, but they travel with feelings of great ambivalence about the relationships left behind. Both characters have a longing for knowledge and an exquisite desire and love for beauty. Yezierska's protagonist, like the author herself, seems stuck in undefined space—not quite the Anglo pioneer she aspires to be, but not able to unburden herself from what she sees as the weight of her father and of the generations before him. She lacks a political vision and an alternative paradigm to bourgeois life. Smedley's Marie is also searching for models and a way out of poverty. This novel ends with a packing-up and a leave-taking: Marie leaves with feelings of acute loneliness but also with a certain consciousness, a certain knowledge that she will carry with her from Colorado to New York to China to the world, that she is forever connected to those who die "*not* for the sake of beauty." They die for other reasons: "exhausted by poverty, victims of wealth and power, fighters in a great cause" (4).

Smedley had little use for what she called "salon Socialists" (MacKinnon and MacKinnon 151) and contempt for those from privileged circumstances who blamed poverty on the proletarian's unwillingness to work hard enough. Smedley was able to make a consciousness leap that Yezierska in her idealization of the American Adam could or would not make, that is, seeing her parents' poverty as linked to a much larger international struggle of the oppressed many against the powerful few. In a letter written in 1930, Smedley says, "Always I think that I shall write one more book before I die—just one book in which I shall, many years from now, try to show what the capitalist system, with its imperialist development, has done to the human being—how it has turned him into a wolf" (MacKinnon and MacKinnon 145).

I suggest that out of the dialectics of these two working-class novels, we can discern possibilities for doing our work in the world. It is possible to leave and look back without turning to stone. When traveling working class, we need to pack a critical class consciousness and solidarity that go beyond identity politics.

Our work is not about celebration. It is full of ambiguity and contradiction. It is a bildungsroman with a working-class difference. It is about building on what is already there, about girding and sustaining, not replacing or rejecting working-class identity. Raymond Williams and Tillie Olsen and many others have marked the way. What is new is what is happening in places like Youngstown, Ohio, where there are opportunities to make that space official. Within the confines of what we call institutional knowledge, we cannot claim authority if we exclude working-class epistemology. This is more than memory recollected, more than the inheritance of grit and stamina, more even than our own survival. It is the institutionalized relationship between knowledge and justice, and hence this working-class journey.

Now, since we are in charge of our own mapping, we also have to be alert to traps and dead ends. The first one is getting stalled at the junction of reciting class injuries. Stories about class prejudice and ignorance abound. I hear many and tell a few myself. Unnamed class prejudice seems endemic to the academy. Watch how waitresses or cleaners or cabdrivers are treated at academic conferences. Are they even visible? Well, what can be expected in a society with so few positive images of working people and where there are such false dichotomies between physical and intellectual labor. It is important to recognize and name incidents of class prejudice, hatred even, but it is just as important to use those occasions as compost for other projects. In other words, let us not linger too long on the hidden and not so hidden injuries of class. I am not saying that we should not affirm our life experiences, but there is a danger of getting stalled at the personal injury stop and not taking on other issues.

Another trap is language, particularly academic language. I have seen intelligent, good-willed academicians get together to discuss important issues and never get beyond the definition stage. What is class? How do we define it? Who is or isn't working class? These are questions that I think about a great deal, but I suspect there are other ways to answer them than with either a plodding academic approach or an intoxication with highly theoretical language that is not grounded in a lived reality. Class experience is real and not necessarily textual. Any study of working-class culture should certainly include orality and also the nontextual expressions of how the working-class body speaks. How do we bring, for example, the physicality of the working body into the academic classroom? I am arguing for a more complex intellectuality, always conscious of how knowledge is framed and how pervasive bourgeois sensibilities are.

It may be a good thing for us not to feel at home in the academic habitat in order to retain a sense of the strategic importance of our work. It reminds us of how much we don't know. That the whole story is always out of reach. That we, as Tillie Olsen writes, "will never total it all" (12). That we realize, as Raymond Williams puts it, "the most uneventful life would take a library of books to transcribe" (207).

DESTINATIONS

Obviously, determining final destinations for working-class studies cannot and should not be the work of any one person. But I want to offer some considerations for our work together. To be sure, the journey is not going to be easy. But it never was.

One of the many complications we face is the absence of a parallel political movement outside the academy to match our work inside it. For example, women's studies as a field might not have found credibility without the street action of the women's liberation movement—which in turn was influenced by the antiwar movement, which was influenced by the Civil Rights movement. But we cannot wait for a grand movement. We have to begin somewhere, perhaps even leading in the building of an international working-class labor movement both inside and outside the academy.

Another daunting aspect of our work is selection and representation. Contrary to bourgeois notions of working-class people's having "no class," we have an abundance of culture: a wealth of writing, much of it now in print; oral, social, industrial, and community histories; and a long legacy of music and visual and folk art. These stories and histories have extraordinary power. With this cultural plenty come hard questions of selection and issues of representation—how to account for the lived experiences of literally millions of people.

How we organize this material, how we think about time, is another consideration. Our selection of working-class materials might be guided by a reciprocal sense of time, of how one moment informs, another, how the future and the past are held in the present. This is a dialogue or conversation with other voices around particular historical moments, what I call the "I, they, and we" of working-class voices. We have many narrative and poetic contemporary retellings of specific events in labor history, for example. This is not an appropriation of the past but an internalizing of time to reinform the creative act in the present.

To be sure, it is a great responsibility but also an extraordinary opportunity for cultural workers to define the territory for working-class studies. We have the power of our grandparents' stories—and we know how to use the technology to get them out.

What might working-class studies look like in its many geographic sites and cultural permutations? I want to offer a few brief observations from my own travels, in the form of intersections and interventions. I want to stop traveling for a while, get off the train, and notice some fields of intersection, clearings where meadow and forest meet and various species commingle.

It seems to me that a key but overlooked area for building working-class studies is with children. Perhaps we should develop more programs and contacts with elementary school teachers. So much labor history has been lost. My college seniors had never heard of the Ludlow massacre or the Triangle fire, for example. Perhaps if we start early enough talking about the ongoing class war in American history, a generation of young people might find some things in common with their elders. Certainly we can provide alternatives to civic pablum about Betsy Ross sweetly sewing the flag or George Washington not telling a lie about cutting down the cherry tree. A lot of lies have been told, but they're not really about cherry trees.

Also, the practice at Youngstown University of moving the classroom into the work site is an important point of intersection. We might consider it a mutual exchange of literacies. Teachers have knowledge about how to form ideas into written and spoken language, and workers have the knowledge of specific labor practices and concerns, particularly safety and health issues, underemployment and unemployment and job scarcity. We also need to listen better, to use oral history and personal narratives in our classes so that we can build into our courses the voices of people whose lives are not located in the university.

Another crucial point of intersection and alliance is with multiculturalism and women's studies. We should structure our academic practices—our courses and our selected texts—so that we can offer models of what I call reciprocal visibility. Our study of class must be informed by differences of race, ethnicity, sexuality, and gender. Class is multicultural. In particular, we need more study and exposure of the relationship between race and class and how the race card is used by the dominant class to deflect worker solidarity. An international capitalist system has hierarchies of humanity. We need to identify those forces that block a collective consciousness. There are many opportunities for informed comparative readings if we focus on work, labor, and jobs in multicultural texts. I also suggest that we take a transnational and postcolonial perspective in our development of working-class studies, especially as we look at what constitutes "home"—the transitory, unpredictable, slippery nature of home. We can get to intersections of gender, race, and class if we begin with home and work.

Next, we need to intersect with the producers of progress and technology. I suggest that we engage in discursive practices (that is, talk) to computer experts, scientists, and engineers. I even would welcome critical alliances. Jeremy Rifkin and others are predicting that these knowledge elites are among the few who will have meaningful work in the near future. We need to establish spaces, places of intersection, for conversations about technology, progress, and work. We need to question the Forrest Gump view of PROGRESS, a big wave of change (as in the Kodak layoff comic) that just happens. We can draw on our scholarship in literature and history to critique commonplace notions of progress (hand every engineer a copy of Kurt Vonnegut's *Player Piano*). Progress is not an engineless train—it is driven by identifiable business and government interests. Progress is inseparable from power relations. It seems to me that who defines and controls "progress," who profits from it, and who is destroyed by it is at the heart of working-class studies.

I suspect that it might be easier to intersect with engineers and computer scientists about working-class studies than it would be to convince the Modern Language Association to make working-class literature a permanent discussion group. Engineers and computer scientists can be reached not only because many of them are just a generation or two away from their own working-class roots but also because a case can be made that they will miss crucial pieces of knowledge if they don't recognize working-class craft and labor practices. That is, solving technical problems depends on workers' knowledge.[1]

Philosopher Simone Weil went to work in a factory (and risked her health) in order to internalize the physicality of the working body into her mind and consciousness. About technology she wrote, "All technological problems should be viewed within the context of what will bring about the best working conditions. The whole of society should be first constituted so that work does not demean those who perform it" (McLellan).

Finally, we circle back in this journey to the historicity and future of work. The theologian Dorothee Soelle offers this:

> All workers act within a particular society and culture. All have inherited tools, technology, knowledge from past generations of workers. . . .
> To develop a historical sense of what work has been, to know what our grandparents did and the path they took to their achievements, is the aim of an educational process that puts self-understanding and human worth before capital. Yet this approach to work is almost unheard of in a nation like the United States, which evaluates labor primarily in terms of productivity. . . . Work is communal not only in the space of a given community but also in time, as the shared memory of what we have received from the past that accompanies us into the future. (94–95)

I conclude by extending a wish—it is the same wish that I have for my children, for myself, for all of us—I wish you good work. By that, I mean work that is creative, not destructive; work that is safe (something millions of people cannot take for granted); work in which you are the subject, not the object; work with a sense of history; work that offers fair compensation, autonomy, and space to hone your craft; work that allows you time to develop your humanity—to read, think, listen to music, observe nature, plant gardens; work that makes a clear distinction between human beings and things, that does not turn human beings into things. And finally, work that offers small occasions for big acts, opportunities to give something back and to make a contribution to our common humanity. I cannot think of a better final destination.

NOTE
This essay was originally given as a keynote address at the "Working-Class Lives/Working-Class Studies" conference at Youngstown State University, Youngstown, Ohio, 1995.

1. Eugene Ferguson, a mechanical engineer and historian of technology, concludes his book *Engineering and the Mind's Eye* by arguing that human abilities and limitations need to be designed into systems, not designed out of them.

WORKS CITED
Ferguson, Eugene. *Engineering and the Mind's Eye*. Cambridge: MIT Press, 1993.
Gould, Stephen Jay. *Time's Arrow Time's Cycle: The Myth and Metaphor in the Discovery of Geological Time*. Cambridge: Harvard University Press, 1987.
MacKinnon, Janice R., and Stephen R. MacKinnon. *Agnes Smedley: The Life and Times of an American Radical*. Berkeley and Los Angeles: University of California Press, 1988.
McDaniel, Wilma Elizabeth. "The Academic Career of Orville Kincaid." In *Liberating Memory: Our Work and Our Working-Class Consciousness*, edited by Janet Zandy. New Brunswick, N.J.: Rutgers University Press, 1995.
McLellan, David. *Utopian Pessimist: The Life and Thought of Simone Weil*. New York: Poseidon Press, 1990.
Morrison, Toni. *Song of Solomon*. New York: Alfred A. Knopf, 1977.
Olsen, Tillie. "I Stand Here Ironing." In *Tell Me a Riddle*. Reprint, New York: Delta, 1994.
Portelli, Alessandro. *The Death of Luigi Trastulli and Other Stories*. New York: State University of New York Press, 1991.
Smedley, Agnes. *Daughter of Earth*. 1929. Reprint, New York: The Feminist Press, 1973.
Soelle, Dorothee, with Shirley A. Cloyes. *To Work and to Love*. Philadelphia: Fortress Press, 1988.
Vonnegut, Kurt. *Player Piano*. 1952. Reprint, New York: Laurel/Dell, 1980.
Williams, Raymond. "Creative Practice." In *Marxism and Literature*. New York: Oxford University Press, 1977.
Wood, Denis. *The Power of Maps*. New York: Guilford Press, 1992.
Yezierska, Anzia. *Bread Givers*. 1925. Reprint, New York: Persea, 1975.

Building a Center for Working-Class Studies at Youngstown State University

Sherry Lee Linkon and John Russo

In the early 1990s, several faculty at Youngstown State University (YSU) with overlapping interests in American culture studies, labor history, and working-class culture organized a conference on the 1930s. Cosponsored by the English and history departments, the conference attracted about one hundred people, most from literary studies. The conference featured art exhibits, panels, a keynote address by Tillie Olsen, and a roundtable of labor organizers and writers who reflected on their own memories of the 1930s. Participants were enthusiastic, many commenting that they would like to see more events like this.

Encouraged by this response, the organizers planned another conference in 1995, Working-Class Lives/Working-Class Studies. At the conference's closing plenary, John Russo led an open discussion asking, "If we were to start a center for working-class studies here, what should it look like?" Answers ranged from offering educational programs for local unions to creating a journal in working-class studies, from promoting attention to class in academic organizations to starting a class revolution. The participants' enthusiasm was clear, and many commented that the Youngstown conference provided them with a sense of belonging that they were not finding in other academic conferences or at their home institutions.

At the same time, led by John Russo, the YSU team applied to be part of a project on diversity and democracy sponsored by the Association of American Colleges and Universities (AAC&U). The group's application raised a key question: Would class be invited to the diversity banquet? At the AAC&U summer seminar that year, the YSU team, including Sherry Linkon, Bill Mullen, John Russo, and Linda Strom, was the only group whose work emphasized class. Later that year, the group organized itself into the Center for Working-Class Studies (CWCS). Susan Russo was also part of the initial center group, and Beverly Gray joined within a year. The CWCS became the only center in the United States devoted to the study of working-class life and culture.

The center's goal was to redress the erasure of class in American culture by creating opportunities for academic and public conversations about class, work, and identity; intersections between class and other categories of identity; studies of working-class culture; and approaches to teaching that emphasize class as both content and a key element of classroom dynamics. Since 1995, the CWCS has served as a clearinghouse and meeting place for academics, artists, students, and organizers whose work focuses on class, and its programs have generated lively discussions at public presentations and conferences, on-line and in the classroom, about class and work.

The information sharing and explorations sponsored by the CWCS do not simply celebrate working-class culture. Rather, the center helps to raise critical questions about the social significance of class, the denial of economic and political opportunities to working-class people, and the sometimes contentious relationship between class, race, gender, and sexuality. The CWCS seeks to link academic study of class and work with the workplace, the classroom, and the community. Through these conversations, the CWCS aims to create a culture of organizing and education within working-class institutions and communities.

The CWCS has also played a leadership role in developing a new approach to the study of working-class life and culture. This new working-class studies uses an interdisciplinary approach to address four areas: the role of class within multiculturalism, the role of culture in working-class history, cultural representations of class and work, and teaching of and about the working class. At the forefront of this emerging field have been scholars such as Robin D. G. Kelley, David Roediger, Manning Marable, Janet Zandy, Don Mitchell, and George Lipsitz. New working-class studies interrogates the relationships between class, gender, sexuality, and race in labor history, literature, geography, education, and popular culture. Such scholarship offers more complex understandings of multiculturalism, new theoretical models for understanding class, deeper understanding of how the media and education construct ways of seeing class and work, and greater awareness of the role of class in education and community.

Higher education has begun to take notice of this new working-class studies. The *Chronicle of Higher Education* published a major story on the field by Jeff Sharlett, which focused on the 1999 CWCS conference and sponsored an online colloquy that generated more than fifty responses. A number of new books have appeared in recent years, including two on working-class pedagogy by CWCS members, suggesting that academic publishing is taking note of this increased interest in class. Attendance at CWCS conferences (now held every other year) has increased steadily, and at least three other conferences focusing on issues of class have been offered by other programs around the country in the past few years. Several other schools have formed or are beginning plans to create study groups and centers on working-class studies. In part because of support from the CWCS, working-class studies interest groups and caucuses have been organized within professional societies. In 2000, the work of the CWCS was recognized by the Ford Foundation, with a major grant that will support several new projects, including the development of a new general education course on diversity, cosponsored with the Africana, American, and women's studies programs and the Partners for Workplace Diversity project at YSU; an oral history project that will focus on the GM-Lordstown plant near Youngstown; a summer institute for high school teachers; creation of materials for distance learning; an annual arts exhibit; and publication of a book of essays representing the field's development.

The CWCS is located at Youngstown State University in Youngstown, Ohio. YSU is an accredited, state-affiliated comprehensive university with an outstanding record of academic achievement and public service. Located in a 130-acre urban campus midway between Pittsburgh and Cleveland, YSU primarily serves northeastern Ohio and western Pennsylvania. This area, often referred to as the "Ruhr Valley of America," was once dominated by the steel industry. In recent years, the area has become more economically diversified to include auto assembly, light manufacturing, metal fabrication, service, and small business while retaining its distinctive working-class and tightly bound ethnic communities. Today, YSU serves 12,000 students, many of whom are first-generation college students from families with strong working-class and ethnic roots.

Youngstown is uniquely situated at the center of new working-class studies, in part because the area has been the subject of many studies of working-class culture. In the past decade, many labor historians, artists, and social scientists have studied the working class in the Youngstown area. Much of that research has centered around the steel industry, the struggles to save the mills in the early 1980s, and the impact of the closings on individuals and the community. For example, labor historians and political scientists like Bruce Nelson of Dartmouth College and Robert Bruno of the University of Illinois studied Youngstown's steelworkers in an effort to develop a more dynamic analysis of the working class that stresses its ability to shape society and its own consciousness; Youngstown activist Staughton Lynd has written about building community coalitions and mobilizing workers in an attempt to stop plant closings; Pulitzer prize–winning journalists Dale Maharidge and Michael Williamson used Youngstown as the starting point for tracing the movements of industrial migrant workers in the book *Journey to Nowhere: Saga of the New Underclass*; and artists such as sculptor Bryn Zellers and musician Bruce Springsteen have used Youngstown as inspiration for their representations of the plight of the industrial working class. CWCS members have also contributed important scholarship focused on Youngstown: Donna DeBlasio has written on Youngstown's working-class housing, and CWCS directors John Russo and Sherry Linkon are currently writing a book on representations of work in Youngstown (under contract with the University Press of Kansas).

At present, the center has four core members: Sherry Linkon (coordinator, American studies/English), Beverly Gray (psychology), Donna DeBlasio (coordinator, historic preservation), and John Russo (coordinator, labor studies/management). In addition to the core faculty, the CWCS has seven affiliated faculty from the art, English, history, geography, and marketing departments. The CWCS also has community affiliates representing religious and labor institutions and artists interested in working-class life and culture.

One of the center's primary interests has been the development of working-class pedagogy, an approach that, as Janet Zandy explains, rests in part "on old cultural practices of self-education and group study, union organizing, summer schools for workers, and cultural expression." This emphasis on pedagogy is appropriate for Youngstown State University, a comprehensive university in an urban setting with a strong commitment to teaching. The CWCS has developed a number of new courses that focus on work and the working class. A one-year graduate certificate in working-class studies will become available in fall 2001. The CWCS has also created new models for adult education, such as a program that offers courses in composition, math, labor history, labor studies, and

American studies at a local union hall, with a schedule adjusted to meet the needs of steelworkers whose shifts change every week. The program not only accommodates the workers' schedules, it also features a curriculum that advocates critical literacy by tailoring courses to students' interests and experiences. CWCS members have produced important scholarship on working-class pedagogy based in part on their experiences teaching at YSU, including *Second Shift: Teaching Writing to Working Adults*, a book-length study of workplace-based college education by Kelly Belanger and Linda Strom, and *Teaching Working Class*, a collection of essays on teaching working-class students and working-class studies, edited by Sherry Linkon.

The center's research activities involve gathering and analyzing materials that contribute to an understanding of the cultural, social, economic, psychological, and political conditions and experiences of working-class people. CWCS members have applied their research to instructional and community activities. Center members have helped initiate a diversity-training program, Partners for Workplace Diversity, for area businesses and organizations; provided training for United Auto Workers members through a national program organized by Ford and the UAW; produced a series of programs on working-class studies for the local public radio affiliate; sponsored public programs on intersections among health, race, and class; and sponsored public exhibits of working-class art and history. CWCS members have also served as consultants on working-class history and culture for the Ohio Department of Transportation, area museums, journalists, filmmakers, and artists.

The CWCS offers an annual public lecture series that has featured poetry readings, slide presentations, and discussions of films, as well as more formal academic presentations on history, philosophy, geography, and labor studies. Each visiting speaker is cosponsored by an appropriate department or program on campus or in the community. For both the conferences and the lecture series, the CWCS tries to involve individuals outside the academic community who are attempting to explore or chronicle their own lives, struggles, and history, and/or community members who are addressing working-class concerns and issues.

The center has also developed a web site (www.as.ysu.edu/~cwcs), an e-mail discussion group (CWCS-L@ysub.ysu.edu), and a newsletter, *Working-Class Notes*. The web site contains information about upcoming national events and conferences, announcements of center activities, listings of labor and working-class museums, an exhibit created by YSU students on working-class culture in Youngstown, sample syllabi for courses in working-class studies, and an on-line bibliography. The unmoderated e-mail discussion group provides a network to stimulate discussions of research questions, share research information, and compare pedagogical and community activities. The center's newsletter is published twice a year and contains an update of the center's activities, book reviews, and announcements of upcoming events. Currently, more than 750 individuals around the world subscribe to *Working-Class Notes*.

For many who have felt isolated as the only person studying class at their institutions, Youngstown has provided an intellectual home. This may be the most significant of the center's accomplishments: helping students, artists, and academics pursue creative and critical explorations of working-class life and culture simply by providing support, opportunities to present their work, and ways to connect with others who share their interests.

REFERENCES

Belanger, Kelly, and Linda Strom. *Second Shift: Teaching Writing to Working Adults.* Portsmouth, N.H.: Boynton/Cook, 1999.

Bruno, Robert. *Steelworker Alley: How Class Works in Youngstown.* Ithaca: Cornell University Press, 1999.

Linkon, Sherry Lee, ed. *Teaching Working Class.* Boston and Amherst: University of Massachusetts Press, 1999.

Lynd, Staughton. *The Fight Against Shutdowns: Youngstown's Steel Mill Closings.* San Pedro, Calif.: Singlejack Books, 1982.

Maharidge, Dale, and Michael Williamson. *Journey to Nowhere: The Saga of the New Underclass.* New York: Hyperion, 1996.

Nelson, Bruce. *Divided We Stand: American Workers and the Struggle for Black Equality.* Princeton: Princeton University Press, 2000.

Sharlett, Jeff. "Seeking Solidarity in the Culture of the Working Class." *Chronicle of Higher Education* 23 July 1999, sec. A19.

Springsteen, Bruce. "Youngstown." *The Ghost of Tom Joad.* Columbia Records, 1995.

Zandy, Janet. "Toward Working-Class Studies." In *The Heartlands Today*, edited by Larry Smith. Huron, Oh.: Firelands Writing Center, 1997, 158–62.

The Rochester Education Alliance of Labor Work-Based Curriculum Project

Douglas D. Noble

The Work-Based Curriculum Project (WBC) is a long-term, still-evolving project of the Rochester, New York, Labor Council that began in the mid-1990s with workshops to help local urban teachers and counselors teach about work from a critical, working-class, worker-oriented perspective. The original intentions of the project's two coordinators—Jonathan Garlock, a labor historian/activist, and myself, a teacher/researcher—were threefold: (1) to encourage teachers and counselors to think of themselves as workers by reflecting on their own working-class histories and current workplace struggles in sustained, democratic collaboration with other local union workers; (2) to develop curriculum, based on participants' own workplace realities, that might educate students about work issues and class-based realities (rather than simply prepare them for a job); and (3) to develop an antidote to the business-led "school-to-work" enterprise then spreading throughout the United States as the result of state initiatives and federal legislation. We were concerned about the corporate agenda behind most school-to-work initiatives, which were designed, it seemed, to link schooling to a fanciful new "high performance" world of work, and to blame students' uncertain futures, especially students historically disenfranchised, on their own lack of new workplace skills or proper attitudes of loyalty, responsibility, and adaptability.

We knew enough about the realities of people's work, or lack of work, from our own experiences and from such accounts as Rifkin's *The End of Work* and Aronowitz and DiFazio's *The Jobless Future* to identify the pernicious fiction in these scenarios, despite their seductiveness. And we were less concerned with blaming students or with mindlessly grooming them for a fanciful future than with providing them with an *education* about work that respected their own work experiences, addressed honestly and critically their own questions about their future, and encouraged them to imagine alternative work possibilities. We were aware that work as a subject in the school curriculum is almost invisible, despite the centrality of work in people's lives. And we were concerned that for schoolteachers and counselors, too, caught up in an unlikely curriculum preparing students for a fanciful world of work, critical reflection on workplace realities was not even on the table.

Drawing inspiration from a book by Canadian scholars called *Learning Work*, which lays out a critical pedagogy for teaching students about work, we began holding workshops called Teaching Work, which focused on teachers' collective reflections about their own work and on issues facing workers, present and future. We wanted teachers to look to their own work and working histories for insights into how to teach their students about work, rather than relying on corporate

258

workplace images and agendas. In typical school-to-work professional development, teachers were viewed as having an impoverished sense of the world of work; they were blank slates needing to be informed about "real" workplaces in business and industry. This belied the obvious fact that teachers are workers, too (although many have lost this sense of identification) and many of them have held a variety of jobs throughout their lives. Although they have much to learn about other occupational opportunities for their students, they know precisely as much or as little about other workers' jobs as those workers know about the job of teaching. With teachers as with their students, we believed, the place to start in learning about work, and how to teach about it, is one's own work and one's own identity and experience as a worker.

One initial intent was to replace corporate fictions celebrating work with hard-nosed realities—downsizing, underemployment, contingent labor, intensified workloads, erosion of benefits—while somehow crafting an education about work that was still hopeful and full of promise. The single most frequently expressed concern of teachers and counselors, strongly committed to the lives of their disenfranchised urban students, was how to engage students with these difficult truths and uncertainties without dashing their already fragile hopes. Teachers, understandably, also wanted concrete skills-based strategies that would prepare their students for jobs. And frequently they lamented their students' woeful lack of preparation for the "world of work," in particular their lack of social skills: attendance and punctuality, motivation, work ethic, and polite behavior. We understood that these concerns were very real and would have to be addressed. Thus began our continuing balancing act of trying to encourage a progressive, labor-oriented perspective based on critical awareness and respect for students and teachers, while addressing teachers' daily experience with student disengagement and incivility, their own uncritical assumptions about the work ethic and employer expectations, and the relentlessly pressing demands on teachers' everyday working lives.

In the first few years of the project, groups of teachers, counselors, and other union workers, many of whom attended our initial workshops and were eager to unlock new possibilities for students, met to share their work experiences and issues, to read critical articles on work, and to develop curriculum materials. One pivotal activity involved each of us sketching out and then sharing with one another our own circuitous career histories, tracing key influences, privileges, and obstacles along the path; this activity demonstrated the simplifications underlying the career-planning curriculum typically used with students. Many participants also conducted interviews with a wide range of workers in the community, compiling a collection of insider profiles of various occupations from workers' perspectives. In several schools, participating teachers and counselors conducted interviews with a range of other school workers, including secretaries, custodians, nurses, and food-service workers, in order to more fully understand the complex realities and interdependence of workers within their own workplace. Others developed curriculum materials, including a module for high school students on occupational health and safety, an activity booklet for teachers called "Imagining Work" that poses work issues through the use of photos and other images, and a coloring book featuring detailed line drawings of local workers.[1]

One group met for a year to examine work values and the work ethic, reading related articles, tracing their own family legacies of work, and examining the deeper meanings of their working lives. They put together a professional development handbook for teachers, "The Meaning and Value of Work," using autobiographical pieces as well as fiction and poetry. Several groups of teachers and other union workers were convened over two years to develop two volumes of critical study guides for a hard-hitting series of nationally televised videos called *We Do the Work*. One group came together to develop an extensive activity guide for the handbook *It's Your Job . . . And These Are Your Rights* of the American Federation of Labor–Congress of Industrial Organizations (AFL-CIO), which deals with young people's rights on the job. Other groups have met more recently to develop modules on work issues and work-related fiction adaptable to current social studies and literature curricula. Another group developed an extensive curriculum on the realities of urban teaching called "Teachers and the World of Work," to be used in teacher education programs.

One large group of teachers and union workers developed a work guide for high school students that addressed students' own questions about work, compiled from interviews with hundreds of students. This work guide was entitled "The REAL WorkGuide" because it was the first publication of the Rochester Education Alliance of Labor (REAL), formed by the Rochester Labor Council as a countermeasure against the Rochester Business Education Alliance, a key promoter of local corporate school-to-work initiatives that offered decidedly unreal images of work opportunities. Most recently, another REAL group has compiled a comprehensive local "Labor History Map/Guide" and accompanying study guide for teachers.

In all of these activities, our goal has been twofold: to develop curriculum that promotes teachers' and students' critical reflection and investigation about work, and to forge sustained collaboration between teachers from various schools and disciplines and other union workers from the manufacturing and service sectors. For all their work, participants have been paid through grants from federal and state agencies and the Ford Foundation. We have also held annual conferences on work and education issues for all work-based curriculum participants; guest speakers have included Barbara Garson, author of *The Electronic Sweatshop*; William DiFazio, coauthor of *The Jobless Future*; Tom Wayman, Canadian author of numerous volumes of poetry about work; and Maude Barlow, chair of the Council of Canadians and coauthor of *Class Warfare*.

Over the years, the project has taken many twists and turns, based on shifting funding priorities and on changes in direction determined by collaborative participants. With funding from the State Education Department for math, science, and technology professional development, interdisciplinary teams of teachers were recruited, through word of mouth, in two urban high schools, one middle school, and three colleges. Each team met regularly to discuss work-related issues

in these disciplines, to pilot work-based curriculum materials, to gather information on occupational opportunities for their students, and to explore various
strategies of interdisciplinary collaboration—from reciprocal classroom visits to
team teaching and planning. Each team was encouraged to develop its own
agenda and direction, based on its own workplace issues and specific pedagogical
concerns. Secondary school teams also met jointly in larger forums to exchange
ideas, curriculum materials, and work experiences. It is worth noting that the collaboration of each of these school teams was a grassroots effort, accomplished
largely without the sanction of school administration, because these teachers are
wary from prior experience of administrative interference in worthwhile projects.
Teams often met outside of school, typically in local taverns.

For two years, each of the three secondary school teams were partnered with a
team of union workers—auto workers from the United Auto Workers (UAW),
metal fabrication workers from the Union of Needletrades, Industrial, and
Textile Employees (UNITE), and hospital workers from the Service Employees
International Union (SEIU) 1199. The partners meet regularly to learn about
one another's work, to engage in team-building activities and reciprocal site visits, and to identify common issues and concerns in their work—from speed-ups to
layoffs to grievance procedures. Teachers and counselors were eager to learn
about workplace expectations and opportunities for their students and to enlist
outside help in their efforts to reach their students, while their union partners
wanted to learn about and to support the daily work of teachers and to inform
students about workplace expectations and union opportunities. Together they
developed strategies to help students understand work and workers, through col-
laborating on technology projects, importing industry problem-solving and team-
work strategies to the classroom, sharing their own education and occupational
histories with students, teaching kids about labor history and workplace rights,
and coordinating career-day presentations in the manufacturing skilled trades.

Although some of these partnered activities continue, including expanded
union-based career-day events in local middle schools and classroom visits, the
formal partnerships between teams, initially so promising, have been discontinued for a number of reasons. First, teachers and unionized skilled trades and service workers come from different cultures, and there has been a struggle linking
them. Expectations of classroom discipline and young people's behavior differed
widely, and teachers felt judged inadequate by their union counterparts. Teachers
questioned their union partners' underlying commitment to urban students,
while the industrial union workers have been frustrated by what they perceive to
be chaotic routines and diluted skill expectations. Second, teachers' diverse and
pressing educational concerns often distracted their attention from specific student work and career issues. A year-long professional development partnership,
ultimately fruitless, established between REAL teacher teams and other teacher
teams across the country, coordinated through the TeachNET project of the
University of Wisconsin, further diverted participating teachers' focus on work-
based concerns shared with labor partners, despite repeated efforts to keep linkages alive.

Finally, major struggles faced by all three participating unions with local employers—including lockouts, layoffs, outsourcing, restructuring, unfair labor practices, and intractable negotiations—seriously diverted union partners' efforts from concerns for public education. Teachers in the school teams, too, are dealing with serious morale problems and job security issues in their schools, which takes its toll on their commitment to any efforts of this kind. The two high school teams discontinued their school-specific team efforts as it became clear that the team could not effect change in the school, given administrative obstacles and lack of support. Ironically, while teachers and union workers have been concerned about the uncertain futures of city students, their own job futures sometimes seem to be just as uncertain. So, despite recognition by the AFL-CIO as being in the forefront of efforts to link organized labor with the schools, and despite the dissemination of our work-based curriculum materials throughout the United States, these teams and partnerships, centerpieces of the project, have been discontinued.

As a collaborative for teacher professional development, however, the project continues to thrive, although not with its original school-specific, labor-oriented focus. We have been documenting the project's changing directions with support from a Spencer/MacArthur professional development research and documentation grant. One clear observation is that when we have had specific work-based curriculum to develop—the study guides, the work guide, the modules—it has been comparatively easy to get a dozen or so teachers and union partners together, map out a plan of action over a few months, designate tasks and deadlines, and produce some excellent curriculum materials. But with the ongoing teacher-worker collaborative teams and self-directed school teams, things were much less clear, and we have felt ourselves continually rebuilding the collaboration as we go along. We have sometimes lost our way and teachers and other workers have become frustrated because they didn't know what they were doing. One problem has been the lack of clear top-down direction, because each team is recruited by word of mouth and its goals and directions are determined by the team, reflecting school-specific realities that often get in the way of focused, collaborative, work-related curriculum goals.

We have found that tying project goals as much as possible to individual teachers' own professional goals and classroom needs greatly enhances their overall commitment. Still, our collaboration takes a great deal of nurturing, personal attention, reminders, restated objectives, individualized assignments, team-building activities, and clear deadlines to work effectively, and we have also found it best to establish flexible arrangements that allow teachers to move in and out of the collaborative as their work and home lives permit from year to year.

The teachers and counselors are also a varied lot, who join the project for a variety of reasons. Because much of the funding for school teams has come from math, science, and technology (MST) professional development grants, some teachers have demonstrated more interest in these areas than in the original labor and work-based agendas of the project. In fact, only a few participants are committed to labor unions and progressive political ideology; most are committed simply, though deeply, to whatever might improve the educational and occupational prospects for their disenfranchised students. Indeed, many participants hold deep-seated assumptions and engage in traditional practices antithetical to more progressive agendas. Furthermore, few project teachers and counselors are disposed toward substantive critical reflection on their own practice and assumptions, probably because such critical reflection was largely absent in their own education and because it is anathema within their current school regimes.

Within the last year, the structure and focus of the project have shifted yet again. Participants continue to meet as a full collaborative four or five times a year, to ensure the ongoing identity of the project and to enable cross-fertilization of ideas and contacts. But rather than having school-based teams, cross-school and cross-level working groups have been established that focus specifically on various areas of interest that have arisen within the collaborative.

With encouragement from project coordinators, concerned about the project's departure from its original focus on critical, worker-oriented reflection, participants have agreed that the focus of these working groups should be on substantive professional development, through shared readings, critical inquiry, reflection, and discussion. Starting with a "summer of inquiry," all working groups have become solidly established, with monthly meetings and focused agendas. These include a preservice teacher education group, focused on the preparation of teacher education students for the realities of urban teaching; a reading group for critical reading and discussion of books related to teachers' work and educational issues; a math/science/technology group experimenting with progressive pedagogies in math, science, and technology; and a job preparation group investigating possibilities for urban middle school vocational programs.

While the project continues to engage participants, through myriad course corrections toward its original goals, we might ask just what it has accomplished. We have certainly produced some excellent critical curriculum materials, and disseminated them widely. The teachers and counselors in the project find it a "refuge," rarely found in their own schools, for sustained solidarity and professional validation, for sharing of curriculum and instruction, and for discussion of ideas among diverse teachers with widely varied years of experience and from different disciplines and teaching levels. Despite the discontinuation of their partnerships, teachers and other workers on various teams, in their words, had their eyes opened about larger forces affecting education, and they began to see themselves as coworkers, with new respect for and understanding of each other's work and with mutual issues and concerns. And teachers and counselors have expanded their horizons about a range of hitherto invisible occupational pathways for students not going to college directly from high school. But the changes in teachers' assumptions and teaching have been slight, especially with respect to the project's original progressive goals. So just how all this translates, down the road, into better, more critically aware, more worker- and student-centered teaching and learning in classrooms, and into greater opportunities for Rochester's disenfranchised young people, remains to be seen.

NOTES

I dedicate this essay to the memory of John J. Tiby Jr. (1950–2000), a fiercely committed teacher and champion of the working class.

This essay was written with support from a Spencer/MacArthur Professional Development Research and Documentation Program grant.

1. REAL Work-Based Curriculum products include: "The Meaning and Value of Work: Personal/Critical Investigations for Teachers"; "Imagining Work" (a handbook for teachers); "Our Community of Workers" (a coloring book and handbook for students); "We Do the Work," volumes 1 and 2 (teachers' study guides for a video series by the California Working Group); "Teachers and the World of Work: A Preservice Teachers' Curriculum"; "The REAL WorkGuide" (a handbook on work issues for students); "Rochester Labor History Map/Guide" (for teachers and students); and "Study/Activity Guide" for It's Your Job . . . And These Are Your Rights (published by the AFL-CIO Working for America Institute and the U.S. Department of Labor).

REFERENCES

Aronowitz, S., and W. DiFazio. The Jobless Future: Sci-Tech and the Dogma of Work. Minneapolis: University of Minnesota Press, 1994.

Barlow, M., and H. J. Robertson. Class Warfare: The Assault on Canada's Schools. Toronto: Key Porter Books, 1994.

Garson, B. The Electronic Sweatshop: How Computers Are Transforming the Office of Today into the Factory of the Past. New York: Penguin, 1989.

Rifkin, J. The End of Work. New York: G.P. Putnam's Sons, 1995.

Simon, R. I., et al. Learning Work: A Critical Pedagogy of Work Education. New York: Bergin and Garvey, 1991.

Honor Thy Students

The Power of Writing

Edvige Giunta

It's a Sunday, late April, and I am waiting for the students from my memoir class to come to my house for an evening of closure to the fifteen weeks of the term. The students have been looking forward to this evening: excitement, eagerness, and a bit of nervousness, even fear. One student has decided not to go to her cousin's wedding so that she will not miss this event. This is the culmination of months of hard work: mine, but, above all, theirs. The class is now running itself. I have done my part.

Years ago, when I was teaching in a liberal arts college in upstate New York (quite different from an urban institution like New Jersey City University, where I currently teach), a colleague shared with me what he described as the greatest thrill of teaching: "It's that moment in which students are in awe of me and my knowledge. It's when I look at them looking at me and I see they are mesmerized." "Funny," I replied, "for me, instead, the most exciting moment in teaching occurs when I almost disappear and the students are in awe of themselves, of their knowledge and power." Which is what I hope will happen on this particular spring evening in my home in Jersey City. And if I have provided the framework, the guidance, and the support, enforced the rules and encouraged the self-discipline, it's my students' enthusiasm, determination, bravery, and compassion that make their success possible.

To nurture students' recognition of their learning power is pedagogically necessary in any school setting, but it is especially important with working-class and minority students. Such students often carry the baggage of cultural marginalization and denigration that insidiously shapes their self-perception. Appropriating memory is a crucial step for all marginalized groups. Over the last several years, the memoir has established itself as a forum in which authors can address traditionally unspeakable topics such as political and cultural oppression, poverty, disability, interracial relationships, homosexuality, and physical and sexual violence. Through writing, students can grasp the intricate ways in which story and history, private and public, intersect.

Memoirs interweave explorations of social issues with intimate life narratives. My memoir students learn to write about their lives *critically* and, in doing so, come to "own" the very experiences of violence, abuse, and disempowerment that have erased—or partly constituted—their sense of selfhood. I emphasize "critically" because memoir is not simply about writing the facts of one's life. Memoir requires, as I understand and teach it, creating frameworks in which to place one's life, frameworks that enable the writer to shift from the position of object to that of subject, a narrating subject who views and interprets the world from newly created perspectives. This is one class in which students become "experts," as they teach themselves and their peers about historical events and geographical regions that are often unfamiliar to most of the class. Their diverse backgrounds—African, Palestinian, Guatemalan, Italian, Salvadoran, among others—represent sources for interchange: acceptance of and respect for cultural differences—one's own and others'—enrich the fabric of this community of young writers.

For the first eleven weeks of the term, students wrote weekly assignments: memoir "moments" the length of which increased as the weeks went by.[1] Every week, two students presented their work and benefited from insightful suggestions and comments offered by the class. Everyone had to respond. We devised our own ground rules: respondents could not talk about or draw comparisons with their own life experiences or even comment on the author's experiences described in the memoir; the focus had to be on how a particular autobiographical event had been crafted as a written piece. During the last four weeks, students worked on a longer final piece (15–20 pages) that they presented to the class toward the end of the term.

A week before our final meeting at my house, as we were discussing the length of time each student would read, some students expressed their concern over the discomfort they might feel in sharing the intimate details of their lives that had made their way into the final memoir pieces. After much discussion, one student exclaimed that she had come to trust this group so much that she expected that trust to be reciprocated. The fact that my students have become so vocal about their work and so intent on shaping the context for the presentation of that work represents, in my mind, a victorious moment in their efforts to gain power and exercise it. In the end, while I encouraged everyone to avoid self-censorship, I told them that if they felt it necessary, they could edit on the spot: they should leave the options open.

As much as I believe in democratic teaching, I do not underestimate the reality that, in the classroom, I am in charge and will, ultimately, evaluate the students' work. Nevertheless, many decisions, such as ground rules for editorial responses, were made collectively. Although students submitted their memoir moments to me weekly for comments (no grades were given on these shorter pieces), I gave them my immediate responses in class as well, after everyone else had responded. I also intervened to help someone refocus or redirect an excessively vague or personal response: I was, after all, the facilitator of this writing group. Yet, in order to facilitate, I had to monitor my own role in and influence on the class. For example, I debated about whether to respond at the beginning or the end of each session. Because this was a writing workshop, I wanted to be sure not to interrupt the flow of class responses with my own comments. In addition, I find that in contrast to students from more affluent backgrounds, who will have their voices heard in one way or another, students at New Jersey City University tend to silence themselves and rarely interrupt the teacher to express their own views. I feared that by being the first to respond, I would prevent the students from forming and freely articulating their responses. The weight of authority must be delicately balanced. So, although by responding last I risked giving the "final" word, I felt that this was the option that would be least damaging to the atmosphere of a student-centered workshop. The students' comments became increasingly sharper: their growth as writers matched their growth as readers.

Exploratory discussions increased in number and intensity throughout the term. I witnessed a shift in class dynamics as the students came to occupy a different place in the classroom. By the end of the term they recognized that the class belonged to them and that the work they produced there was meaningful and beautiful. Whether it is a question of sexual identity or homelessness, of being an immigrant, a political exile, or a rape, incest, or war survivor, students in memoir courses have important things to say, and most of them are not aware of these things until they begin writing.

My students each developed an appreciation for the power they had achieved through writing—a power to understand their lives in contexts that are familial and societal, personal and political, but also a power to articulate such an understanding in eloquent prose. Although only a small fraction of my students plan to become professional writers, they have all come to regard themselves as "writers" and have come to view writing as a powerful means for situating and understanding themselves in history. When historically disempowered people write memoirs, in claiming a space for their voices and their memory, they obliquely—and not so obliquely—claim a space for those who are, in turn, empowered by reading their memoirs. Writing memoir involves writing one's history, but very often also dismantling the historical constructions that have been handed down to us. In writing memoir, writers claim for themselves the role of interpreter and historian—indeed, reader—of their families and communities, a role often fraught with productive contradictions.

Laura McKeon, one of my students, described her experience with the memoir class as follows: "We all suffer from certain degrees of historical, social, and familial amnesia. Through memoir writing, one can learn to fill in the blanks and, in the process, reclaim his or her past honestly. . . . The greatest gift I received from my course experience was the sense of validation, trust, and community I garnered from my fellow classmates. . . . I came away with the sense that our personal struggles, although different in detail, bound us together as survivors of our own life experiences." My memoir students develop not only an appreciation for their work as writers, but also a respect for the work—and lives—of their peers, lives they have come to know through writing.

My students have become better readers and writers; they have become writers in their own right. I became acutely aware of these newly achieved identities as I observed my students engage in lively, mature conversations with a number of writers who came on campus, thanks to two university grants. My students chatted comfortably with Jacqueline Woodson, Louise DeSalvo, and Cheryl Boyce Taylor, whose works—of memoir, poetry, and fiction—articulate a deeply felt awareness of class politics. They talked about these writers' work as well as their own work with competence, enthusiasm, dignity, and confidence: writers speaking to writers.

I cook lasagna and chicken Marbella. They bring wine, cookies, and a cake. I am moved by the inscription on this cake: "Celebrating Writing & Healing."

The memoirs are astounding: beautifully crafted, moving, powerful stories. These memoirs are neither self-congratulatory nor self-indulgent. Many of them engage American identity by questioning its central mythologies, by exploring, for example, the ruptures in the narratives of success and individualism. One of the students, a particularly shy and self-deprecating young woman whose early work in the class might have been considered mediocre, surprises everyone with a marvelous, incredibly lucid piece that weaves together memories of her childhood with a violent, alcoholic father, and reflections on her present renegotiation with her past. The process my students embarked upon with apprehension has yielded its inevitable results. I feel honored to be able to witness and be part of this victorious journey. I am elated. In the end, they ask me to read from my own memoir. I have been writing with them throughout the term, but have not shared my writing with them yet. It is time. As I read, surprised by my own trepidation, I realize that I have come to respect these young writers. I trust their judgment. I look forward to their comments.

They leave rather late. This has been our longest class: over six hours. We have eaten, read, listened, laughed, and cried. I feel a satisfying sense of closure, but most of all a sense of appreciation for the possibilities that teaching and learning can create. I sit down to write the words that have echoed in my head this night: Honor thy students and their work—and they will, too.

NOTE

1. This weekly memoir "moment" assignment draws from Louise DeSalvo's teaching practice at Hunter College. DeSalvo's approach to teaching memoir has influenced and shaped mine in fundamental ways. See Louise De Salvo, *Writing as a Way of Healing: How Telling Our Stories Transforms Our Lives* (New York: Harper San Francisco, 1999).

Mining Class
A Bibliographic Essay
Laura Hapke

For many of us the final object of our work is to create a world in which working people can make their own life and their own history, rather than to have it made for them by others, including academics.

—Nick Salvatore[1]

Blue Collar: The Literature of Labor. 3 credits. Essay Assignment #1. A Hypothetical Labor Situation

It is (a cold) spring, and you have dutifully participated in class discussion on struggles in coal mining. To further a course requirement in your major, whether it is education, history, sociology, anthropology, politics, industrial relations, or social work, you are doing a "service learning" internship in a company town in western Pennsylvania in which workers have consistently, if mysteriously, voted down union locals. (In a variant assignment, you may choose a venue that is solidly pro–United Mine Workers [UMW].) You have been sent to teach American civilization at a community college with a business and otherwise vocational mission.

Your students, who have heard all too often the term "white trash," are largely blank when asked about John L. Lewis, attend fitfully, look inattentive, and have accents you have difficulty understanding. You ask them to talk about their coal-mining fathers, and, in fewer cases, mothers. As the weeks go by, you are less of an outsider. Your syllabus guide, issued by the American history department, makes no reference to such signature mining history as Avondale, the Molly Maguires, Mother Jones at Cripple Creek, Matewan, and Harlan County. Nor is there reference to songs by Aunt Molly Jackson, "I Am a Union Woman," and Florence Reese, "Which Side Are You On?" or to the classic documentary Out of Darkness: The Mine Workers Story.[2]

In any way you see fit, comment in writing on your plan of action. Begin with what your students might read in your class. Consider carefully how you will explain your approach to your internship director, to your instructor, and to yourself.

In the Hollywood imagination, gutsy miners' daughters rise from Appalachian coal dust to stardom, and brilliant scholarship boys emerge from the strip-mined landscape to soar as rocket scientists. Even in independent films with mainstream distribution, handsome Industrial Workers of the World (IWW) organizers come from afar and whip the Mingo County workers into strike shape. The difficult and often tragic lived experience of a century and a half of anthracite and bituminous coal workers and their families, however, is quite other.[3] As one of the most representative industries to form the battleground on which struggles by and within the working class play out, authentic mining stories have little to do with competitive individualism or the success ethic.

Rather, these varied U.S. labor narratives, in Janet Zandy's phrase, create spaces for workers to represent themselves. If, as Freud observed, no memory is without motive, this little-known body of working-class literature constantly recovers a labor history erased in periods of comparative national prosperity, such as today's. By the 1970s, coal miners were little better off—and in some ways worse off—than in the days when the Wagner Act had permitted the collective bargaining that Taft-Hartley subsequently outlawed. Songwriter Florence Reese stood up at a 1972 convention and sang the protest song she had composed for the 1930s protest, "Which Side Are You On?"[4] Such a question would have particularly ironic overtones in an industry in which internecine struggles occurred between Communist-led mine unions and the United Mine Workers; racial division often replaced class solidarity; and gender stratification limited women to lives above ground but in the domestic or piecework mode.

Still, in have-not places like Harlan County, 1970 was 1930 and, if anything, with de-skilling, mine closings, and striker replacement acts, generation after generation of militant miners have concurred with the mining-town proletarian novelist of the 1930s Jack Conroy's wish that if he rise, it will be with his class.

In the twenty-first century classroom, there is more than coal dust coating the ongoing struggles in coal. Instructors in working-class studies discover that even (and sometimes especially) students with working-class roots have routinely never heard the term "dignity of labor," are neutral or hostile toward unionization, look through rather than at the many janitorial and cafeteria workers they "meet" in campus hallways or stand next to in elevators. Although there are students from prolabor backgrounds, their understanding of the terms "industrial and labor relations," "human resources," and "public policy" is managerial: Taylorism, not Socialism.

What follows is a modest attempt to revive the power and the glory of the mining narrative. This interdisciplinary bibliography, used over the years in numerous labor studies classrooms, generates student interest at the very least and an outraged eloquence at best. Selective rather than exhaustive, may it serve as a model of similarly trade-based cross-racial, multicultural, bi-gender lists in clothing, textiles, rubber, automobiles, and meatpacking, as these are all industries crucial to an understanding of organized and insurgent labor in this "classless" society. Obviously, a "Congress of Industrial Organizations (CIO) approach" to working-class texts is also imperative, as are syllabi on texts of industrial, electronic, urban, and rural marginalization, to cite a few. But a scrutiny of the titles below will reveal what might be loosely termed "the UMW narrative."

The following highly selective titles can constitute or provide a segment of an entire basic, elective, or interdisciplinary course, or a supplementary reading list, as the occasion suits. All prove, however, that the story of the mines has the kind of depth that the new century's prolabor Americanists might well find of use. Where I cite the press the book is still in print.

BY WAY OF INTRODUCTION: TWO INITIAL TEXTS

As a prologue to the fractious unionism, industrial conditions, and warring camps of the mining world, I suggest excerpts from this pair of texts:

Allan Pinkerton. *The Mollie Maguires and the Detectives*. New York: Dover, 1975. Dover has done a great service in reprinting this 1877 diatribe against the Mollies, which combines primitive ethnography, political jeremiad, semifictive melodramatic plotting, and the famed detective agency's characteristic self-aggrandizement.

Anthony Bimba. *The Molly Maguires*. New York: International Publishers, 1932. Although not usually so classified, this groundbreaking study is one of many useful retrospectives produced during the New Deal years. It provides, at the very least, a sympathetic cultural context for this historically liminalized group.

THE MASTER SPEAKS

Melvyn Dubofsky and Warren Van Tine. *John L. Lewis*. Urbana: University of Illinois Press, 1986. John L. Lewis ruled the UMW for forty years, beginning in 1919. One could construct a course solely around the man's various representations—official, political, cultural, literary, and so on. This is the best biography of the still-ambiguous figure (was he the *vir bonus* or the sellout of mining unionism?). At times too laudatory, its thoroughness and insight are unrivaled.

USEFUL OUT-OF-PRINT NOVELS FROM WHICH TO CULL EXCERPTS:

C. M. Cornwall. *Free, Yet Forging Their Own Chains*. 1876. This is an early antilabor cross-class romance treatment of the violent, failed 1876 Central Pennsylvania Anthracite Coal Strike, the allegedly terrorist Molly Maguires, the Avondale Disaster of 1869, and the pre–UMW Miners' National Association (MNA).

Serialized in magazines aimed at working-class consumption were 1876 dime novels on the Molly Maguires: Albert Aiken, "The Molly Maguires"; William Mason Turner, "The Masked Miner," and so on.[5] Michael Denning, who identified these titles, notes that many "shift attention away from the acts of the Mollies themselves; without exonerating" them but criticizing monopolists and mine bosses (Denning 128).

JOURNALISTIC VIGNETTE

Stephen Crane. "In the Depths of a Coal Mine." *McClure's*, 1894. The author of *Red Badge of Courage* and *The Open Boat* finds struggles between elemental forces in a Pennsylvania mine shaft. Crane's family owned coal stock, and the sketch was in part a reproof to them.

"PROLETARIAN" MINING FICTION: FROM THE PROGRESSIVES TO THE POST–COLD WAR ERA

Cross-Class Writing

Upton Sinclair. *King Coal.* 1917. Reprint, New York: Signet, 1991. A contradictory novel based on the Rockefeller-fueled squelching of "Bloody Ludlow," the mine strikes of Colorado, 1913–14. In it, a kind of Fabian Socialism intersects uneasily with Sinclair's signature outrage. He reinvents the Rockefeller figure as a benevolent paternalist, while appending the muckraking Industrial Commission findings on Ludlow (mines owned by Rockefeller) to the text. It is useful, though, for two reasons: it is a bridge from the genteel to the proletarian treatment of mining and it is in paperback, unlike other period fare such as Walter Hurt's Cripple Creek mass-circulation novel *The Scarlet Shadow* (1907). Perhaps excerpts from both authors can suit.

The Golden Age of Worker Writing

Jack Conroy. *The Disinherited.* 1933. Reprint, Columbia: University of Missouri Press, 1991. Part 1 of this proletarian picaresque is a tribute to Conroy's coal-mining Missouri father, killed in an overtime accident. The novel's strongest section, it is a virtual ethnography of the early-twentieth-century mining camp surround. As his biographer persuasively claims, Conroy fell out of favor, ironically, in the mid-1930s for being too much the worker-writer.[6]

Tom Tippett. *Horseshoe Bottoms.* 1935. This historical novel of British coal miners transplanted to Kickapoo Creek, Illinois, retains Conroy's immense respect for the father sacrificed to capitalist greed. Although it illustrates the variations on the lost-miner theme, this is hagiography rather than call to action.

Lauren Gilfillan. *I Went to Pit College.* 1934. Gilfillan, writes Alan Wald, disguised herself as a miner's child, among other guises, to gather material for her book.[7] Wald's forthcoming two-volume history of the formation of the left tradition in the 1930s and World War II era contains a fine reappraisal of this once-maligned fictive autobiography and provides much-needed historical context: in this case, the "Great Coal Strike" of 1931 in Avella, Pennsylvania.

After the House Un-American Activities Committee (HUAC): Carrying On

John Yount. *Hardcastle.* Dallas: Southern Methodist University Press, 1990. A gem, misunderstood by post–Cold War critics, is the unfairly neglected novel *Hardcastle*. Set in the strife-torn coalfields of eastern Kentucky in the waning months of the Hoover presidency, it both modernizes and historicizes the doomed conflict. It reads like what it is: a proletarian novel for nonproletarian times.

Denise Giardina. *The Unquiet Earth.* New York: Ivy Books, 1992. Giardina, who writes frequently on the betrayal of modern coal mining (see her introduction to *Women of Coal* [University Press of Kentucky, 1996]), provides an often lyrical novel here. It opens with Dillon Freeman, a prototypical coal miner's son summoning up Depression-era courage by tapping the spirit of his own long-dead union-organizer father. Giardina takes him and the Blackberry Creek, West Virginia, denizens of Mining Camp Number 13 through fifty years of draining wildcat labor strife characterized by company wage cuts of 50 percent, lockouts at rifle point, and retaliatory industrial sabotage. Responsive to feminist issues as well, Giardina is eloquent on the post–Taft-Hartley labor militant.

James Lee Burke. *To the Bright and Shining Sun.* New York: Hyperion, 1966.; John Sayles, *Union Dues.* New York: Harper Torchbooks, 1977. Two of their most important fellow writers contextualize white laboring men within a lost radical UMW tradition in the coalfields of eastern Kentucky and nearby West Virginia. Burke and Sayles link the working miner's erosion of spirit to the twilight of their worker fathers: reduced to a white-trash subsistence when they rightly belong in the artisan tradition of the dignified workman.

PERIOD DOCUMENTS: THE UMW AND WORKING-CLASS HISTORY

Theodore Dreiser and the National Committee for the Defense of Political Prisoners, comps. *Harlan Miners Speak: Report on Terrorism in the Kentucky Coal Fields.* 1930. Reprint, New York: Da Capo Press, 1970. Compiled by Dreiser and an ad-hoc leftist writers group, the anti-UMW (and pro-National Miners Union) National Committee for the Defense of Political Prisoners, this book consists of transcripts of trial testimony and essays by various hands on "class war in Kentucky," "living conditions in the coal fields," and transcribed interviews with miners.

John H. M. Laslett, ed. *The United Mine Workers of America: A Model of Industrial Solidarity?* University Park: Pennsylvania State University Press, 1996. This substantial collection, while it contains many essays critical of "Big Labor" in the mines, also draws on UMW archives, including material about the Southwest Virginia Pittston Strike of 1989–99, widely perceived in labor quarters as a revivifying union victory.

Edward M. Steel Jr., ed. *The Court-Martial of Mother Jones.* 1913. Reprint, Lexington: University Press of Kentucky, 1995. This scholarly paperback edition includes an introduction and an annotated transcription of the celebrated labor agitator Mary Harris (Mother Jones) at the 1913 Paint Creek and Cabin Creek, West Virginia, strikes. The book is especially useful in describing "radicals'" ambiguous relationship with the UMW, and important events in the history of mining-town militance.

THE NEW WORKING-CLASS HISTORY: HISTORICAL REVISIONISM ON THE MINES

Joshua Freeman, et al., eds. *Who Built America?* New York: Pantheon, 1992. References to mining appear frequently in this two-volume book generated under the aegis of the dean of working-class historians, Herbert Gutman, by his American Social History Project. This beautifully written, detailed survey reenvisions history "from the bottom up." Although at times overstating the significance and prevalence of union victories, it is still unsurpassed in the undergraduate classroom. A revised edition is scheduled to appear soon.

There is a wealth of new social history available to those studying the mining narrative. Some currently available texts, already classics of labor history, include Ronald L. Lewis, *Black Coal Miners in America: Race, Class, and Community*

Conflict, 1780–1980 (Lexington: University Press of Kentucky, 1987); David Alan Corbin, *Life, Work, and Rebellion in the Coal Fields: The Southern West Virginia Miners, 1880–1922* (Urbana: University of Illinois Press, 1981); Joe William Trotter Jr., *Coal, Class, and Color: Blacks in Southern West Virginia, 1915–32* (Urbana: University of Illinois, 1990). Particularly in the context of fiction, all these studies are user-friendly to the undergraduate classroom and include much bibliographical information, including primary sources in federal and state history, oral interviews, period newspapers, and archival sources.

TWO FINAL COMPANION TEXTS

Peter Oresick and Nicholas Coles, eds. *Working Classics: Poems on Industrial Life*. Urbana: University of Illinois Press, 1990. I suggest a quartet of moving and rather documentary poems by Ed Ochester in this work, which prompted one of my students, herself a coal miner's daughter watching her father denied UMW benefits for black lung disease, to write: "Ochester provides the precise feeling that my father has experienced the majority of his life." Both her father and Ochester's subjects are "left with disabled bodies and disappointed souls."[8]

Contrast the sincerity of the above texts with the disappointed cynicism of Robert Schenkkan's nostalgic but corrupt UMW leader in the Pulitzer prize–winning play *The Kentucky Cycle* (New York: Plume/New American Library, 1992). What should be an exhilarating theatrical experience, interestingly, is in part an elegy to the lost John L. Lewis of the early union decades.

NOTES

1. Nick Salvatore, "Herbert Gutman's Narrative of the American Working Class: A Reevaluation," *International Journal of Business, Politics, and Society* 12, no. 1 (1998): 46.

2. An excellent guide to labor films, and soon to be issued in a second edition, is Tom Zaniello, *Working Stiffs, Union Maids, Reds, and Riffraff: An Organized Guide to Films about Labor* (Ithaca: ILR Press, 1996).

3. Copper miners (particularly those in the Southwest and in Idaho's famed 1892 Coeur d'Alene protest), who waged Western Federation of Miners and Industrial Workers of the World struggles, could easily form another article.

4. See Janet Zandy, ed., *Calling Home: Working-Class Women's Writing* (New Brunswick, N.J.: Rutgers University Press, 1990), 62, in which the 1930s Reese song is reprinted.

5. Michael Denning, *Mechanic Accents: Dime Novels and Working-Class Culture in America* (London: Verso, 1987), 121; hereafter cited in text.

6. Douglas Wixson, *Worker-Writer in America: Jack Conroy and the Tradition of Midwestern Literary Radicalism, 1898–1990* (Urbana: University of Illinois Press, 1994).

7. Alan Wald, H-Labor LISTSERV, 23 September 1999.

8. Rebecca Roach, "Ochester's 'Retired Miners,'" term paper, Literature 102, Prof. Laura Hapke, Pace University, 11 November 1993.

Working, Buying, and Becoming
Race, Labor, and the High Life from the Plantation to the Internet

Todd Vogel

I originally called this class "Race, Labor, and Literature" but found that many students don't, at first blush, think they are interested in labor. I changed the title—and little else in the course—to "Working, Buying, and Becoming," and enrollments swelled. Once students see the relationship between people's work and their sense of who they are in society, they see themselves in these questions and they develop interest. I stoke that interest on the first day by giving them oral histories of workers in the year 2000 from the volume Gig. A Kinko's worker, an advertising executive, and a dominatrix talk about themes that Crèvecoeur and Melville brought up more than 150 years before. Students then have current representations attached to these enduring issues. We move back in time and work forward. The class then shows, with stories and other cultural artifacts, the ways that work has defined us. It also shows how the source of that definition migrates from work-as-a-means-to-serve-society to work-as-a-means-to-consume. Along the way, students get a more nuanced understanding of class and they see the myriad ways race and gender intrude on our everyday lives.

How do writers talk about what we do for a living, and how do we use race, gender, and material goods to define ourselves? Which tells the most about us—our skin color, our sex, our job, or our Jeep Cherokee? This class seeks to understand how these factors influence our perceptions of who we are and how we fit into society. Race, gender, and the market economy—and the ways these concepts change throughout American history—will become key issues for us to consider. Our reading will cover a broad swath of time, from Crèvecoeur and Equiano in the eighteenth century, to Thoreau and Frederick Douglass in the nineteenth century, and to Richard Wright and "Rivethead" in the twentieth century.

Also key in understanding this process will be a shifting understanding of human rights. As we investigate labor and consumption in literature, we will investigate the artistic expression of societal conflict over human rights. Indeed, writers interested in human rights throughout American history have found ample material in the labor issues of their day. Abolitionists deployed a human rights argument to end slavery. After late-nineteenth-century crises such as the Civil War, Reconstruction, and the Great Southwest Railroad strike focused public attention on the labor protection and freedoms workers deserved, W. E. B. Du Bois's writing, like a literary Geiger counter, registered social fault lines. In the twentieth-century age of mass production and consumerism, the issue becomes more important still. Products that many people buy come from factories where the workers labor in terrible conditions, and writers from W. H. Auden to George

Saunders have used this paradox as fuel for their art. Secretary of State Madeleine Albright gave a September 1999 speech before the Advisory Committee on Labor Diplomacy that played catch-up with artists when she cited the "vital importance of labor in this changing, shrinking world."

To begin to address these questions, the readings will include pieces of history and cultural criticism—documents from the period such as slave narratives and school catalogs, human rights resolutions, journalism, novels, and short stories. The course will move through time, from the yeoman farmers of the American Revolution to a Nike-financed sweatshop, and will weave information about human rights ideals of the time into each section.

WHAT THIS CLASS WILL HELP YOU LEARN TO DO

• Analyze people and their way of life. Reading about how race, gender, and class combine to shape American literature gives you a more subtle understanding of how people and the world work. If you can gain more analytical precision in your thinking (and that's what this course strives to give you), you will move in the world more sure of yourself and your place in it.

• Understand how ideas about human rights affect us today. Human rights have shaped the artistic expression of writing about labor for hundreds of years. These concepts burble beneath the surface, subaquatic, and it's up to each of us to bring the concept of human rights to the surface, inspect it, and decide how the concrete reality of our own lives intersects with it.

• Understand our society. How does class, for example, affect racial groups differently? To be "upper class" in the black community during the antebellum period meant someone who worked as a barber—a class position far different in the white community. What do these distinctions mean? Again, understanding the historical grounding of these kinds of distinctions helps us see the world more clearly.

• See how historical context helps us understand the present. In 2000 both Al Gore and George Bush reached to "historical precedent" to prove whatever point they wanted to make. But when we understand, for example, how American ideas about race, gender, and class changed throughout the eighteenth, nineteenth, and twentieth centuries, as did the definitions of jobs, citizenship, and domestic work, we see that candidates' superficial references to "precedent" help us very little.

• Analyze what you read, see, and hear. Develop close reading skills for various types of primary and secondary texts, and learn how to read all of these texts against one another. For example, how does testimony about workers' abilities change our understanding of antebellum free blacks' exhortations about labor and uplift? These skills of reading and synthesis form the foundation of nearly all work in the liberal arts.

• Hone analytical skills. You will learn to create critical questions, interrogate the text for answers, and draw on outside sources to buttress your analysis. Your final paper requires you to root out new primary sources to shed light on the text you investigate and to place all the primary material in a historically informed setting.

GETTING THERE

To achieve these goals, I expect you to come to every class prepared to contribute something to the group—a comment, a passage that made you excited or confused, or a doubt about something you've read. No exceptions. No excuses.

View our class meetings as the culmination of work that we do on our own. Alone, each of us huddles up with the course packet or the assigned reading for the week. We finish the reading early to give ourselves time to think: What is the central argument of what I just read—or, what is the writer trying to evoke? How do the various kinds of readings fit together? Can I connect them to the last thing we read? Can I connect it to the material we read at the beginning of the semester? Do the readings make some broader sense? Have I learned anything in this class—or in another class—that challenges what the author or artist is arguing? What evidence would I offer to refute this?

By thinking hard about the material and integrating it with how you see the world, you are beginning to gain command of it. This is the process that allows you to make the material your own and reap the benefits listed above. While this process is one of the most rewarding things about taking a class, it is not easy. But like a hard run or a challenging bike ride, you get a thrill of accomplishment— and its benefits don't wear off as quickly.

OUR FLIGHT PLAN

INTRODUCTION

Session 1

Intro Discussion—Defining Class, major themes and periods of the course.
Group Discussions: Selections from Word.com's *Gig: Americans Talk About Their Jobs at the Turn of the Millennium*. New York: Crown Publishers, 2000: Kinko's worker, software engineer, telephone psychic, dominatrix, advertising executive, MC Medusa.

SECTION I: FOUNDING TO 1815—HOUSEHOLD PRODUCTION AND SLAVERY

A. The Standard American Narrative—And Then Some

Session 2

Thomas Paine. *The Rights of Man*. 1792. Reprint, *The Human Rights Reader: Major Political Writings, Essays, Speeches, and Documents from the Bible to the Present*, edited by Micheline R. Ishay. New York: Routledge, 1997, 134–38.
Thomas Paine. "African Slavery in America." 1775. Reprint, *The Human Rights Reader*, 130–33.

Michel-Guillaume-Jean de Crèvecoeur [J. Hector St. John, pseud.] *Letters from an*
    American Farmer. In *Heath Anthology of American Literature*, edited by Paul Lauter.
    Boston: Heath, 1998, 892–925.
Thomas Jefferson. "Jefferson on Manufacturing." Circa 1785. Reprint in *Working in*
    America: A Humanities Reader, edited by Robert Sessions and Jack Wortman. Notre
    Dame, Ind.: University of Notre Dame Press, 1992, 332–34.
Alexis de Tocqueville. "That Aristocracy May Be Engendered by Manufactures." Reprint
    in *Working in America*, 324–28.
"'Learn Them to Be Domestic': Raising Republican Women." *Independent Mechanic* 14
    September 1811.

B. The Standard Narrative, Slavery and Variations

Session 3

Benjamin Franklin. "Advice to a Young Tradesman." Reprint in *Working in America*,
    58–60.
Olaudah Equiano. Selection from *The Interesting Narrative of the Life of Olaudah Equiano,
    Or, Gustavus Vassa, the African*. 1791. Reprint in *The Classic Slave Narratives*, edited by
    Henry Louis Gates Jr. New York: Penguin, 1987, 85–125.

Session 4

WPA interviews with slaves—"Work and Slave Life: 'From Can to Can't.'" In
    *Remembering Slavery: African Americans Talk About Their Personal Experiences of Slavery
    and Freedom*, edited by Ira Berlin, Marc Favreau, and Steven F. Miller. New York: New
    Press, 1998, 71–96. (Also, WPA interviews on tape from *Remembering Slavery* on
    reserve.)

Session 5

John Vlasch. "Plantation Landscape Ensembles." In *Back of the Big House: The Architecture
    of Plantation Slavery*. Chapel Hill: University of North Carolina Press, 1993, 183–227.

SECTION II: 1815 TO CIVIL WAR—SLAVERY AND THE DEVELOPING MARKET ECONOMY

Session 6

Henry David Thoreau. "Economy" and selections. In *Walden*. 1845. Reprint in *Thoreau*.
    New York: Library of America, 1985, 325–85.

Session 7

Herman Melville. "Bartleby the Scrivener." In *Bartleby the Scrivener and Benito Cereno*.
    New York: Dover Publications, 1990.
George Lippard. Selection of columns and "Black Sampson." In *Washington and His
    Generals*. 1847. Reprint in *George Lippard, Prophet of Protest: Writings of an American*

Radical, 1822–1854, edited by David S. Reynolds. New York: P. Lang, 1986, 47–54, 123–28.

Session 8

Rebecca Harding Davis. *Life in the Iron Mills*. 1860. Reprint, edited by Tillie Olsen, New York: The Feminist Press, 1972.

John Roach. "Senate Testimony from Iron Foundry Proprietor." 1883. Reprint in *Life in the Iron Mills*, Bedford Cultural Edition, edited by Cecelia Tichi. New York: Bedford Books, 1998, 97–102.

Session 9

Fanny Fern. "Sewing Machines." 1853. "The Working-Girls of New York." 1867. Reprint in *Life in the Iron Mills*, 156–59.

Herman Melville. "The Paradise of Bachelors and the Tartarus of Maids." Reprint in *Melville*. New York: Library of America, 1984, 1257–79.

Session 10

Eric Lott. "White Kids and No Kids at All: Languages of Race in Antebellum U.S. Working-Class Culture." In *Rethinking Class: Literary Studies and Social Formations*, edited by Wai Chee Dimock and Michael T. Gilmore. New York: Columbia University Press, 1994, 175–211.

Recommended: David Roediger. "White Slaves, Wage Slaves, and Free White Labor." In *The Wages of Whiteness*. New York: Verso, 1991, 65–92.

Session 11

Articles from the Black Press. Accessible Archives, Malvern, Pa. Online. Available: <http://www.accessible.com/>. 15 Nov. 2000:

"From Bennett's N.Y. Herald: Great Abolition Movement—Manifesto of the Negroes." *The North Star*, 10 Nov. 1848.

"Henry Boyd—The Carpenter." *The Colored American*. New York, 17 Aug. 1839.

"Capacity of Negroes to Take Care of Themselves." *The Colored American*. New York, 11 March 1837.

"On Training." *The Colored American*. New York, 11 May 1839.

"Colored Students." *The Colored American*. New York, 2 Sept. 1837.

Session 12

Frederick Douglass. *Narrative of the Life of Frederick Douglass*. 1845. Reprint, edited by David Blight, Boston: Bedford Books of St. Martin's Press, 1993.

Session 13

Finish *Narrative of the Life of Frederick Douglass*.

Session 14

T. Thomas Fortune. "Land and Labor in the South." In *Black and White: Land, Labor, and Politics in the South*. 1884. Reprint in *The Negro Caravan*, edited by Sterling A. Brown, Arthur P. Davis, and Ulysses Lee, 1941; reprint, New York: Arno Press, 1969, 880–84.

Booker T. Washington. "Industrial Education for the Negro." September 1903. Online. Available: <http://douglass.speech.nwu.edu/wash_b04.htm>. 15 Nov. 2000.

Booker T. Washington. *Nineteenth Annual Report of the Principal of the Tuskegee Normal and Industrial Institute, Tuskegee, Alabama: May 31, 1900*. Library of Congress, Daniel Murray Pamphlet Collection. Online. Available: <http://memory.loc.gov/ammem/ammemhome.html>. Digital ID: (h) lcrbmrp t1704. 15 Nov. 2000.

SECTION III: RECONSTRUCTION, BLACKS, AND NEW FREEDOMS?

Session 15

W. E. B. Du Bois, *The Souls of Black Folk*. 1903. Reprint, New York: Library of America, 1990.

Session 16

Catalog. Tennessee Agricultural and Industrial State Normal School, Nashville, Tenn. 1913–14. Mimeographed.

Jesse Claxton, J. G. Going, and N. R. Fielding. "Senate Testimony from Workers of Color." 1883. Reprint in *Life in the Iron Mills*, 114–22.

SECTION IV: THE GREAT DEPRESSION

Session 17

Meridel Le Sueur. "I Was Marching." In *Ripening: Selected Work, 1927–1980*, edited by Elaine Hedges. New York: The Feminist Press, 1982, 158–65.

Richard Wright. "I Have Seen Black Hands." *Working in America*, 92–94.

Ira Katznelson. "Working-Class Formation: Constructing Cases and Comparisons." In *Working-Class Formation: Nineteenth-Century Patterns in Western Europe and the United States*, edited by Ira Katznelson and Aristide R. Zolberg. Princeton: Princeton University Press, 1986, 3–41.

Session 18

Lizabeth Cohen. "Encountering Mass Culture at the Grassroots." *American Quarterly* 41, no. 1 (March 1989): 6–33.

J. Walter Thompson Company Competitive Advertisements Collection of the John W. Hartman Center for Sales, Advertising, and Marketing History in Duke University's Rare Book, Manuscript, and Special Collections Library, 1911–1955. Online. Available: <http://scriptorium.lib.duke.edu/adaccess/>. 15 Nov. 2000.

Louis Untermeyer. "Portrait of a Machine." 1923. Reprint in *Working in America*, 82–83.

Robert Frank. "In the UPS Man, Some Women Find a Complete Package." *The Wall Street Journal,* 8 Feb. 1995, sec. A1.

Session 19

Neil Foley. "The Darker Phases of Whiteness: The New Deal, Tenant Farmers, and the Collapse of Cotton Tenancy, 1933–1940." In *The White Scourge: Mexicans, Blacks, and Poor Whites in Texas Cotton Culture.* Berkeley: University of California Press, 1997, 163–83.

United Nations. *Universal Declaration of Human Rights.* 1948. Online. Available: <http://www.hrweb.org/legal/udhr.html>. 15 Nov. 2000.

Session 20

Francisco Jiménez. "The Circuit." 1997. Reprint in *Literature, Class, and Culture: An Anthology,* edited by Paul Lauter and Ann Fitzgerald. New York: Longman, 2001, 133–37.

Library of Congress Archives. "America From the Great Depression to World-War II: Photographs from the Farm Security Administration, 1935–1945." Online. Available: <http://lcweb2.loc.gov/ammem/fsahtml/fahome.html>. 15 Nov. 2000.

Session 21

The United Nations International Covenant on Economic, Social, and Cultural Rights. 1966. Online. Available: <http://www.hrweb.org/legal/escr.html>. 15 Nov. 2000.

Robert Trout. "Sounds from the 1944 Democratic Convention." Broadcast, *All Things Considered.* National Public Radio, 15 Aug. 2000. Online. Available: <http://www.npr.org/ramfiles/atc/20000815.atc.16.ram>. 15 Nov. 2000.

Franklin Delano Roosevelt. "State of the Union Address, 1944." Reprint in *The Roosevelt Reader; Selected Speeches, Messages, Press Conferences, and Letters of Franklin D. Roosevelt,* edited by Basil Rauch New York: Holt, Rinehart, and Winston, 1964.

Joe Glazer. Songs from *Don't Mourn: Organize!* Washington, D.C.: Smithsonian/Folkways, 1992.

SECTION V: POSTWAR AMERICA

Session 22

Tillie Olsen. "I Stand Here Ironing." In *Tell Me a Riddle.* 1956. Reprint, New York: Delta, 1994.

Elaine Tyler May. "Introduction" and "Chapter 1: Containment at Home: Cold War, Warm Hearth." In *Homeward Bound: American Families in the Cold War Era,* 1988, 1–36.

Session 23

Studs Terkel. "Waitress Dolores Dante." In *Working: People Talk About What They Do All Day and How They Feel About What They Do.* New York: Pantheon Books, 1974, 47–48.

Barbara Ehrenreich. "Nickel-and-Dimed: On (Not) Getting By in America." *Harper's Magazine* (January 1999): 37–52.

Nancy Fraser. "After the Family Wage: What Do Women Want in Social Welfare?" *Social Justice* 21, no. 1 (spring 1994): 80–86.

Bruce Springsteen. "Galveston Bay." *The Ghost of Tom Joad*. Columbia Records, 1995.

Session 24

Ben Hamper. *Rivethead: Tales from the Assembly Line*. New York: Warner Books, 1991.

Fenton Johnson. "The Daily Grind." In *Working in America*, 80–81.

Session 25

Finish *Rivethead*.

Session 26

George Saunders. "Winky." In *Pastoralia*. New York: Riverhead Books, 2000.

Microsoft Advertisement in *Wired Magazine*. 2000.

"Netslaves: Horror Stories of Working the Web." Online. Available: <http://www.disobey.com/netslaves/> 15 Nov. 2000.

Working-Class Studies and the Question of Proletarian Literature in the United States

A Graduate Seminar in American Literature

Will Watson

Since the first Conference on Working-Class Studies at Youngstown State University in 1993, this (inter)discipline has redefined and reinvigorated certain literary, interpretive, historical, and pedagogical questions that had lain dormant since the heydey of "Proletarian Literature" in the late 1930s. In working-class studies, traditional and neo-Marxism(s) contend with late-twentieth-century critical theories of race, nationality, ethnicity, gender, culture, and sexual practice. Thus, traditional questions about proletarian literature—for instance, "Is it literature about, by, or for workers?" and "Can a middle-class writer really identify with the struggle of workers?"—have exfoliated into such questions as "How do specific literary works construct class identities?" "How do gender politics inform a writer's understanding of class struggle?" and "How does a literary work look when situated within a working-class–oriented interpretive framework?"

In this class I want to sample a range of such issues, both new and traditional-Marxist, raised by the re-theorization of class and the emergence of working-class studies. To do so, we will read, discuss, and write about various types of text: writings that directly report working-class experience; memoirs/autobiographies of workers and professionals from working-class backgrounds; literary writings that construct class identity; theoretical works that inform current dialogues about class; and historiographical narratives of the working class.

BOOK LIST

Corbin, David. *Life, Work, and Rebellion in the Coal Fields: The Southern West Virginia Miners 1880–1922*. Urbana: University of Illinois Press, 1981.

Davis, Rebecca Harding. *Life in the Iron Mills and Other Stories*, edited by Tillie Olsen. New York: The Feminist Press, 1972, 1985.

Dimock, Wai-Chi, and Michael T. Gilmore, eds. *Rethinking Class: Literary Studies and Social Formations*. New York: Columbia University Press, 1994.

DiDonato, Pietro. *Christ in Concrete*. New York: Signet Classics, 1993.

Ellison, Ralph. *Invisible Man*. New York: Modern Library, 1994.

Fitzgerald, F. Scott. *The Great Gatsby*. New York: Scribner's, 1995.

Giardina, Denise. *Storming Heaven*. New York: Ivy Books, 1987.

Hurston, Zora Neale. *Their Eyes Were Watching God*. New York: HarperCollins, 1990.

Kadi, Joanne. *Thinking Class: Sketches from a Cultural Worker*. Boston: South End Press, 1996.

Olsen, Tillie. *Yonnondio*. New York: Dell Publishing, 1989.

Oresick, Peter, and Nicholas Coles, eds. *Working Classics: Poems on Industrial Life*. Urbana: University of Illinois Press, 1990.

Sinclair, Upton. *The Jungle*. Chicago: University of Illinois Press, 1988.

Smedley, Agnes. *Daughter of Earth*. New York: The Feminist Press, 1987.

Zandy, Janet, ed. *Liberating Memory: Our Work and Our Working-Class Consciousness*. New Brunswick, N.J.: Rutgers University Press, 1994.

Zinn, Howard. *A People's History of the United States*. New York: Harper Perennial 1990.

SEMINAR REQUIREMENTS

- Oral reports on secondary readings and individual research projects: 20% of grade
- Out-of-class midterm exam essay: 30% of grade
- Term essay of approximately 5,000 words: 50% of grade

READING AND ASSIGNMENT SCHEDULE

Meeting 1: Class Introduction; view *Saturday Night Fever*.

Meeting 2: Zinn, *People's History*, chs. 10 and 11; Kadi, *Thinking Class*, pp. 5–26, 39–59; Zandy, *Liberating Memory*, pp. xi–15, 64–73; Davis, *Life in the Iron Mills*.

Meeting 3: Davis, *Life in the Iron Mills*; Olsen, "Biographical Introduction" to *Life in the Iron Mills*; Kadi, *Thinking Class*, pp. 69–107; Smedley, *Daughter of Earth*.

Meeting 4: Smedley, *Daughter of Earth*; Zandy, *Liberating Memory*, pp. 86–128 (Daniels, McCarriston, Vasconcellos).

Meeting 5: Zinn, *People's History*, chs. 12–14; Giardina, *Storming Heaven*; Corbin, *Life, Work, and Rebellion*, chs. 7–9.

Meeting 6: Sinclair, *The Jungle*; Dimock and Gilmore, *Rethinking Class*, 1–15.

Meeting 7: Fitzgerald, *The Great Gatsby*; midterm essay topics handed out.

Meeting 8: Fitzgerald, *The Great Gatsby*; student presentations; midterm essays due.

Meeting 9: DiDonato, *Christ in Concrete*.

Meeting 10: DiDonato, *Christ in Concrete*; student presentations.

Meeting 11: Olsen, *Yonnondio*.

Meeting 12: Zinn, *People's History*, chs. 2 and 9. Hurston, *Their Eyes Were Watching God*.

Meeting 13: Hurston, *Their Eyes Were Watching God*; student presentations.

Meeting 14: Zinn, *People's History*, ch. 17; Ellison, *Invisible Man*.

Meeting 15: Ellison, *Invisible Man*; student presentations.

Women and Work in U.S. History

Peter Rachleff

Since the foundation of the British colonies in North America, women's work has been an important part of economic and social life. Sometimes it has taken place in the home; sometimes it has taken place in factories, offices, hospitals and nursing homes, or retail businesses. Sometimes it has been waged; sometimes it has been unpaid. All sorts of women have worked—daughters, mothers, single women, married women. Immigrant women and women of color have had work experiences similar to—and different from—those of white women. Changes in family structures, workplace technologies, and economic dynamics have also affected which women have worked and what kind of work they have done.

Women's work—in all of its incarnations—has been central to working-class life. Women's performance of unwaged "reproductive" labor in the home has made it possible for working-class men and girls to seek wage work outside the home. Some of this work in the home has been extended into "productive" activities—taking in boarders, selling surplus canned goods, and performing the outwork of stitching and assembling for piece wages, for example—which bring needed additional income into working-class households. Those women who have earned wages outside the home have also contributed to family income in addition to earning a living for themselves. There is a third category of work, beyond "reproductive" and "productive" (and equally central to working-class life), which we might call "community building." By helping to birth babies; generating economic support for churches, trade unions, and other community institutions; and creating a safety net for other community members, women's work in midwifery, quilting bees, bake sales, auxiliaries, and the like has woven a fabric that gives coherence to working-class communities.

The basic premise of this course is that all these elements are best understood in a historical context. Despite broad patterns and common threads, all these activities have changed over time, all have shifted as the larger dynamics and underlying structures of the American political economy and the composition of the American working class have changed. While there may not be a directional pattern to these changes (such as "progress"), there is no denying that the late twentieth/early twenty-first century is profoundly different from the late eighteenth century. Although we will be primarily interested in change over time— what I consider to be the real content of historical study—we will not overlook the common threads as they speak to us in important ways about the continuing status—and struggles—of working women.

We will rely on a rich variety of readings (and an admittedly heavy reading load). This field has stimulated considerable exciting research in recent years, and our studies will benefit from it. We will draw on this new scholarship, and we will rely on primary historical documents, often reaching for our own interpretations.

The writing assignments will give you an opportunity to work with some of these materials and a chance to explore the interpretations provided by course readings. I hope you will tackle some of these writing assignments in groups of two or three, and I strongly encourage you to talk to one another in even larger groups as you prepare your papers. Class sessions will also provide you with opportunities to try out your own interpretations and challenge those of the scholars we are reading as well as the teacher's, as we will work in small groups and discussion formats far more often than in lectures. Although I am not assuming or requiring any prior experience in U.S. history on your part, I do read your registration for this course as an indication that you are bringing a high degree of interest to the subject matter and a commitment to pursue that interest through a substantial workload. What you get out of this course will depend largely on what you put into it.

The following books are available on reserve at the library and will provide valuable background for the entire course:

Amott, Teresa, and Julie Matthaie, *Race, Gender, and Work: A Multicultural Economic History of Women in the U.S.* Boston: South End Press, 1996.
Kessler-Harris, Alice. *Out to Work.* New York: Oxford University Press, 1982.

The following books are available at the bookstore and on reserve at the library:

Boydston, Jeanne. *Home and Work.* New York: Oxford University Press, 1990.
Cobble, Dorothy Sue. *Dishing It Out.* Urbana: University of Illinois Press, 1991.
Dublin, Tom. *Transforming Women's Work.* Ithaca: Cornell University Press, 1994.
Faue, Elizabeth. *Community of Suffering and Struggle.* Chapel Hill: University of North Carolina Press, 1991.
Gilpin, Toni, et al. *On Strike for Respect.* Urbana: University of Illinois Press, 1995.
Glenn, Evelyn Nakano. *Issei, Nisei, War Bride.* Philadelphia: Temple University Press, 1986.
Green, Nancy. *Ready to Wear and Ready to Work.* Durham N.C.: Duke University Press, 1997.
Hochschild, Arlie. *The Time Bind.* New York: Metropolitan Books, 1997.
Hunter, Tera. *To 'Joy My Freedom.* Cambridge: Harvard University Press, 1997.
Lemke-Santangelo, Gretchen. *Abiding Courage.* Chapel Hill: University of North Carolina Press, 1996.
Swerdlow, Marian. *Underground Woman.* Philadelphia: Temple University Press, 1998.
Ulrich, Laurel Thatcher. *A Midwife's Tale.* New York: Alfred A. Knopf, 1990.
Zavella, Patricia. *Women's Work and Chicano Families.* Ithaca: Cornell University Press, 1987.

SYLLABUS

Sessions I–V: Women and Work in Preindustrial America

Resources

Ulrich, *A Midwife's Tale*—read and discuss in class.
Video of "A Midwife's Tale" (New York: PBS, 1997)—view and discuss in class.

First Writing Assignment

Write a 2–3-page reaction paper to A *Midwife's Tale* in which you discuss the following questions: What is Ulrich's central argument? What sources, in addition to Martha Ballard's diary, does she use to support it? How does she interpret and employ these sources?

Sessions VI–IX: The Industrial Revolution and Women's Work

Resources

Boydston, *Home and Work*; and Dublin, *Transforming Women's Work*—read and discuss in class.
Primary documents selected from Rosalyn Baxandall, et al., *America's Working Women* (New York: Vintage, 1976).

Second Writing Assignment

Using the Manuscript Census of Population for Richmond, Virginia, 1880, analyze the different work situations of native-born white, foreign-born white, and African American women.

Sessions X–XI: Race and Women's Work in the Late Nineteenth Century

Resources

Hunter, *To' Joy My Freedom*—read and discuss in class.
Richmond Manuscript Census of Population—explore for essay paper and discuss in class.

Sessions XII–XIV: Mass Production, Consumerism, and Women's Work

Resources

Green, *Ready to Wear and Ready to Work*—read and discuss in class.
Primary documents selected from Margaret Byington, *Homestead: Households of a Mill Town* (Pittsburgh: University of Pittsburgh Press, 1974).

Third Writing Assignment

Write a 2–3-page reaction paper on Green, *Ready to Wear and Ready to Work*, in which you discuss the following questions: What is Green's central argument? What sources does she use to support her argument? How does she interpret and use these sources?

Sessions XV–XVI: Race, Ethnicity, Class, and Gender

Resources

Glenn, *Issei, Nisei, War Bride*—read and discuss in class.

Sessions XVII–XX: Women Workers and the Labor Movement

Resources

Cobble, *Dishing It Out*—read and discuss in class.
Faue, *Community of Suffering and Struggle*—read and discuss in class.
Primary documents from Meridel LeSueur, *Ripening* (New York: The Feminist Press, 1990).
View and discuss videos *Union Maids* (New York: Educational Broadcasting Corp., 1977) and *With Babies and Banners* (New York: New Day Films, 1978).

Fourth Writing Assignment

Using the course readings and lectures, present an argument that analyzes whether women workers in the 1930s and 1940s employed ways of organizing that differed from those employed by male workers.

Sessions XXI–XXIV: Race and Women's Work, WWII–1970s

Resources

Lemke-Santangelo, *Abiding Courage*—read and discuss in class.
Zavella, *Women's Work and Chicano Families*—read and discuss in class.
View and discuss videos *Rosie the Riveter* (Los Angeles: Direct Cinema Ltd., 1987) and *Salt of the Earth* (Oak Forest, Ill.: MPI Home Video, 1987).

Fifth Writing Assignment

Select an oral history interview with a working-class woman, available at the Minnesota Historical Society. Discuss how her race and/or ethnicity influenced her work and labor movement experiences.

Sessions XXV–XXVI: Women Enter Nontraditional Occupations

Resources

Swerdlow, *Underground Woman*—read and discuss in class.
Discuss tables about women's occupations in the twentieth century in Amott and Matthaei, *Race, Gender, and Work*.

Sessions XXVII–XXVIII: Peering into the Future

Resources

Hochschild, *The Time Bind*—read and discuss in class.
Gilpin et al., *On Strike for Respect*—read and discuss in class.

Final Writing Assignment

Drawing on diverse materials from throughout the course, present an argument about what have been the key elements of change and what have been the key elements of continuity in U.S. women's work experiences during the past 200 years.

Poor in America

Chuck Barone

The biblical reference to the poor always being with us seems to be borne out by the experience of the United States. From the 1800s to the present, poverty has been a persistent fact of life for too many Americans despite the many efforts over time, both private and public, to eliminate it. In fact, the only thing that seems to change is the public's recognition of the problem. Poverty keeps getting rediscovered by the nonpoor who become suitably outraged.

Poor people, after "disappearing" in the 1950s, were rediscovered living in large numbers (the exact number was hotly debated) in 1960s America. The nonpoor were appalled and a public War on Poverty was declared in 1968. Almost before this "war" began, people lost interest, victory was declared by the war's proponents, and the poor were conveniently forgotten once again.

In the 1990s, Americans once again rediscovered large numbers (the exact number is hotly debated) of poor people in our midst, what some call "The New American Poverty." The response to this discovery was, once again, outrage, only this time there has been a public declaration of war *against* the poor in which the public programs designed to help the poor (remnants of the old War on Poverty) have been blamed for causing poverty. The poor themselves are also being blamed as individually flawed and culturally inferior. The major federal welfare program Aid to Families with Dependent Children (AFDC), has been abolished, "ending welfare as we know it." The new replacement program, the 1996 Personal Responsibility and Work Opportunity Act changes some things and leaves other things unchanged.

This course will examine the nature, degree, and causes of poverty in the United States. However, this course is about more than poverty; it is about the nature of our economy and society; about how we view wealth and poverty; about ourselves and our values; and ultimately about the economic foundations of the right to life, liberty, and the pursuit of happiness.

REQUIRED TEXTS

Albelda, Randy, Robert Drago, and Jason Shulman. *Unlevel Playing Fields*. New York: McGraw-Hill, 1997.

MacLeod, Jay. *Ain't No Makin' It*. Rev. ed. Boulder, Colo.: Westview Press, 1995.

Mishel, Lawrence, Jared Bernstein, and John Schmitt. *The State of Working America*, 2000–2001 Edition. Armonk, N.Y.: M. E. Sharpe, 2001.

Pollin, Robert, and Stephanie Luce. *The Living Wage*. New York: New Press, 1998.

Poor in America Reader. Duplicated course readings, college store.

Rodgers, Harrell. *Poor Women Poor Children*, 3d ed. Armonk, N.Y.: M.E. Sharpe, 1996.

Schiller, Bradley. *The Economics of Poverty and Discrimination*, 8th ed. New York: Prentice-Hall, 2001.

Steinberg, Stephen. *The Ethnic Myth*. 2d ed. Boston: Beacon Press, 1989.

REQUIREMENTS

• Course participation will count for 15% of the final grade. Participation includes attendance, the quality and quantity of your discussion, and your attentiveness.

• There will be five writing projects of varying length assigned throughout the semester. Combined, they will make up 85% of the final grade.

• There are no class examinations planned for the course. However, the writing projects will combine elements of both take-home exams and essays.

COURSE OUTLINE

I. WEALTH AND POVERTY IN THE U.S.: AN OVERVIEW

A. U.S. Distribution of Income and Wealth

Mishel and Bernstein, chs. 1–2, 5.

B. The American Rediscovery of Poverty

1. The Poverty Count

Mishel and Bernstein, ch. 6.
Schiller, ch. 2.

2. The Poverty Debates

Schiller, chs. 1, 7.

Paper Due

II. AMERICAN BELIEFS ABOUT EQUALITY VS. INEQUALITY

A. Social Psychology of Inequality

Michael Lewis, *The Culture of Inequality*. Amherst: Universtiy of Massachusetts Press, 1978, chs. 1–3. Course reader.

B. Philosophy of Inequality

(Handout) William Ryan. *Equality*. New York: Pantheon, 1981, chs. 1–3.

Paper Due

III. ECONOMIC MOBILITY: PAST AND PRESENT

A. Historical Mobility

Steinberg, all chapters.

B. Contemporary Mobility

MacLeod, all chapters.

C. Downward Mobility

Katherine Newman. *Falling from Grace*. New York: Free Press, 1988, ch. 3. Course reader.

Paper Due

IV. WHAT DO ECONOMISTS SAY ABOUT WHO GETS WHAT AND WHY?

A. Introduction

Drago and Shulman, part I.
Mishel and Bernstein, ch. 3.

B. Neoclassical Economic Theory: "You Get What You Deserve"

Drago and Shulman, part II: Basic Theory: ch. 3; Work and Wages: ch. 4; Discrimination: ch. 5.

C. Political Economy Theory: "Them That Has, Gits"

Drago and Shulman, part III: Basic Theory: ch. 6; Work and Wages: ch. 7; Discrimination: ch. 8.

D. Applied Economics: Labor Supply

1. Participation Rates

Schiller, chs. 3–4.

2. Human Capital

Schiller, chs. 8–9.
Jonathan Kozol. *Savage Inequalities*. New York: Crown, 1991, Intro, chs. 1, 4. Course reader.

E. Applied Economics: Labor Demand

Mishel and Bernstein, ch. 4.

F. Applied Economics: Gender and Race

Schiller, ch. 10.

Randy Albelda and Chris Tilly. "The Glass Ceiling and the Sticky Floor: Obstacles to Women in the Workforce." *Glass Ceilings and Bottomless Pits: Women's Work, Women's Poverty.* Boston: South End Press, 1997. Course reader.

Paper Due

V. SOCIAL WELFARE POLICY

Schiller, chs. 11–15.

Chris Tilly. "Beyond Patching the Safety Net." *Dollars and Sense.* Online. Available: (Go to <www.igc.apc.org/dollars/1999> and click on 221tilly). Fall 1999.

Randy Albelda. "What Welfare Reform Has Wrought." *Dollars and Sense.* Online. Available: (Go to <www.igc.apc.org/dollars/1999> and click on 221albelda). Fall 1999.

Children Defense League and National Coalition for the Homeless Report. "Welfare to What? Early Findings on Family Hardship and Well-Being." Children Defense League. December 1998. Online. Available: (Go to <www.childrensdefense.org>, click on publications, and then scroll down to assigned report). Fall 1999.

Sarah Brauner and Pamela Loprest. "Where Are They Now? What States' Studies of People Who Left Welfare Tell Us." Urban Institute. May 1999. Online. Available: (Go to <www.urban.org> and click on Assessing the New Federalism icon. Find the assigned report from the list of reports). Fall 1999.

Final Paper Due

American Capitalism

Chuck Barone

Drawing on political economy, American studies, and sociology, this interdisciplinary course critically examines how power is structured in American capitalism. Although there is a growing recognition that in the face of skyrocketing CEO salaries the rich seem to be getting richer, leaving everyone else behind, there is little awareness of just how power is structured and exercised in American capitalism and how such power affects economic outcomes. This course begins with an examination of the patterns of income and wealth inequality in the United States and proceeds to explain these patterns of inequality by analyzing the way power is constituted in the social relations of capitalist production and distribution. Special attention will then be given to the ways powerful economic elites and organizations are able to control economic decision-making as well as influence government policy-making and culture-making institutions such as the mass media. The class dimensions of the criminal justice system will be explored also. Finally, oppositional forms of power will be examined, focusing on worker power and resistance.

REQUIRED TEXTS

Bowles, Samuel, and Richard Edwards. *Understanding Capitalism: Competition, Command, and Change in the U.S. Economy*. 2d ed. New York: HarperCollins, 1993.

Brouwer, Steve. *Sharing the Pie*. New York: Henry Holt, 1998.

Dollars and Sense. Special issue: "Democratizing Labor." Cambridge, Mass.: Economic Affairs Bureau, Sept./Oct. 1998.

Domhoff, G. William. *Who Rules America?* 3d ed. Mountain View, Calif.: Mayfield, 1998.

Parenti, Christian. *Lockdown America: Police and Prisons in the Age of Crisis*. New York: Verso, 1999.

Puette, William. *Through Jaundiced Eyes*. Ithaca: ILR Press, 1992.

Yates, Michael. *Why We Need Unions*. New York: Monthly Review Press, 1998.

REQUIREMENTS

Class participation will count for 15% of the final grade. Participation includes your attentiveness and the seriousness with which you engage the course materials. Being able to participate well requires an intellectual engagement with the course materials prior to class meetings.

You will be required to keep a class journal that records your reactions to the assigned readings. You should write at least one page for each class assignment. Journals are to be typed and handed in every three weeks. Journals will be evaluated in terms of the quality and depth of your engagement of the course materials. Journals count for 30% of the final grade.

There will be a mid-term exam (25%) and final exam/project (30%).

COURSE OUTLINE

I. FEEDING AT THE TROUGH: DISTRIBUTION OF WEALTH AND INCOME IN THE U.S.

Brouwer, part I.

II. "THEM THAT HAS, GITS": POWER IN THE CAPITALIST ECONOMY

A. Historical Evolution of Capitalism

Bowles and Edwards, ch. 1.

B. Political Economy Methodology

Bowles and Edwards, ch. 2.

C. Social Surplus, Classes, and Economic Systems

Bowles and Edwards, chs. 4, 6, 7 (pp.110–20).

D. Production and Profits, Wages and Work

Bowles and Edwards, chs. 8–10.
Brouwer, chs. 6–7.

E. Technology, Control, and Class Conflict

Bowles and Edwards, ch. 11.

III. CAPITALISM'S MACRODYNAMIC FORCES

A. Accumulation and Change

Bowles and Edwards, ch. 7 (pp. 120–25), ch. 18.
Brouwer, chs. 8–13.

B. The Dispossessed/Deindustrialization

Jacqueline Jones. *The Dispossessed*. New York: Basic Books, 1992. Intro., ch. 9 (library reserve).
Lillian Rubin. *Families on the Fault Line*. New York: HarperCollins, 1994. Chs. 6–7 (library reserve).
Video: *Roger and Me*. 1989. Michael Moore, director.

IV. FORMS OF CAPITALIST SOCIAL CONTROL
A. How a Power Elite Rules America

Bowles and Edwards, ch. 17.
Domhoff, chs. 1–4, 6–7.
Brouwer, chs. 14–16.

B. Capitalist Control of Ideology: U.S. Media

Puette, all chapters.
Domhoff, ch. 5.
Video: *Fear and Favor in the Newroom*. California Newsreel, 1996.
Norman Solomon. "What If We Didn't Need Labor Day." *Media Beat*. 1999. Online.
    Available: <www.fair.org/media-beat>.
Scott Sherman. "An Appeal to Reason." *The Nation*. 3 Oct. 1997. Online. Available:
    <www.thenation.com/issue/97031/0310sher>.

C. The Prison-Industrial Complex: The Creation of a Permanent Prison Class

Parenti, all chapters.
Eric Schlosser. "The Prison-Industrial Complex." *Atlantic Magazine*. Dec. 1998. Online.
    Available: <www.theatlantic.com/issues/98dec/prisons>.

V. SOURCES OF WORKER POWER AND RESISTANCE

Yates, all chapters.
Video: *Out of Darkness*. United Mine Workers of America, United Mine Workers Union,
    1995.

VI. TOWARD A MORE JUST ECONOMY AND SOCIETY

Brouwer, chs. 17–20.
Domhoff, ch. 8.
"Workplace Democracy" in *Dollars and Sense*, pp. 28–48.
Frank Lindenfeld. "Vision Statement." *GEO Newsletter*. Undated. Online. Available:
    <www.geonewsletter.org/frankvis>.
Len Krimerman interview. "Building a Democratic Economy and Culture: Second
    Thoughts." *GEO Newsletter*. Undated. Online. Available: <www.geonewsletter.org/len>.
Marc Cooper. "The Boys and Girls of (Union) Summer." *The Nation*. 12 Aug. 1996.
    Online. Available: <www.thenation.com/issue/9608102/0812coop>.
AFL-CIO. "Answers to Common Questions About Union Summer." AFL-CIO 2000.
    Online. Available: <www.aflcio.org/unionsummer/qapage>.
Neil Lahaie. "Labor Party First Constitutional Convention." Labor Party 1999. Online.
    Available: <http://igcf.igc.org>.
David Bacon. "Will the Labor Party Work: At the Founding Convention." *The Nation*.
    8 July 1996. Online. Available: <www.thenation.com/issue/960708/0708baco>.

New Party. "The New Party Principles." New Party, 1999. Online. Available: <www.new-party.org/about_the_np>.

Labor/Economic/Social Justice Web Sites

Association of Community Organizations for Reform Now (ACORN): <www.acorn.org>.
Democratic Socialists of America: <www.dsausa.org>.
Industrial Workers of the World: <www.iww.org>.
Institute for Global Communication (IGC) Internet: A Progressive Web Site Connecting People Who Are Changing the World: <www.igc.org/igc/gateway/index>.
Jobs With Justice: <www.jwj.org/corepage>.
National Interfaith Committee for Worker Justice: <www.nicwj.org>.
Stop Sweatshops: <www.uniteunion.org/sweatshops/sweatshop>.
Student Action: <www.nlcnet.org/student/index>.
Sweatshop Watch: <www.igc.apc.org/swatch>.
United for a Fair Economy: <www.stw.org>.
United Students Against Sweatshops: <www.umich.edu/~sole/usas>.

Who Does the Work?

A One-Day Introduction to American Working-Class Literature

Julia Stein

This course is a one-day, one-unit workshop that introduces students to a neglected part of American literature: working-class literature. We will take a multimedia approach, using novels, poetry, autobiography, and a film. The focus is on issues of labor, women, race, and class in literature. We will look at how political and social issues affected writers in both the nineteenth and the twentieth century. How do popular genres—adventure stories, sea stories, literature of reform, crime stories, sensational stories, and films—affect serious writers and contribute to American literature?

We'll read short sections from the following prose works: Louisa May Alcott's novel *Work*, in which the heroine first works as a housemaid; Herman Melville's writing about mutinous sailors on a whaling ship in *Omoo*; Jack London's "South of the Slot," a short story about a University of California–Berkeley professor who has a double life as a labor organizer in San Francisco; Richard Wright's autobiography, *Black Boy*, on how a Mississippi black boy moves north to Chicago in the mid-1920s; and Anzia Yezierska, a Jewish immigrant novelist in America who writes about surviving the Depression in her autobiographical novel *Red Ribbon on a White Horse*.

We'll read and discuss many poets: Whitman, who writes an epic about ordinary Americans in "Song of Myself"; Albert Hayes on being jobless in the Depression; Wilma Elizabeth McDaniel, an Okie poet who traveled to California in 1936, when she was eighteen, writing about the great Okie migration west. And we'll discuss a whole group of contemporary multicultural poets: Garret Hongo about his working-class father in Gardena, California; Tato Laviera on Puerto Ricans; Fred Voss on working as a machinist in Long Beach; Joan Jobe Smith on working as a go-go dancer, also in Long Beach; Jimmy Santiago Baca on being a Chicano orphan in New Mexico; Jim Daniels on growing up in an auto workers' family in Detroit; Marge Piercy on ordinary women; and Etheridge Knight on Mississippi black boys.

We'll also look at a film: an excerpt from John Ford's great film, *Grapes of Wrath*, starring Henry Fonda—the film version of John Steinbeck's novel about Okies migrating west in the Depression.

REQUIREMENTS

- Please read the five prose pieces by Alcott, Melville, London, Wright, and Yezierska prior to the meeting. Read them carefully and be prepared to discuss them in class. Look for similarities and differences in subjects, approaches, and ideas about labor, race, gender, resistance, and the American Dream. Many of the introductions to the writers, the Jack London story, and poems by Garrett Hongo, Tato Laviera, Marge Piercy, Etheridge Knight, and Alfred Hayes are in *The Heath Anthology of American Literature*, which will be available as an optional book in the bookstore.

• Attend and participate in the meeting. This class will have much discussion of the prose, the film, and the poems. We will read the poems in class.

• After the meeting, write an 8–10 page paper that details your familiarity with the readings, both prose and poetry. You can write a critical student learning paper discussing your own work experiences. The paper must be submitted within thirty days of the workshop.

PAPER

Some of the issues that the writers deal with are honesty and lying at work, friendship with coworkers, joblessness, migration, losing one's parents, having a double life or feeling caught between two classes, feeling degraded or empowered by work, and resistance to the workplace. Your paper can focus on any one of these concepts or a number of them, but discuss both your understanding of the readings and how the readings connect with your own work experience.

• For example, if you have participated in a trade union or other political organizing at work, does Melville's description of a mutiny, London's description of labor organizing, or Yezierska's description of the unemployed organizing in the 1930s help illuminate your experience?

• Are there common gender issues in Alcott, Yezierska, and Smith?

• Are there similarities or differences in the stories of McDaniel and Wright about migrating across the country in search of work and a better life? Have you migrated for these reasons?

• When can work be empowering? Which of the authors gives us such an image of work? Have you experienced work as empowering?

• All assignments must be finished; no incompletes will be granted.

SHORT BIBLIOGRAPHY OF WORKING-CLASS NOVELS, POETRY, AND AUTOBIOGRAPHY

Alcott, Louisa May. *Alternative Alcott*. New Brunswick, N.J.: Rutgers University Press, 1988.
———. *Work*. New York: Shocken Books, 1977.
Baca, Jimmy Santiago. *Martin and Meditations on the South Valley*. New York: New Directions, 1986.
Christopher, Renny, et al., eds. *Women's Studies Quarterly*, "Working-Class Lives and Cultures," 26 (spring/summer 1998).
Daniels, Jim. *M-80*. Pittsburgh: University of Pittsburgh Press, 1993.
Lauter, Paul, et al., eds. *The Heath Anthology of American Literature*. 3d ed. 2 vols. Boston: Houghton Mifflin, 1998.
McDaniel, Wilma Elizabeth. *A Prince Albert Wind*. Albuquerque, N.M.: Mother Road Publications, 1994.

Melville, Herman. *Omoo*. New York: The Heritage Press, 1967.

Nelson, Cary. *Modern American Poetry and the Politics of Cultural Memory 1910–1945*. Madison: University of Wisconsin Press, 1989.

Reynolds, David S. *Beneath the American Renaissance: The Subversive Imagination in the Age of Emerson and Melville*. Cambridge: Harvard University Press, 1988.

Smith, Joan Jobe. *Jehovah Jukebox*. Desert Hot Springs, Calif.: Events Horizon Press, 1993.

Voss, Fred. *Goodstone*. Desert Hot Springs, Calif.: Events Horizon Press, 1991.

Wright, Richard. *Black Boy*. New York: Harper Perennial, 1993.

Yezierska, Anzia. *Red Ribbon on a White Horse*. New York: Charles Scribner's Sons, 1950.

Zandy, Janet. *Calling Home: Working-Class Women's Writing: An Anthology*. New Brunswick, N.J.: Rutgers University Press, 1990.

———, ed., "Working-Class Studies," *Women's Studies Quarterly*, 22 (spring/summer 1995).

WHO DOES THE WORK? AN INTRODUCTORY READER IN AMERICAN WORKING-CLASS LITERATURE

Contents

Prose

Alcott, *Work*, chs. 1, 2.

Melville, *Omoo*, chs. 1–13 (pp. 5–45).

Jack London, "South of the Slot," *Heath Anthology*, pp. 47–58.

Wright, *Black Boy*, chs. 15, 16.

Yezierska, *Red Ribbon on a White Horse*, "The Silent Years," chs. 1–6 (pp. 137–64).

Poems

Walt Whitman, excerpt from "Song of Myself," *Heath Anthology*.

Alfred Hayes, "In a Coffee Pot," *Heath Anthology*, pp. 1356–57.

McDaniel, poems from *A Prince Albert Wind*, pp. 14–17; 19–25; 30–31.

Garrett Hongo, "Yellow Light," "Off from Swing Shift," and "Who Among You Knows the Essence of Garlic," *Heath Anthology*, pp. 2800–2801.

Tato Laviera, "Latero Story," *Heath Anthology*, pp. 3080–81.

Baca, part 7 of "Martin" from *Martin and Meditations on the South Valley*.

Fred Voss, poems from *Goodstone*, pp. 2–3; 6–7; 10–11.

Smith, poems from *Jehovah Jukebox*, pp. 1–2; 23; 32–34; 60–61.

Daniels, poems from *M-80*, pp. 70; 76–81.

Marge Piercy, "The Woman in the Ordinary," "Unlearning Not to Speak," "To Be of Use," *Heath Anthology*, pp. 70; 76–81.

Etheridge Knight, "The Idea of Ancestry," "The Violent Space," "Ill, the Talking Drum," "A Poem for Myself (Or Blues for a Mississippi Black Boy)," *Heath Anthology*, pp. 2686–87.

Film

Grapes of Wrath. Directed by John Ford. Starring Henry Fonda. With Jane Darwell, John Carradine, Charley Grapewin, et al. Cinematography by Gregg Toland. 1940. A brilliant adaptation of John Steinbeck's novel about a dust-bowl Okie family's migration from Oklahoma to California during the 1930s.

Working-Class Literature and Film

Larry Smith

This is a course in literature within the study of humanities. In it we will examine and reveal the nature of writing and film about working-class culture—as statement and literature: stories, novels, memoirs, plays, poems, films, and personal essays. Our goal is to mutually reveal the art and values of the working-class world. We recognize that the very term *working class* is an evolving concept. We will look at themes, values, customs, and rites as patterns in our individual and social behavior and outlook. Although a work's content or significance should not be separated from its form and style, as a method of study we will most often look at how the writer approaches and treats the theme of working-class life. You should gain an ability to talk and write about literature in a revealing way. While focusing on a major aspect or area of literature, we will seek to integrate it into the larger world of society and art. An increased understanding is the goal of this course—both in terms of the literature and of working-class worlds. In understanding our cultural diversity we come to appreciate ourselves more fully.

THE TEXTS

Cisneros, Sandra. *The House on Mango Street*. New York: Vintage, 1989.
Oresick, Peter, and Nicholas Coles, eds. *For a Living: The Poetry of Work*. Urbana: University of Illinois Press, 1995.
Olsen, Tillie. *Tell Me a Riddle* (3 stories). 1961. Reprint, New York: Delta, 1971.
Daniels, Jim Ray. *No Pets: Stories*. Huron, Oh.: Bottom Dog Press, 1999.
Shevin, David, Janet Zandy, and Larry Smith, eds. *Writing Work: Writers on Working-Class Writing*. Huron, Oh.: Bottom Dog Press, 1999.
Course booklet: Working-Class Short Stories, including works by Toni Cade Bambara, John Fante, Grace Paley, Chris Offutt, Barbara Kingsolver, Dorothy Allison, John Sayles, Bobbie Ann Mason, and others.
We will examine closely the art of film and watch and study these films: *October Sky, Two Bits, Good Will Hunting, Tell Me a Riddle, No Pets, Frankie and Johnny*, and *Roger and Me*.

COURSE REQUIREMENTS

You will be asked to do some writing, as a way of both learning and revealing your understanding and as a sharing of your own perceptions about the writings, the films, and the working class. We have a web page for sharing our out-of-class responses (go on once a week with short responses; avoid judgmental reactions). "Message Board": After the first week, you will be asked to go online each week to give a paragraph response to the readings and films, or to share your thoughts on working-class culture.

PROJECTS

You will write a personal essay on your own sense of class values and culture and a review of a working-class film; you will also do a documentary project in which you interview and photograph two workers. We will post your results in a gallery showing of Working People's Photographs. All outside-the-classroom writing is to be typed and in good English form and style.

In some cases we will both read the book and watch the film made of it, and you will be asked to compare and contrast the film adaptations. In other cases we will watch, discuss, and review working-class films. It is important to stay up on readings so that we can have a full class discussion. At times we will break into small discussion groups, and you will be expected to actively contribute. There will be writing exercises and quizzes asking you to use your understanding and to demonstrate your ability to analyze the work at hand. You will choose an author and write an interesting and comprehensive "book or film review" of one of his or her works (700–800 words). Choose an author about whom you can get enthused (see Working-Class Fiction and Working-Class Films listings on our homepage for leads—http://members.aol.com/smithcours/film).

TESTS

There will be three periodic tests on the material covered in readings, classroom lectures, and discussions. We will host some writers and editors as part of this class.

Your participation is important and part of the essential and emerging "text" of this course.

DAILY SYLLABUS

Session 1

In class: Working-class literature (introductions and participants); working-class concept and values (talk); Cisneros, *The House on Mango Street*, ch. 1; discussion of what goes into making a film; *October Sky* (film).
Assignments: Working-Class Matters (sheets); finish *House on Mango Street*; *Writing Work*, essays by Mackall, Shayla, Rapp (pp. 8–32).

Session 2

In class: discuss Cisneros, *The House on Mango Street*; Distancing Concept (role playing); Working-Class Values (sheet); study guide for literature and film; "What Makes a Working-Class Text" by Janet Zandy, from "The Skin of the Worker," forthcoming, in *Hands: Working-Class Bodies Speak* (Rutgers University Press).
Assignments: *Writing Work*, Smith essay (pp. 206–22); John Fante, "First Communion" and Chris Offutt, "Sawdust" (short stories).

Session 3

In class: List of working-class films and characteristics from Smith essay in *Writing Work* (talk); discuss stories by Fante and Offutt; *Two Bits* (film) and discussion.

Assignments: Write a personal essay that reveals *your* awareness of "class culture" (500–700 words—due session 5); *Writing Work*, essays by Christensen, Pendarvis, Springsteen (pp. 45–58, 98–120).

Session 4

In class: Discussion of working-class awareness; Bruce Springsteen, "The Ghost of Tom Joad" and "Youngstown" (songs); Poetry Analysis (sheet) and practice; Jim Daniels, "Short Order Cook" (poem).

Assignments: Essays are due; Grace Paley, "An Interest in Life" and Toni Cade Bambara, "The Lesson" (short stories).

Session 5

In class: short story discussion; *Good Will Hunting* (film); discussion of film as working-class art; essays are due.

Assignment: essay exam over first unit.

Session 6

In class: Essay exam over first unit of course; go over some of Olsen's writing in *Silences*.

Assignment: Tillie Olsen, *Tell Me a Riddle*.

Session 7

In class: small group discussions of four stories in Olsen, *Tell Me a Riddle*; *Tell Me a Riddle* (film); distribute student essays on working class as a packet.

Assignment: Daniels, *No Pets* (pp. 9–77).

Session 8

In class: discussion of Daniels, *No Pets*; ask for student volunteers to read their stories of working class aloud; discussion.

Assignment: finish reading *No Pets*.

Session 9

In class: author Jim Ray Daniels will join the class to read from *No Pets* and discuss his work; *No Pets* (film)

Assignment: scene from *Frankie and Johnny at the Claire de Lune*.

Session 10

In class: discussion of Terrence McNally, *Frankie and Johnny;* on writing a film or book review: guide and samples; *Frankie and Johnny* (film) and discussion; photo project explained and demonstrated; *The Photography of Dorothea Lange* (film).
Assignments: Write a film review of *Frankie and Johnny;* poets A–L, *For a Living;* interview two people at work and photograph them for display (5x7; include profile).

Session 11

In class: small group discussion of poets from *For a Living;* present to the class; present poems from Chris Llewellyn's *Fragments from the Fire: The Triangle Shirtwaist Factory Fire of March 25, 1911* (Bottom Dog Press—photocopied); Llewellyn poetry reading (recording).
Assignments: poets M–Z, *For a Living;* exam over second unit of course.

Session 12

In class: essay exam over second unit.
Assignment: *Trash* (Firebrand Books), Preface and Dorothy Allison, "I'm Working on My Charm" (short story) (pp. 7–12).

Session 13

In class: Discussion of Dorothy Allison as working-class writer; film scenes from *Bastard out of Carolina,* based on a Dorothy Allison novel.
Assignments: short stories: John Sayles, "7-10 Split"; Barbara Kingsolver, "Why I Am a Danger to the Public"; Bobbie Ann Mason, "Shiloh."

Session 14

In class: Michael Moore's *Roger and Me* (film); small group discussion of one of the short stories; present to the group; photos and profiles are due.

Session 15

In class: course review—adjourn to hall gallery; exhibit of Working-Class Lives Photos; each student tells of each worker photographed; final exam.

STUDENT ESSAYS ON CLASS AND CULTURE

Students were asked to tell a story of their coming to an awareness of class. The assignment was deliberately left open, but some models from the *Writing Work* text were suggested. The results were duplicated and presented in a packet to all members of the class. Some were read and discussed in class. This assignment proved to be a revealing and opening experience for all, as did the photo-interview projects.

Understanding

Carolyn J. Garcia

As long as she can remember, she wanted to be a doctor. The money didn't matter, her family didn't have any, and she wouldn't know what to do with much. She wanted to be a doctor, a physician, because that would be doing something important. She watched "Ben Casey, M.D.," "Dr. Kildare," "Medical Center," (the one with Chad Everett) while growing up. Everyone looked up to The Doctor. He always did the right thing, always snapped out the right orders that everyone followed without fail, without question.

By the time "Marcus Welby, M.D." came along, she had been working in the medical field long enough to know how bogus all that was.

Cynicism followed disillusionment and disappointment when she found out just what it took to go to college. She absolutely hated high school, and just couldn't see herself spending eight or ten more years in a classroom. Besides, there was no money, and no support system. She gave up that easily.

During elementary school, her class went on a field trip to the Fanny Farmer candy factory in Norwalk. She loved chocolate, and the thought of being around it all day long was a dream come true. It was even better than being a doctor. She was so enthusiastic that evening at home, she told her mother that that was what she wanted to do: work at Fanny Farmer the rest of her life. Her mother told her that she had higher expectations for her children.

That was the beginning and the end of the motivation she got from her parents. She still doesn't know what her parents wanted for her, her three sisters, and her two brothers. Maybe she should have asked, but she thought this was something she should have been told without having to ask.

The only bright spot in her high school career was the two years she spent at the vocational school. Student advisors had to push her into going, but there were no medical classes. They had a dental assisting class, and that was close enough. A year later, they added the medical assisting curriculum. What a nice break.

She stayed with the first doctor's office that would hire a student for twenty-seven years. She billed insurance companies in the time before they paid for anything, the time before diagnosis and procedure coding even existed. She learned things that no college could teach. Medical terminology was like a second language to her. She didn't know everything, but she knew enough that in time she became indispensable. She was giving more phone advice than the nurse. She handled the front desk as well as calling in prescriptions. She made all the referrals, and set patients up with the hospital for their outpatient testing. When managed care invaded their office, she was the one that filled out the credentialing forms, and when the doctor signed these forms he always put her name in the "office manager" spot. The patients liked her and trusted her. She was the one to whom they came when something needed to be done.

She was proud of the job she did, even when she burned out. All the other doctor's office managers had degrees. Yet, because of her many years of experience, she made as much, if not more money than they did. She was proud to be a medical secretary.

She went to coding seminars, billing seminars, management seminars, Blue Cross and Blue Shield Seminars, workers' compensation seminars. These were her continuing education opportunities.

She always bought into the idea that in America anyone can be anything they want. All it took was hard work and a little luck. She believed that America was one big melting pot. There are no social classes in America. Everyone had the same opportunities as anyone else. A little time in the real world chipped her idealism until she actually became quite cynical for awhile. The reality of our society's class structure swam around in her mind for years, unformed, without much substance.

You see, our heroine kept her expectations low enough that when she reached for something, she always made sure she didn't hit any glass ceilings. She knew that she couldn't stand that kind of rejection and she never developed the backbone she needed to fight for what she wanted. She couldn't even compete with herself. She didn't have that fire in her belly, that *want*.

One day, her beloved doctor/boss retired. He made sure that the new doctors who bought the practice kept all the staff, at their present salaries. At first they all thought this was a good arrangement.

One of the great things about the new practice is that they loved having the pharmaceutical reps bring them lunch. The reps got the doctor's undivided attention for sometimes two hours, and everyone got to eat on the drug company tab (yes, that's probably one of the reasons drugs cost so much).

One day, after lunch was finished, Doc and the Rep were still talking. The "girls" went back to work, and as women are in the habit of doing, they started to clear the conference table of trash and leftovers. Johnny Rep had taken two pieces of pizza and during the whole meal had taken one bite. It was obvious to the Medical Secretary that he was more interested in pushing his products than eating lunch. That was okay, they were all like that. Intending to clear the table, the Medical Secretary, with her one hand full of lunch paraphernalia, interrupted his pitch to ask him if he wanted his lunch, knowing full well he did not. He said no, and at the same time made that impatient, sweeping gesture with his hand. He probably did it all the time to every waitress he ever had. He didn't even look at her when he did it.

With that one careless gesture of his hand, J. Rep dismissed the Medical Secretary. Didn't he know who he was dismissing? Who did this guy think he was? The ink on his diploma wasn't even dry yet. With that one gesture he minimized, not just the Medical Secretary, but all working women. This was the place in time where her understanding of our classless society jelled. She knew it then that she could not work for these doctors any longer. She stood there with her hand poised to take J. Rep's plate, and, just for a second, she almost laughed out loud. Not that she thought this was in the least bit funny. She now understood that the main difference between the man she would always regard as her real boss, and her new doctors was not one of practice philosophy, or even skill. The real difference was the fact that her old boss came from a working-class family, and had grown up with working-class values. His father was a tool and die maker. Doc worked in factories and did lots of things before he started his practice. These were values the Medical Secretary identified with, and believed noble.

The new doctor came from a well-to-do family. Not that this is bad, but his attitudes about patients and employees were very different. He was more interested in volume and early retirement.

She didn't lose her four weeks paid vacation or her salary, but the duties and responsibilities were taken away from her. Insurance and patient billing, all gone. Control over medical records, all gone. No longer allowed to give medical advice, or call in prescriptions. Office policy is communicated by memo from the main office, which is located in a different town. They don't even want her input. The Medical Secretary became the overqualified, overpaid receptionist.

She left that practice, went to another. The Medical Secretary then realized that she had become obsolete. Nobody wanted a person who could "do it all."

After floundering a little, she started working for a billing service. It was a good move, she had just as much responsibility as everyone else, no more, no less. The other, less experienced billers, seek her advice. It makes her feel needed again. But the money sure sucks.

Maybe they don't expect us to make the job our whole life, but they do expect us to kiss up, and some wouldn't mind if we curtsied when they walked into the room, and they don't care to know us at all.

Dad's Home!

Julia Morton

Those reassuring two words my brother or I would yell upon seeing our Dad pull in the drive. It was a daily contest. The stakes were high—first one to Dad got the goods. That sliver of pie he had saved or that extra cookie still wrapped neatly in waxed paper from the lunch my Mother lovingly packed for him each morning at 5:00 A.M.

I can still see him walking toward the house with his large gray lunch box and stainless steel Thermos tucked under his arm. After hugs and kisses shared, he'd set that lunch box and Thermos on the kitchen counter. My Dad never showed the wear and tear of his job when he was young, but his stainless steel Thermos told the story for him.

It stood tall, like a tower next to the lunch box. It would wobble a little when he sat it down. The bottom edge wasn't level; there was a dent in it. The green color on the outside had scratches and lots of places that were pushed in, kind of like craters. The cup screwed on top, which he drank his coffee from, and had a dent on it that matched the one on the bottom. The Thermos bore the scar of the job site.

Dad knew how most of those dents, dings, and scratches got on his Thermos. He would say, "Oh, I left it in the bed of the truck and I could hear it rolling around all the way home," or "That one came from it falling two stories off a steel I-beam while I was having lunch up with the iron workers," or "I forgot I had put it on top of the truck, but it reminded me it was there when I put on the brakes and it bounced off the hood onto the road." One day he was sure it was gone for good. He watched as another operator ran over it unknowingly with a bulldozer. Dad expected the worst, but to his surprise the soft topsoil had swallowed it up to keep it away from the teeth and tracks of the dozer. He ran to where it was, lifted it from its soft bed, brushed it off, carried it home.

The suit my Dad wore to work didn't have to be dry cleaned. His suit was cleaned with Lestoil. My mother used it to get diesel fuel spots off his coveralls. There was always a bottle in the basement. His suit was layered, especially in the cold winter months. Long underwear, flannel shirt, wool socks, jeans, Carhart coveralls and a Carhart jacket. A baseball-style hat covered his head, one that always said something like "John Deere" or "Cat-Diesel Powered." His lace-up work boots, which he always put on at the kitchen table, completed his ensemble.

I never really knew how much money my Dad made. I didn't need to. We didn't have brand-new cars, a big boat, summer vacation spots. What we did have was plenty of food, a warm house, and a sense of pride instilled in us by my Dad. Most importantly, he gave me wonderful memories like these, by sharing stories from work with us at the supper table.

I asked him once, "How old were you Dad when you first started to work?" his reply, "Honey, I was so young I had to carry diapers in my lunch pail."

Crossing the Lines

Gina Parmer

There is a broken, blurred line between the class I grew up in and rebelled against, and the class in which I now live. The gauge I use to measure the line is called Money: not in and of itself, but the *communication* revolving around it. How much is said about money is one measurement, and how much is *not* said is at the other end of the scale. For me, this defines class much more than does an economic wage scale.

My husband, John, is from a down-to-earth working-class family. His father was a steelworker who worked swing shifts and his mother stayed at home. John was aware at an early age that his family lived "week-to-week" and struggled to pay bills. My parents lived a middle-class lifestyle on working-class wages. My dad was a Ford worker and my mom was a cashier at a local drugstore. Growing up, I never saw a bill or heard any struggles concerning money. They were there, but my family never talked about them. My parents lived as if they had more money than they did, and my husband's parents lived from day-to-day. We fall somewhere in-between and over either edge.

I am bluntly honest about the money we have or don't have. I like to tell how my whole outfit only cost one dollar because my shoes were hand-me-downs from my best friend's daughter, my pants were given to me, my shirt was from a garage sale, and my underclothes were bought with a gift certificate. I enjoy explaining how we got our dining room table and chairs because my husband did some woodwork for a woman who traded the set for it. Our children know we are behind on bills and that I sometimes only have twenty dollars to buy groceries for the week.

My dad quit school in ninth grade to help his family out. My mom quit school in eleventh grade to marry Dad. They were both from working poor families in Mississippi. After the Army and Korea, Dad was proud to get a job at the Memphis Ford plant as a paint sprayer. When Ford told him to report to work in Lorain, Ohio, he and mom sold their furniture and moved 800 miles north. You went where the job went.

They married in 1953, moved to Ohio in 1958, and adopted me in 1961. My brother was born to them in 1963. We lived in Valley View, a subdivision in Vermillion built just for the new incoming Ford families. It was a nicer, middle-class neighborhood.

Supper was on the table at 6:00 every night. My brother and I ran in, ate, and ran back out to play. Dad would tell stories about men named Bubble Eyes or Slim, but never talked much about the work he did. He was a painter for fifteen years, then became a quality control inspector. All I knew about his change was, instead of bringing me paint chips, he brought me pens with rubber stamps on the ends.

We were raised never to tell a soul what we paid for anything and, even more, what we *owed* anyone. My friends thought we were "well-off" because my brother and I each had a stereo and a small television in our rooms and wore school clothes from Sears and Penney's—middle-class stores—while they wore clothes from K-Mart and Hills—working-class stores.

Sometimes I think Dad was working class and Mom was middle class. Dad taught me to be generous, "not to look out for number one," but to look around for someone to help. He always gave me extra money when I went out with friends so that I could pay someone else's way.

Mom spends a lot to keep up appearances of middle class. Their house and yard keep getting bigger and better, filled with furniture they don't sit on, cars that wear out before they're paid for, and clothes they don't have enough closets to fill.

My own family falls somewhere in between. I take the good working-class values, live them, and pass them on to my kids by example. We work hard at our jobs, we give more than 100 percent, we are on time, we strive to be the best. I hold two jobs, one as a working-class waitress, and one as a more middle-class piano accompanist at a high school. Both jobs are important to me, and both fulfill a need I have to do good, honest work and to use my talents in a productive way. I am honest about the work I do and the money I have and lack and the struggles that come from living in-between two classes and trying to find where I fit in.

Plastic Shoes

Mary E. Pentridge

"Don't sit by her! She's one of those welfare kids with the plastic shoes!" Plastic shoes? As soon as I got off the bus, I ran the half mile home, quickly removed my white tennis shoes with the powder pink graphics and checked the tag. There was no mention of plastic anywhere on the label. The recipe for my sneakers clearly read, "All vinyl and other man-made materials." Those other fifth graders were obviously mistaken.

As I told my mother of the allegations the other children were making, her face looked as though it would melt onto the floor. My mother explained to me with what seemed to be an apologetic, or even regretful tone, that vinyl was in fact plastic. I felt the last piece of dignity slipping through my fingers.

I had been so excited when mother came home that September, a few weeks after school started, she carried giant bags of our clothes from Hills Department store, that had been on layaway all summer. The extra treat was the Pick-Way shoe store bag. I knew that inside that bag was my new pair of tennis shoes. My school shoes. I wanted to wear them right away, but Mom made me continue to wear my "play shoes." Those were my sneakers from last year, that played peek-a-boo with my toes as I walked out into the yard. I understood. Between my brother, sister, and me, we had to take precautions to make our clothes last, because my father constantly reminded us that, "Money don't grow on trees."

As an eleven-year-old, I felt very confident that I looked clean and well put together every day for school. I did my best to keep my hair brushed, so it wouldn't look like a "rat's nest" on the bus ride home. I knew those girls with the L.A. Gear and British Knight leather shoes, and the permed, curly hair would definitely be watching for anything to taunt me about during the hour journey home.

From that day on, my only defense was my "comebacks" for my tormentors. I told those kids, "that one day you'll be picking up my plastic shoes and mopping the floor beneath them if you spent all your time taunting me instead of doing your school work." They went on teasing about my plastic shoes for two years. Even after I got my British Knight leather tennis shoes for Christmas. Regardless of what I said or what I wore, I was one of the welfare kids.

We were never really on welfare, however, as I look in retrospect, we were probably at or below the poverty level during a great portion of my childhood. My house was always filled with love, and that's what mattered most to my siblings and me. Fortunately, when I look back at my childhood, I'm generally fond of the memories. After those years of verbal torture, I promised myself that my children would never have to endure that type of disrespect, nor give it to anyone else.

To this very day, I can't help but check the tags on the inside of shoes before I buy them. Subconsciously those incidents probably guide me in my monetary decisions today. As an adult, I've worked very hard to rise above the lower-middle-class label. Only now, as an adult, do I recall those times when the reality of my family's financial stability was thrown in my face. I am the first person on either side of my family to attend college. The more knowledge I absorb, the better job I will be able to obtain. As a result, my children will not have to be teased and I will not have to tell them that they wear plastic shoes.

Labor Documentaries

A Filmography

Tom Zaniello

Key to Distributors: The following abbreviations are used for distributors and sources for rental and purchase of the films as well as two other important notations (chain video stores and unavailability). If an entry has no abbreviation, then the film may be available in selected public or university libraries.

A = Appalshop <www.appalshop.org>
CG = Cinema Guild <www.cinemaguild.com>
CN = California Newsreel <www.newsreel.org>
FL = Filmakers Library <www.filmakers.com>
I = Icestorm International <www.icestorm-video.com>
MU = Movies Unlimited <www.moviesunlimited.com>
NL = National Labor Committee <www.nlcnet.org>
ND = New Day Films <www.newday.com>
U = unavailable
VS = available in most chain video stores
WMM = Women Make Movies <www.wmm.com>

FILMS

America and Lewis Hine, 1984: the premier photographer of early urban immigrant life and labor conditions. (CG)

American Dream, 1989: Local P9 versus almost everybody in Hormel meatpackers' strike; filmed by Academy Award winner Barbara Kopple. (MU)

Año Nuevo, 1981: illegal migrant workers at a California flower farm challenge their boss in U.S. courts. (CG)

A. Philip Randolph, 1996: the great civil rights and labor leader (cofounder of the Brotherhood of Sleeping Car Porters). (CN)

At the River I Stand, 1993: Memphis sanitation workers' strike as crucial background to civil rights struggles and King's assassination. (CN)

Automation, 1957: Edward R. Murrow television documentary on changes in assembly-line manufacturing, especially in the auto industry.

The Awful Truth, 2000: Michael Moore's guerilla television exposés of corporate America and other targets. (MU)

Belfast, ME, 2000: Frederick Wiseman's slow but thorough look at work in a small seaport.

The Big One, 1997: Michael Moore on tour for his best-selling book satirizing the corporate 1990s (*Downsize This!*), in which he visits various strike locations and downsized workforces. (VS; MU)

Blue Collar and Buddha, 1989: Rockford, Illinois worker-class town and its hatred toward Laotian immigrants. (FL)

Brass Valley, 1984: the beginning and end of the important brass industry in Connecticut.

British Sounds, 1969: Jean-Luc Godard's banned British television documentary visits Ford workers discussing factory problems and university students making revolutionary posters. (U)

Buffalo Creek Flood, 1974, and *Buffalo Creek Revisited*, 1984: two films analyze the Pittston Company dam, which collapsed, killing 125 West Virginians in 1972.

The Business of America, 1987: the collapse of the American steel industry. (CN)

Chaos, 1999: agitprop documentary on Association of Flight Attendants' innovative strike strategy.

Chemical Valley, 1991: Union Carbide, who caused the Bhopal, India, refinery catastrophe, runs a similar plant in an African American community in the town of Institute, West Virginia. (A)

Children of Golzow, 1980: long-running East German feature, part of series focusing on (mostly) working-class youths in one (formerly) East German town as they become adults in a (former) socialist economy. (I)

Coalmining Women, 1982: women miners in Kentucky and Colorado. (A)

Coal Wars: The Battle in Rum Creek, 1992: militant West Virginia United Mine Worker (UMWA) local's fight against two coal companies during the 1989–90 strikes. (ND)

Collision Course, 1988: struggle between Frank Lorenzo's Texas Air and the international Association of Machinists. (CN)

Computers in Context, 1987: computers as *tools* for workers not *substitutes*. (CN)

Controlling Interest: The World of the Multinational Corporation, 1975: political interpretation, emphasizing the corporate reasons behind the overthrow of Allende in Chile. (CN)

Down and Out in America, 1985: 1986 Emmy winner on homelessness, lost farms, and squatters.

The Electric Valley, 1983: the Tennessee Valley Authority (TVA) and its economic and social impact.

Evelyn Williams, 1995: an Afri-lachian woman's life, work, and organizing efforts from Eastern Kentucky to Brooklyn. (A)

Fallen Champ: The Untold Story of Mike Tyson, 1993: Barbara Kopple television film on Mike Tyson and his working-class roots. (MU)

Fast Food Women, 1992: older women in "part-time" jobs working hard for low wages. (A)

The Fight in the Fields, 1996: exploration of Cesar Chavez's career and the difficulties and successes of the United Farm Workers. (CG)

Finally Got the News, 1970: Black revolutionaries organize Detroit autoworkers in the 1960s. (CN)

Final Offer, 1985: negotiations between the Canadian United Auto Workers (UAW) and General Motors end up fracturing the solidarity between Canadian and American autoworkers. (CN)

42 Up, 1999: one of Michael Apted's continuing series of films (every seven years) on British youth (now forty-two years old). (VS)

Free Voice of Labor: The Jewish Anarchists, 1980: Jewish immigrant workers in New York City. (CG)

Gandy Dancers, 1994: black railroad workers. (CG)

Goin' to Chicago, 1994: the Great Migration of African Americans from the rural South to the cities of the North and West. (CN)

The Golden Cage: A Story of California's Farmworkers, 1989: a history of the United Farm Workers specifically and an exposé of migrant labor in general. (FL)

The Great Depression (Road to Rock Bottom), 1993: features the 1933 Bonus March of WWI veterans and unemployed workers.

Harlan County, USA, 1977: Academy Award–winning film by Barbara Kopple of the Eastern Kentucky miners' struggles. (MU)

Harry Bridges: A Man and His Union, 1992: history of the charismatic west coast dockers' leader. (CG)

Harvest of Shame, 1960: Edward R. Murrow's classic (often imitated, rarely matched) exposé of migrant labor in America.

Hoffa: The True Story, 1992: controversial portrait of the great Teamsters leader.

The Inheritance, 1964: story of the immigrants' "Golden America—half dream, half nightmare."

JFK, Hoffa, and the Mob, 1992: another anti-Hoffa conspiracy film.

Justice in the Coalfields, 1995: the UMWA's great Pittston Strike in the 1990s. (A)

Land Without Bread, 1932: Buñuel classic about severely depressed Spanish peasants in the 1930s. (MU)

Leather Soul: Working for Life in a Factory Town, 1992: the history of leather workers in Peabody, Massachusetts. (FL)

Legacy of Shame, 1995: another CBS exposé of migrant labor conditions.

The Life and Times of Rosie the Riveter, 1980: WWII women workers' documentary.

Making Steel, 1988: the Nova Scotia steel industry.

Mickey Mouse Goes to Haiti, 1996: agitprop exploration of sweatshop conditions. (NL)

Miles of Smiles, Years of Struggles: The Untold Story of the Black Pullman Porter, 1982: the struggles to maintain and unionize successful black jobs. (CN)

Mine War on Blackberry Creek, 1986: a bitter UMWA strike against the A. T. Massey Coal Company, in the same locale as the events of John Sayles's feature film *Matewan*.

Moving Mountains, 1981: women handling giant open-pit earthmovers.

New Deal Documentaries, 1934–1940, 1997: Depression classics by Pare Lorentz ("The River" and "The Plow that Broke the Plains"), Joris Ivins ("Power and the Land"), and H. B. McClure ("The New Frontier"). (MU)

New Harvest, Old Shame, 1990: revisiting Edward R. Murrow's classic *Harvest of Shame*.

On Our Own Land, 1988: the "broadform" deeds that permitted strip-mining of private lands in Kentucky and throughout Appalachia. (A)

On to Ottawa, 1992: historic Depression march of the unemployed.

Out at Work, 1996: gay union workers fight legal and illegal job discrimination. (FL)

Out of Darkness: The Mine Worker's Story, 1990: history of UMWA and their workers, by Barbara Kopple.

Perestroika from Below, 1990: ex-Soviet workers attempt to democratize their factories.

Que Viva México! 1979: a version of Eisenstein's peasant Mexican masterpiece of the 1930s. (MU)

The Richest Man in the World, 1997: the contradictions in the life and work of the master capitalist, Andrew Carnegie.

Riding the Rails, 1998: exploration of youth on the bum in the Depression.

The River Ran Red, 1993: the great Pennsylvania Homestead Strike of 1892.

Roger & Me, 1989: filmmaker Michael Moore pursues the chairman of General Motors through Flint, Michigan. (VS; MU)

The Rouge, 1998: history of the Ford plant that was once the largest industrial complex in the world. (FL)

Rough Side of the Mountain, 1997: the demise and partial comeback of two company towns in southwestern Virginia. (A)

Roving Pickets, 1991: dislocation in the Appalachian mining industry of the 1950s and the agitation in the 1960s that led to President Johnson's War on Poverty. (A)

Salesman, 1969: high-pressure Bible salesmanship in cinema verité.

Shout Youngstown, 1984: the closing of Youngstown's steel plants. (CG)

Sit Down and Fight: Walter Reuther and the Rise of the Auto Workers Union, 1993: history of the auto industry and its most famous organizer.

Standing Tall, 2000: women organizing Mississippi catfish industry. (FL)

Struggles in Steel, 1996: black steelworkers in Pittsburgh. (FL)

Surviving the Good Times, 2000: two Milwaukee families—one white, the other one black—coping with layoffs.

Taylor Chain, 1980, 1984: a pair of films that follow a Chicago local union's ups and downs in collective bargaining. (ND)

These Hands, 1992: film from Tanzania depicting women refugees from Mozambique crushing stone in a quarry. (CN)

35 Up, 1991: another snapshot of the British youngsters who "star" in a film every seven years. (MU)

Troublesome Creek: A Midwestern, 1997: coping with the economic squeeze on an Iowa family farm. (VS; MU)

TV Nation, 1995–96: Michael Moore's anticapitalist television satires begin where *Roger & Me* left off. (MU)

Union Maids, 1976: radical activist women reminisce about the 1930s. (ND)

The Uprising of '34, 1995: textile workers' ill-fated strike in South Carolina.

Voices from a Steeltown, 1984: filmmaker Tony Buba on his hometown (Braddock) near Pittsburgh. (ND)

We Dig Coal: A Portrait of Three Women, 1982: underground pioneers in Pennsylvania coalfields. (CG)

Who Killed Vincent Chin? 1989: unemployed Detroit workers kill Chin because they think he is Japanese. (FL)

The Wilmar Eight, 1981: Minnesota "pink-collar" employees say "enough" and strike. (CN)

With Babies and Banners, 1978: Flint, Michigan, women of the Sit-Down Strike of the 1930s. (ND)

Wittstock, Wittstock, 1997: latest in a continuing series on a former East German industrial town and its workers. (U)

The Wobblies, 1979: portrait of the radical "One Big Union."

Women of Steel, 1985: Homestead, Pennsylvania pioneer workers who broke the gender barrier. (WMM)

The Women of Summer, 1986: garment and other workers in the 1920s in an unusual summer school for women.

Wrath of Grapes, 1986: controversial United Farmworkers' agitprop film about pesticides, withdrawn after court fight.

American Working-Class Literature
A Selected Bibliography
Nicholas Coles

As Janet Zandy writes in *Calling Home: An Anthology of Working-Class Women's Writing*, "Despite its diversity and unconventional literary forms, working-class literature is not a mass of dangling parts, but a collective body of work."[1] One of the ways to discern a body of work, to gather its parts and begin to articulate the connections among them, is to make lists. I've been working on versions of the list that follows for most of the fifteen years since I wrote an article for *College English* arguing that we need to teach this literature in our English classes.[2] I've used the list in workshops and have given it to students in my courses, adding and cutting books every time I used it.

My strategy in creating a version for publication—given the diversity and shifting shape of this "collective body of work"—has been to treat the work of selecting titles for the bibliography as a collective activity in itself. I have correlated my lists with those of the scholars and publishers whose views of working-class literature have informed my own. In particular, I have drawn on bibliographies and indexes by Laura Hapke, Paul Lauter, Cary Nelson, and Janet Zandy.[3] I have consulted the extensive list of working-class novels compiled by Eric Schocket on the web site of the Center for Working-Class Studies at Youngstown State University (www.as.ysu.edu/~cwcs) and Cheryl Cline's annotated bibliography of working-class women's autobiographies (in this volume). I have also drawn on the book lists of university presses and smaller independent publishers—especially Arté Público Press, Bottom Dog Press, The Feminist Press, and West End Press—that have reissued older working-class texts along with an expanding list of contemporary literature by ethnic and worker writers.

Despite these debts, I am of course responsible for whatever inclusions to and omissions from the list may seem idiosyncratic or simply wrongheaded. Compiling a list of this kind entails hundreds of tiny decisions about what to leave in and what to leave out. Let me try to articulate the criteria I have used in selecting texts for the bibliography that follows, knowing that each of the distinctions and decisions outlined here is debatable and deserves more thorough discussion.[4]

- As in Paul Lauter's pioneering bibliography of working-class women's writing,[5] my list includes literature both by and about working-class people. However, there are far fewer books here by middle- or upper-class authors writing about the working class, than books written from an insider's perspective. In including middle-class writers such as Harding Davis, Sinclair, and Le Sueur, I chose those whose perspective is not only sympathetic but whose "trespass vision" across class lines (in Tillie Olsen's phrase) achieves what Zandy calls "close political and cultural identification with working-class life."[6]

- The operating definition of "working class" here is broad enough to represent the majority of Americans: blue collar, white collar, the rural and urban poor, the "underclass." I have been guided in this by "Notes Toward an Overview" (in this volume) by Constance Coiner, who in turn is guided by Lauter's categories. Whether or not the writing demonstrates "working-class consciousness" in the classic sense, this literature consciously addresses issues of class and their consequences in the lives of working people. Working-class literature overlaps with, but is not identical to, "labor," "proletarian," and "radical" literature.

- Rather than calling this body of work "working-class writing" (favored by Coiner), I'm sticking with the word *literature*, despite its élite history and connotations. Even by traditional definitions of literature as "well-written" and "creative" work of a certain cultural importance, the texts below qualify. And if we take a step further, following Raymond Williams, and think of *literature* as the name for an activity—the social practices of reading, writing, and publishing—then the works listed here can be seen as belonging to a living literary tradition in which all of us can potentially participate.[7]

- The range of genres represented in this literature is as broad as the variety of forms of cultural expression used by working-class people, including essays, fiction, memoir and autobiography, oral history, plays, poetry, reportage, song lyrics, work narratives, and texts composed in multiple genres. If the list below includes more poetry than in other published bibliographies, this emphasis reflects a desire to revise a habitual view of working-class literature as represented primarily by the naturalistic fiction of the "proletarian" tradition.

- The list also includes more contemporary writing than is typical—in part, again, because I have wanted to limit the association of working-class literature as primarily with the industrial past. As a result—and also out of a desire to assert "working class" as a missing or silent category within "multiculturalism"—the list includes a number of writers who are African American, Asian American, Native American, and Americans with roots in Latin America and the Caribbean. It includes "worker-writers" along with established, professional writers from the working class.

While these criteria work in the direction of making the bibliography relatively inclusive, two other decisions I have made limit its scope. First, I have listed only published full-length books—no articles or journal and magazine publications, no chapbooks, and no unpublished manuscripts. This means that, for example, the California worker-writer Carol Tarlen does not have an entry (though her poems can be found in the listed anthologies edited by Zandy and myself). Second, I have listed in the first section, "Books by Individual Authors," only books that are currently in print (with one or two exceptions: I hope Judy Grahn's *The Work of the Common Woman*, for example, will be reprinted soon). My reason for this decision is a preference toward texts that are available for classroom use by teachers and students. The major problem with this restriction is, of course, that it essentially cedes decisions about value to the economics of the publishing industry which, until recently, has not done well by working-class writers. It also privileges the moment, the turn of the year 2001, in which I happen to be putting the list together. On the other hand, the pleasure of assembling such a bibliography at this moment is that there is so much more to choose from than when I began list-making fifteen years ago. We now have a wealth of compelling working-class literature, new and old, available to study, learn from, and enjoy.

BOOKS BY INDIVIDUAL AUTHORS

Allen, Paula Gunn. *Life Is a Fatal Disease: Selected Poems, 1962–1995*. Albuquerque: West End Press, 1996.

Allison, Dorothy. *Trash*. Ithaca: Firebrand, 1988. Short fiction.

———. *Bastard out of Carolina*. New York: Dutton, 1992. Novel.

Anderson, Edward. *Hungry Men*. 1935. Reprint, Norman: University of Oklahoma Press: 1993. Novel.

Anzaldúa, Gloria. *Borderlands/ La Frontera: The New Mestiza*. San Francisco: Aunt Lute, 1987. Multigenre.

Arnow, Harriette. *The Dollmaker*. 1954. Reprint, New York: Avon, 1999. Novel.

Attaway, William. *Blood on the Forge*. 1941. Reprint, New York: Monthly Review, 1987. Novel.

Baca, Jimmy Santiago. *Immigrants in Our Own Land*. New York: New Directions, 1990. Poetry.

———. *Working in the Dark: Reflections of a Poet of the Barrio*. Santa Fe, N.M.: RedCrane, 1992.

Bambara, Toni Cade. *The Salt Eaters*. New York: Vintage, 1980. Novel.

———. *Gorilla, My Love*. New York: Vintage, 1992. Short Fiction.

Barrio, Raymond. *The Plum Plum Pickers*. 1981. Reprint, Tempe, Ariz.: Bilingual Review Press, 1984. Novel.

Bell, Thomas. *Out of This Furnace*. 1940. Reprint, Pittsburgh: University of Pittsburgh Press, 1976. Novel.

Bencastro, Mario. *Odyssey to the North*. Translated by Susan Giersbach Rascon. Houston: Arte Público Press, 1998. Novel.

Berlin, Lucia. *Homesick: New and Selected Stories*. Santa Rosa, Calif.: Black Sparrow Press, 1990. Short fiction.

Bonosky, Phillip. *Burning Valley*. 1953. Reprint, Urbana: University of Illinois Press, 1998. Novel.

Bontemps, Arna Wendell, and Jack Conroy. *Anyplace but Here*. 1966. Reprint, Columbia: University of Missouri Press, 1997. History/oral history.

Box-Car Bertha. *Sister of the Road: The Autobiography of Box-Car Bertha*. As told to Dr. Ben L. Reitman. 1937. Reprint, New York: AMOK Press, 1988.

Brady, Maureen. *Folly*. 1982. Reprint, New York: The Feminist Press, 1994. Novel.

Brant, Beth. *Mohawk Trail*. Ithaca: Firebrand Books, 1985. Multigenre.

Brill, Ernie. *I Looked Over Jordan and Other Stories*. Boston: South End Press, 1980. Short fiction.

Brown, Claude. *Manchild in the Promised Land*. 1965. Reprint, New York: Simon and Shuster, 1999. Autobiography.

Brown, Sterling A. *The Collected Poems of Sterling A. Brown*. Edited by Michael Harper. Evanston, Ill.: Triquarterly Books, 1996.

Bryant, Dorothy. *Miss Giardino*. 1978. Reprint, New York: The Feminist Press, 1997. Novel.

Burke, Fielding. *Call Home the Heart*. 1932. Reprint, New York: The Feminist Press, 1983.

Cahan, Abraham. *The Rise of David Levinsky*. 1917. Reprint, New York: Penguin, 1993. Novel.

Chute, Carolyn. *The Beans of Egypt, Maine*. 1985. Reprint, New York: Harcourt, 1995. Novel.

———. *Letourneau's Used Auto Parts*. New York: Harper, 1988. Novel.

Cisneros, Sandra. *The House on Mango Street*. New York: Vintage, 1984. Short fiction.

———. *Woman Hollering Creek and Other Stories*. New York: Vintage, 1991. Short fiction.

Coleman, Wanda. *African Sleeping Sickness*. 1979. Reprint, Santa Rosa, Calif.: Black Sparrow Press, 1990. Stories and poems.

Conroy, Jack. *The Disinherited.*1933. Reprint, Columbia: University of Missouri Press, 1991. Novel.

Crane, Stephen. *Maggie: A Girl of the Streets, and Other Bowery Tales*. 1893. Reprint, New York: Random, 2001. Novella.

Curran, Mary Doyle. *The Parish and the Hill*. 1948. Reprint, New York: The Feminist Press, 1986. Novel.

Daniels, Jim. *Punching Out*. Detroit: Wayne State University Press, 1989. Poems.

———. *No Pets: Stories*. Huron, Ohio: Bottom Dog Press, 1999. Short fiction.

Davis, Rebecca Harding. *Life in the Iron Mills*. 1861. Reprint, New York, The Feminist Press, 1972. Novella.

Denby, Charles. *Indignant Heart: A Black Worker's Journal*. Detroit: Wayne State University Press, 1989. Autobiography.

De Rosa, Tina. *Paper Fish*. 1980. Reprint, New York: The Feminist Press, 1996. Novel.

Diaz, Junot. *Drown and Other Stories*. New York: Riverhead, 1996. Short fiction.

DiDonato, Pietro. *Christ in Concrete*. 1939. Reprint, New York: Signet, 1993. Novel.

Dobler, Patricia. *Talking to Strangers*. Madison: University of Wisconsin Press, 1986. Poems.

Doro, Sue. *Heart, Home, and Hardhats*. Minneapolis: Midwest Villages and Voices, 1986. Stories and poems.

———. *Blue Collar Goodbyes*. 1992. Reprint, Huron, Oh.: Bottom Dog Press, 2000. Poems.

Dos Passos, John. *USA: The 42nd Parallel/1919/The Big Money*. New York: Library of America, 1996. Trilogy of novels.

Doubiago, Sharon. *Hard Country*. 1982. Reprint, Tucson, Ariz.: University of New Mexico Press, 1999. Poem.

Dreiser, Theodore. *Sister Carrie*. 1900. Reprint, New York: Signet, 2000. Novel.

Eisenberg, Susan. *Pioneering: Poems from the Construction Site*. Ithaca: ILR Press, 1998. Work narrative.

———. *We'll Call You if We Need You: Experiences of Women Working Construction*. Ithaca: ILR Press, 1999.

Ellison, Ralph. *Invisible Man*. 1952. Reprint, New York: Vintage, 1995.

Espada, Martin. *City of Coughing and Dead Radiators*. New York: Norton, 1994. Poems.

Farrell, Thomas. *Studs Lonigan: A Trilogy Comprising Young Lonigan, the Young Manhood of Studs Lonigan, and Judgement Day*. 1933–35. Reprint, Urbana: University of Illinois Press, 1993. Trilogy of novels.

Fell, Mary. *The Persistence of Memory*. New York: Random House, 1984. Poems.

Fuchs, Daniel. *The Williamsburg Trilogy*. 1934–37. Reprint, Berkeley: Carroll and Graf, 1983. Trilogy of novels.

Gardner, Leonard. *Fat City*. 1969. Reprint, Berkeley: University of California Press, 1996. Novel.

Garson, Barbara. *All the Livelong Day: The Meaning and Demeaning of Routine Work*. 1975. Reprint, New York: Penguin, 1994. Reportage/oral history.

Giardina, Denise. *Storming Heaven: A Novel*. New York: Ballantine, 1988.

————. *The Unquiet Earth: A Novel*. New York: Norton, 1992.

Gold, Michael. *Jews Without Money*. 1930. Reprint, Berkeley, Calif.: Carroll and Graf, 1996. Novel.

Goldman, Emma. *Living My Life*. 2 vols. New York: Dover, 1930. Autobiography.

Grahn, Judy. *The Work of a Common Woman*. New York: St. Martin's Press, 1978. Poems.

Gwaltney, John Langston, ed. *Drylongso: A Self-Portrait of Black America*. 1980. Reprint, New York: New Press, 1993. Oral history.

Hamper, Ben. *Rivethead: Tales from the Assembly Line*. 1986. Reprint, New York: Warner, 1992. Work narrative.

Herbst, Josephine. *Pity Is Not Enough*. Urbana: University of Illinois Press, 1998. Novel.

Himes, Chester. *If He Hollers Let Him Go*. 1945. Reprint, New York: Thunder's Mouth Press, 1995. Novel.

Hughes, Langston. *Good Morning Revolution: Uncollected Writings of Social Protest*. Edited by Faith Berry. Secaucus, N.J.: Citadel Press, 1992.

————. *The Political Plays of Langston Hughes*. Edited by Susan Duffy. Carbondale: Southern Illinois University Press, 2001.

Hurston, Zora Neale. *I Love Myself When I'm Laughing . . . and Then Again When I Am Looking Mean and Impressive: A Zora Neale Hurston Reader*. Edited by Alice Walker. New York: The Feminist Press, 1989. Stories/articles.

————. *Their Eyes Were Watching God*. 1937. Reprint, New York: Harper, 1998. Novel.

Jones, Mary Harris. *The Autobiography of Mother Jones*. 1925. Reprint, Chicago: C.H. Kerr Publishing, 1990.

Karr, Mary. *The Liars' Club: A Memoir*. New York: Penguin,1995.

Kelley, Edith Summers. *Weeds*. 1923. Reprint, New York: The Feminist Press, 1982. Novel.

Kingsolver, Barbara. *The Bean Trees*. New York: Harper, 1988. Novel.

————. *Holding the Line: Women in the Great Arizona Mine Strike of 1983*. Ithaca: ILR Press, 1997. History/oral history.

Kingston, Maxine Hong. *China Men*. New York: Vintage, 1989. Multigenre.

Kromer, Tom. *Waiting for Nothing*. 1935. Reprint, Athens: University of Georgia Press, 1986. Novel.

Larcom, Lucy. *A New England Girlhood, Outlined from Memory*. 1889. Reprint, Boston: Northeastern University Press, 1986.

Le Sueur, Meridel. *Ripening: Selected Work, 1927–1980*. 1982. Reprint, New York: The Feminist Press, 1990. Stories/articles.

————. *The Girl*. 1938. Reprint, Albuquerque: University of New Mexico Press, 2000. Novel.

Levine, Philip. *What Work Is*. New York: Alfred A. Knopf, 1992. Poems.

Llewellyn, Chris. *Steam Dummy and Fragments From the Fire: The Triangle Shirtwaist Company Fire of March 25, 1911*. 1987. Reprint, Huron, Oh.: Bottom Dog Press, 1993. Poems.

London, Jack. *Martin Eden*. 1884. Reprint, New York: Penguin, 1993. Novel.

Lorde, Audre. *Zami: A New Spelling of My Name*. Freedom, Calif.: Crossing Press, 1983. Autobiography.

Lumpkin, Grace. *To Make My Bread*. 1932. Reprint, Urbana: University of Illinois Press, 1995. Novel.

Lynn, Loretta, with George Vecsey. *Coal Miner's Daughter*. 1976. Reprint, New York: Da Capo Press, 1996. Autobiography.

Malkiel, Theresa S. *The Diary of a Shirtwaist Worker*. 1910. Reprint, Ithaca: Cornell University Press, 1990.

Marshall, Paule. *Brown Girl, Brownstones*. 1959. Reprint, New York: The Feminist Press, 1981. Novel.

Mason, Bobbie Ann. *In Country*. New York: Harper, 1993.

McCarriston, Linda. *Eva-Mary*. Evanston, Ill.: Triquarterly Books, 1994. Poems.

McDaniel, Wilma Elizabeth. *The Last Dust Storm*. Brooklyn: Hanging Loose Press, 1995. Poems.

McKenney, Ruth. *Industrial Valley*. 1939. Reprint, Ithaca: Cornell University Press, 1992. Novel.

Meriwether, Louise. *Daddy Was a Numbers Runner*. New York: The Feminist Press, 1986.

Miner, Valerie. *Winter's Edge*. New York: The Feminist Press, 1997.

Moraga, Cherrie. *Heroes and Saints and Other Plays*. Albuquerque, N.M.: West End Press, 1994.

Naylor, Gloria. *The Women of Bewster Place: A Novel in Seven Stories*. New York: Penguin, 1983.

Ng, Fae Myenne. *Bone*. New York: Harper, 1994. Novel.

Noyes, Henry. *Hand Over Fist*. Boston: South End Press, 1980. Novel.

Odets, Clifford. *Waiting for Lefty/Collected Plays*. 1935. Reprint, New York: Grove Press, 1993. Play.

Olsen, Tillie. *Yonnondio: From the Thirties*. 1974. Reprint, New York: Delacorte Press, 1979. Unfinished novel.

———. *Tell Me a Riddle*. 1961. Reprint, New Brunswick, N.J.: Rutgers University Press, 1995. Short fiction.

Page, Myra. *Daughter of the Hills*. 1950. Reprint, New York: The Feminist Press, 1983. Novel.

Pancake, Breece. *The Stories of Breece D'J Pancake*. 1983. Reprint, New York: Henry Holt, 1988. Short fiction.

Petry, Ann Lane. *The Street*. 1946. Reprint, Boston: Houghton Mifflin, 1988. Novel.

Pinzer, Maimie. *The Maimie Papers: Letters from an Ex-Prostitute*. New York: The Feminist Press, 1997.

Porter, Connie. *All Bright Court*. New York: Harper, 1991. Novel.

Potrebenko, Helen. *Taxi!* Vancouver, B.C.: New Star Press, 1989. Short fiction.

———. *Hey Waitress and Other Stories*. Vancouver, B.C.: Lazara Press, 1990.

Richardson, Dorothy. *The Long Day: The Story of a New York Working Girl*. 1904. Reprint, Charlottesville: University Press of Virginia, 1990.

Rivera, Tomas. *. . . y no se lo trago la tierra/ . . . And the Earth Did Not Devour Them*. Houston: Arte Público Press, 1987. Bilingual novel.

Rodriguez, Luis. *Always Running: La Vida Loca: Gang Days in L.A.* New York: Touchstone, 1994. Memoir.

Rolvag, Ole. *Giants in the Earth: A Saga of the Prairie*. 1927. Reprint, New York: Harper Collins, 1999. Novel.

Rose, Wendy. *The Halfbreed Chronicles and Other Poems*. Albuquerque: University of New Mexico Press, 1986.

Roth, Henry. *Call It Sleep*. 1934. Reprint, New York: Noonday Press, 1992. Novel.

Sanchez, Sonia. *Homegirls and Handgrenades*. 1984. Reprint, New York: Thunder's Mouth Press, 1997.

Sapphire (Ramona Lofton). *PUSH: A Novel*. New York: Vintage Contempraries, 1997.

Sayles, John. *The Anarchists' Convention: Stories*. 1979. Reprint, New York: Harper, 1992. Short fiction.

Saxton. Alexander. *The Great Midland*. 1948. Reprint, Urbana: University of Illinois, 1997. Novel.

Silko, Leslie Marmon. *Ceremony*. New York: Penguin, 1989. Novel.

———. *Storyteller*. Champaign, Ill.: Arcade, 1989. Multigenre.

Sinclair, Jo. *The Seasons: Death and Transfiguration*. New York: The Feminist Press, 1993. Memoir.

Sinclair, Upton. *The Jungle*. 1906. Reprint, New York: Bantam Classics, 1981. Novel.

Smedley, Agnes. *Daughter of Earth*. 1929. Reprint, New York: The Feminist Press, 1987. Novel.

Spewack, Bella. *Streets: A Memoir of the Lower East Side*. New York: The Feminist Press, 1995.

Stein, Julia. *Under the Ladder to Heaven*. Albuquerque, N.M.: West End Press, 1984. Poems.

Steinbeck, John. *In Dubious Battle*. 1936. Reprint, New York: Penguin, 1992. Novel.

Swados, Harvey. *On the Line: Stories About a Life on the Assembly Line*. 1957. Reprint, Urbana: University of Illinois, 1990. Short stories.

Thomas, Piri. *Down These Mean Streets*. 1967. Reprint, New York: Vintage, 1997. Autobiography.

Viramontes, Helen. *The Moths and Other Stories*. Houston: Arte Público Press, 1995.

Vorse, Mary Heaton. *Rebel Pen: The Writings of Mary Heaton Vorse*. Edited by Dee Garrison. New York: Monthly Review Press, 1986.

Walker, Alice. *The Color Purple*. 1982. Reprint, New York: Washington Square Press, 1996. Novel.

Wayman, Tom. *Introducing Tom Wayman: Selected Poems, 1973–1980*. Seattle, Wash.: Left Bank Books, 1980.

———. *I'll Be Right Back: New and Selected Poems, 1980–1996*. New York: Ontario Review Press, 1997.

Wideman, John Edgar. *Brothers and Keepers*. New York: Vintage, 1995. Memoir.

Wilson, August. *Fences*. 1986. Reprint, New York: New American Library, 1995. Play.

Wilson, Harriet. *Our Nig: Or, Sketches from the Life of a Free Black*. Edited by Henry Louis Gates Jr. 1859. Reprint, New York: Random House, 1983. Novel.

Wong, Nellie. *The Death of Long Steam Lady*. Los Angeles: West End Press, 1986. Poems.

Wright, Richard. *Native Son*. 1940. Reprint, New York: HarperCollins, 1989. Novel.

———. *Uncle Tom's Children: Four Novellas*. 1938. Reprint, New York: Harper, 1993.

———. *Black Boy (American Hunger)*. 1944. Reprint, New York: Harper, 1998. Autobiography.

Yamauchi, Wakako. *Songs My Mother Taught Me*. New York: The Feminist Press, 1994. Songs/Plays/Memoir.

Yezierska, Anzia. *The Open Cage: An Anzia Yezierska Collection*. Edited by Alice Kessler-Harris. New York: Persea, 1979. Short fiction.

———. *Bread Givers*. 1925. Reprint, New York: Persea Press, 1995. Novel.

Anthologies and Collections

Banks, Ann, ed. *First Person America*. 1981. Reprint, New York: Norton, 1991. Oral history from the Federal Writers Project.

Berkinow, Louise, ed. *The World Split Open: Four Centuries of Women Poets in England and America, 1552–1950*. New York: Vintage, 1974.

Byerly, Victoria. *Hard Times Cotton Mill Girls: Personal Histories of Womanhood and Poverty in the South*. Ithaca: ILR Press, 1987.

Carlsson, Chris, and Mark Leger, eds. *Bad Attitude: The Processed World Anthology*. New York: Verso, 1990.

Carson, Robert, ed. *The Waterfront Writers: The Literature of Work*. San Francisco: Harper and Row, 1979. Poems/Stories/Play/Work narratives.

Coles, Nicholas, and Peter Oresick, eds. *For a Living: The Poetry of Work*. Urbana: University of Illinois Presss, 1995.

Delacoste, Frederique, and Pricilla Alexander. *Sex Work: Writings by Women in the Sex Industry*. 1987. Reprint, Pittsburgh: Cleis Press, 1998.

Eisler, Benita, ed. *The Lowell Offering: Writings by New England Mill Women, 1840–1845*. 1980. Reprint, New York: Norton, 1997.

Espada, Martin, ed. *Poetry like Bread: Poets of the Political Imagination*. Willimantic, Conn.: Curbstone Press, 2000.

Foner, Philip, and Ronald L. Lewis. *American Labor Songs of the Nineteenth Century*. Urbana: University of Illinois Press, 1975.

Fowke, Edith, and Joe Glazer. *Songs of Work and Protest*. 1960. Reprint, New York: Dover Publications, 1973.

Grahn, Judy, ed. *True to Life Adventure Stories*. Santa Cruz, Calif.: Crossing Press, 1983.

Hoffman, Nancy, and Florence Howe. *Women Working: An Anthology of Stories and Poems*. New York: The Feminist Press, 1979.

Hourwich, Andria Taylor, and Gladys L. Palmer. *I Am a Woman Worker: A Scrapbook of Autobiographies*. 1936. Reprint, Manchester, N.H.: Ayer Publishing, 1980.

Lauter, Paul, and Ann Fitzgerald. *Literature, Class, and Culture: An Anthology*. New York: Longman, 2001.

Lerner, Gerda. *Black Women in White America: A Documentary History*. 1973. Reprint, New York: Vintage, 1992.

Lomax, Alan, Woody Guthrie, and Pete Seeger, eds. *Hard Hitting Songs for Hard Hit People*. 1967. Reprint, Lincoln: University of Nebraska Press, 1999.

Lynd, Staughton, and Alice Lynd, eds. *Rank and File: Personal Histories by Working-Class Organizers*. 1981. Reprint, Ithaca: ILR Press, 1999.

Martz, Sandra. *If I Had a Hammer: Women's Work in Poetry, Fiction, and Photographs*. Watsonville, Calif.: Paper Mache Press, 1990.

Mill Hunk Editorial Committee, *Overtime: Punchin' Out with the Mill Hunk Herald Magazine (1979–1989)*. Tucson, Ariz.: University of New Mexico Press, 1990.

Moraga, Cherrie, and Gloria Anzaldúa. *This Bridge Called My Back: Writings by Radical Women of Color*. 1981. Reprint, Latham, N.Y.: Kitchen Table Press, 1984.

Nekola, Charlotte, and Paula Rabinowitz, eds. *Writing Red: An Anthology of American Women Writers, 1930–1940*. New York: The Feminist Press, 1987.

North, Joseph, ed. *New Masses: An Anthology of the Rebel Thirties*. New York: International Publishers, 1969.

Oresick, Peter, and Nicholas Coles, eds. *Working Classics: Poems on Industrial Life*. Urbana: University of Illinois Press, 1990.

Raffo, Susan, ed. *Queerly Classed: Gay Men and Lesbians Write about Class*. Boston: South End Press, 1997.

Salzman, Jack, ed. *Years of Protest: A Collection of American Writings of the 1930s*. New York: Pegasus, 1967.

Seeger, Pete, and Bob Reiser. *Carry It On: A History in Song and Pictures of America's Working Men and Women*. New York: Simon and Shuster, 1985.

Shevin, David, and Larry Smith, eds. *Getting By: Stories of Working Lives*. Huron, Oh.: Bottom Dog Press, 1996.

Sinclair, Upton, Edward Sagarin, and Albert Teichner, eds. *The Cry for Justice: An Anthology of the Literature of Social Protest*. 1915. Reprint, Fort Lee, N.J.: Barricade Books, 1996.

Smith, Barbara. *Homegirls: Black Feminist Anthology*. 1983. Reprint, New Brunswick, N.J.: Rutgers University Press, 2000.

Smith, Larry. *Our Working Lives: Short Stories of People and Work*. Huron, Oh.: Bottom Dog Press, 2000.

Solomon, Barbara, ed. *The Haves and the Have-Nots: 30 Stories About Money and Class in America*. New York: Signet, 1999.

Terkel, Studs. *Working: People Talk About What They Do All Day and How They Feel About What They Do*. 1972. Reprint, New York: New Press, 1997. Interviews.

Washington, Mary Helen, ed. *Invented Lives: Narratives of Black Women, 1860–1960*. New York: Anchor, 1987.

———. *Memory of Kin: Stories about Families by Black Writers*. New York: Anchor Press, 1991.

Wayman, Tom, ed. *Going for Coffee: Poetry on the Job*. Seattle, Wash.: Left Bank Books, 1981.

———. *Paperwork*. Madiera Park, B.C.: Harbour Press, 1991.

Wolf, Robert, ed. *An American Mosaic: Prose and Poetry by Everyday Folk*. New York: Oxford University Press, 1999.

Wray, Matt, and Annalee Newitz, eds. *White Trash: Race and Class in America*. New York: Routledge, 1997. Essays.

Zandy, Janet, ed. *Calling Home: Working-Class Women's Writings, An Anthology*. New Brunswick, N.J.: Rutgers University Press, 1990.

———. *Liberating Memory: Our Work and Our Working-Class Consciousness*. New Brunswick, N.J.: Rutgers University Press, 1994.

COMMENTARIES ON WORKING-CLASS LITERATURE

Aaron, Daniel. *Writers on the Left: Episodes in American Literary Communism*. 1961. Reprint, New York: Columbia University Press, 1992.

Allison, Dorothy. *Skin: Talking About Sex, Class, and Literature*. Ithaca: Firebrand, 1994.

Bromell, Nicholas Knowles. *By the Sweat of the Brow: Literature and Labor in Ante-Bellum America*. Chicago: University of Chicago Press, 1993.

Coiner, Constance. *Better Red: the Writing and Resistance of Tillie Olsen and Meridel Le Sueur*. New York: Oxford University Press, 1995.

Denning, Michael. *Cultural Front: The Laboring of American Culture in the Twentieth Century*. New York: Verso, 1998.

Ellis, Jacqueline. *Silent Witnesses: Representations of Working-Class Women in the United States*. Bowling Green, Oh.: Bowling Green State University Press, 1998.

Foley, Barbara. *Radical Representations: Politics and Form in U.S. Proletarian Fiction, 1929–1941*. Durham, N.C.: Duke University Press, 1993.

Halker, Clark D. *For Democracy, Workers, and God: Labor Song-Poems and Labor Protest*. Urbana: University of Illinois Press, 1991.

Hapke, Laura. *Tales of the Working Girl: Wage-Earning Women in American Literature, 1890–1925*. New York: Twayne, 1992.

———. *Daughters of the Great Depression: Women, Work, and Fiction in the American 1930s*. Athens: University of Georgia Press, 1995.

———. *Labor's Text: The Worker in American Fiction*. New Brunswick, N.J.: Rutgers University Press, 2001.

Hollis, Karen. *Resisting Voices: Writing at the Bryn Mawr Summer School for Women Workers, 1921–1938*. Englewood Cliffs, N.J.: Prentice-Hall, 1996.

hooks, bell. *Where We Stand: Class Matters*. New York: Routledge, 2000.

Jones, Jacqueline. *Labor of Love, Labor of Sorrow: Black Women, Work, and the Family from Slavery to the Present*. New York: Basic Books, 1985.

Klaus, Gustav, ed. *The Literature of Labor: Two Hundred Years of Working-Class Writing*. New York: St. Martin's Press, 1985.

Lauter, Paul. *Canons and Contexts*. New York: Oxford University Press, 1991.

Linkon, Sherry, ed. *Teaching Working Class*. Amherst: University of Massachusetts Press, 1999.

Mirabella, M. Bella, and Lennard Davis, eds. *Left Politics and the Literary Profession*. New York: Columbia University Press, 1991.

Murphy, James. *The Proletarian Moment: The Controversy over Leftism in Literature*. Urbana: University of Illinois Press, 1991.

Nelson, Cary. *Repression and Recovery: Modern American Poetry and the Politics of Cultural Memory*. Madison: University of Wisconsin Press, 1989.

———. *Modern Poems We Have Wanted to Forget: Recovering the Literature of the American Left*. New York University Press, 2001.

Olsen, Tillie. *Silences*. 1978. Reprint, New York: Bantam Doubleday Dell, 1989.

Prestridge, Victoria. *The Worker in American Fiction: An Annotated Bibliography*. Champaign: University of Illinois Press, 1954.

Rabinowitz, Paula. *Labor and Desire: Women's Revolutionary Fiction in Depression America*. Chapel Hill: University of North Carolina Press, 1991.

Rideout, Walter. *The Radical Novel in the United States, 1900–1954: Some Interrelations of Literature and Society*. New York: Columbia University Press, 1992.

Robinson, Lillian. *Sex, Class, and Culture*. Bloomington: Indiana University Press, 1978.

Scully, James. *Line Break: Poetry as Social Practice*. Seattle: Bay Press, 1988.

Shepard, Alan, John McMillan, and Gary Tate. *Coming to Class: Pedagogy and the Social Class of Teachers*. Portsmouth, N.H.: Boynton/Cook, 1998.

Walker, Alice. *In Search of Our Mothers' Gardens*. New York: Harcourt, 1983.

Wayman, Tom. *Inside Job: Essays on the New Work Writing*. 1983. Reprint, Toronto: University of Toronto Press, 1986.

Wixson, Douglas C. *Worker-Writer in America: Jack Conroy and the Tradition of Midwestern Literary Radicalism, 1898–1990*. Urbana: Illinois University Press, 1994.

Zaniello, Tom. *Working Stiffs, Union Maids, Reds, and Riffraff: An Organized Guide to Films about Labor*. Ithaca: Cornell University Press, 1996.

NOTES

1. Janet Zandy, *Calling Home: An Anthology of Working-Class Women's Writing* (New Brunswick, N.J.: Rutgers University Press, 1990), 9.

2. Nicholas Coles, "Democratizing Literature: Issues in Teaching Working-Class Literature," *College English* 48 (November 1986): 664–80.

3. See Paul Lauter, "Working-Class Women's Literature: An Introduction to Study," in *Women in Print I*, eds. Joan E. Hartman and Ellen Messer-Davidow (New York: Modern Language Association of America, 1982); Paul Lauter and Ann Fitzgerald, *Literature, Class, and Culture: An Anthology* (New York: Longman, 2001); Cary Nelson, *Repression and Recovery: Modern American Poetry and the Politics of Cultural Memory* (Madison: University of Wisconsin Press, 1989); Janet Zandy, *Calling Home: Working-Class Women's Writings* (New Brunswick, N.J.: Rutgers University Press, 1990); Laura Hapke, personal correspondence, but see *Tales of the Working Girl* and *Labor's Text*, cited under "Commentaries."

4. In addition to the works cited above by Hapke, Lauter, Nelson, and Zandy see Constance Coiner's "Notes Toward an Overview" in this volume, for further discussion of the shape of working-class literature as a field.

5. Cited in note 3.

6. Zandy, *Calling Home*, 8.

7. Raymond Williams, *Keywords: A Vocabulary of Culture and Society* (New York: Oxford University Press, 1983), 183–88.

Biographical Notes

Marilyn Anderson is an activist-photographer, author of *Guatemalan Textiles Today* (1978), and coauthor, with Jon Garlock, of *Granddaughters of Corn* (Curbstone Press). As a team, they collaborate in an ongoing project to document workers in Rochester, New York. She has recently published a bilingual English/Spanish coloring book about the arts and crafts of Guatemala, and a Mayan languages/Spanish edition is soon to appear.

Chuck Barone is a professor of political economy at Dickinson College who has published articles on the personal and social dynamics and the economic foundations of class and classism. He is the director of the National Coalition Building Institute (NCBI), Dickinson College Diversity Training Team, and is actively engaged in International Re-evaluation Co-Counseling, a peer-based counseling community.

Carolyn Chute, once a Maine poultry worker, is the author of *The Beans of Egypt, Maine* (1985, 1989, 1995); *Letourneau's Used Auto Parts* (1988, 1995); *Merry Men* (1994, 1995); *New York Times* Notable Book, *Snowman* (1999, 2000); and *The School on Heart's Content Road* (forthcoming); all are published by Harcourt Brace. She lives in Maine.

Cheryl Cline maintains *Payday*, a web site devoted to working-class life and art (http://www.steamiron.com/payday), and is part owner of Diablo Books in Walnut Creek, California. She is the author of *Women's Diaries, Journals, and Letters: An Annotated Bibliography* (Garland, 1989) and is compiling a bibliography of North American working-class autobiographies.

Constance Coiner (1948–1996) was associate professor of English at SUNY-Binghamton. She authored *Better Red: The Writing and Resistance of Tillie Olsen and Meridel Le Sueur* (1995, available in paper from the University of Illinois), and earned Binghamton's and the SUNY Chancellor's Awards for Excellence in Teaching in 1995. During her life, Constance Coiner energetically assumed many roles: activist, mother, daughter, teacher, scholar, and partner. Her collaboration with Diana Hume George on a second book, *The Family Track* (University of Illinois, 1998), represents her commitment to changing the world and to challenging herself and others to reflect, engage, and enact during her lifetime. She is greatly missed.

Nicholas Coles is associate professor of English at the University of Pittsburgh, where he directs the Western Pennsylvania Writing Project, a site of the National Writing Project. In recognition of his work with the Writing Project, Coles received a Chancellor's Distinguished Public Service Award in 1998. With Peter Oresick, he coedited the anthology, *Working Classics: Poems of Industrial*

Life (1990) and a companion volume, *For a Living: The Poetry of Work* (1995), both from Illinois University Press. He is coediting with Janet Zandy an anthology of American working-class literature, to be published by Oxford University Press.

Edvige Giunta is assistant professor of English at New Jersey City University and a founding member of the Collective of Italian American Women. She has edited a special issue of *Voices in Italian Americana* devoted to women authors and coedited *A Tavola: Food, Tradition, and Community Among Italian Americans* (1998). She is coeditor, with Louise DeSalvo, of an anthology of writings by Italian American women about food (The Feminist Press) and, with Maria Rosa Cutrufelli and Caterina Romeo, of a special issue of *tutteStorie* devoted to Italian American women. She is completing a book on contemporary Italian American Writers, *Writing with an Accent*, to be published by St. Martin's Press.

Laura Hapke is a professor of English at Pace University. The winner of two *Choice* magazine Outstanding Academic Book awards, she is the author of *Tales of the Working Girl: Wage Earning Women in American Literature, 1890–1925* (1992), *Daughters of the Great Depression: Women, Work, and Fiction in the American 1930s* (1995), and other books on labor and working-class studies. Her newest book is *Labor's Text: The Worker in American Fiction* (2001), published by Rutger's University Press.

Safia Henderson-Holmes is assistant professor at the Graduate Creative Writing Program at Syracuse University. She has published two collections of poetry, *Daily Bread* and *Madness and a Bit of Hope*, which won the Poetry Society of America's William Carlos Williams Award. Her work has appeared in numerous newsletters, magazines, and anthologies.

Karyn Hollis directs the Writing Program at Villanova University. She is currently researching labor union women's literacy practices. Her book on the writing of the students at the Bryn Maur Summer School for Women Workers is forthcoming from Southern Illinois University Press (2002).

Barbara Horn, who grew up in rural Missouri, is professor of English at Nassau Community College of the State University of New York, where she coordinates a Women's Studies Project. She has published in *Women's Studies Quarterly, Iowa Woman, Calyx, Belles Lettres, Esprit, Potpourri*, and *Nassau Review*. She wrote an afterword for the reissue of Dorothy Bryant's novel, *Ella Price's Journal* (The Feminist Press, 1997) and currently is working on a monograph on this writer. Her research interests include images of rural and aging women in American literature.

Florence Howe became closely involved with the women's movement after her active participation in the civil rights and antiwar movements of the 1960s. She became a founding mother of the women's studies movement during the 1970s and 1980s, while serving as professor of English at Goucher College and the College at Old Westbury/SUNY. She is now professor of English and women's studies at The Graduate Center/CUNY and director and publisher emerita of The Feminist Press at CUNY. She is author of *Myths of Coeducation* and editor of *No More Masks! An Anthology of Twentieth-Century American Women's Poetry*.

Joyce L. Kornbluh is the retired director of the Women and Work Program, Institute of Labor and Industrial Relations at the University of Michigan. She currently serves as an adjunct faculty member for the National Labor College and Goddard College and has been a workers' educator for more than fifty years. She is the author of *A New Deal for Labor Education* (University of Illinois Press, 1985), the editor of *Rebel Voices: An I.W.W. Anthology* (University of Michigan Press, 1963), and coeditor (with Mary Frederickson) of *Sisterhood and Solidarity* (Temple University Press, 1990).

Kristin Kovacic is a writer and editor in Pittsburgh. Her essays, poetry, and fiction can be found in *Cimmarron Review*, *Kansas Quarterly*, *Gulf Stream*, *Third Coast*, and other magazines. She teaches at the Pittsburgh High School for the Creative and Performing Arts.

Sherry Lee Linkon is a professor of English, coordinator of American Studies, and codirector of the Center for Working-Class Studies at Youngstown State University. Her research and teaching focus on working-class pedagogy and representations of class and work. She is the editor of three books, including *Teaching Working Class* (University of Massachusetts Press, 1999), which was selected by readers of *Lingua Franca* as one of the ten best academic books of the 1990s. She is currently completing an interdisciplinary study of images of work and loss of work in Youngstown, Ohio, with John Russo.

Wilma Elizabeth McDaniel was born in 1918 in Stroud, Oklahoma, the fourth child in a sharecropper's family of eight children. McDaniel, with her family, made the dust-bowl trek to the San Joaquin Valley of California in 1936. Reluctant to give interviews, she writes, "Did a lot of hard, thankless, practically payless work, always a poet and a storyteller, have written twelve books of poetry, four books of stories, one novella, one play." Her first book of poetry was published in 1973. Her books include: *A Primer for Buford* (1990), *Sister Vayda's Song* (1982), *A Girl from Buttonwillow* (1990), *Tollbridge* (1980), *A Prince Albert Wind* (1994), and *Vito and Zona* (1993). Since 1995, she has published dozens of poems. A documentary of her life and work is forthcoming.

Douglas D. Noble is coordinator of the Rochester Education Alliance of Labor Work-Based Curriculum Project, teacher coordinator at Cobblestone School, learning support specialist at Rochester Institute of Technology, and senior research associate at SUNY-Geneseo. He has written extensively on issues of education, work, and technology, including *The Classroom Arsenal: Military Research, Technology, and Public Education*.

Brigid O'Farrell is a senior fellow at the Women's Research and Education Institute. Recent publications include "Women in Blue Collar and Related Occupations at the End of the Millennium," in *The Quarterly Review of Economics and Finance* (1999) and, with Betty Friedan, *Beyond Gender: The New Politics of Work and Family* (Johns Hopkins University Press/Wilson Center Press, 1997).

Lisa Orr is an assistant professor of English at Utica College of Syracuse University. She coedited *Working-Class Studies II: Expanding the Field*, a special issue of *Women's Studies Quarterly* (1998). Her essay, "'Cotton Patch Strumpets' and Masculine Women: Performing Classed Genders," recently appeared in the journal *Race, Gender, and Class* (2000).

Joann Quinones is a graduate of Rutgers University. She hopes to attend graduate school for a Ph.D. degree in English.

Peter Rachleff has taught at Macalester College in St. Paul, Minnesota since 1982. He teaches courses in U.S. Labor History, African American History, Immigration and Ethnicity in U.S. History, the United States in the 1930s, and American Labor Radicalism, as well as Women and Work in U.S. History, for which he provided a syllabus in this volume. He is the author of *Black Labor in Richmond, Virginia, 1865–1890* (University of Illinois Press, 1989) and *Hard-Pressed in the Heartland: The Hormel Strike and the Future of the Labor Movement* (South End Press, 1993). He is currently working, with Beth Cleary (associate professor of Dramatic Arts at Macalester), on an analysis of the work of a troupe of African American marionetteers who worked with "white" and "black" puppets in 1930s Buffalo, New York. In addition to his academic work, Rachleff engages in labor educational work with a variety of unions, particularly the American Postal Workers Union, and chairs the "Meeting the Challenge" Labor Educational Committee in St. Paul, Minnesota.

Roxanne Rimstead writes about poverty and literature, cultural and textual resistance, working-class intellectuals, cultural memory, autobiography, and oral histories. She has published internationally on cultural studies, feminist criticism, resistant genres of writing, and Canadian Literature(s) and is the author of *Remnants of Nation: On Poverty Narratives by Women* (University of Toronto Press, 2000). It develops radical ways of reading poverty and gender in literary texts, popular culture, and ordinary utterances. She teaches comparative and cultural studies at l'Université de Sherbrooke, Québec, Canada.

Melida Rodas is a student at New Jersey City University. The memoir published here is an excerpt from her memoir-in-progress, *Me llamo Guadalupe*. She has published her work in *Paths* and *Women on Campus*. She has also presented it in many forums, including the Newark Museum, Barnes and Noble, Rutgers University, the GAIN Spring Festival, and the 1999 Urban Mission Conference at NJCU. Her artwork has been exhibited at the Courtney Gallery, Barnes and Noble, ArtSpace, The Bayonne Public Library, and elsewhere.

John Russo is the coordinator of labor studies and codirector of the Center for Working-Class Studies at Youngstown State. He has written widely of labor and social issues and is recognized as a national expert on labor unions. His current research interests involve a comparative study of automobile assembly plants in Mexico and the United States and a book-length study of representations of work and nonwork in Youngstown with Sherry Linkon. Russo has been awarded Distinguished Professorship Awards in both scholarship and public service by Youngstown State University for his research and community activities.

Cy-Thea Sand works as a teaching assistant in the English Department at the University of Otago, New Zealand, where she is finishing a thesis on the rhetorics of self-representation. Her work has been published in several anthologies, journals, and magazines, including *Calling Home: Working-Class Women's Writing* (1990), *Fireweed* (1987), and *Herizons* (1983).

Larry Smith is a professor of English and humanities at Firelands College of Bowling Green State University. He is a poet and the author of two working-class novellas: *Beyond Rust: Novella and Stories* (1995) and *Working It Out* (1998). Smith is the director of Bottom Dog Press and the editor of several books on working-class literature. Most recently, he coedited, with Bonnie Jo Campbell, *Our Working Lives: Short Stories of People and Work* (Bottom Dog Press, 2000).

Julia Stein is a Jewish American poet and critic. Her books of poetry are *Under the Ladder to Heaven* (West End Press, 1984) and *Desert Soldiers* (California Classics, 1992). West End Press is publishing two new volumes of her poetry: *Woman of Valor* and *Walker Woman* in 2001. She writes literary criticism about women's, working-class, and multicultural literature. Stein is writing a book of literary criticism entitled *Wild Radicals of America: Essays in American Literature*. She has taught at the UCLA Extension Writers Program, Antioch University/L.A., and other colleges. Stein is a long-time activist in the labor and anti-sweatshop movements. She successfully fought a libel/slander lawsuit brought by Guess Jeans, and she founded the Los Angeles local of the National Writers Union. She lives in Los Angeles.

Linda Strom is associate professor of English at Youngstown State University, where she teaches courses in women's studies, working-class studies, and composition. In addition to publishing articles in *Radical Teacher* and *Writing Instructor*, she recently coauthored *Second Shift: Teaching Writing to Working Adults* with Kelly Belanger.

Carol Tarlen lives and works in San Francisco. She is a union activist and a clerical worker. Her writing can be found in *Calling Home* (edited by Janet Zandy),

For a Living (edited by Nicholas Cage and Peter Oresick), and *Liberating Memory* (edited by Janet Zandy).

Carole Anne Taylor teaches literature and African American/American cultural studies at Bates College while working for social justice with the Maine People's Alliance, the Maine Rural Workers' Association, and the I.W.W. Books on Roland Barthes and on visual poetics represent her sustained interest in the ideology of literary forms, as do articles on women's narration and subjectivity. *The Tragedy and Comedy of Resistance: Reading Modernity through Black Women's Fiction*(2000) explores the interconnections between a comedy that affirms wholesome normalcy in the face of terror and a tragedy that finds something terribly wrong in the social order itself.

Todd Vogel is visiting assistant professor and director of American studies at Trinity College in Hartford. He is editing a forthcoming book for Rutgers University Press called *The Black Press: New Literary and Historical Essays on Another Front Page*. He is completing a manuscript on marginalized writers and literary whiteness called, *Staging Race and Sabotaging Whiteness*.

Will Watson worked as a laborer in Chicago area steel mills for a decade before attending college. He is currently associate professor of English at the University of Southern Mississippi, Gulf Coast, where he teaches American and postcolonial literatures.

Pat Wynne is a songwriter, performer, voice teacher, union organizer, and instructor in the labor studies programs at City College, San Francisco, and Laney College in Oakland. A founding member of the Freedom Song Network, she is the former West Coast representative of Local 1000 of the American Federation of Musicians. She is now the field representative of the California Faculty Association at San Francisco State University. Wynne performs in a two-woman show called "Working Women's Stories and Songs" and in a one-woman performance piece called "Days of a Red Diaper Daughter," which is based on her memoir of the same name, published in the anthology, *Liberating Memory* (Rutgers University Press, 1995). Her greatest joy is as conductor of the San Francisco Labor Heritage/Rockin' Solidarity Chorus.

Janet Zandy is an associate professor of language and literature at Rochester Institute of Technology, and general editor of *Women's Studies Quarterly* (1997–2001). Her books include *Calling Home: Working-Class Women's Writings* (Rutgers University Press, 1990), *Liberating Memory: Our Work and Our Working-Class Consciousness* (Rutgers University Press, 1995), *Writing Work: Writer's on Working-Class Writing*, coedited with Larry Smith and David Sherin (Bottom Dog Press, 1999), and she is coediting with Nicholas Coles an anthology of American working-class literature to be published by Oxford University Press.

Tom Zaniello is the director of the honors program and professor of English at Northern Kentucky University. He also teaches Images of Labor in Film at the National Labor College at the George Meany Center for Labor Studies. He has published *Working Stiffs, Union Maids, Reds, and Riffraff: An Organized Guide to Films about Labor* (Cornell/ILR) and is completing its sequel, *Organizers, Average Joes, Brassy Dames, Finks, and the Salt of the Earth: The World of Work in Film*.

Publication Acknowledgments

Unless noted below, the pieces included in parts 1–4 of this collection, as well as the introduction, were originally published in *Working-Class Studies*, edited by Janet Zandy, special issue, *Women's Studies Quarterly* 23, nos. 1 and 2 (spring/ summer 1995). Copyright for each contribution © 1995 in the name of the author. Reprinted here by permission of The Feminist Press at The City University of New York.

The publisher gratefully acknowledges the permission of the following publishers and authors:

Carolyn Chute, "Faces in the Hands," originally appeared in *I Was Content and Not Content: The Story of Linda Lord and the Closing of Penobscot Poultry*, edited by Cedric N. Chatterley and Alicia J. Rouverol with Stephen A. Cole (Carbondale: Southern Illinois University Press, 2000). Copyright © 2000 by Carolyn A. Chute. Reprinted by permission of the author and Gelfman Schneider Literary Agents.

Ralph Fasanella, comments on *Family Supper*, copyright © 1997 by Eva Fasanella. Reprinted by permission of Eva Fasanella.

Edvige Giunta, "For Giacomo," originally appeared in *The Paterson Literary Review* 28 (1999). Copyright © by Edvige Giunta. Reprinted by permission of the author and the editor of *The Paterson Literary Review*.

Edvige Giunta, "Honor Thy Students," originally appeared in *The Academic Forum: The Academic Affairs Newsletter of New Jersey City University* 7, no. 1 (1998). Copyright © 1998 by Edvige Giunta. Reprinted by permission of the author.

Safiya Henderson-Holmes, "rituals of spring (for the 78th anniversary of the shirtwaist factory fire)," originally appeared in *Madness and a Bit of Hope: Poems* (New York: Harlem River Press, 1990). Copyright © 1990 by Safiya Henderson-Holmes. Reprinted by permission of the author.

Karyn L. Hollis, "Autobiography and Reconstructing Subjectivity at the Bryn Mawr Summer School for Women Workers, 1921–1938," originally appeared, in slightly different form, in *College Composition and Communication* 45, no. 1 (February 1994): 31–60. Copyright © 1994 by Conference on College Composition and Communication of the National Council of Teachers of English. Reprinted by permission *College Composition and Communication*.

Kristin Kovacic, "Proud to Work in the University," originally appeared in *Focus*, the staff/faculty newspaper of Carnegie Mellon University, September 1990. Copyright © 1990 by Kristin Kovacic. Reprinted by permission of the author.

A Note about the Cover

Family Supper was painted in 1972 by Ralph Fasanella and was bought from the collector by labor unions and installed in the Ellis Island Immigration Museum in 1991.

"It's a typical family of immigrants that came to America around 1910," Fasanella said of the painting. "We had three rooms and eight people in my family. We paid about eight bucks a month, cold water flat. . . . In those days you had a gas meter, you had to put a quarter in and then the light would go on.

"My mother was a buttonhole maker in a dress shop. There in the center, I show a woman tied to a cross with the clothesline, feet in a pan cooling off. Mothers are always working, right?

"And underneath the gas meter is a towel, Pillsbury flour. In those days, we got flour bags, and a lot of families made pillow cases, towels, pants, dresses.

"I put my father on the calendar at the right. Since he was an iceman, I use the symbol I know best—ice tongs. And I have this in his memory: 'The poor bastard died broke and all the other bastards will do the same.' Then I have on top of the refrigerator, 'Good-bye Joe.' I cried when I put that in. I was saying good-bye to my father."